D0678481

forms of desire

forms of desire

sexual orientation and the

social constructionist controversy

edited by **edward stein**

ROUTLEDGE · NEW YORK AND LONDON

First published in 1990 by Garland Publishing Inc.

Published in 1992 by

Routledge
An imprint of Routledge, Chapman and Hall, Inc.
29 West 35 Street
New York, NY 10001

Published in Great Britain by

Routledge
11 New Fetter Lane
London EC4P 4EE

Copyright © 1990 by Edward Stein

Printed in the United States of America

All rights reserved. No part of this book may be reprinted or reproduced or utilized in any form or by any electronic, mechanical or other means, now known or here-after invented, including photocopying and recording, or in any information storage or retrieval system, without permission in writing from the publishers.

Library of Congress Cataloging in Publication Data

Forms of desire : sexual orientation and the social constructionist
  controversey / edited by Edward Stein.
      p.   cm.
  Includes bibliographical references and index.
  ISBN 0-415-90485-4
      1. Homosexuality—United States.   2. Gays—United States—Social
  conditions.   I. Stein, Edward, 1965-
  HQ76.3.U5F67   1992
  306.76′6—dc20   91-37164
                                                              CIP

To Morris Kaplan and Ron Caldwell,
for friendship and fellowship

Contents

Acknowledgements

Several institutions and a great number of people have helped me in a variety of ways on this project. In 1988, the Lesbian and Gay Studies Conference at Yale University was a catalyst for my thinking about gay studies. The conference introduced me to several people and ideas that have influenced me in my approach to the social constructionist controversy and in my work on this anthology. In 1989, with funding from the Massachusetts Institute of Technology, I helped to form a lesbian and gay academics study group. The people I have met through this group, the research and readings I have done for it, and the discussions I have had through it have been of great value to me. During the summer of 1989, the Woodrow Wilson Foundation sponsored a conference for recipients of the Mellon Fellowship in the Humanities. At this conference, there was a discussion on "Lesbians and Gays in the Academy." Several of the participants in that discussion group as well as others at that conference have become friends and colleagues of mine and an informal, inter-institutional network of people interested in lesbian and gay studies arose from it; this network has provided me with a sense of community that has been both directly and indirectly significant to my work on this project. Also, since 1989, I have given five talks on the social constructionist controversy—one at SUNY-Purchase (jointly sponsored by the philosophy department and the gay, lesbian and bisexual student group), one at Brown University (as part of a conference for graduate students doing work in lesbian and gay studies), one at the University of Maryland-College Park (sponsored by the philosophy department), and two at M.I.T. The comments I received at these talks were helpful in developing my ideas for this anthology, especially for the concluding essay.

More important than the institutions that have helped me are the individuals. Without the support, encouragement, advice and criticism of my friends and colleagues, this anthology would have never come to exist. From the earliest moments that I began thinking about this project, Morris Kaplan and Ron Caldwell have provided friendly support and conversation which have been essential to sustaining my efforts. David Halperin has made numerous useful suggestions, made detailed comments on my written work, and engaged me in lengthy discussions that have proved invaluable. Paul Bloom collaborated with me on a project that relates to this anthology; through that collaboration and related discussions, he made a significant impact on my thinking about these issues. Gene Rice provided crucial help and encouragement, especially at the beginning and the end of this project. Also, Bill Percy and Charley Shively have offered encouraging comments and helpful suggestions. As my immediate supervisor on this project, Wayne Dynes has provided the proper combination of support, advice and freedom. Other individuals whose comments have proven important, are: Alyssa Bernstein, Gene Buckley, Steve Greene, Michael Inman, Thomas Kuhn, Peter Lipton, Eric Lormand, Brett McDonnell, Bonnie McElhinny, Richard Mohr, Georges Rey, Sean Walter, and Karen Wynn. Sean Walter provided a great deal of invaluable proofreading and other assistance. Paul Bloom, Tina Blythe, Robert Buerglener, Wayne Dynes, Tracy Isaacs, Ann Liu, Eric Lormand and Karen Wynn as well as Gary Kuris and Phyllis Korper of Garland Publishing have helped me in different ways to get this book physically and typographically ready for publication.

Finally, I thank the contributors who agreed to have their essays reprinted in this volume. Their contributions, of course, made this book possible.

- Edward Stein
Cambridge, MA
March 1990

Preface to the Paperback Edition

The original version of this book appeared in the fall of 1990 published by Garland Publishing, Inc., as volume one in the Garland Gay and Lesbian Series edited by Wayne R. Dynes. This paperback edition is the same as the original with the following exception: several typographical errors have been changed, the series editor's introduction has been removed, and the bibliography has been updated and expanded. In addition to help from some of the people listed in the acknowledgments, the following people have helped me get the paperback version of this book ready: Michael Bronski, Donna Scholes of Garland Publishing and Maureen MacGrogan of Routledge Chapman Hall.

- Edward Stein
Cambridge, MA
October 1991

Forms of Desire

CHAPTER 1:
Edward Stein
Introduction

Sexual Behavior in the Human Male and *Sexual Behavior in the Human Female*, published respectively in 1948 and 1953 and collectively known as the Kinsey reports, revolutionized the way many North Americans think about sex. In particular, these books brought to light the significant number of people who engage in same-sex sexual activities— "only 50 percent of the [white male] population is exclusively heterosexual throughout its adult life."[1]

The discovery of a surprisingly high frequency of same-sex sexual activities led Kinsey and his collaborators to examine the definition of the term 'homosexual.' They wrote:

> For nearly a century the term homosexual in connection with human behavior has been applied to sexual relationships, either overt or psychic, between individuals of the same sex. . . . It would encourage clearer thinking on these matters if persons were not characterized as heterosexual or homosexual, but as individuals who have had certain amounts of heterosexual experience and certain amounts of homosexual experience. Instead of using these terms as substantives which stand for persons, or even as adjectives to describe persons, they may better be used to describe the nature of overt sexual relations, or of the stimuli to which an individual erotically responds.[2]

---

[1] A.C. Kinsey, W.B. Pomeroy, and C.E. Martin, *Sexual Behavior in the Human Male* (Philadelphia: W.B. Saunders Company, 1948), p. 656.
[2] *Ibid.*, pp. 612, 617.

Kinsey's 1948 suggestion not to use the terms
'heterosexual,' 'homosexual' and 'bisexual'[3] as nouns or
adjectives applying to human beings has been, for the most
part, ignored. We quite commonly talk about people as being
homosexual, heterosexual or bisexual. This is true not only in
everyday talk, but in scholarly work as well. For example,
scientists commonly ask what factors (e.g., genetic,
hormonal) make some people into heterosexuals and other
people into homosexuals, historians ask whether some
historical figure (e.g., Walt Whitman, Joan of Arc) was a
homosexual, and sociologists ask about the ways that
homosexuals in a particular society (e.g., Ancient Greece,
Native American cultures) are viewed. The central issue of
this anthology is whether these sorts of questions are
legitimate or whether Kinsey's forty-year-old exhortation
against them was justified.

The issue to which this anthology is devoted is the debate
between social constructionists and essentialists[4] about sexual
orientation. In simplest terms, essentialists think that the
categories of sexual orientation[5] (e.g., heterosexual,

---

[3] See *Ibid.*, pp. 656-659 for the claim that 'bisexual,' like 'homosexual'
and 'heterosexual' should not be applied to individuals.

[4] John Boswell, "Revolutions, Universal and Sexual Categories,"
Salmagundi 58-69, (1982-83), pp. 89-113, and James Weinrich, in his
contribution to this volume (chapter eight), refer to essentialism with
the word 'realism.' Since there are so many views about so many
different questions which go by the name 'realism,' I prefer to use
'essentialism.' My preference, here, should be seen as stylistic rather
than theoretical. The potential problem with this usage is that the term
'essentialism' may suggest that the view entails that there is an *essence*
to sexual orientation. As I use 'essentialism,' no literal sense of
'essence' is implied. See also Boswell's contribution to this volume
(chapter seven).

[5] There has been some dispute within the scholarly community and the
lesbian and gay community about whether it is correct or preferable to
use the phrase 'sexual orientation,' the phrase 'sexual preference' or
some other cognate. I wish to sidestep this dispute. 'Sexual preference'
is ambiguous: on one reading, 'sexual orientation' and 'sexual
preference' are synonyms; on the other, 'sexual preference' refers to more
--->

homosexual and bisexual) are appropriate categories to apply to individuals. According to essentialists, it is legitimate to inquire into the origin of heterosexuality or homosexuality, to ask whether some historical figure was a heterosexual or homosexual, etc. This follows from the essentialist tenet that there are objective, intrinsic, culture-independent facts about what a person's sexual orientation is. In contrast, the social constructionist denies that there are such facts about people's sexual orientation and would agree with the exhortation that it is mistaken to look at an individual as being of a particular sexual orientation in the absence of a cultural construction of that orientation. Thus, social constructionism, if true, has deep ramifications for the historical, scientific, sociological, philosophical, anthropological and psychological studies of sexuality because these studies often assume that the objects of their investigations are natural rather than cultural entities.

The debate about sexual orientation between the social constructionists and the essentialists started fairly recently. In 1968, Mary McIntosh wrote "The Homosexual Role" (reprinted as chapter three of this volume).[6] In this essay, she uses the tools of labelling theory, a sociological approach, to defend social constructionism as applied to homosexuality. In

---

fine-grained erotic desires such as desires for sorts of people (e.g., large-breasted women or muscular men) or for sorts of activities (sado-masochism or being "passive"). For consistency, I will generally use 'sexual preference' in the second sense and not the first sense. To convey the first sense of 'sexual preference,' I will use 'sexual orientation.' That a person has a particular sexual orientation/preference does not entail that she publicly identifies herself as having that particular orientation/preference or that she engages in certain sexual behaviors (she might, for example, be celibate). Sexual orientation, rather than being about self-conscious identity or actual sexual practice, has to do with erotic desires and dispositions. See the contributions of Epstein, pp. 239-40, and Weinrich, p. 179, for brief characterizations of a more standard way of seeing the preference/orientation distinction.

[6] Mary McIntosh, "The Homosexual Role," *Social Problems* 16 (1968), pp. 182-193, reprinted with postscript in Kenneth Plummer, ed., *The Making of the Modern Homosexual* (Totowa, NJ: Barnes and Noble, 1981), pp. 30-49.

1976, Michel Foucault, a noted French philosopher, published the first volume of *The History of Sexuality*.[7] This book has become, for many social constructionists, the *locus classicus* of their program. The section of this book in which Foucault lays out his version of the social constructionist thesis (part two, chapter 2, "The Perverse Implantation") is reprinted as chapter two of this volume. From this double origin, social constructionism has developed as a serious challenge to essentialism.[8]

Social constructionists began by defining their view in contrast to essentialism, but more recently they have developed an independent account of same-sex behavior and desire as it exists today and as it has existed in the past. Some of the essays in this volume—in particular, Robert Padgug's "Sexual Matters: On Conceptualizing Sexuality in History"[9] and Arnold Davidson's "Sex and the Emergence of Sexuality"[10]— have played a role in developing this positive picture. Padgug's essay argues that sexual orientation needs to be located as a construction within a certain social reality while Davidson's essay attempts to formalize and provide support for Foucault's thesis about the emergence of the homosexual as a type of person. Davidson focuses on the distinction between sex and sexuality. Davidson's essay complements Ian Hacking's essay "Making Up People"[11] in which Hacking

---

[7] Michel Foucault, *The History of Sexuality, Volume I: An Introduction*, Robert Hurley, trans. (New York: Pantheon, 1978).

[8] Social constructionism in general, i.e., not just about sexual orientation, has roots in hermeneutics, cultural relativism and other related intellectual movements.

[9] Robert Padgug, "Sexual Matters: On Conceptualizing Sexuality in History," *Radical History Review* 20 (1979), pp. 3-23, reprinted as chapter four.

[10] Arnold Davidson, "Sex and the Emergence of Sexuality," *Critical Inquiry* 14 (Autumn 1987), pp. 16-48, reprinted as chapter six of this volume.

[11] Ian Hacking, "Making Up People," in *Reconstructing Individualism: Autonomy, Individuality and the Self in Western Thought*, Thomas

--->

attempts to develop a general account of the development of
new types of people.

Three of the remaining essays in this volume are in some
way critical of social constructionism. John Boswell, in
"Concepts, Experience and Sexuality" (chapter seven) tries to
mediate between extreme versions of social constructionism
and essentialism through his interpretation of some historical
evidence. James Weinrich tries to do the same thing but his
discussion is informed by a variety of scientific and theoretical
considerations.[12] He discusses a theory called
"interactionism" which shares some features of both
constructionism and essentialism. Wayne Dynes looks at
social constructionism in terms of intellectual history and
compares it to other methodological approaches in history.[13]

The remaining essays are by Steven Epstein, who focuses
on the political ramifications of the social constructionist
controversy,[14] and Leonore Tiefer, who discusses how the
social constructionist perspective has an impact on sexology
and parts of psychology.[15] Finally, in my conclusion (chapter
twelve of this volume), I attempt to pull the various threads of
the debate together, lay out what exactly is in dispute between
essentialists and social constructionists, and suggest what sort
of information would be needed to settle the matter.

Heller, *et al.*, eds. (Stanford: Stanford University Press, 1986), reprinted
as chapter five of this volume.

[12] Weinrich's essay, reprinted as chapter eight of this volume, is chapter
five of his book *Sexual Landscapes* (New York: Charles Scribner's
Sons, 1987).

[13] Dynes's essay, which is reprinted as chapter nine of this volume, is a
modified version of "Wrestling with the Social Boa Constructor," *Out
in Academia* 2 (1988), pp. 18-29.

[14] Steven Epstein, "Gay Politics, Ethnic Identity: The Limits of Social
Constructionism," *Socialist Review* 93/94 (May/August 1987), pp. 9-
54, reprinted as chapter ten of this volume.

[15] Leonore Tiefer, "Social Constructionism and the Study of Human
Sexuality," in *Review of Personality and Social Psychology*, volume
7, P. Shaver and C. Hendrick, eds. (1987), pp. 70-94, reprinted as
chapter eleven of this volume.

Most people who have well-articulated views on the debate between social constructionists and essentialists think that it has been settled. Many scholars in the humanities working in lesbian and gay studies think that the debate is settled in favor of social constructionism while most scientists working on issues relating to sexual orientation as well as, for example, members of the national organization Parents and Friends of Lesbians and Gays (PFLAG) think it is settled in favor of essentialism. Most laypeople seem to have conflicting intuitions—they are essentialist in some ways and constructionist in some others.[16]

One of my aims in assembling this anthology is to show that the debate is far from settled. One of the reasons why it might appear to some of the disputants that it is settled is because the two sides are talking past each other, working with impoverished versions of their rivals' views and resorting to name-calling. By bringing together, for close comparison and scrutiny, essays from disparate journals and books as well as different disciplines and methodologies, I hope that it will become clearer what is really at issue between the social constructionists and essentialists and how to proceed if we are to get to the bottom of this controversy. I also hope to stimulate further discussion, perhaps from a slightly different perspective, of the questions that the essays in this volume raise.

In putting this anthology together, I have tried to represent a variety of viewpoints and disciplines. In doing so, I have left out many interesting and relevant essays that have been written on the topic, not to mention entire disciplines (for example, anthropology) that have addressed themselves to related questions. My selections have been guided by a desire to collect essays that fit together nicely, that are free of unnecessary jargon, and that are often difficult to locate.

With the exception of Dynes's essay which has been substantially rewritten by the author, the reprinted essays in this volume appear largely unaltered. Some stylistic changes

---

[16] In his essay in this volume, Epstein, pp. 239-42, nicely discusses some of these "folk" intuitions about homosexuality.

have been made. First, the format of footnotes and references has been made relatively uniform. Doing so involved renumbering some of the notes. Second, typographical and other obvious errors have been eliminated. Third, single quotation marks are used around words to denote reference to the word itself, rather than the meaning of the word, as in: the word 'homosexual' has ten letters in it. In other contexts, double quotation marks are used.

The essays in this anthology may be read in any order as each is self-contained. All of the essays have appeared before in some form with the exception of Boswell's essay and my two essays. Those who wish to begin with a critical overview of the social constructionism/essentialism debate may want to begin with my concluding essay and then read the others.[17]

---

[17] Thanks to Ron Caldwell, Wayne Dynes, David Halperin, Bonnie McElhinny, Gene Rice and Sean Walter for their comments on an earlier draft of this introduction.

CHAPTER 2
Michael Foucault
The Perverse Implantation

A possible objection: it would be a mistake to see in this proliferation of discourses merely a quantitative phenomenon, something like a pure increase, as if what was said in them were immaterial, as if the fact of speaking about sex were of itself more important than the forms of imperatives that were imposed on it by speaking about it. For was this transformation of sex into discourse not governed by the endeavor to expel from reality the forms of sexuality that were not amenable to the strict economy of reproduction: to say no to unproductive activities, to banish casual pleasures, to reduce or exclude practices whose object was not procreation? Through the various discourses, legal sanctions against minor perversions were multiplied; sexual irregularity was annexed to mental illness; from childhood to old age, a norm of sexual development was defined and all the possible deviations were carefully described; pedagogical controls and medical treatments were organized around the least fantasies, moralists, but especially doctors, brandished the whole emphatic vocabulary of abomination. Were these anything more than means employed to absorb, for the benefit of a genitally centered sexuality, all the fruitless pleasures? All this garrulous attention which has us in a stew over sexuality, is it not motivated by one basic concern: to ensure population, to reproduce labor capacity, to perpetuate the form of social relations: in short, to constitute a sexuality that is economically useful and politically conservative?

From Michel Foucault, *The History of Sexuality, Volume I*. English translation copyright © 1978 by Random House, Inc. Copyright © 1976 by Editions Gallimard. Reprinted with permission of Georges Borchardt, Inc.

I still do not know whether this is the ultimate objective. But this much is certain: reduction has not been the means employed for trying to achieve it. The nineteenth century and our own have been rather the age of multiplication: a dispersion of sexualities, a strengthening of their disparate forms, a multiple implantation of "perversions." Our epoch has initiated sexual heterogeneities.

Up to the end of the eighteenth century, three major explicit codes—apart from the customary regularities and constraints of opinion—governed sexual practices: canonical law, the Christian pastoral, and civil law. They determined, each in its own way, the division between licit and illicit. They were all centered on matrimonial relations: the marital obligation, the ability to fulfill it, the manner in which one complied with it, the requirements and violences that accompanied it, the useless or unwarranted caresses for which it was a pretext, its fecundity or the way one went about making it sterile, the moments when one demanded it (dangerous periods of pregnancy or breast-feeding, forbidden times of Lent or abstinence), its frequency or infrequency, and so on. It was this domain that was especially saturated with prescriptions. The sex of husband and wife was beset by rules and recommendations. The marriage relation was the most intense focus of constraints; it was spoken of more than anything else; more than any other relation, it was required to give a detailed accounting of itself. It was under constant surveillance: if it was found to be lacking, it had to come forward and plead its case before a witness. The "rest" remained a good deal more confused: one only has to think of the uncertain status of "sodomy," or the indifference regarding the sexuality of children.

Moreover, these different codes did not make a clear distinction between violations of the rules of marriage and deviations with respect to genitality. Breaking the rules of marriage or seeking strange pleasures brought an equal measure of condemnation. On the list of grave sins, and separated only by their relative importance, there appeared debauchery (extramarital relations), adultery, rape, spiritual or carnal incest, but also sodomy, or the mutual "caress." As to the courts, they could condemn homosexuality as well as infidelity, marriage without parental consent, or bestiality. What was taken into account in the civil and religious jurisdictions alike was a general unlawfulness. Doubtless acts "contrary to nature," were stamped as especially abominable, but they were perceived simply as an extreme form of acts "against the law"; they were infringements of decrees which were just as sacred as those of marriage, and which had been established for governing the order of things and the plan of beings. Prohibitions bearing on sex were essentially of a juridical nature. The "nature" on which they were based was still a kind of law. For a long time hermaphrodites were criminals, or crime's offspring, since their anatomical disposition, their very being, confounded the law that distinguished the sexes and prescribed their union.

The discursive explosion of the eighteenth and nineteenth centuries caused this system centered on legitimate alliance to undergo two modifications. First, a centrifugal movement with respect to heterosexual monogamy. Of course, the array of practices and pleasures continued to be referred to it as their internal standard; but it was spoken of less and less, or in any case with a growing moderation. Efforts to find out its secrets were abandoned; nothing further was demanded of it than to define itself from day to day. The legitimate couple, with its regular sexuality, had a right to more discretion. It tended to function as a norm, one that was stricter, perhaps, but quieter. On the other hand, what came under scrutiny was the sexuality of children, mad men and women, and criminals; the sensuality of those who did not like the opposite sex; reveries, obsessions, petty manias, or great transports of rage. It was time for all these figures, scarcely noticed in the past, to step forward and speak, to make the difficult confession of what they were. No doubt they were condemned all the same; but they were listened to; and if regular sexuality happened to be questioned once again, it was through a reflux movement, originating in these peripheral sexualities.

Whence the setting apart of the "unnatural" as a specific dimension in the field of sexuality. This kind of activity assumed an autonomy with regard to the other condemned forms such as adultery or rape (and the latter were condemned less and less): to marry a close relative or practice sodomy, to seduce a nun or engage in sadism, to deceive one's wife or violate cadavers, became things that were essentially different. The area covered by the Sixth Commandment began to fragment. Similarly, in the civil order, the confused category of "debauchery," which for more than a century had been one of the most frequent reasons for administrative confinement, came apart. From the debris, there appeared on the one hand infractions against the legislation (or morality) pertaining to marriage and the family, and on the other, offenses against the regularity of a natural function (offenses which, it must be added, the law was apt to punish). Here, we have a likely reason, among others, for the prestige of Don Juan, which three centuries have not erased. Underneath the great violator of the rules of marriage—stealer of wives, seducer of virgins, the shame of families, and an insult to husbands and fathers—another personage can be glimpsed: the individual driven, in spite of himself, by the somber madness of sex. Underneath the libertine, the pervert. He deliberately breaks the law, but at the same time, something like a nature gone awry transports him far from all nature; his death is the moment when the supernatural return of the crime and its retribution thwarts the flight into counternature. There were two great systems conceived by the West for governing sex: the law of marriage and the order of desires—and the life of Don Juan overturned them both. We shall leave it to psychoanalysts to speculate whether he was homosexual, narcissistic, or impotent.

Although not without delay and equivocation, the natural laws of matrimony and the immanent rules of sexuality began to be recorded on two separate registers. There emerged a world of perversion which partook of that of legal or moral infraction, yet was not simply a variety of the latter. An entire sub-race race was born, different—despite certain kinship ties—from the libertines of the past. From the end of the eighteenth century to our own, they circulated through the pores of society; they were always hounded, but not always by laws; were often locked up, but not always in prisons; were sick perhaps, but scandalous, dangerous victims, prey to a strange evil that also bore the name of vice and sometimes crime. They were children wise beyond their years, precocious little girls, ambiguous schoolboys, dubious servants and educators, cruel or maniacal husbands, solitary collectors, ramblers with bizarre impulses; they haunted the houses of correction, the penal colonies, the tribunals, and the asylums; they carried their infamy to the doctors and their sickness to the judges. This was the numberless family of perverts who were on friendly terms with delinquents and akin to madmen.   In the course of the century they successively bore the stamp of "moral folly," "genital neurosis,"   "aberration   of   the   genetic   instinct," "degenerescence," or "physical imbalance."

What does the appearance of all these peripheral sexualities signify? Is the fact that they could appear in broad daylight a sign that the code had become more lax? Or does the fact that they were given so much attention testify to a stricter regime and to its concern to bring them under close supervision? In terms of repression, things are unclear. There was permissiveness, if one bears in mind that the severity of the codes relating to sexual offenses diminished considerably in the nineteenth century and that law itself often deferred to medicine. But an additional ruse of severity, if one thinks of all the agencies of control and all the mechanisms of surveillance that were put into operation by pedagogy or therapeutics.   It may be the case that the intervention of the Church in conjugal sexuality and its rejection of "frauds". against procreation had lost much of their insistence over the previous two hundred years. But medicine made a forceful entry into the pleasures of the couple: it created an entire organic, functional, or mental pathology arising out of "incomplete" sexual practices; it carefully classified all forms of related pleasures; it incorporated them into the notions of "development" and instinctual "disturbances"; and it undertook to manage them.

Perhaps the point to consider is not the level of indulgence or the quantity of repression but the form of power that was exercised.   When this whole thicket of disparate sexualities was labeled, as if to disentangle them from one another, was the object to exclude them from reality? It appears, in fact, that the function of the power exerted in this instance was not that of interdiction, and that it involved four operations quite different from simple prohibition.

1. Take the ancient prohibitions of consanguine marriages (as numerous and complex as they were) or the condemnation of adultery, with its inevitable frequency of occurrence; or on the other hand, the recent controls through which, since the nineteenth century, the sexuality of children has been subordinated and their "solitary habits" interfered with. It is clear that we are not dealing with one and the same power mechanism. Not only because in the one case it is a question of law and penality, and in the other, medicine and regimentation; but also because the tactics employed is [*sic*] not the same. On the surface, what appears in both cases is an effort at elimination that was always destined to fail and always constrained to begin again. But the prohibition of "incests" attempted to reach its objective through an asymptotic decrease in the thing it condemned, whereas the control of infantile sexuality hoped to reach it through a simultaneous propagation of its own power and of the object on which it was brought to bear. It proceeded in accordance with a twofold increase extended indefinitely. Educators and doctors combatted children's onanism like an epidemic that needed to be eradicated. What this actually entailed, throughout this whole secular campaign that mobilized the adult world around the sex of children, was using these tenuous pleasures as a prop, constituting them as secrets (that is, forcing them into hiding so as to make possible their discovery), tracing them back to their source, tracking them from their origins to their effects, searching out everything that might cause them or simply enable them to exist. Wherever there was the chance they might appear, devices of surveillance were installed; traps were laid for compelling admissions; inexhaustible and corrective discourses were imposed; parents and teachers were alerted, and left with the suspicion that all children were guilty, and with the fear of being themselves at fault if their suspicions were not sufficiently strong; they were kept in readiness in the face of this recurrent danger; their conduct was prescribed and their pedagogy recodified; an entire medico-sexual regime took

hold of the family milieu. The child's "vice" was not so much an enemy as a support; it may have been designated as the evil to be eliminated, but the extraordinary effort that went into the task that was bound to fail leads one to suspect that what was demanded of it was to persevere, to proliferate to the limits of the visible and the invisible, rather than to disappear for good. Always relying on this support, power advanced, multiplied its relays and its effects, while its target expanded, subdivided, and branched out, penetrating further into reality at the same pace. In appearance, we are dealing with a barrier system; but in fact, all around the child, indefinite *lines of penetration* were disposed.

2. This new persecution of the peripheral sexualities entailed an *incorporation of perversions* and a *new specification of individuals*. As defined by the ancient civil or canonical codes, sodomy was a category of forbidden acts; their perpetrator was nothing more than the juridical subject of them. The nineteenth-century homosexual became a personage, a past, a case history, and a childhood, in addition to being a type of life, a life form, and a morphology, with an indiscreet anatomy and possibly a mysterious physiology. Nothing that went into his total composition was unaffected by his sexuality. It was everywhere present in him: at the root of all his actions because it was their insidious and indefinitely active principle; written immodestly on his face and body because it was a secret that always gave itself away. It was consubstantial with him, less as a habitual sin than as a singular nature. We must not forget that the psychological, psychiatric, medical category of homosexuality was constituted from the moment it was characterized— Westphal's famous article of 1870 on "contrary sexual sensations" can stand as its date of birth[1]—less by a type of sexual relations than by a certain quality of sexual sensibility,

---

[1] Karl Westphal, "Die Konträre Sexualempfindung: Sypmtom eines neuropathologischen (psychopathischen) Zustandes," *Archiv für Psychiatrie und Nervenkrankheiten*, 2 (1869), pp. 73- 108. [This is the corrected and complete reference. Foucault simply refers to: Carl Westphal, *Archiv für Neuroligie*, 1870.]

a certain way of inverting the masculine and the feminine in oneself. Homosexuality appeared as one of the forms of sexuality when it was transposed from the practice of sodomy onto a kind of interior androgyny, a hermaphrodism of the soul. The sodomite had been a temporary aberration; the homosexual was now a species.

So too were all those minor perverts whom nineteenth-century psychiatrists entomologized by giving them strange baptismal names: there were Krafft-Ebing's zoophiles and zooerasts, Rohleder's auto-monosexualists; and later, mixoscopophiles, gynecomasts, presbyophiles, sexoesthetic inverts, and dyspareunist women. These fine names for heresies referred to a nature that was overlooked by the law, but not so neglectful of itself that it did not go on producing more species, even where there was no order to fit them into. The machinery of power that focused on this whole alien strain did not aim to suppress it, but rather to give it an analytical, visible, and permanent reality: it was implanted in bodies, slipped in beneath modes of conduct, made into a principle of classification and intelligibility, established as a *raison d'être* and a natural order of disorder. Not the exclusion of these thousand aberrant sexualities, but the specification, the regional solidification of each one of them. The strategy behind this dissemination was to strew reality with them and incorporate them into the individual.

3. More than the old taboos, this form of power demanded constant, attentive, and curious presences for its exercise; it presupposed proximities; it proceeded through examination and insistent observation; it required an exchange of discourses, through questions that extorted admissions, and confidences that went beyond the questions that were asked. It implied a physical proximity and an interplay of intense sensations. The medicalization of the sexually peculiar was both the effect and the instrument of this. Imbedded in bodies, becoming deeply characteristic of individuals, the oddities of sex relied on a technology of health and pathology. And conversely, since sexuality was a medical and medicalizable object, one had to try and detect it—as a lesion, a dysfunction, or a symptom—in the depths of the organism, or on the surface of the skin, or among all the

signs of behavior. The power which thus took charge of sexuality set about contacting bodies, caressing them with its eyes, intensifying areas, electrifying surfaces, dramatizing troubled moments. It wrapped the sexual body in its embrace. There was undoubtedly an increase in effectiveness and an extension of the domain controlled; but also a sensualization of power and a gain of pleasure. This produced a twofold effect: an impetus was given to power through its very exercise; an emotion rewarded the overseeing control and carried it further; the intensity of the confession renewed the questioner's curiosity; the pleasure discovered fed back to the power that encircled it. But so many pressing questions singularized the pleasures felt by the one who had to reply. They were fixed by a gaze, isolated and animated by the attention they received. Power operated as a mechanism of attraction; it drew out those peculiarities over which it kept watch. Pleasure spread to the power that harried it; power anchored the pleasure it uncovered.

{ hence { perusity

The medical examination, the psychiatric investigation, the pedagogical report, and family controls may have the over-all and apparent objective of saying no to all wayward or unproductive sexualities, but the fact is that they function as mechanisms with a double impetus: pleasure and power. The pleasure that comes of exercising a power that questions, monitors, watches, spies, searches out, palpates, brings to light; and on the other hand, the pleasure kindles at having to evade this power, flee from it, fool it, or travesty it. The power that lets itself be invaded by the pleasure it is pursuing; and opposite it, power asserting itself in the pleasure of showing off, scandalizing, or resisting. Capture and seduction, confrontation and mutual reinforcement: parents and children, adults and adolescents, educator and students, doctors and patients, the psychiatrist with his hysteric and his perverts, all have played this game continually since the nineteenth century. These attractions, these evasions, these circular incitements have traced around bodies and sexes, not boundaries not to be crossed, but *perpetual spirals of power and pleasure*.

4. Whence those *devices of sexual saturation* so characteristic of the space and the social rituals of the

nineteenth century. <u>People often say</u> that modern society has
attempted <u>to</u> reduce sexuality to the couple—the heterosexual
and, insofar as possible, legitimate couple. There are equal
grounds for saying that it has, if not created, <u>at least outfitted</u>

<u>and made to proliferate</u>, groups with multiple elements and a
<u>circulating sexuality</u>: a distribution of points of power,
hierarchized and placed opposite to one another; "pursued"
pleasures, that is, both sought after and searched out;
compartmental sexualities that are tolerated or encouraged;
proximities that serve as surveillance procedures, and
function as mechanisms of intensification; contacts that
operate as inductors. This is the way things worked in the
case of the family, or rather the household, with parents,
children, and in some instances, servants. Was the
nineteenth-century family really a monogamic and conjugal
cell? Perhaps to a certain extent. But it was also a network of
pleasures and powers linked together at multiple points and
according to transformable relationships. The separation of
grown-ups and children, the polarity established between the
parents' bedroom and that of the children (it became routine
in the course of the century when working-class housing
construction was undertaken), the relative segregation of
boys and girls, the strict instructions as to the care of nursing
infants (maternal breast-feeding, hygiene), the attention
focused on infantile sexuality, the supposed dangers of
masturbation, the importance attached to puberty, the
methods of surveillance suggested to parents, the
exhortations, secrets, and fears, the presence—both valued
and feared—of servants: all this made the family, even when
brought down to its smallest dimensions, a complicated
network, saturated with multiple, fragmentary, and mobile
sexualities. To reduce them to the conjugal relationship, and
then to project the latter, in the form of a forbidden desire,
onto the children, cannot account for this apparatus which, in
relation to these sexualities, was less a principle of inhibition
than an inciting and multiplying mechanism. Educational or
psychiatric institutions, with their large populations, their
hierarchies, their spatial arrangements, their surveillance
systems, constituted, alongside the family, another way of
distributing the interplay of powers and pleasures; but they

too delineated areas of extreme sexual saturation, with privileged spaces or rituals such as the classroom, the dormitory, the visit, and the consultation. The forms of a nonconjugal, nonmonogamous sexuality were drawn there and established.

Nineteenth-century "bourgeois" society—and it is doubtless still with us—was a society of blatant and fragmented perversion. And this was not by way of hypocrisy, for nothing was more manifest and more prolix, or more manifestly taken over by discourses and institutions. Not because, having tried to erect too rigid or too general a barrier against sexuality, society succeeded only in giving rise to a whole perverse outbreak and a long pathology of the sexual instinct. At issue, rather, is the type of power it brought to bear on the body and on sex. In point of fact, this power had neither the form of the law, nor the effects of the taboo. On the contrary, it acted by multiplication of singular sexualities. It did not set boundaries for sexuality; it extended the various forms of sexuality, pursuing them according to lines of indefinite penetration. It did not exclude sexuality, but included it in the body as a mode of specification of individuals. It did not seek to avoid it; it attracted its varieties by means of spirals in which pleasure and power reinforced one another. It did not set up a barrier; it provided places of maximum saturation. It produced and determined the sexual mosaic. Modern society is perverse, not in spite of its puritanism or as if from a backlash provoked by its hypocrisy; it is in actual fact, and directly, perverse.

In actual fact. The manifold sexualities—those which appear with the different ages (sexualities of the infant or the child), those which become fixated on particular tastes or practices (the sexuality of the invert, the gerontophile, the fetishist), those which, in a diffuse manner, invest relationships (the sexuality of doctor and patient, teacher and student, psychiatrist and mental patient), those which haunt spaces (the sexuality of the home, the school, the prison)—all form the correlate of exact procedures of power. We must not imagine that all these things that were formerly tolerated attracted notice and received a pejorative designation when the time came to give a regulative role to the one type of sexuality that was capable of reproducing labor power and the form of the family. These polymorphous conducts were actually extracted from people's bodies and from their pleasures; or rather, they were solidified in them; they were drawn out, revealed, isolated, intensified, incorporated, by multifarious power devices. The growth of perversions is not a moralizing theme that obsessed the scrupulous minds of the Victorians. It is the real product of the encroachment of a type of power on bodies and their pleasures. It is possible that the West has not been capable of inventing any new pleasures, and it has doubtless not discovered any original vices. But it has defined new rules for the game of powers and pleasures. The frozen countenance of the perversions is a fixture of this game.

Directly. This implantation of multiple perversions is not a mockery of sexuality taking revenge on a power that has thrust on it an excessively repressive law. Neither are we dealing with paradoxical forms of pleasure that turn back on power and invest it in the form of a "pleasure to be endured." The implantation of perversions is an instrument-effect: it is through the isolation, intensification, and consolidation of peripheral sexualities that the relations of power to sex and pleasure branched out and multiplied, measured the body, and penetrated modes of conduct. And accompanying this encroachment of powers, scattered sexualities rigidified, became stuck to an age, a place, a type of practice. A proliferation of sexualities through the extension of power; an optimization of the power to which each of these local sexualities gave a surface of intervention: this concatenation, particularly since the nineteenth century, has been ensured and relayed by the countless economic interests which, with the help of medicine, psychiatry, prostitution, and pornography, have tapped into both this analytical multiplication of pleasure and this optimization of the power that controls it. Pleasure and power do not cancel or turn back against one another; they seek out, overlap, and reinforce one another. They are linked together by complex mechanisms and devices of excitation and incitement.

We must therefore abandon the hypothesis that modern industrial societies ushered in an age of increased sexual repression. We have not only witnessed a visible explosion of unorthodox sexualities; but—and this is the important point—a deployment quite different from the law, even if it is locally dependent on procedures of prohibition, has ensured, through a network of interconnecting mechanisms, the proliferation of specific pleasures and the multiplication of disparate sexualities. It is said that no society has been more prudish; never have the agencies of power taken such care to feign ignorance of the thing they prohibited, as if they were determined to have nothing to do with it. But it is the opposite that has become apparent, at least after a general review of the facts: never have there existed more centers of power; never more attention manifested and verbalized; never more circular contacts and linkages; never more sites where the intensity of pleasures and the persistency of power catch hold, only to spread elsewhere.

CHAPTER 3:
Mary McIntosh
The Homosexual Role

Recent advances in the sociology of deviant behaviour have not yet affected the study of homosexuality, which is still commonly seen as a condition characterizing certain persons in the way that birthplace or deformity might characterize them. The limitations of this view can best be understood if we examine some of its implications. In the first place, if homosexuality is a condition, then people either have it or do not have it. Many scientists and ordinary people assume that there are two kinds of people in the world: homosexuals and heterosexuals. Some of them recognize that homosexual feelings and behaviour are not confined to the persons they would like to call "homosexuals" and that some of these persons do not actually engage in homosexual behaviour. This should pose a crucial problem, but they evade the crux by retaining their assumption and puzzling over the question of how to tell whether someone is "really" homosexual or not. Lay people too will discuss whether a certain person is "queer" in much the same way as they might question whether a certain pain indicated cancer. And in much the same way they will often turn to scientists or to medical men for a surer diagnosis. Thus one psychiatrist, discussing the definition of homosexuality, has written:

> I do not diagnose patients as homosexual unless they have engaged in overt homosexual behaviour. Those who also engage in heterosexual activity are diagnosed as bisexual. An isolated experience may not warrant the diagnosis, but repetetive [sic]

© 1968 by the Society for the Study of Social Problems. Reprinted from *Social Problems* 16 (Fall 1968), pp. 182-192.

homosexual behaviour in adulthood, whether sporadic or
continuous, designates a homosexual.[1]

Along with many other writers, he introduces the notion of
a third type of person, the "bisexual," to handle the fact that
behavior patterns cannot be conveniently dichotomized into
heterosexual and homosexual. But this does not solve the
conceptual problem, since bisexuality too is seen as a
condition (unless as a passing response to unusual situations
such as confinement in a one-sex prison). In any case there is
no extended discussion of bisexuality; the topic is usually
given a brief mention in order to clear the ground for the
consideration of "true homosexuality."
To cover the cases where the symptoms of behaviour or of
felt attractions do not match the diagnosis, other writers have
referred to an adolescent homosexual phase or have used such
terms as 'latent homosexual' or 'pseudo homosexual.' Indeed
one of the earliest studies of the subject, by Krafft-Ebing,[2]
was concerned with making a distinction between the "invert"
who is congenitally homosexual and others who, although
they behave in the same way, are not true inverts.
A second result of the conceptualization of homosexuality
as a condition is that the major research task has been seen as
the study of its aetiology. There has been much debate as to
whether the condition is innate or acquired. The first step in
such research has commonly been to find a sample of
"homosexuals" in the same way that a medical researcher
might find a sample of diabetics if he wanted to study that
disease. Yet after a long history of such studies, the results
are sadly inconclusive, and the answer is still as much a matter
of opinion as it was when Havelock Ellis's *Sexual Inversion*
was published seventy years ago. The failure of research to

---

[1] Irving Bieber, "Clinical Aspects of Male Homosexuality," in *Sexual Inversion: The Multiple Roots of Homosexuality*, J. Marmor, ed. (New York: Basic Books, 1965), p. 248.

[2] Richard von Krafft-Ebing, *Psychopathia Sexualis: A Medico-Economic Study*, M.E. Wedeck, trans. (New York: G.P. Putnam's and Sons, 1965).

answer the question has not been due to lack of scientific rigour or to any inadequacy of the available evidence; it results rather from the fact that the wrong question has been asked. One might as well try to trace the aetiology of "committee chairmanship" or "Seventh Day Adventism" as of "homosexuality."

The vantage point of comparative sociology enables us to see that the conception of homosexuality as a condition is, in itself, a possible object of study. This conception and the behaviour it supports operate as a form of social control in a society in which homosexuality is condemned. Furthermore the uncritical acceptance of the conception by social scientists can be traced to their concern with homosexuality as a social problem. They have tended to accept the popular definition of what the problem is, and they have been implicated in the process of social control.

The practice of the social labeling of persons as deviant operates in two ways as a mechanism of social control.[3] In the first place it helps to provide a clear-cut, publicized and recognizable threshold between permissible and impermissible behaviour. This means that people cannot so easily drift into deviant behaviour. Their first moves in a deviant direction immediately raise the question of a total move into a deviant role with all the sanctions that this is likely to elicit. Second, the labeling serves to segregate the deviants from others, and this means that their deviant practices and their self-justifications for these practices are contained within a relatively narrow group. The creation of a specialized, despised and punished role of homosexual keeps the bulk of society pure in rather the same way that the similar treatment of some kinds of criminals helps keep the rest of society law-abiding.

However, the disadvantage of this practice as a technique of social control is that there may be a tendency for people to become fixed in their deviance once they have become labeled.

---

[3] This is a grossly simplified account. Edwin Lemert provides a far more subtle and detailed analysis in his *Social Pathology* (New York: McGraw-Hill, 1951), chapter 4, "Sociopathic Individuation."

This too is a process that has become well-recognized in discussion of other forms of deviant behaviour, such as juvenile delinquency and drug taking, and indeed of other kinds of social labeling, such as streaming in schools and racial distinctions. One might expect social categorizations of this sort to be to some extent self-fulfilling prophecies: if the culture defines people as falling into distinct types—black and white, criminal and non-criminal, homosexual and normal— then these types tend to become polarized, highly differentiated from each other. Later in this paper I shall discuss whether this is so in the case of homosexuals and "normals" in the United States today.

It is interesting to notice that homosexuals themselves welcome and suppose the notion that homosexuality is a condition. For just as the rigid categorization deters people from drifting into deviancy, so it appears to foreclose on the possibility of drifting back into normality and thus removes the element of anxious choice. It appears to justify the deviant behaviour of the homosexual as being appropriate for him as a member of the homosexual category. The deviancy can thus be seen as legitimate for him and he can continue in it without rejecting the norms of the society.[4]

The way in which people become labeled as homosexual can now be seen as an important social process connected with mechanisms of social control. It is important therefore that sociologists should examine this process objectively and not lend themselves to participation in it, particularly since, as we have seen, psychologists and psychiatrists on the whole have not retained their objectivity but have become involved as diagnostic agents in the process of social labeling.[5]

---

[4] For discussion of situations in which deviants can lay claim to legitimacy, see Talcott Parsons, *The Social System* (New York: Free Press, 1951), pp. 292-3

[5] The position taken here is similar to that of Irving Goffman in his discussion of becoming a mental patient in *Asylums: Essays on the Social Situation of Mental Patients and Other Inmates* (New York: Anchor Books, 1961), pp. 128-46.

It is proposed that the homosexual should be seen as playing a social role rather than as having a condition. The role of "homosexual," however, does not simply describe a sexual behaviour pattern. If it did, the idea of a role would be no more useful than that of a condition. For the purpose of introducing the term 'role' is to enable us to handle the fact that behaviour in this sphere does not match popular beliefs: that sexual behaviour patterns cannot be dichotomized in the way that the social roles of homosexual and heterosexual can.

It may seem rather odd to distinguish in this way between role and behaviour, but if we accept a definition of role in terms of expectations (which may or may not be fulfilled), then the distinction is both legitimate and useful. In modern societies where a separate homosexual role is recognized, the expectation, on behalf of those who play the role and of others, is that a homosexual will be exclusively or very predominantly homosexual in his feelings and behaviour. In addition there are other expectations that frequently exist, especially on the part of nonhomosexuals, but affecting the self-conception of anyone who sees himself as homosexual. These are the expectation that he will be effeminate in manner, personality, or preferred sexual activity, the expectation that sexuality will play a part of some kind in all his relations with other men, and the expectation that he will be attracted to boys and very young men and probably willing to seduce them. The existence of a social expectation, of course, commonly helps to produce its own fulfillment. But the question of how far it is fulfilled is a matter for empirical investigation rather than *a priori* pronouncement. Some of the empirical evidence about the chief expectation—that homosexuality precludes heterosexuality—in relation to the homosexual role in America is examined in the final section of this paper.[6]

In order to clarify the nature of the role and demonstrate that it exists only in certain societies, we shall present the cross-cultural and historical evidence available. This raises awkward

---

[6] For evidence that many self confessed homosexuals in England are not effeminate and many are not interested in boys, see Michael Schofield, *Sociological Aspects of Homosexuality* (Boston: Little, Brown, 1965).

problems of method because the material has hitherto usually been collected and analyzed in terms of culturally specific modern Western conceptions.

The Homosexual Role in Various Societies

To study homosexuality in the past or in other societies we usually have to rely on secondary evidence rather than on direct observation. The reliability and the validity of such evidence is open to question because what the original observers reported may have been distorted by their disapproval of homosexuality and by their definition of it, which may be different from the one we wish to adopt.

For example, Marc Daniel[7] tries to refute accusations of homosexuality against Pope Julian II by producing four arguments: the Pope had many enemies who might wish to blacken his name; he and his supposed lover, Alidosi, both had mistresses; neither of them was at all effeminate; and the Pope had other men friends about whom no similar accusations were made. In other words Daniel is trying to fit an early sixteenth century Pope to the modern conception of the homosexual as effeminate, exclusively homosexual and sexual in relation to all men. The fact that he does not fit is, of course, no evidence, as Daniel would have it, that his relationship with Alidosi was not a sexual one.

Anthropologists too can fall into this trap. Marvin Opler, summarizing anthropological evidence on the subject, says:

> Actually, no society, save perhaps Ancient Greece, pre-Meiji Japan, certain top echelons in Nazi Germany, and the scattered examples of such special status groups as the *berdaches*, Nata slaves and one category of Chuckchee shamans, has lent sanction in any real sense to homosexuality.[8]

---

[7] Marc Daniel, "Essai de Methodologie pour l'etude des aspects homosexuals de l'historie," *Arcadie* 133 (January 1965), pp. 31-37.

[8] Marvin Opler, "Anthropological and Cross Cultural Aspects of Homos," in *Sexual Inversion*, p.174.

Yet he goes on to discuss societies in which there are reports of sanctioned adolescent and other occasional "experimentation." Of the Cubeo of the North West Amazon, for instance, he says, "*true* homosexuality among the Cubeo is rare if not absent," giving as evidence the fact that no males with persistent homosexual patterns are reported.[9]

Allowing for such weaknesses, the Human Relations Area Files are the best single source of comparative information. Their evidence on homosexuality has been summarized by Ford and Beach,[10] who identify two broad types of accepted patterns: the institutionalized homosexual role and the liaison between men and boys who are otherwise heterosexual. The recognition of a distinct role of *berdache* or transvestite is, they say, "the commonest form of institutionalized homosexuality." This form shows a marked similarity to that in our own society, though in some ways it is even more extreme. The Mojave Indians of California and Arizona, for example, recognized both an *alyha*, a male transvestite who took the role of the woman in sexual intercourse, and a *hwame*, a female homosexual who took the role of the male.[11] People were believed to be born as *alyha* or *hwame*, hints of their future proclivities occurring in their mothers' dreams during pregnancy. If a young boy began to behave like a girl and take an interest in women's things instead of men's, there was an initiation ceremony in which he would become an *alyha*. After that he would dress and act like a woman, would be referred to as "she" and could take "husbands."

But the Mojave pattern differs from ours in that although the *alyha* was considered regrettable and amusing, he was not condemned and was given public recognition. The attitude was that "he was an *alyha*, he could not help it." But the "husband" of an *alyha* was an ordinary man who happened to

---

[9] *Ibid.*, p. 117

[10] C.S. Ford and F. Beach, *Patterns of Sexual Behavior* (New York: Harper, 1951).

[11] G. Devereux, "Institutional Homosexuality of the Mohave Indians," *Human Biology* 9 (1937), pp. 498-627.

have chosen an *alyha*, perhaps because they were good housekeepers or because they were believed to be "lucky in love," and he would be the butt of endless teasing and joking.

This radical distinction between the feminine, passive homosexual and his masculine, active partner is one which is not made very much in our own society,[12] but which is very important in the Middle East. There, however, neither is thought of as being a "born" homosexual, although the passive partner, who demeans himself by his feminine submission, is despised and ridiculed while the active one is not. In most of the ancient Middle East, including among the Jews until the return from the Babylonian exile, there were male temple prostitutes.[13] Thus even cultures that recognize a separate homosexual role may not define it in the same way as our culture does.

Many other societies accept or approve of homosexual liaisons as part of a variegated sexual pattern. Usually these are confined to a particular stage in the individual's life. Among the Aranda of Central Australia, for instance, there are long-standing relationships of several years' duration between unmarried men and young boys, starting at the age of 10 to 12 years.[14] This is rather similar to the well-known situation in classical Greece, but there, of course, the older man could have a wife as well. Sometimes, however, as among the Siwans of North Africa,[15] all men and boys can and are

---

[12] The lack of cultural distinction is reflected in behaviour Gordon Westwood found that only a small proportion of his sample of British homosexuals engaged in anal intercourse, and many of these had been active and passive and did not have a clear preference. See Westwood [alias for Michael Schofield], *A Minority Report on the Life of the Male Homosexual in Great Britain* (London: Longmans, 1960), pp. 127-34).

[13] G. R. Taylor, "Historical and Mythological Aspects of Homosexuality", in *Sexual Inversion* and F. Henriques, *Prostitution and Society*, volume 1 (London: MacGibbon and Kee, 1962), pp. 341-343.

[14] *Patterns of Sexual Behavior*, p. 132

[15] *Ibid.*, p. 131-32.

expected to engage in homosexual activities, apparently at every stage of life. In all of these societies there may be much homosexual behaviour, but there are no "homosexuals."

The Development of the Homosexual Role in England

The problem of method is even more acute in dealing with historical material than with anthropological, for history is usually concerned with "great events" rather than with recurrent patterns. There are some records of attempts to curb sodomy among minor churchmen during the medieval period,[16] which seem to indicate that it was common. At least they suggest that laymen feared on behalf of their sons that it was common. The term 'catamite,' meaning "boy kept for immoral purposes," was first used in 1593, again suggesting that this practice was common then. But most of the historical references to homosexuality relate either to great men or to great scandals. However, over the last seventy years or so various scholars have tried to trace the history of sex,[17] and it is possible to glean a good deal from what they have found and also from what they have failed to establish.

Their studies of English history before the seventeenth century consist usually of inconclusive speculation as to whether certain men, such as Edward II, Christopher Marlowe, William Shakespeare, were or were not homosexual. Yet the disputes are inconclusive not because of lack of evidence but because none of these men fits the modern stereotype of the homosexual.

It is not until the end of the seventeenth century that other kinds of information become available, and it is possible to

---

[16] G. May, *Social Control of Sex* (New York: Morrow and Company, 1931), pp. 65, 101.

[17] See especially H. Ellis, *Studies in the Psychology of Sex*, volume 2: *Sexual Inversion* (New York: Random House, 1936), I. Bloch (F. Uuhren, pseud.), *Sexual Life in England: Past and Present* (London: Francis Adler, 1938), G.R. Taylor, *Sex in History* (New York: Vanguard, 1954), N.I. Garde, *Jonathan to Gide: The Homosexual History* (New York: Vantage, 1964).

move from speculations about individuals to descriptions of homosexual life. At this period references to homosexuals as a type and to a rudimentary homosexual subculture, mainly in London, begin to appear. But the earliest descriptions of homosexuals do not coincide exactly with the modern conception. There is much more stress on effeminacy and in particular on transvestism, to such an extent that there seems to be no distinction at first between transvestism and homosexuality.[18] The terms emerging at this period to describe homosexuals—Molly, Nancy-boy, Madge-cull—emphasize effeminacy. In contrast the modern terms—like fag, queer, gay, bent—do not have this implication.[19]

By the end of the seventeenth century, homosexual transvestites were a distinct enough group to be able to form their own clubs in London.[20] Edward Ward's *History of the London Clubs* (1896), first published in 1709, describes one called "The Mollie's Club" which met "in a certain tavern in the City" for "parties and regular gatherings." The members "adopt[ed] all the small vanities natural to the feminine sex to such an extent that they try to speak, walk, chatter, shriek and scold as women do, aping them as well in other respects." The other respects apparently included the enactment of marriages and childbirth. The club was discovered and broken up by agents of the Reform Society.[21] There were a number

---

[18] Evelyn Hooker has suggested that in a period when homosexual grouping and a homosexual subculture have not yet become institutionalized, homosexuals are likely to behave in a more distinctive and conspicuous manner because other means of making contact are not available. This is confirmed by the fact that lesbians are more conspicuous than male homosexuals in our society, but does not seem to fit the seventeenth century, where the groups are already described as "clubs."

[19] However, 'fairy', and 'pansy,' the commonest slang terms used by non-homosexuals, have the same meaning of effeminate as the earlier terms.

[20] Bloch, *Sexual Life in England: Past and Present*, p. 328, gives several examples, but attributes their emergence to the fact that "the number of homosexuals increased."

[21] *Sex in History*.

of similar scandals during the course of the eighteenth century as various homosexual coteries were exposed.

A writer in 1729 describes the widespread homosexual life of the period:

> They also have their Walks and Appointments, to meet and pick up one another, and their particular Houses of Resort to go to, because they dare not trust themselves in an open Tavern. About twenty of these sort of Houses have been discovered, besides the Nocturnal Assemblies of great numbers of the like vile Persons, what they call the Markets, which are the Royal Exchange, Lincoln's Inn, Bog Houses, the south side of St James's Park, the Piazzas in Covent Garden, St Clement's Churchyard, etc.
> It would be a pretty scene to behold them in their clubs and cabals, how they assume the air and affect the name of Madam or Miss, Betty or Molly, with a chuck under the chin, and "Oh you bold pullet, I'll break your eggs," and then frisk and walk away.[22]

The notion of exclusive homosexuality became well established during this period:

> Two Englishmen, Leith and Drew, were accused of paederasty. . .
> The evidence given by the plaintiffs was, as was generally the case in these trials, very imperfect. On the other hand the defendants denied the accusation, and produced witnesses to prove their predeliction for women. They were in consequence acquitted.[23]

This could only have been an effective argument in a society that perceived homosexual behaviour as incompatible with heterosexual tastes.

During the nineteenth century there are further reports of raided clubs and homosexual brothels. However, by this time the element of transvestism had diminished in importance. Even the male prostitutes are described as being of masculine

---

[22] *Ibid.*, p. 142
[23] *Sexual Life in England: Past and Present*, p. 334.

build, and there is more stress upon sexual licence and less upon dressing up and play-acting.

The Homosexual Role and Homosexual Behavior

Thus a distinct, separate, specialized role of "homosexual" emerged in England at the end of the seventeenth century, and the conception of homosexuality as a condition which characterizes certain individuals and not others is now firmly established in our society. The term role is, of course, a form of shorthand. It refers not only to a cultural conception or set of ideas but also to a complex of institutional arrangements which depend upon and reinforce these ideas. These arrangements include all the forms of heterosexual activity, courtship and marriage as well as the labeling processes— gossip, ridicule, psychiatric diagnosis, criminal conviction— and the groups and networks of the homosexual subculture. For simplicity we shall simply say that a specialized role exists. How does the existence of this social role affect actual behaviour? And, in particular, does the behaviour of individuals conform to the cultural conception in the sense that most people are either exclusively heterosexual or exclusively homosexual? It is difficult to answer these questions on the basis of available evidence because so many researchers have worked with the preconception that homosexuality is a condition, so that in order to study the behaviour they have first found a group of people who could be identified as "homosexuals." Homosexual behaviour should be studied independently of social roles, if the connection between the two is to be revealed. This may not sound like a particularly novel programme to those who are familiar with Kinsey's contribution to the field. He, after all, set out to study "sexual behaviour"; he rejected the assumptions of scientists and laymen:

> . . . that there are persons who are "heterosexual" and persons who are "homosexual," that these two types represent antitheses in the sexual world and that there is only an insignificant class of "bisexuals" who occupy an intermediate position between the other groups. . . that every individual is innately—inherently—

either heterosexual or homosexual. . . [and] that from the time of
birth one is fated to be one thing or the other. . . .[24]

But although some of Kinsey's ideas are often referred to,
particularly in polemical writings, surprisingly little use has
been made of his actual data.

Most of Kinsey's chapter on the "Homosexual Outlet"
centers on his "heterosexual-homosexual rating scale." His
subjects were rated on this scale according to the proportion of
their "psychologic reactions and overt experience" that was
homosexual in any given period of their lives. It is interesting
and unfortunate for our purposes, that this is one of the few
places in the book where Kinsey abandons his behaviouristic
approach to some extent. However, "psychologic reactions"
may well be expected to be affected by the existence of a social
role in the some way as overt behaviour. Another problem
with using Kinsey's material is that although he gives very full
information about sexual behaviour, the other characteristics of
the people he interviewed are only given in a very bald form.[25]
But Kinsey's study is undoubtedly the fullest description there
is of sexual behavior in any society, and as such it is the safest
basis for generalizations to other Western societies.

The ideal way to trace the effects on behaviour of the
existence of a homosexual role would be to compare societies
in which the role exists with societies in which it does not.
But as there are no adequate descriptions of homosexual
behaviour in societies where there is no homosexual role, we
shall have to substitute comparisons within American society.

---

[24] A.C. Kinsey, W.B. Pomeroy, and C.E. Martin, *Sexual Behavior in
the Human Male* (Philadelphia, W.B. Saunders, 1948), pp. 636-7

[25] The more general drawbacks of Kinsey's data, particularly the problem
of the representativeness of his sample, have been thoroughly canvassed
in a number of places; see especially W.G. Cochran, F. Mosteller, and
J.W. Tukey, *Statistical Problems of the Kinsey Report* (Washington,
D.C.: American Statistical Society, 1954).

Polarization

If the existence of a social role were reflected in people's behaviour, we should expect to find that relatively few people would engage in bisexual behaviour. The problem about investigating this empirically is to know what is meant by "relatively few." The categories of Kinsey's rating scale are, of course, completely arbitrary. He has five bisexual categories, but he might just as well have had more or less, in which case the number falling into each would have been smaller or larger. The fact that the distribution of his scale is U-shaped, then, is in itself meaningless (see Table A).

Table A

Heterosexual-homoseual rating: active incidence by age

% of each age group having each rating

Age	(1) X	(2) 0	(3) 1	(4) 2	(5) 3	(6) 4	(7) 5	(8) 6	(9) 1-6
15	23.6	48.4	3.6	6.0	4.7	3.7	2.6	7.4	28.0
20	3.3	69.3	4.4	7.4	4.4	2.9	3.4	4.9	27.4
25	1.0	79.2	3.9	5.1	3.2	2.4	2.3	2.9	19.8
30	0.5	83.1	4.0	3.4	2.1	3.0	1.3	2.6	16.4
35	0.4	86.7	2.4	3.4	1.9	1.7	0.9	1.6	12.9
40	1.3	86.8	3.0	3.6	2.0	0.7	0.3	2.3	11.9
45	2.7	88.8	2.3	2.0	1.3	0.9	0.2	1.8	8.5

X=unresponsive to either sex; 0=entirely heterosexual 1=largely heterosexual but with incidental homosexual history; 2=largely heterosexual but with a distinct homosexual history; 3=equally heterosexual and homosexual; 4=largely homosexual but with distinct heterosexual history; 5=largely homosexual but with incidental heterosexual history; 6=entirely homosexual

Source: Based on Kinsey et al. (1948), p. 652, Table 148

It is impossible to get direct evidence of a polarization between the homosexual and the heterosexual pattern, though we may note the suggestive evidence to the contrary that at every age far more men have bisexual than exclusively homosexual patterns. However, by making comparisons between one age group and another and between men and women, it should be possible to see some of the effects of the role.

Age comparison

As they grow older, more and more men take up exclusively heterosexual patterns, as Table A, column 2 shows. The table also shows that *each* of the bisexual and homosexual categories, columns 3-8, contains fewer men as time goes by after the age of 20. The greatest losses are from the fifth bisexual category, column 7, with responses that are "almost entirely homosexual." It is a fairly small group to begin with, but by the age of 45 it has almost entirely disappeared. On the other hand, the first bisexual category, column 3, with only "incidental homosexual histories" has its numbers not even halved by the age of 45. Yet at all ages the first bisexual category represents a much smaller proportion of those who are almost entirely heterosexual (columns 2 and 3) than the fifth category represents of those who are almost entirely homosexual (columns 7 and 8). In everyday language it seems that proportionately more "homosexuals" dabble in heterosexual activity than "heterosexuals" dabble in homosexual activity and such dabbling is particularly common in the younger age groups of 20 to 30. This indicates that the existence of the despised role operates at all ages to inhibit people from engaging in occasional homosexual behaviour, but does not have the effect of making the behaviour of many "homosexuals" exclusively homosexual.

On the other hand, the overall reduction in the amount of homosexual behaviour with age can be attributed in part to the fact that more and more men become married. While the active incidence of homosexual behaviour is high and increases with age among single men, among married men it is low and decreases only slightly with age. Unfortunately the Kinsey figures do not enable us to compare the incidence of homosexuality among single men who later marry and those who do not.

Comparison between men and women

The notion of a separate homosexual role is much less well developed in women than it is for men, and so too are the attendant techniques of social control and the deviant subculture and organization. So a comparison with women's sexual behaviour should tell us something about the effects of the social role on men's behaviour.

Table B

Comparison of male and female heterosexual-homosexual ratings: active incidence at selected ages

% of each age group having each rating

Age	(1) X	(2) 0	(3) 1	(4) 2	(5) 3	(6) 4	(7) 5	(8) 6	(9) 1-6
Male } 20	3.3	69.3	4.4	7.4	4.4	2.9	3.4	4.9	27.4
Female	15	74	5	2	1	1	1	1	11
Male } 35	0.4	86.7	2.4	3.4	1.9	1.7	0.9	2.6	12.9
Female	7	80	7	2	1	1	1	1	13

Source: Based on Kinsey et al. (1948), p. 652, Table 148, and Kinsey
   (1953), p. 499, Table 142. For explanation of the ratings, see Table A.

Fewer women than men engage in homosexual behaviour. By the time they are 45, 26 percent of women have had *some* homosexual experience, whereas about 50 percent of men have. But this is probably a cause rather than an effect of the difference in the extent to which the homosexual role is crystallized, for women engage in less non-marital sexual activity of any kind than men. For instance, by the time they marry, 50 percent of women have had some pre-marital heterosexual experience to orgasm, whereas as many as 90 percent of men have.

The most revealing contrast is between the male and female distributions on the Kinsey rating scale, shown in Table B. The distributions for women follow a smooth U-shaped pattern, while those for men are uneven with an increase in numbers at the exclusively homosexual end. The distributions for women are the shape that one would expect on the assumption that homosexual and heterosexual acts are randomly distributed in a ratio of 1 to 18.[26] The men are relatively more concentrated in the exclusively homosexual category. This appears to confirm the hypothesis that the existence of the role is reflected in behaviour.

Finally, it is interesting to notice that although at the age of 20 far more men than women have homosexual and bisexual patterns (27 percent as against 11 percent), by the age of 35 the figures are both the same (13 percent). Women seem to broaden their sexual experience as they get older whereas more men become narrower and more specialized. None of this, however, should obscure the fact that, in terms of behaviour, the polarization between the heterosexual man and the homosexual man is far from complete in our society. Some polarization does seem to have occurred, but many men manage to follow patterns of sexual behaviour that are between the two, in spite of our cultural preconceptions and institutional arrangements.

Conclusion

This paper has dealt with only one small aspect of the sociology of homosexuality. It is, nevertheless, a fundamental one. For it is not until he sees homosexuals as a social category, rather than a medical or psychiatric one, that the sociologist can begin to ask the right questions about the specific content of the homosexual role and about the

---

[26] This cannot be taken in a rigorously statistical sense, since the categories are arbitrary and do not refer to numbers, or even proportions, of actual sexual acts.

organization and functions of homosexual groups.[27] All that has been done here is to indicate that the role does not exist in many societies, that it only emerged in England towards the end of the seventeenth century, and that, although the existence of the role in modern America appears to have some effect on the distribution of homosexual behavior, such behavior is far from being monopolized by persons who play the role of homosexual.

---

[27] But an interesting beginning has been made by Evelyn Hooker, "The Homosexual Community" in *Sexual Deviance*, J.H. Gagnon and W.S. Simon, eds. (New York: Harper & Row, 1967) and "Male Homosexuals and Their 'Worlds'" in *Sexual Inversion: The Multiple Roots of Homosexuality*, pp. 83-107; there is much valuable descriptive material in D. W. Cory (pseud. for Edward Sararin) *The Homosexual Outlook: A Subjective Approach* (New York: Greenberg, 1951) and in *A Minority Report on the Life of the Male Homosexual in Great Britain*, as well as elsewhere.

CHAPTER 4:
Robert Padgug
Sexual Matters:
On Conceptualizing Sexuality in History

Sexuality—the subject matter seems so obvious that it hardly appears to need comment. An immense and ever-increasing number of "discourses" has been devoted to its exploration and control during the last few centuries, and their very production has, as Foucault points out,[1] been a major characteristic of bourgeois society. Yet, ironically, as soon as we attempt to apply the concept to history, apparently insurmountable problems confront us.

To take a relatively simple example, relevant to one aspect of sexuality only, what are we to make of the ancient Greek historian Alexis's curious description of Polykrates, sixth-century B.C. ruler of Samos?[2] In the course of his account of the luxurious habits of Polykrates, Alexis stresses his numerous imports of foreign goods, and adds: "Because of all this there is good reason to marvel at the fact that the tyrant is not mentioned as having sent for women or boys from anywhere, despite his passion for liaisons with males. . ." Now, that Polykrates did not "send for women" would seem to us to be a direct corollary of "his passion for liaisons with

---

[1] Michel Foucault, *The History of Sexuality, Volume I: An Introduction*, Robert Hurley, trans. (New York: Pantheon, 1978)

[2] As reported in Athenaeus, *Deipnosophistae* 12.450, in Felix Jacoby, *Fragmente der Griech. Historiker* (Leiden: Brill, 1954-1964) no. 539, fragment no. 2.

This article originally appeared in *Radical History Review* 20 (Spring/Summer 1979), pp. 3-23. It is reprinted with the permission of MARHO: The Radical Historians' Organization.

males." But to Alexis—and we know that his attitude was shared by all of Greek antiquity[3]—sexual passion in any form implied sexual passion in all forms. Sexual categories which seem so obvious to us, those which divide humanity into "heterosexuals" and "homosexuals," seem unknown to the ancient Greeks.

A problem thus emerges at the start: the categories which most historians normally use to analyze sexual matters do not seem adequate when we deal with Greek antiquity. We might, of course, simply dismiss the Greeks as "peculiar"—a procedure as common as it is unenlightening—but we would confront similar problems with respect to most other societies. Or, we might recognize the difference between Greek sexuality and our own, but not admit that it creates a problem in conceptualization. Freud, for example, writes:

> The most striking distinction between the erotic life of antiquity and our own no doubt lies in the fact that the ancients laid the stress upon the instinct itself, whereas we emphasize its object. The ancients glorified the instinct and were prepared on its account to honor even an inferior object; while we despise the instinctual activity in itself, and find excuses for it only in the merit of the object.[4]

Having made this perceptive comment, he lets the subject drop: so striking a contrast is, for him, a curiosity, rather than the starting point for serious critique of the very categories of sexuality.

Most investigators into sexuality in history have in fact treated their subject as so many variations on a single theme, whose contents were already broadly known. This is not only

---

[3] For other examples, see Lucian, "The Ship," in Loeb Classical Library edition of Lucian, volume VI, p. 481, or Plutarch, "The Love Stories," in *Moralia* 771E-775E, which provides pairs of similar love tales, each consisting of one involving heterosexual love and one involving homosexual love.

[4] Sigmund Freud, *Three Essays on the Theory of Sexuality*, James Strachey, trans. (New York: Basic Books, 1964), p. 38; the footnote was added in the 1910 edition.

true of those who openly treat the history of sexuality as a species of entertainment, but even of those whose purpose is more serious and whose work is considered more significant from an historical point of view. One example chosen from the much-admired *The Other Victorians* of Steven Marcus,[5] is typical. Marcus describes a very Victorian flagellation scene which appears in the anonymous *My Secret Life*. After describing its contents, he states categorically:

> But the representation in *My Secret Life* does something which pornography cannot. It demonstrates how truly and literally childish such behavior is; it shows us, as nothing else that I know does, the pathos of perversity, how deeply sad, how cheerless a condemnation it really is. It is more than a condemnation; it is—or was—an imprisonment for life. For if it is bad enough that we are all imprisoned within our own sexuality, how much sadder must it be to be still further confined within this foreshortened, abridged and parodically grotesque version of it.

Marcus already *knows* the content and meaning of sexuality, Victorian or otherwise. It was not *My Secret Life* which gave him his knowledge, but rather his predetermined and prejudged "knowledge" which allowed him to use *My Secret Life* to create a catalogue of examples of a generalized and universal sexuality, a sexuality which was not the result but the organizing principle of his study. Given this pre-knowledge, sexuality in history could hardly become a problem—it was simply a given.

Not surprisingly, for Marcus as well as for many other "sex researchers"—from Freudians to positivists—the sexuality which is "given," which is sexuality *tout court*, is what they perceive to be the sexuality of their own century, culture, and class, whether it bears a fundamentally "popular" stamp or comes decked out in full scientific garb.

---

[5] Steven Marcus, *The Other Victorians: A Study of Sexuality and Pornography in Mid-Nineteenth Century England*, second edition (New York: Basic Books, 1974), p. 127

In any approach that takes as predetermined and universal the categories of sexuality, real history disappears. Sexual practice becomes a more or less sophisticated selection of curiosities, whose meaning and validity can be gauged by that truth—or rather truths, since there are many competitors—which we, in our enlightened age, have discovered. This procedure is reminiscent of the political economy of the period before, and all too often after, Marx, but it is not purely bourgeois failing. Many of the chief sinners are Marxists.

A surprising lack of a properly historical approach to the subject of sexuality has allowed a fundamentally bourgeois view of sexuality and its subdivisions to deform twentieth-century Marxism. Marx and Engels themselves tended to neglect the subject and even Engels's *Origins of the Family, Private Property and the State* by no means succeeded in making it a concern central to historical materialism. The Marxism of the Second International, trapped to so great a degree within a narrow economism, mainly dismissed sexuality as merely superstructural. Most later Marxist thought and practice, with a few notable exceptions—Alexandra Kollontai, Wilhelm Reich, and Frankfurt School—has in one way or another accepted this judgment.

In recent years questions concerning the nature of sexuality have been re-placed on the Marxist agenda by the force of events and movements. The women's movement, and, to an increasing degree, the gay movement, have made it clear that a politics without sexuality is doomed to failure or deformation; the strong offensive of the American right-wing which combines class and sexual politics can only re-enforce this view.[6] The feminist insistence that "the personal *is* political," itself a product of ongoing struggle, represents an immense step forward in the understanding of social reality, one which must be absorbed as a living part of Marxist attitudes toward sexuality. The important comprehension that sexuality, class, and politics cannot easily be disengaged from one another

---

[6] See Linda Gordon and Allen Hunter, "Sex, Family and the New Right," *Radical America* 11/12 (November 1977/February 1978), pp. 9-26.

must serve as the basis of a materialist view of sexuality in
historical perspective as well.

Sexuality as Ideology

The contemporary view of sexuality which underlies most
historical work in this field is the major stumbling block
preventing further progress into the nature of sexuality in
history. A brief account of it can be provided here, largely in
the light of feminist work, which has begun to discredit so
much of it. What follows is a composite picture, not meant to
apply as a whole or in detail to specific movements and
theories. But the general assumptions which inform this view
appear at the center of the dominant ideologies of sexuality in
twentieth-century capitalist societies, and it is against these
assumptions that alternative theories and practices must be
gauged and opposed.

In spite of the elaborate discourses and analyses devoted to
it, and the continual stress on its centrality to human reality,
this modern concept of sexuality remains difficult to define.
Dictionaries and encyclopedias refer simply to the division of
most species into males and females for purposes of
reproduction; beyond that, specifically human sexuality is only
described, never defined. What the ideologists of sexuality
describe, in fact, are only the supposed spheres of its
operation: gender; reproduction, the family, and socialization;
love and intercourse. To be sure, each of these spheres is
thought by them to have its own essence and forms ("*the*
family," for example), but together they are taken to define the
arena in which sexuality operates.

Within this arena, sexuality as a general, over-arching
category is used to define and delimit a large part of the world
in which we exist. The almost perfect congruence between
those spheres of existence which are said to be sexual and
what is viewed as the "private sphere" of life is striking. As
Carroll Smith-Rosenberg, working partly within this view of
sexuality, puts it, "The most significant and intriguing
historical questions relate to the events, the causal patterns, the
psychodynamics of private places: the household, the family,

the bed, the nursery, and kinship systems."[7]   Indeed, a general definition of the most widely accepted notion of sexuality in the later twentieth century might easily be "that which pertains to the private, to the individual," as opposed to the allegedly "public" spheres of work, production, and politics.

This broad understanding of sexuality as "the private" involves other significant dualities, which, while not simply translations of the general division into private and public spheres, do present obvious analogies to it in the minds of those who accept it. Briefly, the sexual sphere is seen as the realm of psychology, while the public sphere is seen as the realm of politics and economics; Marx and Freud are often taken as symbolic of this division. The sexual sphere is considered the realm of consumption, the public sphere that of production; the former is sometimes viewed as the site of use value and the latter as that of exchange value. Sexuality is the realm of "nature," of the individual, and of biology; the public sphere is the realm of culture, society, and history. Finally, sexuality tends to be identified most closely with the female and the homosexual, while the public sphere is conceived of as male and heterosexual.

The intertwined dualities are not absolute, for those who believe in them are certain that although sexuality properly belongs to an identifiable private sphere, it slips over, legitimately or, more usually, illegitimately, into other spheres as well, spheres which otherwise would be definitely desexualized. Sexuality appears at one and the same time as narrow and limited and as universal and ubiquitous. Its role is both overestimated as the very core of being and underestimated as a merely private reality.

Both views refer sexuality to the individual, whom it is used to define. As Richard Sennett suggests:

> Sexuality we imagine to define a large territory of who we are and what we feel. . .Whatever we experience must in some way

---

[7] Carroll Smith-Rosenberg, "The New Woman and the New History," *Feminist Studies* 3 (1976), p. 185.

touch on our sexuality, but sexuality *is*. We uncover it, we discover it, we come to terms with it, but we do not master it.[8]

Or, as Foucault rather more succinctly states, "In the space of a few centuries, a certain inclination has led us to direct the question of what we are to sex."[9] This is, after all, why we write about it, talk about it, worry about it so continuously.

Under the impulse of these assumptions, individuals are encouraged to see themselves in terms of their sexuality. This is most easily seen in such examples of "popular wisdom" as that one must love people for their inner, that is, sexual, selves, and not for "mere incidentals," like class, work, and wealth, and in the apparently widespread belief that the "real me" emerges only in private life, in the supposedly sexual spheres of intercourse and family, that is, outside of class, work, and public life. Sexuality is thereby detached from socio-economic and class realities, which appear, in contrast, as external and imposed.

The location of sexuality as the innermost reality of the individual defines it, in Sennett's phrase, as an "expressive state," rather than an "expressive act."[10] For those who accept the foregoing assumptions, it appears as a *thing*, a fixed essence, which we possess as part of our very being; it simply *is*. And because sexuality is itself seen as a thing, it can be identified, for certain purposes at least, as inherent in particular objects, such as the sex organs, which are then seen as, in some sense, sexuality itself.

But modern sexual ideologues do not simply argue that sexuality is a *single* essence; they proclaim, rather, that it is a *group* of essences. For although they tell us that sexuality as a general category is universally shared by all of humanity, they insist that sub-categories appear within it. There are thus said to be sexual essences appropriate to "the male," "the female," "the child," "the homosexual," "the heterosexual" (and indeed

---

[8] Richard Sennett, *The Fall of the Public Man* (New York: Random House, 1977), p. 7.

[9] *History of Sexuality*, p. 78.

[10] *Fall of the Public Man*, p. 7.

to "the foot-fetishist," "the child-molester," and on and on). In this view, identifiable and analytically discrete groups emerge, each bearing an appropriate sexual essence, capable of being analyzed as a "case history," and given a normative value. Krafft-Ebing's *Psychopathia Sexualis* of 1886 may still stand as the *logical* high-point of this type of analysis, but the underlying attitude seems to permeate most of contemporary thought on the subject.

In sum, the most commonly held twentieth-century assumptions about sexuality imply that it is a separate category of existence (like "the economy," or "the state," other supposedly independent spheres of reality), almost identical with the sphere of private life. Such a view necessitates the location of sexuality within the individual as a fixed essence, leading to a classic division of individual and society and to a variety of psychological determinisms, and, often enough, to a full-blown biological determinism as well. These in turn involve the enshrinement of contemporary sexual categories as universal, static, and permanent, suitable for the analysis of all human beings and all societies. Finally, the consequences of this view are to restrict class struggle to non-sexual realms, since that which is private, sexual, and static is not a proper arena for public social action and change.

Biology and Society

The inadequacies of this dominant ideology require us to look at sexuality from a very different perspective, a perspective which can serve both as an implicit critique of the contemporary view as well as the starting point for a specific Marxist conceptualization.

If we compare human sexuality with that of other species, we are immediately struck by its richness, its vast scope, and the degree to which its potentialities can seemingly be built upon endlessly, implicating the entire human world. Animal sexuality, by contrast, appears limited, constricted, and pre-defined in a narrow physical sphere.

This is not to deny that human sexuality, like animal sexuality, is deeply involved with physical reproduction and with intercourse and its pleasures. Biological sexuality is the necessary precondition for human sexuality. But biological sexuality is only a precondition, a set of potentialities, which is never unmediated by human reality, and which becomes transformed in qualitatively new ways in human society. The rich and ever-varying nature of such concepts and institutions as marriage, kinship, "love," "eroticism," in a variety of physical senses and as a component of fantasy and religious, social, and even economic reality, and the general human ability to extend the range of sexuality far beyond the physical body, all bear witness to this transformation.

Even this bare catalogue of examples demonstrates that sexuality is closely involved in *social* reality. Marshall Sahlins makes the point clearly, when he argues that sexual reproduction and intercourse must not be

> considered *a priori* as a biological fact, characterized as an urge of human nature independent of the relations between social persons. . .[and] acting *upon* society from without (or below). [Uniquely among human beings] the process of "conception" is always a double entendre, since no satisfaction can occur without the act and the partners as socially defined and contemplated, that is, according to a symbolic code of persons, practices and proprieties.[11]

Such an approach does not seek to eliminate biology from human life, but to absorb it into a unity with social reality. Biology as a set of potentialities and insuperable necessities[12] provides the material of social interpretations and extensions; it does not *cause* human behavior, but conditions and limits it. Biology is not a narrow set of absolute imperatives. That it is malleable and broad is as obvious for animals, whose nature is altered with changing environment, as for human beings.[13]

---

[11] Marshall Sahlins, *New York Review of Books* (November 23, 1978), p. 51

[12] On biology as a realm of necessary, see Sebastiano Timpanaro, *On Materialism* (London: NLB, 1978).

[13] Helen H. Lambert, "Biology and Equality," *Signs* 4 (1978), pp. 97-117, especially 104.

The uniqueness of human beings lies in their ability to create the environment which alters their own—and indeed other animals'—biological nature.

Human biology and culture are both necessary for the creation of human society. It is as important to avoid a rigid separation of "Nature" and "Culture" as it is to avoid reducing one to the other, or simply uniting them as an undifferentiated reality. Human beings are doubly determined by a permanent (but not immutable) natural base and by a permanent social mediation and transformation of it. An attempt to eliminate the biological aspect is misleading because it denies that social behavior takes place within nature and by extension of natural processes. Marx's insistence that "men make their own history but they do not make it just as they please" applies as well to biological as to inherited social realities.[14] An attempt—as in such disparate movements as Reichian analysis or the currently fashionable "sociobiology"—to absorb culture into biology is equally misleading, because, as Sahlins puts it

> Biology, while it is an absolutely necessary condition for culture, is equally and absolutely insufficient, it is completely unable to specify the cultural properties of human behavior or their variations from one human group to another.[15]

It is clear that, with certain limits, human beings have no fixed, inherited nature. We *become* human only in human society. Lucien Malson may overstate his case when he writes, "The idea that man has no nature is now beyond dispute. He has or rather is a history,"[16] but he is correct to focus on history and change in the creation of human culture

---

[14] These points are strongly insisted upon by Timpanaro, *On Materialism.* See also Raymond Wilson, "Problems of Materialism," *New Left Review* 109 (1978), pp. 3-18.

[15] M. Sahlins, *The Use and Abuse of Biology* (Ann Arbor: University of Michigan Press, 1976), p. xi.

[16] L. Malson, *Wolf Children and the Problem of Human Nature* (New York: Monthly Review Press, 1972), p. 9.

and personality. Social reality cannot simply be "peeled off" to reveal "natural man" lurking beneath.[17]

This is true of sexuality in all its forms, from what seem to be the most purely "natural" acts of intercourse[18] or gender differentiation and hierarchy to the most elaborated forms of fantasy or kinship relations. Contrary to a common belief that sexuality is simply "natural" behavior, "nothing is more essentially transmitted by a social process of learning than sexual behavior," as Mary Douglas notes.[19]

Even an act which is apparently so purely physical, individual, and biological as masturbation illustrates this point. Doubtless we stroke our genitals because the act is pleasurable and the pleasure is physiologically rooted, but from that to masturbation, with its large element of fantasy, is a social leap, mediated by a vast set of definitions, meanings, connotations, learned behavior, shared and learned fantasies.

Sexual reality is variable, and it is so in several senses. It changes within individuals, within genders, and within societies, just as it differs from gender to gender, from class to class, and from society to society. Even the very meaning and content of sexual arousal varies according to these categories.[20] Above all, there is continuous *development and transformation* of its realities. What Marx suggests for hunger is equally true of the social forms of sexuality: "Hunger is hunger, but the hunger gratified by cooked meat eaten with a knife and fork is a different hunger from that which bolts down raw meat with the aid of hand, nail and tooth."[21]

---

[17] See *Ibid.*, p. 10.

[18] See *Ibid.*, p. 48.

[19] Mary Douglas, *Natural Symbols: Explorations in Cosmology*, (New York: Pantheon Books, 1973), p. 93.

[20] W.H. Davenport, "Sex in Cross-Cultural Perspective," in F. Beach, ed., *Human Sexuality in Four Perspectives* (Baltimore: Wiley, 1977), chapter 5.

[21] Karl Marx, *Grundrisse*, Martin Nicolaus, ed., (New York: Random House, 1973), p. 92.

There do exist certain sexual forms which, at least at a high level of generality, are common to all human societies: live, intercourse, kinship, can be understood universally on a very general level. But that both "saint and sinner" have erotic impulses, as George Bataille rightly claims,[22] or that Greece, Medieval Europe, and modern capitalist societies share general sexual forms, do not make the contents and meaning of these impulses and forms identical or undifferentiated. They must be carefully distinguished and separately understood, since their inner structures and social meanings and articulations are very different. The content and meaning of the eroticism of Christian mysticism is by no means reducible to that of Henry Miller, nor is the asceticism of the monk identical to that of the Irish peasants who delay their marriages to a relatively late age.[23]

The forms, content, and context of sexuality always differ. There is no abstract and universal category of "the erotic" or "the sexual" applicable without change to all societies. Any view which suggests otherwise is hopelessly mired in one or another form of biologism, and biologism is easily put forth as the basis of normative attitudes toward sexuality, which, if deviated from, may be seen as rendering the deviant behavior "unhealthy" and "abnormal." Such views are as unenlightening when dealing with Christian celibacy as when discussing Greek homosexual behavior.

Sexuality as Praxis (I)

When we look more directly at the social world itself, it becomes apparent that the general distinguishing mark of human sexuality, as of all social reality, is the unique role played in its construction by language, consciousness, symbolism, and labor, which, taken together—as they must

---

22 Georges Bataille, *Death and Sensuality: A Study of Eroticism and Taboo*, (New York: Arno Press, 1962).

23 See the important analysis of this and similar points in Denis de Rougemont, *Love in the Western World* (New York: Pantheon, 1956), p. 159ff.

be—are *praxis*, the production and reproduction of material life. Through *praxis* human beings produce an ever-changing human world within nature and give order and meaning to it, just as they come to know and give meaning to, and, to a degree, change, the realities of their own bodies, their physiology.[24] The content of sexuality is ultimately provided by human social relations, human productive activities, and human consciousness. The *history* of sexuality is therefore the history of a subject whose meaning and contents are in a continual process of change. It is the history of social relations.

For sexuality, although part of material reality, is not itself an object or thing. It is rather a group of social relations, of human interactions. Marx writes in the *Grundrisse* that "Society does not consist of individuals, but expresses the sum of interrelations, the relations within which these individuals stand."[25] This seems to put the emphasis precisely where it should be: individuals do exist as the constituent elements of society, but society is not the simple multiplication of isolated individuals. It is constituted only by the relationships between those individuals. On the other hand, society does not stand outside of and beyond the individuals who exist within it, but is the expression of their complex activity. The emphasis is on activity and relationships, which individuals ultimately create and through which, in turn, they are themselves created and modified. Particular individuals are both subjects and objects within the process, although in class societies the subjective aspect tends to be lost to sight and the processes tend to become reified as objective conditions working from outside.

Sexuality is relational.[26] It consists of activity and interactions—active social relations—and not simply "acts," as

---

[24] See Adolfo Sanchez Vazques, *The Philosophy of Praxis*, Mike Gonzales, trans. (London: Merlin Press, 1977).

[25] *Grundisse*, p. 265.

[26] See the work of the so-called "symbolic interactionists," best exemplified by Kenneth Plummer, *Sexual Stigma* (London: Routledge and Kegan Paul, 1975). Their work, although not Marxist and too

--->

if sexuality were the enumeration and typology of an individual's orgasms (as it sometimes appears to be conceived of in, for example, the work of Kinsey and others), a position which puts the emphasis back within the individual alone. "It" does not do anything, combine with anything, appear anywhere; only people, acting within specific relationships create what we call sexuality. This is a significant aspect of what Marx means when he claims, in the famous Sixth Thesis on Feuerbach, that "the essence of man is no abstraction inherent in each single individual. In its reality it is the ensemble of the social relations."[27] Social relations, like the biological inheritance, at once create, condition, and limit the possibilities of individual activity and personality.

Praxis is fully meaningful only at the level of socio-historical reality. The particular interrelations and activities which exist at any moment in a specific society create sexual and other categories which, ultimately, determine the broad range of modes of behavior available to individuals who are born within that society. In turn, the social categories and interrelations are themselves altered over time by the activities and changing relationships of individuals. Sexual categories do not make manifest essences implicit within individuals, but are the expression of the active relationships of the members of entire groups and collectives.

We can understand this most clearly by examining particular categories. We speak, for example, of homosexuals and heterosexuals as distinct categories of people, each with its sexual essence and personal behavioral characteristics. That these are not "natural" categories is evident. Freud, especially in the *Three Essays on the Theory of Sexuality*, and other psychologists have demonstrated that the boundaries between the two groups in our own society are fluid and difficult to define. And, as a result of everyday experience as well as the

---

focused on individuals *per se*, does represent a major step forward in our understanding of sexuality as interpersonal.

27 Karl Marx, "Sixth Thesis on Feuerbach," in Karl Marx and Friedrich Engels, *Collected Works*, volume 5 (New York: International Publishers, 1976), p. 4.

material collected in surveys like the Kinsey reports, we know that the categories of heterosexuality and homosexuality are by no means coextensive with the activities and personalities of heterosexuals and homosexuals. Individuals belonging to either group are capable of performing and, on more or less numerous occasions, do perform acts, and have behavioral characteristics and display social relationships thought specific to the other group.

The categories in fact take what are no more than a group of more or less closely related acts ("homosexual"/"heterosexual" behavior) and convert them into case studies of people ("homosexuals"/"heterosexuals"). This conversion of acts into roles/personalities, and ultimately into entire subcultures, cannot be said to have been accomplished before at least the seventeenth century, and, as a firm belief and more or less close approximation of reality, the late nineteenth century.[28] What we call "homosexuality" (in the sense of the distinguishing traits of "homosexuals"), for example, was not considered a unified set of acts, much less a set of qualities defining particular persons, in pre-capitalist societies. Jeffrey

---

[28] Mary McIntosh, "The Homosexual Role," *Social Problems*, 16 (1968), pp. 182-193, reprinted this volume, the pioneer work in this field, suggests the seventeenth century for the emergence of the first homosexual subculture. Randolph Trumbach, "London's Sodomites: Homosexual Behavior and Western Culture in the Eighteenth Century," *Journal of Social History* 11 (1977/1978), pp. 1-33 argues for the eighteenth century. Jeffrey Weeks, in two important works, "'Sins and Diseases': Some Notes on Homosexuality in the Nineteenth Century," *History Workshop* 1 (1976), pp. 211-219, and *Coming Out: Homosexual Politics in Britain from the Nineteenth Century to the Present*, (London: Quartet Books, 1977), argues, correctly, I think, that the full emergence of homosexual role and subculture occurs only in the second half of the nineteenth century. See also Bert Hansen, "Historical Construction of Homosexuality," *Radical History Review* 20 (1979), pp. 66-73 and Jeffrey Weeks, "Movements of Affirmation: Sexual Meaning and Homosexual Identities," *Radical History Review* 20 (1979), pp. 164-180. All of these works deal with England, but there is little reason to suspect that the general phenomenon, at least, varies considerably in other bourgeois countries.

Weeks, in discussing the act of Henry VIII of 1533 brought sodomy within the purview of statute law, argues that

> the central point was that the law was directed against a series of sexual acts, not a particular type of person. There was no concept of the homosexual in law, and homosexuality was regarded not as a particular attribute of a certain type of person but as a potential in all sinful creatures.[29]

The Greeks of the classical period would have agreed with the general principle, if not with the moral attitude. Homosexuality and heterosexuality for them were indeed groups of not necessarily very closely related acts, each of which could be performed by any person, depending upon his or her gender, status, or class.[30] "Homosexuals" and "heterosexuals" in the modern sense did not exist in their world, and to speak, as is common, of the Greeks, as "bisexual" is illegitimate as well, since that merely adds a new, intermediate category, whereas it was precisely the categories themselves which had no meaning in antiquity.

Heterosexuals and homosexuals are involved in social "roles" and attitudes which pertain to a particular society, modern capitalism. These roles do have something in common with very different roles known in other societies— modern homosexuality and ancient pederasty, for example, share at least one feature: that the participants were of the same sex and that sexual intercourse is often involved—but the significant features are those that are not shared, including the entire range of symbolic, social, economic, and political meanings and functions each group of roles possesses.

"Homosexual" and "heterosexual" *behavior* may be universal; homosexual and heterosexual *identity and consciousness* are modern realities. These identities are not inherent in the individual. In order to be gay, for example,

---

[29] *Coming Out*, p. 12.

[30] The best work available on Greek homosexual behavior is K. J. Dover, *Greek Homosexuality* (Cambridge: Harvard University Press, 1975), which contains further bibliography.

more than individual inclinations (however we might conceive of those) or homosexual activity is required; entire ranges of social attitudes and the construction of particular cultures, subcultures, and social relations are first necessary. To "commit" a homosexual act is one thing: to *be* a homosexual is something entirely different.

By the same token, of course, these are changeable and changing roles. The emergence of a gay movement (like that of the women's movement) has meant major alterations in homosexual and heterosexual realities and self-perceptions. Indeed it is abundantly clear that there has always existed in the modern world a dialectical interplay between those social categories and activities which ascribe to certain people a homosexual identity and the activities of those who are so categorized. The result is the complex constitution of "the homosexual" as a social being within bourgeois society. The same is, of course, true of "the heterosexual," although the processes and details vary.[31]

The example of homosexuality/heterosexuality is particularly striking, since it involves a categorization which appears limited to modern societies. But even categories with an apparently more general application demonstrate the same social construction.

For example, as feminists have made abundantly clear, while every society does divide its members into "men" and "women," what is meant by these divisions and the roles played by those defined by these terms varies significantly from society to society and even within each society by class, estate, or social position. The same is true of kinship relations. All societies have some conception of kinship, and use it for a variety of purposes, but the conceptions differ widely and the institutions based on them are not necessarily directly comparable. Above all, the modern nuclear family, with its particular social and economic roles, does not appear to exist in other societies, which have no institution truly

---

[31] See *History of Sexuality*, parts 4-5, as well as Guy Hocquenghem, *Homosexual Desire*, Dangoor Daniella, trans. (New York: Schocken, 1980).

analogous to our own, either in conception, membership, or in articulation with other institutions and activities. Even within any single society, family/kinship patterns, perceptions, and activity vary considerably by class and gender.[32]

The point is clear: the members of each society create all of the sexual categories and roles within which they act and define themselves. The categories and the significance of the activity involved will vary widely as do the societies within whose general social relations they occur, and categories appropriate to each society must be discovered by historians.

Not only must the categories of any single society or period not be hypostatized as universal, but even the categories which are appropriate to each society must be treated with care. Ultimately, they are only parameters within which sexual activity occurs or, indeed, against which it may be brought to bear. They tend to be normative—and ideological—in nature, that is, they are presented as the categories within which members of particular societies *ought* to act. The realities of any society only approximate the normative categories, as our homosexual/heterosexual example most clearly showed. It is both as norms, which determine the status of all sexual activity, and as approximations to actual social reality that they must be defined and explored.

Sexuality as Praxis (II)

Within this broad approach, the relationship between sexual activity and its categories and those that are non-sexual, especially those that are economic in nature, become of great importance. Too many Marxists have tried to solve this

---

[32] On the conceptualization of family, kinship, and household, see the important collective work by Rayna Rapp, Ellen Ross, and Renate Bridenthal, "Examining Family History," *Feminist Studies* 5 (1979), pp. 174-200, as well as Rayna Rapp, "Family Class in Contemporary America," *Science and Society* 42 (1978), pp. 278-300. Also see Mark Poster, *Critical Theory of the Family* (New York: Seabury Press, 1978), and the critique of it by Ellen Ross, "Rethinking 'The Family,'" *Radical History Review* 20 (1979), pp. 76-84.

problem by placing it within a simplified version of the "base/superstructure" model of society, in which the base is considered simply as "the economy," narrowly defined, while sexuality is relegated to the superstructure; that is, sexuality is seen as a "reflex" of an economic base.[33] Aside from the problems inherent in the base/superstructure model itself,[34] this approach not only reproduces the classic bourgeois division of society into private and public spheres, enshrining capitalist ideology as universal reality, but loses the basic insights inherent in viewing sexuality as social relations and activity.

Recently, many theorists, mainly working within a feminist perspective, began to develop a more sophisticated point of view, aiming, as Gayle Rubin put it in an important article,[35] "to introduce a distinction between 'economic' system and 'sexual' system, and to indicate that sexual systems have a certain autonomy and cannot always be explained in terms of economic forces." This view, which represented a great advance, nonetheless still partially accepted the contemporary

---

[33] This appears to be true even of such relatively unorthodox thinkers as Louis Althusser, *Lenin and Philosophy* (New York: Monthly Review Press, 1971), pp. 127-186, E. Balibar and Louis Althusser, *Reading Capital* (London: NLB, 1970), part III, P. Hindess and B. Hirst, *Pre-Capitalist Modes of Production* (London: Routledge and Kegan Paul, 1975), especially chapter 1, and Claude Meillassoux, *Maidens, Meal, and Money: Capitalism and the Domestic Community*, (New York: Cambridge University Press, 1981), part I.

[34] See Raymond Williams, *Marxism and Literature* (New York: Oxford University Press, 1977), especially part II.

[35] Gayle Rubin, "The Traffic in Women: Notes on the 'Political Economy' of Sex," in *Towards an Anthropology of Women*, Rayna Reiter, ed., (New York: Monthly Review, 1975), p. 167. For other similar views, on this point at least, see R. Bridenthal, "The Dialectics of Production and Reproduction in History," *Radical America* 10:2 (1976), pp. 3-11, Nancy Chodorow, "Mothering, Male Dominance and Capitalism," in *Capitalist Patriarchy and the Case for Social Feminism*, Z. Eisenstein, ed. (New York: Monthly Review Press, 1979), pp. 83-106 and Juliet Mitchell, *Woman's Estate* (New York: Pantheon Books, 1972).

distinction between a sphere of work and a sphere of sexuality.

The latest developments of socialist-feminist theory and practice have brought us still further, by demonstrating clearly that both sexuality in all its aspects and work/production are equally involved in the production and reproduction of *all* aspects of social reality, and cannot be easily separated out from one another.[36] Above all, elements of class and sexuality do not contradict one another or exist on different planes, but produce and reproduce each other's realities in complex ways, and both often take the form of activity carried out by the same persons working within the same institutions.

This means, among other things, that what we consider "sexuality" was, in the pre-bourgeois world, a group of acts and institutions not necessarily linked to one another, or, if they were linked, combined in ways very different from our own. Intercourse, kinship, and the family, and gender, did not form anything like a "field" of sexuality. Rather, each group of sexual acts was connected directly or indirectly—that is, formed a part of—institutions and thought patterns which we tend to view as political, economic, or social in nature, and the connections cut across our idea of sexuality as a thing, detachable from other things, and as a separate sphere of private existence.

The Greeks, for example, would not have known how, and would not have thought, to detach "sexuality" from the household (*oikos*), with its economic, political, and religious functions; from the state (especially as the reproduction of

---

[36] Among recent works which come to this conclusion, and whose bibliographies and notes are useful for further study, see Joan Kelly, "The Doubled Vision of Feminist Theory," *Feminist Studies* 5 (1979), pp. 216-227, Lisa Vogel, "Questions on the Woman Question," *Monthly Review* (June 1979), pp. 39-60, Renate Bridenthal, "Family and Reproduction," the third part of a joint essay cited in note 32 above, Eli Zaretsky, *Capitalism and Personal Life* (New York, Harper and Row, 1976), pp. 24ff., and Ann Forman, *Femininity as Alienation: Women and the Family in Marxism and Psychoanalysis* (London: Pluto, 1977).

citizenship); from religion (as the fertility cults or ancestor worship, for example); or from class and estate (as the determiner of the propriety of sexual acts, and the like). Nor would they have been able to distinguish a private realm of "sexuality"; the Greek *oikos* or household unit was as much or more a public institution as a private one.[37] This is even more true of so-called primitive societies, where sexuality (mediated through kinship, the dominant form of social relations) seems to permeate all aspects of life uniformly.

It was only with the development of capitalist societies that "sexuality" and "the economy" became separable from other spheres of society and could be counterposed to one another as realities of different sorts.[38] To be sure, the reality of that separation is, in the fullest sense of the word, ideological; that is, the spheres do have a certain reality as autonomous areas of activity and consciousness, but the links between them are innumerable, and both remain significant in the production and reproduction of social reality in the fullest sense. The actual connections between sexuality and the economy must be studied in greater detail, as must the specific relations between class, gender, family, and intercourse,[39] if the Marxist and sexual liberation movements are to work in a cooperative and fruitful, rather than antagonistic and harmful, manner.

A second major problem-area stands in the way of a fuller understanding of sexuality as *praxis*. The approach to

---

[37] On the oikos and related institutions, see W.K. Lacey, *The Family in Classical Greece* (London: Thames and Hudson, 1968).

[38] See Foucault, *History of Sexuality*, and Zaretsky, *Capitalism and Personal Life*, for attempts to conceptualize the emergence of these categories. On the non-emergence of a separate sphere of the economy in non-capitalist societies, see Georg Lukacs, *History and Class Consciousness* , Rodney Livingstone, trans. (Cambridge: MIT Press, 1972) and Samir Amin, "In Praise of Socialism," in *Imperialism and Unequal Development* (New York: Monthly Review Press, 1979), pp. 73-85.

[39] For the works which begin this process, see those cited in notes 35 and 26 above, plus the articles collected in Eisenstein, *Capitalist Patriarchy*.

sexuality we have outlined does not overcome the apparently insurmountable opposition between society and the individual which marks the ideological views with which we began our discussion. But it overcomes it at a general level, leaving many specific problems unsolved. The most important of these is the large and thorny problem of the determination of the specific ways in which specific individuals react to existing sexual categories and act within or against them. To deal with this vast subject fully, Marxists need to develop a psychology—or a set of psychologies—compatible with their social and economic analyses.[40]

Much the most common approach among western Marxists in the last fifty years toward creating a Marxist psychology has been an attempt, in one manner or another, to combine Marx and Freud. Whether in the sophisticated and dialectical versions of the Frankfurt School, Herbert Marcuse, or Wilhelm Reich, or in what Richard Lichtman has called "the popular view that Freud analyzed the individual while Marx uncovered the structure of social reality,"[41] these attempts arose out of the felt need for a more fully developed Marxist psychology in light of the failure of socialist revolutions in the west.

None of these attempts has, ultimately, been a success, and their failure seems to lie in real contradictions between Marxist and Freudian theory. Both present theories of the relationship between individual and society, theories which contradict each other at fundamental levels.

------

[40] For a full discussion of this need and what it involves, see Lucien Seve, *Marxism and the Theory of Human Personality* (London: Lawrence and Wishart, 1975). Seve is the best on the social conditioning of individual psychology and weakest on individual psychic processes themselves.

[41] "Marx and Freud," part 1, *Socialist Review* 30 (1976), p. 5. This article, along with its two successors in *Socialist Review* 33 (1977), pp. 59-84 and 36 (1977), pp. 37-78, form a good introduction to the study of the relationship between Marx and Freud, arguing for their incompatibility.

Freud does accept the importance of social relations for individual psychology. For him, sexuality has its roots in physiology, especially in the anatomical differences between the sexes, but these distinctions are not in themselves constitutive of our sexuality. Sexuality is indeed a process of development in which the unconscious takes account of biology as well as of society (mediated through the family) to produce an individual's sexuality.[42]

The problems begin here. Society, for Freud, is the medium in which the individual psyche grows and operates, but it is also in fundamental ways antipathetical to the individual, forcing him or her to repress instinctual desires. Freud's theory preserves the bourgeois division between society and the individual, and ultimately gives primacy to inborn drives within an essentially ahistorical individual over social reality. In a revealing passage, Freud argues:

> Human civilization rests upon two pillars, of which one is the control of natural forces and the other the restriction of our instincts. The ruler's throne rests upon fettered slaves. Among the instinctual component which are thus brought into service, the sexual instincts, in the narrow sense of the word, are conspicuous for their strength and savagery. Woe if they should be set loose! The throne would be overturned and the ruler trampled under foot.[43]

---

[42]An important recent attempt to demonstrate the social underpinnings of Freud's thought is Juliet Mitchell, *Psychoanalysis and Feminism* (New York: Pantheon, 1974). Eli Zaretsky, "Male Supremacy and the Unconscious," *Socialist Review* 21/22 (1975), pp. 7-55, demonstrates several defects in Freud's understanding of socio-historical reality, but suggests that they are remediable.

[43]Sigmund Freud, "The Resistance to Psychoanalysis," *The Standard Edition of the Complete Psychological Works of Sigmund Freud*, James Strachey, ed. and trans. (London: Hogarth Press, 1953-1974), volume 19, p. 218.

In spite of the fact that Freud does not view instincts as purely biological in nature,[44] he certainly sees sexuality as an internal, biologically-based force, a thing inherent in the individual. This is a view which makes it difficult to use Freud alongside of Marx in the elucidation of the nature of sexuality. This is not to say that we need necessarily discard all of Freud. The general theory of the unconscious remains a powerful one. Zillah Eisenstein pointed in a useful direction when she wrote, "Whether there can be a meaningful synthesis of Marx and Freud depends on whether it is possible to understand how the unconscious is reproduced and maintained by the relations of the society."[45] But it is uncertain whether the Freudian theory of the unconscious can be stripped of so much of its specific content and remain useful for Marxist purposes. The work of Lacan, which attempts to "de-biologize" the Freudian unconscious by focusing on the role of language, and that of Deleuze and Guattari, in the *Anti-Oedipus*, which attempts to provide it with a more full socio-historical content, are significant beginnings in this process.[46]

At the present time, however, Marxism still awaits a psychology fully adequate to its needs, although some recent developments are promising, such as the publication in English of the important non-Freudian work of the early Soviet psychologist L.S. Vygotskii.[47] But if psychology is to play a significant role in Marxist thought, as a science whose

---

[44]See Freud, "Instincts and Their Vicissitudes," *The Standard Edition*, volume 14, pp. 105-140.

[45]Eisenstein, *Capitalist Patriarchy*, p. 3.

[46]G. Deleuze and F. Guattari, *Anti-Oedipus: Capitalism and Schizophrenia* (New York: Viking Press, 1977). See also the work of Herbert Marcuse, especially *Eros and Civilization* (Boston: Beacon Press, 1955), and Norman O. Brown, *Life Against Death* (Middletown, Conn.: Wesleyan University Press, 1959).

[47]L.S. Vygotskii, *Mind in Society: The Development of Higher Psychological Processes* (Cambridge: Harvard University Press, 1977). See also Stephen Toulmin's essay on Vygotskii, "The Mozart in Psychology," *New York Review of Books*, September 28, 1978, pp. 51-57.

object is one of the dialectical poles of the individual/society unity, then it must have a finer grasp of the nature of that object. At this point, we can only agree with Lucien Seve that the object of psychology has not yet been adequately explored.[48]

---

[48] This essay represents a condensed and reworked version of the introduction to a much longer work on the nature of sexuality in history. The author wishes to thank Betsy Blackmar, Edwin Burrows, Victoria de Grazia, Elizabeth Fee, Joseph Interrante, Michael Merrill, David Varas, and Michael Wallace for their invaluable comments on earlier drafts. He dedicates the essay to David Varas, without whose help and encouragement it would have been impossible to write it.

CHAPTER 5:
Ian Hacking
Making Up People

Were there any perverts before the latter part of the
nineteenth century? According to Arnold Davidson, "The
answer is NO. . . . Perversion was not a disease that lurked
about in nature, waiting for a psychiatrist with especially acute
powers of observation to discover it hiding everywhere. It
was a disease created by a new (functional) understanding of
disease."[1] Davidson is not denying that there have been odd
people at all times. He is asserting that perversion, as a
disease, and the pervert, as a diseased person, were created in
the late nineteenth century. Davidson's claim, one of many
now in circulation, illustrates what I call making up people.

I have three aims: I want a better understanding of claims as
curious as Davidson's; I would like to know if there could be a
general theory of making up people, or whether each example
is so peculiar that it demands its own nongeneralizable story;
and I want to know how this idea "making up people" affects
our very idea of what it is to be an individual. I should warn
that my concern is philosophical and abstract; I look more at
what people might be than at what we are. I imagine a

---

[1] Arnold Davidson, "Closing Up the Corpses: Diseases of Sexuality and
the Emergence of the Psychiatric Style of Reasoning," in *Meaning and
Method: Essays in Honor of Hilary Putnam*, George Boolos, ed.
(Cambridge: Cambridge University Press, 1990).

Reprinted from *Reconstructing Individualism: Autonomy,
Individuality and the Self in Western Thought*, Thomas Heller,
Morton Sosna, and David Wellbery, eds., with the permission
of Stanford University Press. © 1986 by the Board of
Trustees of the Leland Stanford Junior University.

philosophical notion I call dynamic nominalism, and reflect too
little on the ordinary dynamics of human interaction.

First we need more examples. I study the dullest of
subjects, the official statistics of the nineteenth century. They
range, of course, over agriculture, education, trade, births,
and military might, but there is one especially striking feature
of the avalanche of numbers that begins around 1820. It is
obsessed with *analyse morale*, namely, the statistics of
deviance. It is the numerical analysis of suicide, prostitution,
drunkenness, vagrancy, madness, crime, *les misérables*.
Counting generated its own subdivisions and rearrangements.
We find classifications of over 4,000 different crisscrossing
motives for murder and requests that the police classify each
individual suicide in 21 different ways. I do not believe that
motives of these sorts or suicides of these kinds existed until
the practice of counting them came into being.[2]

New slots were created in which to fit and enumerate
people. Even national and provincial censuses amazingly
show that the categories into which people fall change every
ten years. Social change creates new categories of people, but
the counting is no mere report of developments. It elaborately,
often philanthropically, creates new ways for people to be.

People spontaneously come to fit their categories. When
factory inspectors in England and Wales went to the mills,
they found various kinds of people there, loosely sorted
according to tasks and wages. But when they had finished
their reports, millhands had precise ways in which to work,
and the owner had a clear set of concepts about how to employ
workers according to the ways in which he was obliged to
classify them.

I am more familiar with the creation of kinds among the
masses than with interventions that act upon individuals,

---

2 Ian Hacking, "Biopower and the Avalanche of Printed Numbers,"
Humanities in Society 5 (1982), pp. 279-95; "The Autonomy of
Statistical Law," in *Scientific Explanation and Understanding: Essays
on Reasoning and Rationality in Science*, N. Rescher, ed. (Lanham,
MD: University Press of America, 1983), pp. 3-20; "How Should We
Do the History of Statistics?," *Ideology & Consciousness*11.

though I did look into one rare kind of insanity. I claim that multiple personality as an idea and as a clinical phenomenon was invented around 1875: only one or two possible cases per generation had been recorded before that time, but a whole flock of them came after. I also found that the clinical history of split personality parodies itself—the one clear case of classic symptoms was long recorded as two, quite distinct, human beings, each of which was multiple. There was "the lady of MacNish," so called after a report in *The Philosophy of Sleep*, written by the Edinburgh physician Robert MacNish in 1832, and there was one Mary R. The two would be reported in successive paragraphs as two different cases, although in fact Mary Reynolds was the very split-personality lady reported by MacNish.[3]

Mary Reynolds died long before 1875, but she was not taken up as a case of multiple personality until then. Not she but one Félida X got the split-personality industry under way. As the great French psychiatrist Pierre Janet remarked at Harvard in 1906, Félida's history "was the great argument of which the positivist psychologists made use at the time of the heroic struggles against the dogmatism of Cousin's school. But for Félida, it is not certain that there would be a professorship of psychology at the Collège de France."[4] Janet held precisely that chair. The "heroic struggles" were important for our passing conceptions of the self, and for individuality, because the split Félida was held to refute the dogmatic transcendental unity of apperception that made the self prior to all knowledge.

After Félida came a rush of multiples. The syndrome bloomed in France and later flourished in America, which is still its home. Do I mean that there were no multiples before Félida? Yes. Except for a very few earlier examples, which

---

[3] Ian Hacking, "The Invention of Split Personalities," in *Human Nature and Natural Knowledge*, Alan Donagan, Anthony Perovich, Jr., and Michael Wedin, eds. (Dordrecht: D. Reidel, 1986), pp. 63-85.

[4] Pierre Janet, *The Major Symptom of Hysteria* (New York: Hafner, 1965), p. 78.

after 1875 were reinterpreted as classic multiples, there was no such syndrome for a disturbed person to display or to adopt.

I do not deny that there are other behaviors in other cultures that resemble multiple personality. Possession is our most familiar example—a common form of Renaissance behavior that died long ago, though it was curiously hardy in isolated German villages even late in the nineteenth century. Possession was not split personality, but if you balk at my implication that a few people (in committee with their medical or moral advisers) almost choose to become splits, recall that tormented souls in the past have often been said to have in some way chosen to be possessed, to have been seeking attention, exorcism, and tranquility.

I should give one all-too-tidy example of how a new person can be made up. Once again I quote from Janet, whom I find the most open and honorable of the psychiatrists. He is speaking to Lucie, who had the once-fashionable but now-forgotten habit of automatic writing. Lucie replies to Janet in writing without her normal self's awareness:

> *Janet*. Do you understand me ?
> *Lucie (writes)*. No.
> *J*. But to reply you must understand me.
> *L*. Oh yes, absolutely.
> *J*. Then what are you doing?
> *L*. I don't know.
> *J*. It is certain that someone is understanding me.
> *L*. Yes.
> *J*. Who is that ?
> *L*. Somebody besides Lucie.
> *J*. Another person. Would you like to give her a name?
> *L*. No.
> *J*. Yes. It would be far easier that way.
> *L*. Oh well. If you want: Adrienne.
> *J*. Then, Adrienne, do you understand me?
> *L*. Yes.[5]

---

[5] Pierre Janet, "Les Actes inconsistents et le dedoublement de la personnalité pendant le somnambulisme provoqué," *Revue Philosophique* 22 (1886), p. 581.

If you think this is what people used to do in the bad old days, consider poor Charles, who was given a whole page of *Time* magazine on October 25, 1982 (p. 70). He was picked up wandering aimlessly and was placed in the care of Dr. Malcolm Graham of Daytona Beach, who in turn consulted with Dr. William Rothstein, a notable student of multiple personality at the University Hospital in Columbia, South Carolina. Here is what is said to have happened:

> After listening to a tape recording made in June of the character Mark, Graham became convinced he was dealing with a multiple personality. Graham began consulting with Rothstein, who recommended hypnosis. Under the spell, Eric began calling his characters. Most of the personalities have been purged, although there are three or four being treated, officials say. It was the real personality that signed a consent form that allowed Graham to comment on the case.[6]

Hypnosis elicited Charles, Eric, Mark, and some 24 other personalities. When I read of such present-day manipulations of character, I pine a little for Mollie Fancher, who gloried in the personalities of Sunbeam, Idol, Rosebud, Pearl, and Ruby. She became somewhat split after being dragged a mile by a horse car. She was not regarded as especially deranged, nor in much need of "cure." She was much loved by her friends, who memorialized her in 1894 in a book with the title *Mollie Fancher, The Brooklyn Enigma: An Authentic Statement of Facts in the Life of Mollie J. Fancher, The Psychological Marvel of the Nineteenth Century.*[7] The idea of making up people has, I said, become quite widespread. *The Making of the Modern Homosexual* is a good example;

---

[6] *The State*, Columbia, S.C., October 4, 1982, p. 3A. I apologize for using a newspaper story, but the doctors involved created this story for the papers and do not reply to my letters requesting more information.

[7] Abraham H. Dailey, *Mollie Fancher, the Brooklyn Enigma* (Brooklyn: Eagle Book Printing Department, 1894).

'Making' in this title is close to my 'making up.'[8] The contributors by and large accept that the homosexual and the heterosexual as kinds of persons (as ways to be persons, or as conditions of personhood), came into being only toward the end of the nineteenth century. There has been plenty of same-sex activity in all ages, but not, *Making* argues, same-sex people and different-sex people. I do not wish to enter the complexities of that idea, but will quote a typical passage from this anthology to show what is intended:

> One difficulty in transcending the theme of gender inversion as the basis of the specialized homosexual identity was the rather late historical development of more precise conceptions of components of sexual identity. [Footnote:] It is not suggested that these components are 'real' entities, which awaited scientific 'discovery.' However once the distinctions were made, new realities effectively came into being.[9]

Note how the language here resembles my opening quotation: "not a disease ... in nature, waiting for ... observation to discover it" versus "not ... 'real' entities, which awaited scientific 'discovery.'" Moreover, this author too suggests that "once the distinctions were made, new realities effectively came into being."

This theme, the homosexual as a kind of person, is often traced to a paper by Mary McIntosh, "The Homosexual Role" which she published in 1968 in *Social Problems*.[10] That journal was much devoted to "labeling theory," which asserts that social reality is conditioned, stabilized, or even created by the labels we apply to people, actions, and communities.

---

[8] K. Plummer, ed., *The Making of the Modern Homosexual* (Totowa, NJ: Barnes and Noble).

[9] John Marshall, "Pansies, Perverts and Macho Men: Changing Conceptions of the Modern Homosexual," in *The Making of the Modern Homosexual*, pp. 150, 249, note 6.

[10] Reprinted in *The Making of the Modern Homosexual*, pp. 30-43, with postscript; originally published in *Social Problems*, 16 (1968), pp. 182-192, reprinted in this volume.

Already in 1963 "A Note on the Uses of Official Statistics" in the same journal anticipated my own inferences about counting.[11] But there is a currently more fashionable source of the idea of making up people, namely, Michel Foucault, to whom both Davidson and I are indebted. A quotation from Foucault provides the epigraph—following one from Nietzsche—for *The Making of the Modern Homosexual*; and although its authors cite some 450 sources, they refer to Foucault more than anyone else. Since I shall be primarily concerned with labeling, let me state at once that for all his famous fascination with discourse, naming is only one element in what Foucault calls the "constitution of subjects" (in context a pun, but in one sense the making up of the subject): "We should try to discover how it is that subjects are gradually, progressively, really and materially constituted through a multiplicity of organisms, forces, energies, materials, desires, thoughts etc."[12]

Since so many of us have been influenced by Foucault, our choice of topic and time may be biased. My examples dwell in the nineteenth century and are obsessed with deviation and control. Thus among the questions on a complete agenda, we should include these two: is making up people intimately linked to control? Is making up people itself of recent origin? The answer to both questions might conceivably be yes. We may be observing a particular medico-forensic-political language of individual and social control. Likewise, the sheer proliferation of labels in that domain may have engendered vastly more kinds of people than the world had ever known before.

Partly in order to distance myself for a moment from issues of repression, and partly for intrinsic interest, I would like to abstract from my examples. If there were some truth in the descriptions I and others have furnished, then making up

---

[11] John Kituse and Aaron V. Cewrel, "A Note on the Uses of Official Statistics," *Social Problems* 11 (1963), pp. 131-139.

[12] Michel Foucault, *Power/Knowledge*, C. Gordon, ed. (New York: Pantheon, 1980), p. 97. The translation of this passage is by Alessandro Fontana and Pasquale Pasquino.

people would bear on one of the great traditional questions of philosophy, namely, the debate between nominalists and realists.[13] The author I quoted who rejects the idea that the components of the homosexual identity are real entities, has taken a time-worn nominalist suggestion and made it interesting by the thought that "once the distinctions were made, new realities effectively came into being. You will recall that a traditional nominalist says that stars (or algae, or justice) have nothing in common except our names ('stars', 'algae', 'justice'). The traditional realist in contrast finds it amazing that the world could so kindly sort itself into our categories. He protests that there are definite sorts of objects in it, at least stars and algae, which we have painstakingly come to recognize and classify correctly. The robust realist does not have to argue very hard that people also come sorted. Some are thick, some thin, some dead, some alive. It may be a fact about human beings that we notice who is fat and who is dead, but the fact itself that some of our fellows are fat and others are dead has nothing to do with our schemes of classification.

The realist continues: consumption was not only a sickness but also a moral failing, caused by defects of character. That is an important nineteenth-century social fact about TB. We discovered in due course, however, that the disease is transmitted by bacilli that divide very slowly and that we can kill. It is a fact about us that we were first moralistic and later made this discovery, but it is a brute fact about tuberculosis that it is a specific disease transmitted by microbes. The nominalist is left rather weakly contending that even though a particular kind of person, the consumptive, may have been an artifact of the nineteenth century, the disease itself is an entity in its own right, independently of how we classify.

---

[13] After the conference, my colleague Bert Hansen (who has helped me a number of times with this paper) remarked that the relation of the nominalist/realist dispute to homosexuality is used by John Boswell, "Revolutions, Universal and Sexual Categories," *Salmagundi* 58-59 (1982-83), pp. 89-114.

It would be foolhardy, at this conference ["Reconstructing Individualism," Stanford University, February 18-20, 1984], to have an opinion about one of the more stable human dichotomies, male and female. But very roughly, the robust realist will agree that there may be what really are physiological borderline cases, once called "hermaphrodites." The existence of vague boundaries is normal: most of us are neither tall nor short, fat nor thin. Sexual physiology is unusually abrupt in its divisions. The realist will take the occasional compulsive fascination with transvestitism, or horror about hermaphrodites (so well described by Stephen Greenblatt in this volume [*Reconstructing Individualism*][14]), as human (nominalist) resistance to nature's putative aberrations. Likewise the realist will assert that even though our attitudes to gender are almost entirely nonobjective and culturally ordained, gender itself is a real distinction.

I do not know if there were thoroughgoing, consistent, hard line nominalists who held that every classification is of our own making. I might pick that great British nominalist Hobbes out of context: "How can any man imagine that the names of things were imposed by their natures?"[15] or I might pick Nelson Goodman.[16]

---

[14] Stephen Greenblatt, "Fiction and Friction," in Thomas Heller, et. al., *Reconstructing Individualism: Autonomy, Individuality, and the Self in Western Thought* (Stanford: Stanford University Press), pp. 30-52.

[15] Thomas Hobbes, *Elements of Philosophy*, II, 4.

[16] Trendy, self-styled modern nominalists might refer to his *Ways of Worldmaking* (Indianapolis: Hackett, 1978), but the real hard line is his *Fact, Fiction and Forecast* (Cambridge, MA: Harvard University Press, 1955)—a line so hard that few philosophers who write about the "new riddle of induction," of that book appear even to see the point. Goodman is saying that the only reason to project the hypothesis that all emeralds are green rather than grue—the latter implying that those emeralds, which are in the future examined for the first time, will prove to be blue—is that the word 'green' is entrenched, i.e., it is a word and a classification that we have been using. Where the inductive skeptic Hume allowed that there is a real quality, greenness, that we project out

--->

Let me take even the vibrant Hobbes, Goodman, and their scholastic predecessors as pale reflections of a perhaps nonexistent static nominalist, who thinks that all categories, classes, and taxonomies are given by human beings rather than by nature and that these categories are essentially fixed throughout the several eras of humankind. I believe that static nominalism is doubly wrong: I think that many categories come from nature, not from the human mind, and I think our categories are not static. A different kind of nominalism—I call it dynamic nominalism—attracts my realist self, spurred on by theories about the making of the homosexual and the heterosexual as kinds of persons or by my observations about official statistics. The claim of dynamic nominalism is not that there was a kind of person who came increasingly to be recognized by bureaucrats or by students of human nature but rather that a kind of person came into being at the same time as the kind itself was being invented. In some cases, that is, our classifications and our classes conspire to emerge hand in hand, each egging the other on.

Take four categories: horse, planet, glove, and multiple personality. It would be preposterous to suggest that the only thing horses have in common is that we call them horses. We may draw the boundaries to admit or to exclude Shetland ponies, but the similarities and difference are real enough. The planets furnish one of T. S. Kuhn's examples of conceptual change.[17] Arguably the heavens looked different after we grouped Earth with the other planets and excluded Moon and Sun, but I am sure that acute thinkers had discovered a real difference. I hold (most of the time) that strict nominalism is unintelligible for horses and the planets. How could horses and planets be so obedient to our minds? Gloves are something else: we manufacture them. I know not which came first, the thought or the mitten, but they have evolved hand in hand. That the concept "glove" fits gloves so well is

of habit, for Goodman there is only our practice of using the word 'green' (*Fact, Fiction and Forecast*, chapter 4).

[17] T.S. Kuhn, *The Structure of Scientific Revolutions* (Chicago: University of Chicago Press, 1962), p. 115.

no surprise; we made them that way. My claim about making up people is that in a few interesting respects multiple personalities (and much else) are more like gloves than like horses. The category and the people in it emerged hand in hand.

How might a dynamic nominalism affect the concept of the individual person? One answer has to do with possibility. Who we are is not only what we did, do, and will do but also what we might have done and may do. Making up people changes the space of possibilities for personhood. Even the dead are more than their deeds, for we make sense of a finished life only within its sphere of former possibilities. But our possibilities, although inexhaustible, are also bounded. If the nominalist thesis about sexuality were correct, it simply wasn't possible to be a heterosexual kind of person before the nineteenth century, for that kind of person was not there to choose. What could that mean? What could it mean in general to say that possible ways to be a person can from time to time come into being or disappear? Such queries force us to be careful about the idea of possibility itself.

We have a folk picture of the gradations of possibility. Some things, for example, are easy to do, some hard, and some plain impossible. What is impossible for one person is possible for another. At the limit we have the statement: "With men it is impossible, but not with God, for with God, all things are possible" (Mark 10:27). (Christ had been saying that it is easier for a camel to pass through the eye of a needle than for a rich man to enter the kingdom of heaven.) Degrees of possibility are degrees in the ability of some agent to do or make something. The more ability, the more possibility, and omnipotence makes anything possible. At that point, logicians have stumbled, worrying about what were once called "the eternal truths," and are now called "logical necessities." Even God cannot make a five-sided square, or so mathematicians say, except for a few such eminent dissenters as Descartes. Often this limitation on omnipotence is explained linguistically, being said to reflect our unwillingness to call anything a five-sided square.

There is something more interesting that God can't do. Suppose that Arnold Davidson, in my opening quotation about

perversion, is literally correct. Then it was not possible for
God to make George Washington a pervert. God could have
delayed Washington's birth by over a century, but would that
have been the same man? God could have moved the medical
discourse back 100-odd years. But God could not have
simply made him a pervert, the way He could have made him
freckled or had him captured and hung for treachery. This
may seem all the more surprising since Washington was but
eight years older than the Marquis de Sade—and Krafft-Ebing
has sadomasochism among the four chief categories of
perversion. But it follows from Davidson's doctrine that de
Sade was not afflicted by the disease of perversion, nor even
the disease of sadomasochism either.

Such strange claims are more trivial than they seem; they
result from a contrast between people and things. Except
when we interfere, what things are doing, and indeed what
camels are doing, does not depend on how we describe them.
But some of the things that we ourselves do are intimately
connected to our descriptions. Many philosophers follow
Elizabeth Anscombe and say that intentional human actions
must be "actions under a description."[18] This is not mere
lingualism, for descriptions are embedded in our practices and
lives. But if a description is not there, then intentional actions
under that description cannot be there either: that, apparently,
is a fact of logic.

Elaborating on this difference between people and things:
what camels, mountains, and microbes are doing does not
depend on our words. What happens to tuberculosis bacilli
depends on whether or not we poison them with BCG
vaccine, but it does not depend upon how we describe them.
Of course we poison them with a certain vaccine in part
because we describe them in certain ways, but it is the vaccine
that kills, not our words. Human action is more closely linked
to human description than bacterial action is. A century ago I
would have said that consumption is caused by bad air and
sent the patient to the Alps. Today, I may say that TB is

---

[18] G.E.M. Anscombe, *Intention* (Oxford: Oxford University Press,
1957).

caused by microbes and prescribe a two-year course of injections. But what is happening to the microbes and the patient is entirely independent of my correct or incorrect description, even though it is not independent of the medication prescribed. The microbes' possibilities are delimited by nature, not by words. What is curious about human action is that by and large what I am deliberately doing depends on the possibilities of description. To repeat, this is a tautological inference from what is now a philosopher's commonplace, that all intentional acts are acts under a description. Hence if new modes of description come into being, new possibilities for action come into being in consequence.

Let us now add an example to our repertoire; let it have nothing to do with deviancy, let it be rich in connotations of human practices, and let it help furnish the end of a spectrum of making up people opposite from the multiple personality. I take it from Jean-Paul Sartre, partly for the well-deserved fame of his description, partly for its excellence as description, partly because Sartre is our premium philosopher of choice, and partly because recalling Sartre will recall an example that returns me to my origin. Let us first look at Sartre's magnificent humdrum example. Many among us might have chosen to be a waiter or waitress and several have been one for a time. A few men might have chosen to be something more specific, a Parisian *garçon de café*, about whom Sartre writes in his immortal discussion of bad faith:

> His movement is quick and forward, a little too precise, a little too rapid. He comes toward the patrons with a step a little too quick. He bends forward a little too eagerly, his eyes express an interest too solicitous for the order of the customer.[19]

Psychiatrists and medical people in general try to be extremely specific in describing, but no description of the several classical kinds of split personality is as precise (or as

[19] Jean-Paul Sartre, *Being and Nothingness*, Hazel E. Barnes, trans. (London: Methuen, 1957), p. 59.

recognizable) as this. Imagine for a moment that we are reading not the words of a philosopher who writes his books in *cafés* but those of a doctor who writes them in a clinic. Has the *garçon de café* a chance of escaping treatment by experts? Was Sartre showing or merely anticipating when he concluded this very paragraph with the words: "There are indeed many precautions to imprison a man in what he is, as if we lived in perpetual fear that he might escape from it, that he might break away and suddenly elude his condition." That is a good reminder of Sartre's teaching: possibility, project, and prison are one of a piece.

Sartre's antihero chose to be a waiter. Evidently that was not a possible choice in other places, other times. There are servile people in most societies, and servants in many, but a waiter is something specific, and a *garçon de café* more specific. Sartre remarks that the waiter is doing something different when he pretends to play at being a sailor or a diplomat than when he plays at being a waiter in order to be a waiter. I think that in most parts of, let us say, Saskatchewan (or in a McDonald's anywhere), a waiter playing at being a *garçon de café* would miss the mark as surely as if he were playing at being a diplomat while passing over the french fries. As with almost every way in which it is possible to be a person, it is possible to be a *garçon de café* only at a certain time, in a certain place, in a certain social setting. The feudal serf putting food on my lady's table can no more choose to be a *garçon de café* than he can choose to be lord of the manor. But the impossibility is evidently different in kind.

It is not a technical impossibility. Serfs may once have dreamed of travel to the moon; certainly their lettered betters wrote or read adventures of moon travel. But moon travel was impossible for them, whereas it is not quite impossible for today's young waiter. One young waiter will, in a few years, be serving steaks in a satellite. Sartre is at pains to say that even technical limitations do not mean that you have fewer possibilities. For every person, in every era, the world is a plenitude of possibilities. "Of course," Sartre writes, "a contemporary of Duns Scotus is ignorant of the use of the automobile or the aeroplane. . . . For the one who has no relation of any kind to these objects and the techniques that refer to them, there is a kind of absolute, unthinkable and undecipherable nothingness. Such a nothing can in no way limit the For-itself that is choosing itself; it cannot be apprehended as a lack, no matter how we consider it." Passing to a different example, he continues, "The feudal world offered to the vassal lord of Raymond VI infinite possibilities of choice; we do not possess more."[20]

"Absolute, unthinkable and undecipherable nothingness" is a great phrase. That is exactly what being a multiple personality, or being a *garçon de café*, was to Raymond's vassal. Many of you could, in truth, be neither a Parisian waiter nor a split, but both are thinkable, decipherable somethingnesses. It would be possible for God to have made you one or the other or both, leaving the rest of the world more or less intact. That means, to me, that the outer reaches of your space as an individual are essentially different from what they would have been had these possibilities not come into being.

Thus the idea of making up people is enriched; it applies not to the unfortunate elect but to all of us. It is not just the making up of people of a kind that did not exist before: not only are the split and the waiter made up, but each of us is made up. We are not only what we are but what we might have been, and the possibilities for what we might have been are transformed.

Hence anyone who thinks about the individual, the person, must reflect on this strange idea, of making up people. Do my stories tell a uniform tale? Manifestly not. The multiple personality, the homosexual or heterosexual person, and the waiter form one spectrum among many that may color our perception here.

Suppose there is some truth in the labeling theory of the modern homosexual. It cannot be the whole truth, and this for several reasons, including one that is future-directed and one that is past-directed. The future-directed fact is that after the institutionalization of the homosexual person in law and

---

[20] *Ibid.*, p. 522.

official morality, the people involved had a life of their own, individually and collectively. As gay liberation has amply proved, that life was no simple product of the labeling.

The past-directed fact is that the labeling did not occur in a social vacuum, in which those identified as homosexual people passively accepted the format. There was a complex social life that is only now revealing itself in the annals of academic social history. It is quite clear that the internal life of innumerable clubs and associations interacted with the medico-forensic-journalistic labeling. At the risk of giving offense, I suggest that the quickest way to see the contrast between making up homosexuals and making up multiple personalities is to try to imagine split-personality bars. Splits, insofar as they are declared, are under care, and the syndrome, the form of behavior, is orchestrated by a team of experts. Whatever the medico-forensic experts tried to do with their categories, the homosexual person became autonomous of the labeling, but the split is not.

The *garçon de café* is at the opposite extreme. There is of course a social history of waiters in Paris. Some of this will be as anecdotal as the fact that croissants originated in the cafés of Vienna after the Turkish siege was lifted in 1653: the pastries in the shape of a crescent were a mockery of Islam. Other parts of the story will be structurally connected with numerous French institutions. But the class of waiters is autonomous of any act of labeling. At most the name *garçon de café* can continue to ensure both the inferior position of the waiter and the fact that he is male. Sartre's precise description does not fit the *garçon de café* that is a different role.

I do not believe there is a general story to be told about making up people. Each category has its own history. If we wish to present a partial framework in which to describe such events, we might think of two vectors. One is the vector of labeling from above, from a community of experts who create a "reality" that some people make their own. Different from this is the vector of the autonomous behavior of the person so labeled, which presses from below, creating a reality every expert must face. The second vector is negligible for the split but powerful for the homosexual person. People who write about the history of homosexuality seem to disagree about the relative importance of the two vectors. My scheme at best highlights what the dispute is about. It provides no answers.

The scheme is also too narrow. I began by mentioning my own dusty studies in official statistics and asserted that these also, in a less melodramatic way, contribute to making up people. There is a story to tell here, even about Parisian waiters, who surface in the official statistics of Paris surprisingly late, in 1881. However, I shall conclude with yet another way of making up people and human acts, one of notorious interest tó the existentialist culture of a couple of generations past. I mean suicide, the option that Sartre always left open to the For-itself. Suicide sounds like a timeless option. It is not. Indeed it might be better described as a French obsession.

There have been cultures, including some in recent European history, that knew no suicide. It is said that there were no suicides in Venice when it was the noblest city of Europe. But can I seriously propose that suicide is a concept that has been made up? Oddly, that is exactly what is said by the deeply influential Esquirol in his 1823 medical-encyclopedia article on suicide.[21] He mistakenly asserts that the very word was devised by his predecessor Sauvages. What is true is this: suicide was made the property of medics only at the beginning of the nineteenth century, and a major fight it was too.[22] It was generally allowed that there was the noble suicide, the suicide of honor or of state, but all the rest had to be regarded as part of the new medicine of insanity. By mid-century it would be contended that there was no case of suicide that was not preceded by symptoms of insanity.[23]

This literature concerns the doctors and their patients. It exactly parallels a statistical story. Foucault suggests we think

---

[21] E. Esquirol, "Suicide," *Dictionnare des Science Medicales* (Paris, 1823), LIII, p. 213.

[22] Ian Hacking, "Suicide au XIXe sièle," in *Medicine et probabilitiès*, A. Fagot, ed. (Paris, 1982), pp. 165-86.

[23] C.E. Bourdin, *Du suicide consideré comme maladie* (Batignolles, 1845), p. 19. The first sentence of this book asserts in bold letters: *Le suicide est une monomanie*.

in terms of "two poles of development linked together by a whole cluster of intermediary relations."[24] One pole centers on the individual as a speaking, working, procreating entity he calls an "anatomo-politics of the human body." The second pole, "focused on the species body," serves as the "basis of the biological processes: propagation, births, and mortality, the level of health, life expectancy and longevity." He calls this polarity a "biopolitics of the population." Suicide aptly illustrates patterns of connection between both poles. The medical men comment on the bodies and their past, which led to self-destruction; the statisticians count and classify the bodies. Every fact about the suicide becomes fascinating. The statisticians compose forms to be completed by doctors and police, recording everything from the time of death to the objects found in the pockets of the corpse. The various ways of killing oneself are abruptly characterized and become symbols of national character. The French favor carbon monoxide and drowning; the English hang or shoot themselves.

By the end of the nineteenth century there was so much information about French suicides that Durkheim could use suicide to measure social pathology. Earlier, a rapid increase in the rate of suicide in all European countries had caused great concern. More recently authors have suggested that the growth may have been largely apparent, a consequence of improved systems of reporting.[25] It was thought that there were more suicides because more care was taken to report them. But such a remark is unwittingly ambiguous: reporting brought about more suicides. I do not refer to suicide epidemics that follow a sensational case, like that of von Kleist, who shot his lover and then himself on the Wannsee in 1811—an event vigorously reported in every European capital. I mean instead that the systems of reporting positively created an entire ethos of suicide, right down to the suicide note, an art

---

[24] Michel Foucault, *The History of Sexuality*, volume 1, Robert Hurley, trans. (New York: Random House, 1978), p. 139

[25] A classic statement of this idea is Jack Douglas, *The Social Meanings of Suicide* (Princeton: Princeton University Press, 1967), chapter 3.

form that previously was virtually unknown apart from the rare noble suicide of state. Suicide has of course attracted attention in all times and has invited such distinguished essayists as Cicero and Hume. But the distinctively European and American pattern of suicide is a historical artifact. Even the unmaking of people has been made up.

Naturally my kinds of making up people are far from exhaustive. Individuals serve as role models and sometimes thereby create new roles. We have only to think of James Clifford's contribution to this volume [*Reconstructing Individualism*], "On Ethnographic Self-Fashioning: Conrad and Malinowski."[26] Malinowski's book largely created the participant-observer cultural-relativist ethnographer, even if Malinowski himself did not truly conform to that role in the field. He did something more important—he made up a kind of scholar. The advertising industry relies on our susceptibilities to role models and is largely engaged in trying to make up people. But here nominalism, even of a dynamic kind, is not the key. Often we have no name for the very role a model entices us to adopt.

Dynamic nominalism remains an intriguing doctrine, arguing that numerous kinds of human beings and human acts come into being hand in hand with our invention of the categories labeling them. It is for me the only intelligible species of nominalism, the only one that can even gesture at an account of how common names and the named could so tidily fit together. It is of more human interest than the arid and scholastic forms of nominalism because it contends that our spheres of possibility, and hence ourselves, are to some extent made up by our naming and what that entails. But let us not be overly optimistic about the future of dynamic nominalism. It has the merit of bypassing abstract hand waving and inviting us to do serious philosophy, namely, to examine the intricate origin of our ideas of multiple personality or of suicide. It is, we might say, putting some flesh on that wizened figure, John Locke, who wrote about the origin of ideas while introspecting

---

[26] James Clifford, "On Ethnographic Self-Fashioning: Conrad and Malinowski," in *Reconstructing Individualism*, pp. 140-162.

at his desk. But just because it invites us to examine the intricacies of real life, it has little chance of being a general philosophical theory. Although we may find it useful to arrange influences according to Foucault's poles and my vectors, such metaphors are mere suggestions of what to look for next. I see no reason to suppose that we shall ever tell two identical stories of two different instances of making up people.

CHAPTER 6:
Arnold Davidson
Sex and the Emergence of Sexuality

I.

Some years ago a collection of historical and philosophical essays on sex was advertised under the slogan: Philosophers are interested in sex again. Since that time the history of sexuality has become an almost unexceptionable topic, occasioning as many books and articles as anyone would ever care to read. Yet there are still fundamental conceptual problems that get passed over imperceptibly when this topic is discussed, passed over, at least in part, because they seem so basic or obvious that it would be time badly spent to worry too much about them. However, without backtracking toward this set of problems, one will quite literally not know what one is writing the history of when one writes a history of sexuality.

An excellent example of some of the most sophisticated current writing in this field can be found in *Western Sexuality*, a collection of essays that resulted from a seminar conducted by Philippe Ariès at the Ecole des Hautes Etudes en Sciences Sociales in 1979-80.[1] As one would expect, *Western Sexuality* is characterized by a diversity of methodological and historiographical approaches—social history, intellectual history, cultural history (which one historian I know refers to as the history of bad ideas), historical sociology, the analysis of literary texts, and that distinctive kind of history practiced by Michel Foucault and also in evidence in the short essay by

---

[1] Philippe Ariès and André Béjin, eds., *Western Sexuality: Practice and Perception in Past and Present Times* (Oxford: Basil Blackwell, 1985).

This essay originally appeared in *Critical Inquiry* 14 (Autumn 1987), pp. 16-48. It is reprinted by permission of the author.

Paul Veyne. One perspective virtually absent from this collection is the history of science, and since I believe that the history of science has a decisive and irreducible contribution to make to the history of sexuality, it is no accident that I am going to focus on that connection. But the history of sexuality is also an area in which one's historiography or implicit epistemology will stamp, virtually irrevocably, one's first-order historical writing. It is an arena in which philosophical and historical concerns inevitably run into one another.

In his 1979 Tanner lectures, Foucault writes that he is concerned with the problem of "the relations between experiences (like madness, illness, transgression of laws, sexuality, self-identity), knowledge (like psychiatry, medicine, criminology, sexology, psychology), and power (such as the power which is wielded in psychiatric and penal institutions and all other institutions which deal with individual control)."[2] The question that he places at the center of his work is, "In what way are those fundamental experiences of madness, suffering, death, crime, desire, individuality connected, even if we are not aware of it, with knowledge and power?"[3] In the preface to the second volume of his *History of Sexuality*, attempting to explain the chronological displacement from the eighteenth and nineteenth centuries (the focus of the first volume) to the period of antiquity (in the second and third volumes), Foucault emphasizes that the period around the nineteenth century "when this singular form of experience, sexuality, took shape is particularly complex."[4] In particular, the formation of domains of knowledge and the role of various normative systems had a determining effect on the constitution

---

[2] Michel Foucault, "*Omnes et singulatum*: Towards a Criticism of 'Political Reason,'" in *The Tanner Lectures on Human Values*, Sterling M. McMurrin, ed. (Salt Lake City: Utah University Press, 1981), p. 239.

[3] *Ibid.*, p. 240.

[4] Foucault wrote several prefaces or introductions to the second volume of *History of Sexuality*. This one appears in *The Foucault Reader*, Paul Rainbow, ed. (New York: Pantheon, 1984), p. 338.

of this experience. For a number of reasons, Foucault decided to address himself

> to periods when the effect of scientific knowledge and the complexity of normative systems were less, . . . in order eventually to make out forms of relation to the self different from those characterizing the experience of sexuality. . . Rather than placing myself at the threshold of the formation of the *experience of sexuality* I tried to analyze the formation of a certain mode of relation to the self in the experience of the flesh.[5]

Foucault's distinction between the experience of sexuality and the experience of the flesh is meant to mark the fact that our experience of sexuality has a specific and distinctive historical genesis. Although we take it to be a natural phenomenon, a phenomenon of nature not falling within the domain of historical emergence, our experience of sexuality is a product of systems of knowledge and modalities of power that bear no claim to ineluctability. And an analysis of late antiquity and early Christianity would reveal, according to Foucault, an experience of the flesh quite distinct from, and not to be confused with, our experience of sexuality. The conflation of these experiences is the result of a coarse epistemology whose consequence is a disfiguring, disabling anachronism. Much the same idea is expressed in Veyne's article, "Homosexuality in Ancient Rome," when he argues that the ancient Roman world did not view the experience of homosexuality as "a separate problem," that the question was never homosexuality per se, but being free and not being a passive agent. What we find is "a world in which one's behaviour was judged not by one's preference for girls or boys, but by whether one played an active or a passive role."[6] If we want to isolate the problem of homosexuality, we must jump to the nineteenth century to find it.

---

[5] *Ibid.*, p. 339; my emphasis.

[6] Paul Veyne, "Homosexuality in Ancient Rome," *Western Sexuality*, p. 29.

I want to concentrate on the relation between forms of experience and systems of knowledge, on the way in which what we have come to call "sexuality" is the product of a system of psychiatric knowledge that has its own very particular style of reasoning and argumentation. No complete account of the genesis of sexuality can ignore modalities of nineteenth-century power, what Foucault calls biopower, that have detailed and precise relations to our experience of sexuality, a topic about which I shall have almost nothing to say. But the emergence of sexuality and the emergence of a new psychiatric style of reasoning bear such an intimate connection to one another that our experience must remain opaque until this connection is fully articulated.

In order to provide some understanding, even if only at an intuitive level, of how I understand the notion of a style of reasoning or argumentation, let me give an example of two radically different styles of reasoning about disease—what I call the anatomical and psychiatric styles of reasoning. Like Foucault, I am concerned with how systems of knowledge shape us as subjects, how these systems literally make us subjects. In modern times, categories of sexuality have partially determined how we think of ourselves, the shape of ourselves as subjects. If we take the example of sexual identity and its disorders, we can see two systems of knowledge, exhibiting two styles of reasoning, as they come to be instantiated in the nineteenth century. The particular case of the anatomical style of reasoning that I will consider is one that Foucault has made famous with his publication of the memoirs of the nineteenth-century French hermaphrodite, Herculine Barbin. Foucault claims in his introduction to the memoirs that in the Middle Ages both canon and civil law designated those people "hermaphrodites" in whom the two sexes were juxtaposed in variable proportions. In some of these cases the father or godfather determined the sex of the child at the time of baptism. However, later, when it was time for these hermaphrodites to marry, they could decide for themselves whether they wished to retain the sex that had been assigned them or whether to choose instead the opposite sex. The only constraint was that they could not change their minds again: they had to keep the sex that they had chosen until the end of their lives.[7]   Although Foucault's account applies to only one kind of medieval hermaphrodite (and because of its brevity simplifies the complex relations between the legal, religious, and medical treatment of hermaphroditism in the Middle Ages and Renaissance),[8] his claim simply echoes that of, for example, Ambroise Paré's 1573 *Des Monstres et prodiges.*[9]

As Foucault emphasizes, in the eighteenth and into the nineteenth centuries, all apparent hermaphrodites came to be treated as pseudo-hermaphrodites, and it became the task of the medical expert to decipher "the true sex that was hidden beneath ambiguous appearances" (*HB*, p. viii), to find the one true sex of the so-called hermaphrodite. It is in this context that the case of Herculine Barbin must be placed. Adelaide Herculine Barbin, also known as Alexina or Abel Barbin, was raised as a woman but was eventually recognized as really being a man. Given this determination of his true sexual identity, Barbin's civil status was changed, and, unable to adapt to his new identity, he committed suicide. The details of the case are fascinating, but my concern is with how medical science determined Herculine's real sexual identity. Here are some remarks from the doctor who first examined Barbin, and who published a report in 1860 in the *Annales d'hygiene publique et de medicine legale.* After describing Barbin's genital area, Dr. Chesnet asks,

> What shall we conclude from the above facts? Is Alexina a woman? She has a vulva, labia majora, and a feminine urethra. . .

---

[7] See Foucault, introduction to *Herculine Barbin, Being the Recently Discovered Memoirs of a Nineteenth-Century French Hermaphrodite*, Richard McDougal, trans. (New York: Pantheon, 1980), pp. vii-viii; further references to this work, abbreviated *HB*, will be included in the text.

[8] For a critique of some of Foucault's claims, see Lorraine Daston and Katherine Park, "Hermaphrodites in Renaissance France," *Critical Matrix: Princeton Working Papers in Women's Studies*, 1: 5 (1985).

[9] Ambroise Paré, *Des Monstres et prodiges*, Jean Céard, ed. (Geneva: Droz, 1971), pp. 24-27.

> . . She has a vagina. True, it is very short, very narrow; but
> after all what is it if not a vagina. These are completely
> feminine attributes. Yes, but Alexina has never menstruated; the
> whole outer part of her body is that of a man, and my
> explorations did not enable me to find a womb. . . . Finally, to
> sum up the matter, ovoid bodies and spermatic cords are found by
> touch in a divided scrotum. *These are the real proofs of sex.* We
> can now conclude and say: Alexina is a man, hermaphroditic, no
> doubt, but with an obvious predominance of masculine sexual
> characteristics. (*HB*, pp. 127-28 ; my emphasis).

Notice that the real proofs of sex are to be found in the
anatomical structure of Barbin's sexual organs.

Writing nine years later in the *Journal de l'anatomie et de la
physiologie de l'homme*, Dr. E. Goujon definitively confirms
Chesnet's conclusions by using that great technique of
pathological anatomy, the autopsy. After discussing Barbin's
genital organs, Goujon offers a detailed account of his internal
genital organs:

> Upon opening the body, one saw that only the epididymis of the
> left testicle had passed through the ring; it was smaller than the
> right one; the vasa deferentia drew near each other behind and
> slightly below the bladder, and had normal connections with the
> seminal vesicles. Two ejaculatory canals, one on each side of
> the vagina, protruded from the mucous membrane of the vagina
> and traveled from the vesicles to the vulvar orifice. The seminal
> vesicles, the right one being a little larger than the left were
> distended by sperm that had a normal consistency and color. (*HB*,
> pp. 135 - 36).

All of medical science, with its style of pathological
anatomy, agreed with Auguste Tardieu when he claimed in his
revealingly titled book, *Question médico-légale de l'identité
dans ses rapports avec les vices de conformation des organes
sexuels*, that "to be sure, the appearances that are typical of the
feminine sex were carried very far in his case, but both science
and the law were nevertheless obliged to recognize the error

and to recognize the true sex of this young man" (HB, p. 123).[10]

Let me now bypass a number of decades. It is 1913, and the great psychologist of sex, Havelock Ellis, has written a paper called "Sexo-Aesthetic Inversion" that appears in *Alienist and Neurologist*. It begins as follows:

> By 'sexual inversion,' we mean exclusively such a change in a person's sexual impulses, the result of inborn constitution, that the impulse is turned towards individuals of the same sex, while all the other impulses and tastes may remain those of the sex to which the person by anatomical configuration belongs. There is, however, a wider kind of inversion, which not only covers much more than the direction of the sexual impulses, but may not, and indeed frequently does not, include the sexual impulse at all. This inversion is that by which a person's tastes and impulses are so altered that, if a man, he emphasizes and even exaggerates the feminine characteristics in his own person, delights in manifesting feminine aptitudes and very especially, finds peculiar satisfaction in dressing himself as a woman and adopting a woman's ways. Yet the subject of this perversion experiences the normal sexual attraction, though in some cases the general

---

[10] Tardieu's book was published in 1874. Parts of it had previously appeared in *Annals d'hygiène publique* in 1872. Controversies concerning the identity of an individual's sex often revolved around questions of the person's reproductive capabilities and ultimate suitability for marriage. By the nineteenth century, these determinations subordinated physiological considerations to anatomical ones. To base classifications of hermaphroditism on physiological rather than anatomical facts was thought to be "completely inadmissible in the present state of science." See Isidore Geoffroy Saint-Hilaire, *Histoire générale et particulière des anomalies de l'organisation chez l'homme et les animaux*, 3 volumes (Paris, 1823-37), 3:34n. For a more general discussion of some of these issues, see Pierre Darmon, *Le Tribunal de l'impuissance: Virilité et défaillances conjugales dans l'ancienne France* (Paris, 1979). I am indebted to Joel Snyder for clarification on this point.

inversion of tastes may extend, it may be gradually, to the sexual impulses.[11]

After describing some cases, Ellis writes further,

> The precise nature of aesthetic inversion can only be ascertained by presenting illustrative examples. There are at least two types of such cases; one, the most common kind, in which the inversion is mainly confined to the sphere of clothing, and another, less common but more complete, in which cross-dressing is regarded with comparative indifference but the subject so identifies himself with those of his physical and psychic traits which recall the opposite sex that he feels really to belong to that sex, although he has no delusion regarding his anatomical conformation.[12]

In categorizing disorders, Ellis's clear separation of two distinct kinds of things, anatomical configuration and psychic traits, provides a surface manifestation of a profound and wide-ranging epistemological mutation. It is what makes possible sexo-aesthetic inversion, as a disease, in the first place.

Ellis's discussion descends from the psychiatric style of reasoning that begins, roughly speaking, in the second half of the nineteenth century, a period during which rules for the production of true discourses about sexuality change radically. Sexual identity is no longer exclusively linked to the anatomical structure of the internal and external genital organs. It is now a matter of impulses, tastes, aptitudes, satisfactions, and psychic traits. There is a whole new set of concepts that makes it possible to detach questions of sexual identity from facts about anatomy, a possibility that only came about with the emergence of a new style of reasoning. And with this new style of reasoning came entirely new kinds of sexual diseases and disorders. As little as 150 years ago, psychiatric theories of sexual identity disorders were not false, but rather were not

---

[11] Havelock Ellis, "Sexo-Aesthetic Inversion," *Alienist and Neurologist* 34 (1913), p. 156.

[12] *Ibid.*, p. 159.

even possible candidates of truth-or-falsehood.[13] Only with the birth of a psychiatric style of reasoning were there categories of evidence, verification, explanation, and so on that allowed such theories to be true-or-false. And lest you think that Ellis's discussion is outdated, I should point out that the third edition of the *Diagnostic and Statistical Manual of Mental Disorders* of the American Psychiatric Association discusses disorders of sexual identity in terms that are almost conceptually identical to those of Ellis. It calls these disorders, "characterized by the individual's feelings of discomfort and inappropriateness about his or her anatomic sex and by persistent behaviors generally associated with the other sex," *gender identity disorders.* [14] We live with the legacy of this relatively recent psychiatric style of reasoning, so foreign to earlier medical theories of sex. So-called sex change operations were not only technologically impossible in earlier centuries; they were conceptually impossible as well. Before the second half of the nineteenth century persons of a determinate anatomical sex could not be thought to be really, that is, psychologically, of the opposite sex. Anatomical sex exhausted one's sexual identity; psychological considerations could not have provided the basis for "sex reassignment surgery" since these considerations were not so much as relevant to the question of one's sexual identity. Our current medical concept of sex reassignment would have been unintelligible or incoherent since it could not cohere with the style of reasoning about sexual identity.

The anatomical style of reasoning took sex as its object of investigation and concerned itself with diseases of structural abnormality, with pathological changes that resulted from some macroscopic or microscopic anatomical change. It is for

---

[13] For an explanation of this terminology, see Ian Hacking, "Language, Truth and Reason," in *Rationality and Relativism*, Martin Hollis and Steven Lukes, eds. (Cambridge: MIT Press, 1983), pp. 48-66.

[14] American Psychiatric Association, Task Force on Nomenclature and Statistics, *Diagnostic and Statistical Manual of Mental Disorders*, third edition (Washington, D.C.: American Psychiatric Association, 1980), p. 261.

this reason that hermaphroditism most visibly exemplifies this mode of reasoning. But for sexuality to become an object of clinical knowledge, a new style of psychiatric reasoning was necessary. Ellis's discussion already *takes for granted* the new style of reasoning and so treats sexuality and its attendant disorders, such as sexo-aesthetic inversion, as if they were naturally given. Even as sophisticated a historian as Ariès can conflate these different objects of clinical investigation, with the inevitable historical confusion that results. Writing about homosexuality he declares, "The anomaly condemned was one of sexual ambiguity, effeminate man, the woman with male organs, the hermaphrodite."[15] But any attempt to write a unified history that passed from hermaphroditism to homosexuality would solder together figures that an adequate historical epistemology must keep separate. The hermaphrodite and the homosexual are as different as the genitalia and the psyche. The notion of a style of reasoning helps us to see how this is so.

Indeed, I do not think it would be going too far to defend the claim, paradoxical though it may seem, that sexuality itself is a product of the psychiatric style of reasoning. Sexuality only became a possible object of psychological investigation, theorizing, and speculation because of a distinctive form of reasoning that had a historically specific origin; or to put it another way, statements about sexuality came to possess a positivity, a being true-or-false, only when the conceptual space associated with the psychiatric style of reasoning was first articulated. A somewhat pedestrian, though still surprising, confirmation of this claim is in fact provided by looking at the origin of the word 'sexuality.' The very word 'sexuality,' as well as our concept of sexuality, first appears, according to the *Oxford English Dictionary*, in the late nineteenth century. The *O.E.D.* gives as its first example of 'sexuality,' defined as "possession of sexual powers, or capability of sexual feelings," a statement from 1879 made in J.M. Duncan's *Diseases of Women*: "In removing the ovaries,

---

15 Ariès, "Thoughts on the History of Homosexuality," in *Western Sexuality*, p. 66.

you do not necessarily destroy sexuality in a woman." Nothing could be a better illustration of my claim that sexuality is an object distinct from the anatomical style of reasoning about diseases. A woman's sexuality is not reducible to facts about or to the existence of, her reproductive system, and given this understanding it was necessary to have a way of conceptualizing sexuality that permitted one to say something about it without invoking, in any essential way, those anatomical facts. It is the psychiatric style of reasoning that made such talk possible in medicine, that made it possible to make statements such as Duncan's. Without this style of reasoning we would be forever talking about sex, not about sexuality.

Despite Foucault's remarks to the contrary at the end of volume 1 of *The History of Sexuality*, I think it is of decisive epistemological importance to distinguish carefully between sex and sexuality, where the former is understood, as the *O.E.D.* defines it, as "either of the two divisions of organic beings distinguished as male and female respectively"; an example of this usage is the statement in Crooke's *Body of Man* from 1615, "If wee respect the. . . conformation of both the sexes, the male is sooner perfected. . . in the wombe." The *O.E.D.* gives as another definition of 'sex' what is in effect a further specification of the first definition, "the sum of those differences in the structure and function of the reproductive organs on the ground of which beings are distinguished as male and female, and of the other physiological differences consequent on these"; an example of this usage is a remark of H. G. Wells from a 1912 book on marriage: "The young need. . . to be told. . . all we know of three fundamental things; the first of which is God, . . . and the third sex." These uses are closely connected with the use of the verb "to sex," which the *O.E.D.* defines as "to determine the sex of, by anatomical examination."

Although they are closely related, I am concerned primarily with the concepts of sexuality and sex rather than with the words 'sexuality' and 'sex.' A good example of how the same word may be used to express two distinct concepts is given by the only instance I know of where the notion of sexuality is linked to biology instead of psychology. This occurs in Buck's *Handbook of Medical Science* from 1888: "According to a strict biological definition sexuality is the characteristic of the male and female reproductive elements (genoblasts), and sex of the individuals in which the reproductive elements arise. A man has sex, a spermatozoon sexuality." This statement is so bizarre as to produce puzzlement eventuating in silence. Can a spermatozoon be heterosexual, homosexual, or bisexual? Can it suffer from deviant sexuality, or abnormally increased or decreased sexuality? Can it have masochistic, sadistic, or fetishistic sexual desires? The answer to these questions is neither yes nor no, since the questions get their sense from the psychiatric style of reasoning, which has no application whatsoever to a spermatozoon. We quite literally do not understand the claim that "a man has sex, a spermatozoon sexuality," for there is no such thing as sexuality outside of the psychiatric style of reasoning. The irreducible weirdness or incomprehensibility of Buck's claim is a good example of how specific concepts are produced by distinctive styles of reasoning, of how we think about sexuality, and of how we distinguish between sex and sexuality. In looking for the origin of our concept of sexuality, we do well to heed Oscar Wilde's advice that "it is only shallow people who do not judge by appearances." We should examine the word 'sexuality' in the sites in which it is used, that is, we must look at the sentences in which 'sexuality' appears, and see what is done with these sentences by the various people who use them. Typically, at least when we are dealing with an epistemological break, we will find that the concept under investigation enters into systematic relation with other very specific concepts, and that it is used in distinctive kinds of sentences to perform regular, because often repeated, functions. What we must avoid is the attempt to go behind the appearances, to offer some subtle hermeneutic reconstruction that ignores or overrides the surface of sentences.

If anyone believes that I have so far been talking only about words and not about things, that I have not exited from concepts to the world, it will be helpful at this point to recall some examples of Wittgensteinian criteria. In the most compelling discussion I know of Wittgenstein's notions of criteria and grammar, Stanley Cavell, in *The Claim of Reason*, brings into focus a number of examples, one of which concerns the grammar of 'pain':

> And pain can be deadened (not altered, as an opinion), or obtunded (not dampened, as a mood); you can locate certain pains, or have to, by prodding, i.e., by activating them, causing them afresh, focussing them; we speak of someone as in pain, but not as in pleasure (and as in mourning and in ecstasy, but not as in joy or in rage); you can cause pain but not pleasure, which is given and is taken (like pride and courage, but unlike happiness which can only be found; though you can make someone proud and happy, and so also ashamed and unhappy); and so on.[16]

Is it only part of our concept of pain that we say it can be deadened or obtunded, but not altered or dampened, that we say someone is in pain but not in pleasure, that we cause pain but give pleasure? Or is it in the nature of pain itself that we can say these things of it? Cavell's grammar of pain is meant to show that any such facile distinction collapses under the weight of this example. And in this same chapter, entitled "What a Thing Is (Called)," contrasting what he calls the Austinian kind of object and the Wittgensteinian kind of object, he shows more specifically that

> if you do not know the grammatical criteria of Wittgensteinian objects, then you lack, as it were, not only a piece of information or knowledge, but the possibility of acquiring any information about such objects *überhaupt*; you cannot be told the name of that object because there is as yet no *object* of that kind for you to attach a forthcoming name to.[17]

In these terms, I can formulate my claim by saying that sexuality is a Wittgensteinian object and that no one could

---

[16] Stanley Cavell, *The Claim of Reason: Wittgenstein, Skepticism, Morality and Tragedy* (New York: Oxford University Press, 1979), p. 78.

[17] *Ibid.*, 77.

know the grammatical criteria of this object before the emergence of the psychiatric style of reasoning, which is to say that before this time there was as yet no object for us to attach the name 'sexuality' to.

I recognize that I am defending a very strong, counterintuitive, even seemingly unnatural, thesis here, so let me try to increase its plausibility. I want to approach this issue by discussing some aspects of Leo Steinberg's brilliant book, *The Sexuality of Christ in Renaissance Art and in Modern Oblivion*.[18] Although I am going to focus almost exclusively on a conceptual inadequacy in Steinberg's account, I do not for a moment wish to diminish the major achievement of his book, which transcends the boundaries of any single discipline, articulating issues that take the reader far from the province of art history. His book has an almost unlimited interest, and the kind of provocations it allows is a certain indication of its very rare virtues. The title of Steinberg's book should give us pause since, according to the claim I have just put forward, it seems as though there could not be any such thing as the *sexuality* of a person, Christ included, in the Renaissance. A careful reading of his book shows unambiguously that it is not about the sexuality of Christ, but about the sex of Christ, the representation of Christ's genitalia in Renaissance art. Indeed, Steinberg's argument requires that the paintings he discusses be about the sex of Christ, the fact of his sex.

To briefly summarize his argument, Steinberg believes that these representations of Christ are motivated by the centrality of an incarnational theology, that the representation of the penis of the infant or adult Christ gives visible reality to the mystery of the incarnation. For Christ to redeem humanity by his death, he had to be a man in every respect, and these Renaissance paintings represent him as such: "The rendering of the incarnate Christ ever more unmistakably flesh and blood is a religious enterprise because it testifies to God's greatest

---

[18] Leo Steinberg, *The Sexuality of Christ in Renaissance Art and in Modern Oblivion* (New York: Pantheon, 1983); all further references to this work, abbreviated *SC*, will be included in the text.

achievement. And this must be the motive that induces a Renaissance artist to include, in his presentation of the Christ Child, even such moments as would normally be excluded by considerations of modesty—such as the exhibition or manipulation of the boy's genitalia" (*SC*, p. 10). As Steinberg succinctly put it later in his book, "the evidence of Christ's sexual member serves as the pledge of God's humanation" (*SC*, p. 13). And as he himself recognizes, the dogma of the incarnation requires that Christ be "both deathbound and sexed" (*SC*, p. 13), and these artists allow us to see that he is sexed, by anatomical examination; the argument requires nothing at all about Christ's sexuality. The anatomical fact of Christ's sex, the representation of his penis, is paralleled by Renaissance discussions and sermons about Christ's circumcision and, as André Chastel has pointed out, by the reliquary of the holy foreskin, called the Relic of the Circumcision, in the Holy of Holies at the Lateran, which was stolen in 1527 during the sack of Rome. Again, there is much about sex but nothing about sexuality in these traditions. At one point in his review of Steinberg's book, Chastel accuses him of "an unjustified transfer of a current conception to description of the situation in the fifteenth and sixteenth centuries."[19] But the most blatant and far-reaching such transfer, overlooked by Chastel, occurs in the very title of his work. Of course, one might think that Steinberg is simply being careless in his choice of words, that nothing significant turns on this choice, since whatever words he uses, he clearly means 'sex.' But his choice of 'sexuality,' whether careless or studied, covers something of genuine significance that is all too naturally missed. It is this automatic and immediate application of concepts, as though concepts have no temporality, that allows, and often requires, us to draw misleading analogies and inferences that derive from a historically inappropriate aud conceptually untenable

---

[19] André Chastel, "A Long-Suppressed Episode," review of *The Sexuality of Christ in Renaissance Art and in Modern Oblivion*, David Bellos and Christopher Benfry, trans., *New York Review of Books*, Nov. 22 1984, p. 25, note 2

perspective. So let me turn to some representations of sex and
sexuality in order to underline their radical differences.

The iconographical representation of sex proceeds by
depiction of the body, more specifically by depiction of the
genitalia. The iconographical representation of sexuality is
given by depiction of the personality, and it most usually takes
the form of depiction of the face and its expressions. Figures 1
through 5, all of which appear in Steinberg's book, represent
the sex of Christ by explicitly drawing attention to the fact of
his genitalia. Figure 1 depicts Saint Anne manipulating
Christ's genitalia as Mary and Joseph look on. The work as a
whole bears no trace of scandal or blasphemy, and I believe
Steinberg is correct in interpreting Anne's palpation of Christ's
penis as "palpable proof" of "God's descent into manhood"
(*SC*, p. 8). Notice that Christ's profile is barely visible, his
face turned toward Mary and not a prominent or significant
part of the woodcut. The lengths or depths to which some will
go to deny what is visibly evident is rather remarkable. One
art historian reviewing Steinberg's book has said the following
about his interpretation of the Baldung woodcut:

> The gesture [of Saint Anne] is at the very least ambiguous, in
> that the fingers could well be behind the penis, and not touching
> it at all. Indeed, given that her other fingers are around his knee,
> this is the most likely reading. . . . If they [Baldung's
> contemporaries] had initially supposed that St. Anne was
> fondling Christ's penis, they surely would have looked again to
> see if another, less wildly inappropriate reading was possible.
> They would have noticed not only the position of the other
> finger, but would also have observed that her right hand is under
> the child's back and that she is bending forward to take him from
> her daughter. This is a familiar subject; and once we recognise
> it, we can see that the ambiguously placed left hand cannot
> possibly be touching the genitals. Baldung's composition is a
> little awkward, but it does not represent a subject unique in
> European art.[20]

---

[20] Charles Hope, "Ostentatio Genitalium," *London Review of Books*,
Nov. 15- Dec. 5 1984, p. 20.

FIG. 1.—Hans Baldung Grien, *Holy Family* 1511.

This description, even while acknowledging that Baldung's composition is a "little awkward," shows a reviewer who exemplifies modern oblivion. First of all, Steinberg's reading is not in the least "wildly inappropriate" when framed by his readings of dozens of other paintings and by the visual evidence of the other 245 reproductions in his book. Furthermore, the alternative reading that the fingers "could well be behind the penis" which is supposed to be made "most likely" by the fact that "her fingers are around his knee" is hardly likely at all. If Saint Anne's fingers were actually around Christ's knee, it would be more natural for her thumb to be extended, which it is not, and for her wrist to be angled more toward her body. Moreover, and most important, the placement of her left hand is more than a little awkward if Saint Anne is lifting Christ from Mary's arms. If, on this interpretation, the supporting right hand is actually doing the lifting, then the position of the other hand is entirely unmotivated. The alternative interpretation is that the left hand is supposed to be participating in the lifting. But if one simply places one's hands in the exact position of Saint Anne's and then attempts to lift an infant from the angle from which she is purported to be lifting Christ, one all too quickly sees that the most straightforward function of this placement of the left hand would be to strain or dislocate the child's left knee or hip. Steinberg's historical erudition in interpreting paintings is not made at the expense of the perspicacity of his eye.

Figure 2, a painting by Veronese, depicts, going clockwise, Mary, Saint Joseph, Saint John, and Saint Barbara, with the infant Jesus in the middle. The central image of the painting is Jesus, self-touch, a motif which recurs in many other Renaissance paintings. Although in passing Steinberg describes the infant Jesus in the painting as a "contented baby" the expression on his face is actually rather minimal, bordering on blank, his "contentment" being more a lack of restlessness than anything else. The other central image of the painting is Saint John kissing the infant's toe. There is a long tradition of Christian exegesis and interpretation in which the head and feet represent respectively the divine and the human. So Saint John's kissing Jesus' foot draws attention to his humanity as

FIG. 2.—Veronese, *Holy Family with Saint Barbara and the Infant Saint John*, c. 1560

does the self-touch, and this is enhanced by the gazes of all the protagonists (nobody looks at Jesus' face) and by the fact that his upper body shadowed in a way that his lower body is not. Moreover, as Steinberg points out in another context, "feet" is a standard biblical euphemism for genitalia—Saint Jerome refers to "'the harlot who opens her feet to everyone who passes by'"(*SC*, p. 144)[21]. Figure 3 is one of three paintings by Maerten van Heemskerck depicting Christ, the mystical Man of Sorrows. All three paintings, not to mention others discussed by Steinberg, clearly exhibit a phallic erection. Even though we take erection to represent sexuality, the presence of rising desire, no such equation can be found here,

---

[21] Steinberg's entire excursus 18 is relevant here.

FIG. 3.—Maerten van Heemskerck, *Man of Sorrows*, c. 1525-30.

where the symbolic value of erection is quite different. Steinberg speculates, not at all wildly, that in these paintings erection should he equated with resurrection: "If the truth of the Incarnation was proved in the mortification of the penis, would not the truth of the Anastasis, the resuscitation, be proved by its erection? Would not this be the body's best show of power?" (*SC*, p. 91). Whatever one ultimately thinks about these depictions, one looks in vain for any expression of sexuality. Figures 4 and 5 depict a hand-on-groin gesture of

FIG. 4.—Mattia Preti (?), *Dead Christ with Angels*.

FIG. 5.—David Kindt, *Lamentation*, 1631.

the dead Christ. Although this motif raises many interpretive problems, discussed at length by Steinberg (see *SC*, excursis 38), suffice it to say that dead men can have no sexuality, even if the dead man is Christ exhibiting, by the gesture of his left hand, his sex, his humanity. My motive for reproducing these illustrations is that, like all of Steinberg's iconographical evidence, they can be fully interpreted without invoking the notion of sexuality; indeed, to invoke this notion is to misrepresent what is being depicted.

Contrast these representations with some illustrations from nineteenth-century psychiatric texts.[22] Consider, first, figure 6, which is from an 1879 article by the Hungarian pediatrician Lindner, cited and discussed in the second of Freud's *Three Essays on the Theory of Sexuality*.[23] The central feature of the drawing is the depicted relationship between thumb sucking and genital stimulation, which relationship is intended to exhibit one of the essential components of infantile sexuality. The upper left arm/shoulder and right hand of the girl are contiguous in a way that suggests one single, interconnected, even continuous motion linking thumb sucking and genital manipulation. The drawing demonstrates, as Freud was to emphasize, that sexuality is not to be confused with the genitals, that the facts of sexuality encompass far more than the fact of one's sex. Think of Lindner's reasons for accompanying his article with this drawing—there is no need for visible proof of the little girl's sex; it is not as though one is faced with a hermaphrodite; the fact that one views a female child is unproblematic and unambiguous. But how could Lindner demonstrate the facts of infantile sexuality to his doubting pediatric colleagues? It is that problem to which this drawing is meant to respond. It links, so to speak, by ocular proof the psychological pleasure and satisfaction in thumb sucking with the satisfaction one takes in genital stimulation. There is no plausible explanation of the drawing that doesn't

---

[22] A useful discussion of the iconography of madness can be found in Sander L. Gilman, *Seeing the Insane* (New York: J. Wiley, 1982).

[23] S. Lindner, "Das Saugen an den Fingern, Lippen etc. bei den Kindern (Ludeln): Eine Studie," *Jahrbuch fur Kinderheilkunde und physische Erziehung* 14:68 (1879); see Sigmund Freud, *Three Essays on the Theory of Sexuality*, in *The Complete Psychological Works of Sigmund Freud*, standard edition, 24 volumes, James Strachey, ed. and trans. (London: Hogarth, 1953-74), volume 7, pp. 179 -81

FIG. 6.—From S. Lindner, "Das Saugen an den Fingern, Lippen, etc. bei den Kindern (Ludeln). Eine Studie," *Jb. Kinderheilk*, 1879.

invoke the psychology of sexuality as opposed to the anatomy of sex. Furthermore, the expression on the girl's face, although perhaps showing contentment (it is difficult to determine unequivocally) is primarily one of distraction and self-absorption. Her eyes never fully meet ours; the lack of direction in her gaze expresses her preoccupation with her own activity. This kind of infantile self-absorption more subtly demonstrates another aspect of infantile sexuality—the

psychiatric style of reasoning calls it "auto-erotism." Figures
7 through 9 illustrate the psychiatric emphasis on the face and
its expressions as the way of representing derangements of the
personality. From "Happy, Hilarious Mania" to "impulsive

FIG. 7.—James Crichton Browne, "Happy Hilarious Mania," c. 1869

FIG. 8.—Manic depression. The manic state is on the left, the depressive state on the right. Theodor Ziehen, *Psychiatre für Artze und Studierende bearbeitet*, 1894

insanity," physiognomy was the key to personality. As James Shaw, author of a series of late nineteenth-century articles entitled "Facial Expression as One of the Means of Diagnosis and Prognosis in Mental Disease," put it:

> The face having been examined in repose, it is necessary, in order to study the facial reaction, to engage the patient in conversation, or if he is suffering from much intellectual weakness, to ask him a question or make some statement or movement calculated to arouse his attention, and then to watch the changes of facial expression carefully, or to note their absence. Attention to these simple directions, together with a general knowledge of the facial signs given below, will enable any practitioner to refer most cases to one of the ten great symptomatic groups into which I have divided mental cases for the purposes of this monograph. Many cases will be further capable of diagnosis as to the subdivisions etiological, pathological, or symptomatic, to which they belong, and in most others the medical man will be put on

FIG. 9.—Three studies of impulsive insanity. Henri Dagonet,
Nouveau traité élémentaire et pratique des maladies mentales,
1876

the way to a diagnosis to be confirmed by the patient's speech,
conversation, conduct, and anamnesia (personal and family
history).[24]

---

[24] These articles originally appeared in *The Medical Annual*, 12 (1894),
15 (1897), and 21 (1903). They were republished as *The Physiognomy
of Mental Disease and Degeneracy*, Alexander Morison, ed. (Bristol:
Longman, 1903). The quotation is from the latter.

For my immediate purposes, figure 10 is most interesting. It is the only photograph of sexual perversion among the fifty-five photographs reproduced in Shaw's *Physiognomy of Mental Disease and Degeneracy*. Here is Shaw's commentary on this photograph: "The young deaf mute represented. . . is the subject of a mild form of sexual perversion, leading him to object to wear male attire except under compulsion. His face suggests effeminacy, and his sloping shoulders strengthen the impression. It is often the case that male sexual perverts resemble females, and *vice versa*."[25] There is obviously no question that the resemblance here is one of sexuality, not of sex. The pervert's tastes, impulses, desires, dispositions and so forth exhibit feminine sexuality, emblematized by the effeminacy of his face. A statement such as Duncan's that removing the ovaries does not necessarily destroy a woman's sexuality, thus divorcing sexuality from sex, was part of the conceptual space that made it possible for males to exhibit feminine sexuality and *vice versa*, made it possible for there to be kinds of sexuality that did not correspond to an individual's sex.

Let me return briefly to Steinberg in order to anticipate, without fully answering, a possible objection to my account. There is a sustained Christian tradition of discussions of Christ's virginity and chastity, a tradition present in many Renaissance sermons, and it might appear that this tradition is explicitly directed to Christ's sexuality, not merely his sex. After all, how is one to understand chastity except by inference to sexuality? But as Steinberg emphasizes, chastity consists of physiological potency under check; it is a triumph of the will over the flesh and is exemplary because of the volitional abstinence in the face of the physiological possibility of sexual activity (see *SC*, p. 17 and excursis 15). Commenting on a painting of Andrea del Sarto, Steinberg notices that he "contrasts the Christ Child's stiffer member with that of St. John—a differentiation which suggests the likeliest reason for

---

[25] *Ibid.*

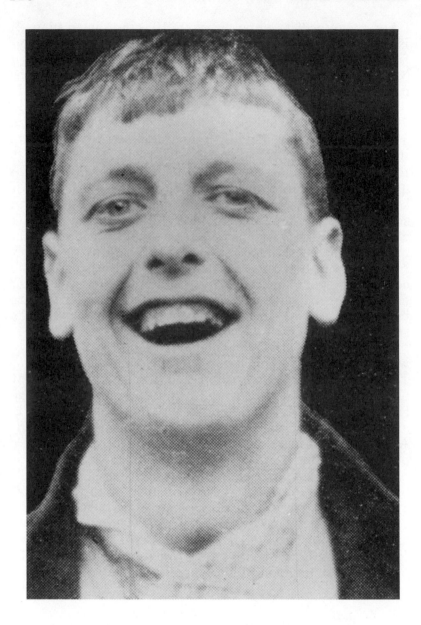

FIG. 10.—Sexual perversion with deaf-mutism. James Shaw, *The Physiognomy of Mental Diseases and Degeneracy*, 1903.

the motif: it demonstrates in the Infant that physiological potency without which the chastity of the man would count for nought" (*SC*, p.79). Chastity and virginity are moral categories denoting a relation between the will and the flesh; they are not categories of sexuality. Although we tend to read back our own categories of sexuality into older moral categories, partly because it is often so difficult for us to distinguish them precisely, it is crucial to my argument that we separate the two. Blurring the two kinds of categories leads to epistemological and conceptual lack of differentiation, and results in the historiographical infection that the great French historian of science Georges Canguilhem has called the "virus of the precursor."[26] We perpetually look for precursors to our categories of sexuality in essentially different domains, producing anachronisms at best and unintelligibility at worst. The distinction between categories of morality and sexuality raises extraordinarily difficult issues, but I think it could be shown, for example, that even Aquinas's discussion of the parts or species of lust in part 2.2, question 154 of the *Summa Theologica* ought not to be assimilated to a discussion of sexuality. One must not suppose that in nineteenth century psychiatry moral deviation was simply transformed into disease. And in the case of chastity one must carefully distinguish it from what Richard von Krafft-Ebing called "anaesthesia of the sexual instinct" in *Psychopathia Sexualis*: "Here all organic impulses arising from the sexual organs, as well as all impulses, and visual, auditory, and olfactory sense impressions fail to sexually excite the individual."[27] This is a disorder of sexuality, not a triumph of the will but a form of psychopathology. Christ most assuredly did not suffer from

---

[26] Georges Canguilhem, "Introduction: L'objet de l'histoire des sciences," *Etudes d'histoire et de philosophie des sciences* (Paris: J. Vrin, 1983), pp. 9-23.

[27] Richard von Krafft-Ebing, *Psychopathia Sexualis, with Especial Reference to the Antipathic Sexual Instinct: A Medico-Forensic Study*, Franklin S. Klaf, trans. (New York: Stein and Day, 1965), p. 34; all further references to this work, abbreviated *PS*, will be included in the text.

it. Of course, in concentrating on the Renaissance and the
nineteenth century, I have passed over many intervening
years. But Steinberg's book is of such importance and can be
used to cast such a clear light on the epistemological contrast I
wish to draw that a detailed discussion of it is worth our
conceptual focus. (The eighteenth century raises its own
intriguing problems and would require an entirely separate
discussion.)

Here is one final piece of visual evidence for the newly
emerging psychiatric style of representing diseases. It was not
uncommon for medical texts up through the nineteenth century
to include drawings depicting hermaphrodites (fig. 11). These

FIG. 11.—Hermaphrodite. James Paris du Plessis, *A Short History of
Human Prodigies and Monstrous Births.* . ., unpublished manuscript,
early seventeenth century

FIG. 12.—Masturbator. D. M. Rozier, *Des Habitudes secrètes ou des maladies produites par l'onanisme chez les femmes*, 1830

poor creatures were shown exhibiting their defective anatomy, the pathological structure of their organs revealing, for all to see, the condition of their diseased sexual identity. Their ambiguous status was an ambiguous anatomical status. But not too many decades later, when a new style of reasoning appeared, we find the radically different iconography of sexual diseases to which I have pointed. A further exemplification of this new iconography is the frontispiece to D. M. Rozier's tract on female masturbation (fig. 12), a nineteenth-century book published, significantly enough, at the threshold of the emergence of the psychiatric style of reasoning.[28] Opening this book, the reader is confronted by a drawing of a young woman. Her head is stiffly tilted toward her left, and her eyes are rolled back, unfocused, the pupils barely visible. She is a habitual masturbator. The depicted portion of her body looks normal, but we can see her psyche, her personality, disintegrating before our eyes. She stands as an emblem of psychiatric disorders, so distinct from her anatomically represented predecessors.

II.

Since there are more seemingly problematic cases for my account than I can possibly discuss here, I want to take one example, returning again to a Renaissance document, in order to show how I would defend my claims against some apparent counterinstances of historical importance. A useful place to begin is with a conversation between Foucault and some members of the department of psychoanalysis at the University of Paris/Vincennes that took place after the publication Foucault's *History of Sexuality*. Towards the end of this conversation, Alan Grosrichard questions Foucault as follows:

> GROSRICHARD: Does what you say in your book about perversions apply equally to sado-masochism? People who have themselves whipped for sexual pleasure have been talked about for a very long time. . .
> FOUCAULT: Listen, that's something that's hard to demonstrate. Do you have any documentation?
> GROSRICHARD: Yes, there exists a treatise *On the Use of the Whip in the Affairs of Venus*, written by a doctor and dating, I think, from 1665, which gives a very complete catalogue of cases. It's cited precisely at the time of the convulsions of St

---

28 D. M. Rozier, *Des Habitudes secrètes ou des maladies produites par l'onanisme chez les femmes* (Paris, 1825). I have not been able to determine in which edition this frontispiece first appears; it does, however, appear by the time of the third edition in 1830.

Médard, in order to show that the alleged miracle actually concealed a sexual story.[29]

Foucault goes on to make the claim that, nevertheless, the pleasure in having oneself whipped was not catalogued in the seventeenth century as a disease of the sexual instinct, and the issue then drops—too soon, in my opinion, to see what is really at stake. Foucault's account of perversion was to have been worked out in what he originally announced as the fifth volume of his *History of Sexuality*, to be titled, appropriately enough, *Perverts*. But he soon reconceived the topics for his projected history of sexuality and so never provided much historical detail to support his claims about perversion. An account of the emergence of sexuality must be supplemented by the story of the emergence of perversion as a disease category, something I have attempted elsewhere.[30] Or to be more precise, our experience of sexuality was born at the same time that perversion emerged as the kind of deviation by which sexuality was ceaselessly threatened. I have argued not only that our medical concept of perversion did not exist prior to the mid-nineteenth century but also that there were no perverts before the existence of this concept. This shift from the emergence of a concept ("perversion") to the emergence of a kind of person (the pervert), to return to an issue I have already mentioned, is underwritten by the doctrine that Ian Hacking has called "dynamic nominalism." Hacking argues that in many domains of the human sciences, "categories of people come into existence at the same time as kinds of people come into being to fit those categories, and there is a two-way interaction between these processes." Dynamic nominalism

---

[29] Michel Foucault, "The Confession of the Flesh," Colin Gordon et al., trans., *Power/Knowledge: Selected Interviews and Other Writings, 1972-1977*, Colin Gordon, ed. (New York: Pantheon Books, 1980), p. 221.

[30] Arnold I. Davidson, "Closing Up the Corpses: Diseases of Sexuality and the Emergence of the Psychiatric Style of Reasoning," in *Meaning and Method: Essays in Honor of Hilary Putnam*, George Boolos, ed. (Cambridge: Cambridge University Press, 1990).

shows how "history plays an essential role in the constitution
of the objects, where the objects are the people and ways in
which they behave," since the human sciences "bring into
being new categories which, in part, bring into being new
kinds of people."[31] Hacking gives multiple personality as an
example of making up people and provides other examples
from the history of statistics.[32] Perverts and the history of
perversion are a still further example of making up people.
Our experience of sexuality is all that there is to sexuality
itself, and this experience was decisively and quite recently
formed by a set of concepts or categories, among them
"perversion," and an associated style of reasoning.

   Since the problem raised by Grosrichard is a good test case
for my claims, I want to turn directly to the treatise he
mentions. In 1629, (or, according to some sources, 1639)
John Henry Meibomius, "a physician of Lubeck," wrote a
short treatise entitled "On the Use of Flogging in Medical and
Venereal Affairs, the Function of the Reins and the Loins." It
begins with a catalog of cases of whipping that bear no relation
to any question of sexuality. Meibomius asserts that whipping
has been used as a cure for melancholy, madness, to help lean
persons "to plump their bodies," to cure relaxed limbs, to
forward the eruption of smallpox, and to cure obstructions in
the belly. After listing these cases, which he takes to be
uncontroversial, he turns to the question of "persons who are
stimulated to venery by strokes of the rod, and worked into a

---

31 Hacking, "Five Parables," in *Philosophy in History: Essays on the
   Historiography of Philosophy*, R. Rorty, et al., ed. (Cambridge:
   Cambridge University Press, 1984), pp. 122, 124.

32 Hacking, "The Invention of Split Personalities," in *Human Nature and
   Natural Knowledge*, Alan Donagan, Anthony Perovich, Jr., and Michael
   Wedin, eds. (Dordrecht: D. Reidel, 1986), pp. 63-85, and "Making Up
   People," in *Reconstructing Individualism: Autonomy, Individuality,
   and the Self in Western Thought*, Thomas Heller, Morton Sosna, and
   David Wellbery, eds. (Stanford: Stanford University Press, 1986), pp.
   222-36, reprinted in this volume. Hacking attributes the doctrine of
   dynamic nominalism to me in this latter paper on the basis of my
   "Closing Up the Corpses."

flame of lust by blows."[33] He establishes the veracity of this kind of case through the testimony of other physicians as well as through his own medical experience. Here is one instance he cites:

> I subjoin a new and late instance, which happened in this city of Lubeck, where I now reside. A citizen of Lubeck, a cheesemonger by trade, was cited before the magistrates, among other crimes, for adultery, and the fact being proved, he was banished. A courtesan, with whom this fellow had often an affair, confessed before the Deputies of the state, that he could never have a forcible erection, and perform the duty of a man, till she had whipped him on the back with rods; and that when the business was over, that he could not be brought to a repetition unless excited by a second flogging. (*FVA*, pp. 20-21)

Having thus established the truth of these instances, he next considers "what reason can be given for an action so odd and uncommon." He first entertains the astrological explanation, namely, that "the man's propensity to Venus was caused in his geniture, and destined to flogging by opposite and threating rays of the stars," only to reject it immediately since "the heavens and the stars are universal causes, and so cannot occasion such particular effects in one or two individuals" (*FVA*, p. 21). He next examines the explanation by custom, the idea that these odd and uncommon acts are due to vicious habits practiced in childhood, "a strange instance of what a power the force of education has in grafting inveterate ill habits on our morals." But this explanation is also rejected because not all youths who are engaged in this practice continue it habitually; and moreover, "neither is it probable that all those boys we mentioned began their youth with exposing their chastity to sale with this reciprocal communication of vice, and used rods at the first to provoke lechery" (*FVA*, p. 22). The most adequate explanation of these strange cases, according to

---

[33] John Henry Meibomius, "On the Use of Flogging in Venereal Affairs" (Chester, Pa., 1961), p. 19; all further references to this work, abbreviated *FVA*, will be included in the text. The English translation of this Latin treatise first appeared in 1801.

Meibomius, can be found by examining the physiology and
anatomy of the reins and loins. After discussing in some detail
the anatomical relations between the reins, loins, the seminal
arteries and veins, and the testicles, as well as determining the
way in which "each in a different manner, are appropriated as
well for the elaborating of the seed as for performing the work
of generation" (*FVA*, p. 23), Meibomius concludes:

> That stripes upon the back and loins, as parts appropriated for the
> generating of the seed, and carrying it to the genitals, warm and
> inflame those parts, and contribute very much to the irritation of
> lechery. From all which, it is no wonder that such shameless
> wretches, victims of a detested appetite such as we have
> mentioned [masturbation], or others exhausted by too frequent
> repetition, their loins and vessels being drained, have sought a
> remedy by flogging. For it is very probable that the refrigerated
> parts grow warm by such stripes, and excite a heat in the seminal
> matter, and that the pain of the flogged parts, which is the reason
> that the blood and spirits are attracted in greater quantity,
> communicate heat also to the organs of generation, and thereby
> the perverse and frenzical appetite is satisfied. Then nature,
> though unwilling, is drawn beyond the stretch of her common
> power and becomes a party to the commission of such an
> abominable crime (*FVA*, p. 30).[34]

In the next paragraph, Meibomius's underlying aim in
writing this treatise becomes clearer. As a physician, he has
evidently cured a number of men, otherwise unable to perform
the act of generation, with this treatment of stripes and strokes
upon the back. This remedy seems to have become the object
of much discussion and questioning among both fellow
physicians and laypersons. Meibomius admits that perhaps
some of those who come to him for treatment are simply
exhausted by excess venery and request his treatment merely
so that they can continue the "same filthy enjoyment." But he
demands of those who question this practice, "You must, in all
conscience, also ask: whether a person who has practised

---

[34] The copy of the text I have cited is mispaginated; page 23 is followed
by page 30.

lawful love, and yet perceives his loins and sides languid, may not, without the imputation of any crime, make use of the same method, in order to discharge a debt which I won't say is due, but to please the creditor?" (*FVA*, p. 30). Meibomius wants to vindicate his practice by arguing that the use of whips in the affairs of Venus can be a justified therapeutic modality, one that physician and patient can practice without the imputation of any crime to either one. These quotations already allow us to anticipate my argument that Meibomius's treatise is not a counterexample to the claim that perversion does not emerge as a medical phenomenon until the nineteenth century. Before I set out this argument, however, let me remind you how masochism was understood by nineteenth-century psychiatry. For this understanding, we do best to turn again to Krafft-Ebing's *Psychopathia Sexualis*, since Krafft-Ebing was, after all, the inventor of the concept of masochism. Here is what Krafft-Ebing says at the beginning of his section on masochism:

> By masochism I understand a peculiar perversion of the psychical sexual life in which the individual affected, in sexual feeling and thought, is controlled by the idea of being completely and unconditionally subject to the will of a person of the opposite sex; of being treated by that person as by a master, humiliated and abused. This idea is colored by lustful feeling; the masochist lives in fantasies, in which he creates situations of this kind and often attempts to realize them. By this perversion his sexual instinct is often made more or less insensible to the normal charms of the opposite sex—incapable of a normal sexual life— psychically impotent. But this physical impotence does not in any way depend upon a horror of the opposite sex, but upon the fact that the perverse instinct finds an adequate satisfaction differing from the normal, in woman, to be sure, but not in coitus. (*PS*, pp. 86-7)

Krafft-Ebing is unequivocal in his assertions that masochism is a special kind of psychopathological disorder that affects the functioning of the sexual instinct in a very particular way. The normal direction of the sexual instinct is blocked in masochism, and this instinct and the psychical sexual life are redirected to an abnormal path which Krafft-

Ebing characterizes by a number of distinctive features. Masochism is one mode of functional deviation of the sexual instinct that picks out a *kind of individual*. Krafft-Ebing's world of sexual psychopathology is peopled not merely by individuals who want to be flagellated but by masochistic individuals, a very specific kind of diseased creature. If we were to list the ways of expressing or instantiating sexuality in Krafft-Ebing's universe, masochism would be on that list. Being a masochist is, in *Psychopathia Sexualis*, a possible way of conceiving of oneself, a possible way of being a person.[35]

Returning to Meibomius's treatise, we find, first of all, that there is not even the slightest implication that people who are whipped, even for venereal purposes, suffer from a disease or disorder which manifests itself in a desire for such whippings. In 1629, there was no possible disease which consisted in the pleasure in having oneself whipped; the very idea of such a disease could not be conceptualized. It is only one of many similar ironies in the history of medicine that far from being a disease, the whipping of patients, and even the desire of some patients for these whippings, was thought to be therapeutically mandated and justified. Moreover, there is absolutely no indication in Meibomius's pamphlet that men who are whipped in venereal affairs constitute a distinct kind of individual, different from other people because of special features of their personality. Anybody may be a candidate for this therapy, depending solely upon whether his languid loins can be, so to speak, activated in no other, simpler way. The question for Meibomius and his interlocutors is whether the lust whipping arouses is always morally prohibited, whether it can ever be so aroused "without the imputation of any crime." The question is not whether there is some kind of person for whom only such whipping provides an adequate psychological satisfaction.

This reading of the treatise is further supported by two additional essays appended to it when it was reprinted in 1669.

---

[35] For further discussion of this terminology, see Hacking's essays cited in note 32.

In neither of these essays is there any anticipation of the set of concepts necessary to describe the phenomenon of masochism. Indeed, all three essays, when not attempting to produce a physiological explanation of the effects caused by whipping, fit squarely into the tradition of moral philosophy and theology that deals with the nature and kinds of lust. Although I cannot discuss this tradition in any detail here, I want to make a few, general background remarks. In book 12 of the *City of God*, Augustine uses the theological concept of perversion to describe evil acts of the will. The will is perversely affected when it fails to adhere to God, when it defects from the immutable to mutable good. Perversion is not intrinsically connected with lust, but describes any act of the will that is contrary to God and so is contrary to nature.[36] In part 2.2, question 154 of the *Summa Theologica*, Aquinas argues that there are unnatural vices that are a determinate species of lust, since they are contrary not merely to right reason, which is common to all lustful vices, but, in addition, "contrary to the natural order of the venereal act as becoming to the human race."[37] However, even in Aquinas's fascinating attempt to distinguish kinds of lust; it is clear that distinct species of lust do not map onto distinct kinds of individuals; we are all subject to all the kinds of lust, and the principle by which we distinguish lusts from one another does not permit us to distinguish different types of people from one another. In this tradition of moral theology, one classifies kinds of sins, not primarily kinds of individuals and certainly not kinds of disorders.

In fact, Krafft-Ebing was quite concerned with the issue of flagellation as it came to be discussed in moral philosophy and theology. He devotes a section of *Psychopathia Sexualis* to distinguishing carefully between passive flagellation and masochism, insisting that the former is a perversity, and therefore an appropriate topic of ethical and legal discussion,

---

[36] Augustine, *Concerning the City of God against the Pagans* (New York: Penguin Books, 1972), book 12.

[37] Thomas Aquinas, *Summa Theologica*, Fathers of the Dominican Province, trans. (Westminster, MD, 1911), 4:1819.

while only the latter is a genuine perversion, a medical phenomenon:

> It is not difficult to show that masochism is something essentially different from flagellation, and more comprehensive. For the masochist the principal thing is subjection to the woman; the punishment is only the expression of this relation— the most intense effect of it he can bring upon himself. For him the act has only a symbolic value, and is a means to the end of mental satisfaction of his peculiar desires. On the other hand, the individual that is weakened and not subject to masochism and who has himself flagellated, desires only a mechanical irritation of his spinal centre. (*PS*, p. 93)

Krafft-Ebing goes on to specify further the characteristics that distinguish the masochist from the "weakened debauchee" who desires passive flagellation, the most significant of these characteristics being psychological. He concludes by claiming that masochism bears to simple flagellation a relation analogous to that between inverted sexual instinct and pederasty; both of these relations are examples of the more general contrast between perversion and perversity, and hence of disease and moral deviation. The phenomenon of masochism, like the general phenomenon of perversion, is a thoroughly modern phenomenon. As Krafft-Ebing remarks, without any further comment, the perversion of masochism was, up until the time of Sacher-Masoch, "quite unknown to the scientific world as such" (*PS*, p. 87).

Let me return one last time to Meibomius's treatise to make a final conceptual point. In this treatise, the adjective 'perverse' occurs twice, once in the phrase 'perverse and frenzical appetite' and a second time in the phrase 'vices of perverse lust' (*FVA*, pp. 30, 22). The context of both occurrences makes it clear that 'perverse' is used as a general term of disapprobation, although precisely what the disapproval consists in is not further specified. Indeed, if one looks at lexical patterns in the treatises of moral philosophy and theology that discuss perversion, and even in the pre-nineteenth-century medical works that seem to deal with this topic, the adjectival, adverbial, and verb forms, 'perverse,' 'perversely,' and 'to pervert,' appear to occur far more predominantly than either the noun form 'perversion' or, especially, the noun form 'pervert.' However, I do not want merely to claim that the numerical occurrences of the noun form are far fewer than adjective, adverb, and verb, although in the works I have examined this appears to be the case. But even apart from looking at and counting lexical patterns, I think it can be argued that the noun had a conceptually derivative place in moral theology but a conceptually central place in nineteenth-century medicine. One could confirm this claim by studying, for instance, the use of this term in Augustine's *City of God*. And just about the time that Meibomius's treatise was published, a common use in English of the noun 'pervert' was as an antonym to 'convert'—a pervert being one that is turned from good to evil, and a convert being the contrary. This usage clearly implies that the primary phenomenon is to be located in the perverse choices and actions of the individual, someone being a pervert or convert depending on the person's ethical choices.

In Krafft-Ebing's *Psychopathia Sexualis*, however, we have a book devoted to the description, indeed the constitution, of four types of characters: the homosexual or invert, the sadist, the masochist, and the fetishist. That is to say, we have a book that sets forth the intrinsic distinguishing characteristics of a new kind of person—the pervert. Krafft-Ebing insisted that to diagnose the pervert correctly one "must investigate the whole personality of the individual" (*PS*, p. 53). He continually emphasizes that diagnosis cannot proceed simply by examining the sexual acts performed. One must rather investigate impulses, feelings, urges, desires, fantasies, tendencies, and so on, and the result of this investigation will be to mark off new kinds of persons, distinct and separate from the normal heterosexual individual. It is the pervert who is primary, perverse choices and actions being subordinated to a conceptually subsidiary role. If in psychiatry the conceptual focus moves from perverse choice to the pervert, and if linguistic forms reflect such conceptual changes, then it should come as no surprise that we find more distinctive and frequent use there of 'pervert' and even 'perversion.'

Connected with this new focus is the fact that nineteenth-century psychiatry often took sexuality to be the way in which the mind is best represented. To know a person's sexuality is to know that person. Sexuality is the externalization of the hidden, inner essence of personality. And to know sexuality, to know the person, we must know its anomalies. Krafft-Ebing was quite clear about this point. In his *Text-book of Insanity*, a massive book that covers the entire field of mental abnormality, he writes, "These anomalies are very important elementary disturbances, since upon the nature of sexual sensibility the mental individuality in greater part depends."[38] Sexuality individualizes, turns one into a specific kind of human being—a sadist, masochist, homosexual, fetishist. This link between sexuality and individuality explains some of the passion with which psychiatry constituted the pervert. The more details we have about the anomalies of perversion, the better we are able to penetrate the covert individuality of the self. Only a psychiatrist, after meticulous examination, could recognize a real pervert. Or to be more accurate, it was also thought that there was one other kind of person who could recognize a true pervert, even without meticulous examination: as if by a kind of hypersensitive perception, a pervert could recognize one of his own kind. Of course, much more historical detail would be needed to produce an unequivocally convincing argument that proves the conceptual shift from perverse choice to the pervert. But anyone who reads a few dozen of the relevant texts in moral theology and psychiatry will, I think, be fully struck by what Foucault once called their "different epistemological texture."[39]

Much of my discussion has been concerned with a rupture in styles of reasoning within medicine, a break from pathological anatomy in all its forms to the emergence of psychiatric reasoning. This rupture delineates a problematic

---

[38] Krafft-Ebing, *Text-book of Insanity Based on Clinical Observations*, Charles Gilbert Chaddock, trans. (Philadelphia: F.A. Davis, Co., 1904), p. 81.

[39] Foucault, "The Confession of the Flesh," p. 221. Foucault uses this expression in a different context than mine, though a related one.

internal to the history of medicine. However, my discussion of Meibomius's treatise and the issues it raises, as well as of Steinberg's remarks on the chastity of Christ, opens up a companion problem, one not internal to the history of medicine but rather centered on medicine's appropriation of an initially related, but unmedicalized domain. It is not that medicine simply took over the study of what had once been a part of morality; moral deviation did not merely transform itself into disease. Instead, the moral phenomenon of the perversity of the will furnished a point of reference that both opened the way for and provided an obstacle to the medical constitution of perversion. This problematic, which has barely begun to be worked out in detail, concerns a crossing of the "threshold of scientificity."[40] Foucault, in *The Archaeology of Knowledge*, has very precisely described the questions that must be answered in attempting to understand how such a threshold can be crossed. Describing not his own position but that of Canguilhem and Gaston Bachelard, the kind of history of science he calls an "epistemological history of the sciences," Foucault writes:

> Its purpose is to discover, for example, how a concept—still overlaid with metaphors or imaginary contents—was purified, and accorded the status and function of a scientific concept. To discover how a region of experience that has already been mapped, already partially articulated, but still overlaid with immediate practical uses or values related to those uses, was constituted as a scientific domain. To discover how, in general, a science was established over and against a pre-scientific level, which both paved the way and resisted it in advance, how it succeeded in overcoming the obstacles and limitations that still stood in its way.[41]

I know of no better succinct description of what is at stake at this level of analysis. An adequate history of the psychiatric

---

[40] Foucault, *The Archaeology of Knowledge and The Discourse of Language*, A.M. Sheridan Smith, trans. (New York: Pantheon, 1972), p. 190.

[41] *Ibid.*

emergence of sexuality will have to look not only to the shifts in styles of reasoning but also to the multilayered relations between our ethical descriptions of sexual practices and their scientific counterparts.[42]

---

[42] I am indebted to Stanley Cavell, Lorraine Daston, Peter Galison, Ian Hacking, Erin Kelly, John McNees, and Joel Snyder for conversations on the topics of this paper.

CHAPTER 7
John Boswell
Categories, Experience and Sexuality

For nearly a decade the historiography of homosexuality has been both enriched and complicated by a controversy over the epistemology of human sexuality, often referred to as the "constructionist/essentialist" debate.[1] It is not actually a debate: one of many ironies about the controversy is that no one deliberately involved in it identifies himself as an "essentialist," although constructionists (of whom, in contrast, there are many)[2] sometimes so label other writers. Even when

---

[1] For an overview of this literature, which is considerable and of uneven quality, see most recently Steven Epstein, "Gay Politics, Ethnic Identity: The Limits of Social Constructionism," *Socialist Review* 93/94 (1987), pp. 9-54, reprinted this volume, the earlier but very articulate overview by Robert Padgug, "Sexual Matters: On Conceptualizing Sexuality in History," *Radical History Review* 20 (1979), pp. 3-33, reprinted this volume, or David Halperin, *One Hundred Years of Homosexuality* (New York: Routledge, 1990).

[2] Jeffrey Weeks, in several books, e.g., *Coming Out: Homosexual Politics in Britain, from the Nineteenth Century to the Present* (London: Quartet Books, 1977), has probably written the most from a constructionist point of view, but see also John D'Emilio, *Sexual Politics, Sexual Communities: The Making of a Homosexual Minority in the United States, 1940-1970* (Chicago: University of Chicago Press, 1983), and the essays in Kenneth Plummer, ed., *The Making of the Modern Homosexual* (Totowa, NJ: Barnes and Noble, 1981). Many others could be mentioned as well (e.g., Padgug and Halperin, cited in previous note, and probably Epstein). Much of the controversy is conducted through scholarly papers: at a conference on "Homosexuality in History and Culture" held at Brown University in February of 1987, of six presentations four were explicitly constructionist; one offered a critique of some constructionist views. Nearly all classicists currently

--->

applied by its opponents the label seems to fit extremely few contemporary scholars.[3] This fact is revealing, and provides a basis for understanding the controversy more accurately not as a dialogue between two schools of thought, but as a critique by revisionists of assumptions believed to underlie traditional historiography.[4]

Most fields of historical enquiry go through phases of self-questioning about basic assumptions, and after an early period of rather simplistic "who-was-and-who-wasn't?" history by and about gay people it was to be expected that there would be a period of reconsideration and an effort to formulate a more sophisticated analytical base. Although welcome and fruitful, this evolution in gay historiography has not been uniformly successful. In some areas it has greatly heightened critical sensibilities on issues of sexuality and sexual identity; in others, the range of opinions and approaches it has produced has blurred rather than refined the focus of discussion.

Like most radical critiques facing the presumed superior numbers and longevity deployed by established, older notions, constructionism wages a kind of guerrilla warfare: its partisans tend to devote more energy to exposing the weaknesses of the "essentialist" position than to articulating and refining their

---

writing on homosexuality at Athens, for example, are constructionist to some degree, except perhaps K.J. Dover, whose views defy easy classification. The few scholars working on Rome, by contrast, tend not to be identifiably constructionist.

[3] Three recent writers on the controversy, Stephen O. Murray, "Homosexual Categorization in Cross-Cultural Perspective," in *Social Theory, Homosexual Realities* (New York: Gay Academic Union, 1984), Epstein, "Gay Politics", and Halperin, *One Hundred Years*, identify among them a dozen or more "constructionist" historians, but Murray and Halperin adduce only a single historian (me) as an example of modern "essentialist" historiography. Epstein, the most sophisticated of the three, can add to this only Adrienne Rich, not usually thought of as a historian. As to whether my views are actually "essentialist" or not, see below.

[4] Many constructionists are consciously influenced by earlier revisionist critiques— e.g., Weeks by that of the class history of E.P. Thompson, others by Foucault's criticisms of western epistemology.

own. This tactic is a bit misleading, since there are few if any works intended to express an "essentialist" position, but it affords constructionism a great defensive strength, since it is very difficult to react to an unidentifiable or deftly moving opponent (opposing one of its manifestations may have no effect on others). It is beneficial to scholarship in the long run, because it does reveal fallacies in earlier writing, but it also makes difficult the task of understanding or defining what newer truth emerges: by the time the reporters have located the "constructionist" camp to interview its leaders, they have usually moved on to a new position.

There are probably as many ways to define "constructionism" as there are "constructionists." Very broadly speaking, they have in common the view that "sexuality" is an artifact or "construct"[5] of human society and therefore specific to any given social situation. Some would argue that there are no underlying diachronic constants of human sexuality involved in this social construction, others that whatever underlying phenomena there may be are of much less importance than social overlay, or cannot be identified and should not be assumed. Part of the reason it is so difficult to identify "essentialists" is that no reasonable person would disagree with the proposition implicit in the constructionist critique that the experience, including the sexual experience, of every human being in every time and place is distinct from that of every other human being, and that the social matrix in which she or he lives will determine that experience in a largely irresistible way, including creating (or not creating) opportunities for sexual expression and possibly even awareness of sexual feelings and desires.

Agreeing on this, however, hardly begins to address the problematic underlying questions, such as whether society is itself responding to sexual phenomena that are generic to humans and *not created* by social structures. In this context

---

[5] Constructionists apparently understand 'construct' as the nominal derivative of the verb 'to construct'; the possibility of derivation from 'to construe,' which would moderate the constructionist position substantially, has not been raised in the literature to my knowledge.

one can see that the controversy is not simply a variant of the ongoing interdisciplinary nature/nurture debate about biological determinism versus social development, because no one who believes that there are biological aspects to human sexuality would claim that there are not also individual psychological, familial and social factors operating alongside and in conjunction with these. Indeed, in any careful epistemology these would have to be considered "biological" as well, since they are a ubiquitous part of the life of human organisms. Constructionists, moreover, can hardly argue that there are not "natural" (i.e., physiological) components to human sexuality in terms of the functioning of body parts, response to stimulus, etc.

It is at the secondary level—where constructionists also disagree among themselves—that the epistemological differences between "constructionists" and the writings they criticize seem most pronounced, although here, too, there is confusion and overlap, and some constructionists seem as far from other constructionists as all do from the so-called "essentialists." Some constructionists argue that a "homosexual identity" did not exist before a certain date (often the second half of the nineteenth century); others that "homosexuality" was not found before such a date; others that although "homosexuality" was known throughout history, "gay people" did not exist until relatively recently.[6] Some writers argue generally that "sexuality" is not a constant; others posit more specifically that social constructs of sexuality are not constant. A more sweeping and profound version of these is that there is no aspect of sexuality that is not socially constructed.

These are all very different propositions, based on distinct premises, presupposing varying definitions of similar terms, and requiring individual analysis. It would be impossible to do justice to this range of views in a brief essay; they are presented here in summary form to help the reader appreciate

---

[6] This is not necessarily a different claim from the first one, although the terminology varies so much that it seems best simply to repeat the propositions in their original form.

their relationship to the idea postulated as the fundamental assumption of "essentialists": that humans are differentiated at an individual level in terms of erotic attraction, so that some are more attracted sexually to their own gender, some to the opposite gender, and some to both, in all cultures.

This is, for example, the assumption usually alleged to make *Christianity, Social Tolerance and Homosexuality*[7] an "essentialist" work: the supposition that there have been in all Western societies "gay people" and "non-gay people."[8] This is not false attribution: it was, in fact, the working hypothesis of the book. Logically this view is not necessarily opposed to all constructionist positions: even if societies create or formulate "sexualities," it might happen that different societies would construct similar ones, as they often construct similar political or class structures; (of course, if a constructionist position holds that "gay person" refers only to a particular, modern identity, it is then, tautologically, not applicable to the past).

Most constructionist critiques, however, assume that the essentialist position necessarily entails a further supposition: that society does not *create* these attractions, but only acts on them. Some other force—genes, psychological influences, etc.—creates "sexuality," which is essentially independent of culture. This was certainly not a working hypothesis of *CSTH*; I can state with reasonable certainty that its author was (and is) agnostic about the *origins* of human sexuality.[9]

---

[7] John Boswell, *Christianity, Social Tolerance and Homosexuality* (Chicago: University of Chicago, 1980), hereafter *CSTH*.

[8] Definitions are at the heart of the controversy, and most constructionists would disagree with my use of 'gay.' I defined 'gay persons' in *CSTH* (p. 44) as those "who are conscious of erotic inclination toward their own gender as a distinguishing characteristic"; I would now simplify this and designate as a gay person anyone whose erotic interest is predominantly directed toward his or her own gender (i.e., regardless of consciousness of this as a distinguishing characteristic). This seems to me the normal meaning of the term among American speakers of English.

[9] *CSTH*, pp. 48-49.

The etiology of human sexual interest could be a crucial facet of the controversy. If a predilection for sexual activity with one gender could be shown to be innate in all humans or fixed in childhood in all (or even many) known cultures, then it would be rather pointless to argue that all "sexuality" is socially constructed.[10] If it could be demonstrated conclusively, on the other hand, that people learn all sexual behavior socially and would be completely non-sexual or undifferentiated in desire if brought up alone on a desert island, then some strains of "constructionism" would be statements of empirical fact rather than critical theory.

For the present, however, data concerning the provenances of human sexuality are so unsatisfactory as to be almost perfectly moot,[11] and if, as seems likely, they turn out ultimately to be a complex interaction of physiological, psychological and cultural factors, it will still be crucial to assess and discuss the extent to which social factors create, shape and determine human sexuality. To do so intelligently requires an appreciation of both the strengths and limitations of the "constructionist" controversy and alternative approaches to the history of human sexuality. It may be helpful to divide them into four different areas: 1) philosophical; 2) semantic; 3) political; and 4) empirical.

Philosophical

Two major philosophical issues underlie much of the constructionist critique of conventional historiography. The

---

[10] On this point see the interesting reply of Halperin to a question about the impact on constructionist theory of data about physiological etiology in "Homosexuality: A Cultural Construct," *Harvard Gay and Lesbian Newsletter* 5 (Fall, 1987), p. 6, where he essentially denies that there could be such findings. [This interview is reprinted, in modified form in David Halperin, *One Hundred Years*. Halperin's revised answer (pp. 49-51) is more equivocal on this point.—ed.]

[11] The most recent overview of such data, along with several original theories, is James Weinrich, *Sexual Landscapes* (New York: Scribners, 1987); chapter 5 of this book is reprinted in this volume.

first is a general reaction against post-enlightenment positivism and its tendency to treat abstractions as concrete signifiers rather than abbreviations for loose generalizations. The reification, for example, of terms like 'capitalism,' 'feudalism,' or 'sexuality'—defensible only as short-hand rubrics for congeries of ideas—can obscure through oversimplification more than is gained through organizational efficiency. This problem is exacerbated, the constructionist critique rightly notes, by anachronistic assumptions that any abstract categories of one culture (e.g., "gender," "class") can be projected onto others.

These problems are both general and specific. They derive from the most basic puzzle of human epistemology: to what extent do the abstractions of human thought and speech correspond to an objective reality? But they also arise from more specific questions about the reality or accuracy of particular concepts and abstractions such as "gender" and "sexuality." Both sorts of questions are useful, but they have played a somewhat confusing role in the constructionist controversy, because they are often adduced in a haphazard and ad hoc way as a criticism of the concept of homosexuality (or sexuality, or "gay person," etc.) alone, without any coherent acknowledgement or exploration of the much broader and more complicated issues they pose for historical writing (and human thought). If constructionists arguing against the transhistorical reality of "sexuality" or "homosexuality" would make clear that they also do not believe there is any such thing as a historical "heterosexuality," "family," "kinship," "state," "government," or other such familiar abstractions, their audience would have a more realistic perception of their position. As it is, readers are usually left with the impression that other diachronic abstractions are accurate as commonly applied, while this one alone is singularly inaccurate.

Almost any thoughtful person would agree with the first point—that all categories are inadequate and abstractions can be misleading; it is the second—namely, this one abstraction is much more removed from reality than any others—that is difficult to accept. If it is not a distortion of their position and constructionists actually believe it, they have yet to demonstrate why this one abstraction is so much less accurate than all others. There is a further subtlety: whatever inadequacies abstract categorizations of sexual experience have transhistorically they may also have in the present. An additional layer of misconception is introduced by implicitly suggesting to readers that it is only across time that conceptual inaccuracy arises, as if "homosexuality" were a perfectly clear and concrete concept in the present.

While it is certainly a valuable intellectual strategy to deflate and refine positivist assumptions, it must be undertaken consistently and with perspective. It is unwise, for example, to ignore the fact that abstractions and their application constitute a useful intellectual strategy in themselves, and are in the long run perhaps the most indispensable element of human thought (all words and terms being, in the most basic sense, abstractions). It is pointless and naive to portray them as inherently false or inimical to accuracy rather than as tools that may be employed well or ill.

A second philosophical problem inherent in the controversy is the issue of "free will." Although it is rarely directly addressed, much discussion about "sexual identity," "sexual orientation," "sexual preference," "homosexuality," "heterosexuality," "sexuality," "gay identity" and related concepts in fact implicitly centers on the extent to which humans determine their own character, preferences, interests, desires, etc., as opposed to passively experiencing or inheriting them. This is one of the oldest riddles of the mind, and has baffled the investigations of philosophers for millennia and psychologists for decades. Introducing it as a casual premise or factor in discussions of human sexuality is jejune and almost guarantees misunderstanding and non-productive argument. Where it is in fact relevant, it needs to be articulated clearly and coherently as a major philosophical difficulty, so that all parties can at least face the real puzzle and not attempt to resolve it obliquely by defining the nature of "sexuality" first and hoping that the question of the will will somehow fall into line.

Semantic

Semantic difficulties are not neatly distinguishable from philosophical problems, but it may be useful to view them from a slightly different perspective. All human disagreements are "semantic" problems in the sense that words are the implements of verbal dispute. A great many different lexical issues make up the constructionist controversy, but some of the most important ones can be subsumed under a single question: is it legitimate to ask questions of the past using the categories of the present, regardless of whether they would have had meaning for the persons being studied, or should the investigator adopt the categories with which denizens of the past would have described their own lives and culture? More simply, should we look at the past through the alembic of our terms or through the alembic of theirs?

Obviously we can not escape our filters entirely, but we could strive to get beyond them. If "sexual orientation" or "gay person" or "homosexual identity" are modern constructs (conceptually or socially, or both) it is grossly misleading, the argument goes, to apply them to premodern people, somewhat like applying the term 'feminist' to Joan of Arc or 'democrat' to Cicero.

Constructionist answers to this question generally presuppose that we should suppress modern categories as irrelevant and focus instead on the categories the ancients would have used themselves, as more reflective of the reality of their structures and experience. This assumes, politely but oddly, that humans are inevitably the best analysts of their own lives and environments. One would have thought that, in fact, the aim of good historical writing was to get beyond the mere descriptions of contemporaries and to organize information in its most revealing way.

To be more concrete: there are few, possibly no words in any ancient or medieval language corresponding precisely to 'gay' or 'homosexual.' Some nouns and verbs categorize homosexual activities or persons involved in them, but the abstractions 'homosexual' or 'homosexuality' are uncommon or unknown in most premodern languages. Constructionists reasonably argue that this is one of a number of indications that these categories did not exist in the past (either conceptually or "really"), and that forcing the modern terms onto data from the past is a distortion. Moreover, the extant indications of sexuality from ancient Greece and Rome suggest categories of organization—e.g., along lines of age or status— quite different from modern patterns. This constitutes, for constructionists, evidence that "sexuality" in such societies was fundamentally different from "sexuality" in the modern West, and should be assessed in its own distinctive terms and categories.

Three problems reduce the value of this line of thought: 1) there may be reasons for the structure of a language other than its reflection of "objective reality"; 2) modern terms for sexuality are not necessarily any more comprehensive or accurate about the present than ancient ones are for the past; 3) application of modern categories to the past, even if they do not match precisely, may be a useful strategy for determining the relationship between the two.

In regard to the first, the absence of a concept can hardly be taken to demonstrate the absence of what it applies to. All languages respond to structural and developmental pressures beyond accurate description. There is no word in French for 'shallow' and no word in Latin for 'religion.'[12] These facts have very different significances. The first is simply a semantic accident: it is hardly the case that there is nothing "shallow" in France or that the French do not recognize "shallowness." They simply happen not to have developed a single word for this concept, and instead use the negation "not deep."

The lack of a word for 'religion' in Rome (and well into the Middle Ages) may be to some extent a semantic accident as well, but it is also related to social reality: there was no "religion" at Rome comparable to "religion" as known in the modern West—i.e., a comprehensive, exclusive system of theology and ethics. Even the word 'cult,' which in the

---

12 The Latin *religio* has a semantic range quite different from 'religion': see discussion in Mary Beard and Michael Crawford, *Rome in the Late Republic* (Ithaca: Cornell University Press, 1985), p. 26.

nineteenth century could be used of Roman religion, now connotes a kind of total commitment which was not an essential component of Roman religion (though not necessarily lacking in it).

Does this mean that there was no "religion" in Rome, and that historians are distorting reality by talking and writing about "Roman religion"? Should some new word, free of the contaminants of modern concepts, be coined to characterize the veneration of Roman deities and the cult of Cybele? No. There was obviously "religion" in Rome, including Christianity itself—which gave us our sense of "religion." That Romans viewed it somewhat differently does not demonstrate that it was, in fact, a different entity. Moreover, to eschew using "religion" for these reasons would imply something completely false about the present—that all adherents of modern "religions" have a uniform commitment utterly unlike anything in the ancient world. Many modern Catholics (e.g., in Italy) entertain attitudes about the official cult of the state highly comparable to those of their ancient counterparts, even if the meaning of the concept "religion" has changed over the centuries. The historian writing about religion in either the modern or the ancient world should attempt to apprize her readers of the meaning she attaches to the term and the extent to which the phenomena she is actually studying do or do not match the definition. It is also helpful to explain what terms the objects of study would have used themselves for the phenomenon at issue. There is no Latin word for 'family' in the modern English sense, and the apparently related word *familia* designates a somewhat different entity. Historians have not, however, concluded that there were no "families" at Rome, but have concentrated instead on understanding the various consonances and dissonances of the ancient and modern concepts.[13]

---

[13] See, for example, David Herlihy, *Medieval Households* (Cambridge, MA: Harvard University Press, 1985), pp.1-28, and the more careful distinctions of Richard Saller, "*Familia, domus*, and the Roman Conception of the Family," *Phoenix* 38 (1984) 336-53.

Is it revealing that Romans and Greeks had many words for age-related sexual categories and no word to describe persons, regardless of gender, involved in what we call "homosexual activity"? Probably not. The relationship of concrete nouns to abstract concepts is not regular or predictable. For example, there is no abstraction in English for both "aunts" and "uncles" in the way that 'sibling' applies to brothers and sisters. Does that mean that we conceive a greater gender difference between aunts and uncles than between brothers and sisters? It is conceivable, but it seems unlikely when one considers the capricious and independent forms of gender pairing in English. There is, for example, no word to distinguish gender for cousins, although all other relatives are so differentiated— brother/sister, father/mother, daughter/son, aunt/uncle, niece/nephew. Should we infer that English speakers do not distinguish between male and female cousins? Of course not; the necessary and relevant information is simply conveyed otherwise—in a name or phrase. 'My cousin Jane' conveys the same amount of information as 'My sister Jane'; the reasons for the difference are linguistically interesting, but not socially significant. Several hundred miles north of New Haven, my contemporaries can make the distinction by saying 'cousin' or 'cousine': is theirs a fundamentally different attitude to gender? No; and since one can not generalize about North America in 1988, we should pause before making inferences from language about "the ancient world."

There is an enormous vocabulary in all ancient languages referring to aspects of homosexuality, and no reason to suppose that the lack of a perfect match with English in terms of its organization proves a fundamental discontinuity either of experience or conceptualizations. It may reveal no more than a linguistic boundary.

Nor should the prevalence of age-related terminology in such languages, in and of itself, be considered evidence of a wholly different sexual structure. Why are 'boyfriend' and 'girlfriend' common English words, while 'manfriend' and 'womanfriend' are not in the language at all? Because friendship is limited to the young? Or because older people usually have younger "friends"? Or because love makes us feel "young" again? In fact, these terms, like many words in all languages, are only very obliquely related to their obvious meaning, and apply less often to "friendship" than to romantic love. Sexual and romantic terminology tends to be deformed by reticence, decorum and taboo, and must be addressed with enormous caution by scholars.[14] 'Boyfriend' and 'girlfriend' are certainly not indications of a general propensity for older persons to date "boys" or "girls" as those terms are understood in English cultures. They are simply conventions, perfectly unambiguous to native speakers even to degrees of great subtlety: the point of 'boyfriend' is in fact to distinguish the person so designated from a "friend," so the "friend" is wholly misleading, and the term is doubly or trebly removed from reality; by contrast, 'girlfriend' could be used of a "friend" by a female or a romantic interest by a male. Scholars of the future would be completely wrong to infer from these terms a preoccupation with younger sexual partners on the part of most English speakers, or to suspect lesbianism in a case where a teenage girl has a "girlfriend," but would be correct to infer homosexuality if a teenage boy had a "boyfriend." These are, moreover, not odd or little used terms; they are the most basic and familiar words for such relationships in our language.

How will we determine, then, whether premodern sexuality was fundamentally different from our experience? Partly by defining our terms, beginning with "fundamentally different." Being a Catholic in Rome in the fourth century, when choosing to join the minority religion incurred the threat of death, was obviously "fundamentally different" from being a Catholic in the fifteenth century, when failing to observe the official Catholic religion meant death, and from being a Catholic in present-day Italy, where it is an ethnic heritage of little moment to many Italians. Is it wrong or misleading to use 'Catholic' to describe all of these categories? On the

---

[14] *'Baiser"* in French, for example, which a century ago meant 'to kiss,' now means 'to fuck,' and *'embrasser'*, formerly 'to hug,' now means 'to kiss.' Future scholars who accepted these words in their nineteenth-century meanings would completely miss the point of statements made (in conversation, at least) in the second half of the twentieth.

contrary, it is necessary, since they are all fundamentally related as well as fundamentally different. The task of the historian is to convey both aspects to readers.

To apply this to constructionism would require separate and lengthy analysis of the use of each of the possible terms relating to sexual identity, orientation, etc. 'Gay' is probably the most problematic and revealing. If by a 'gay person' one means someone having a specific social identity beyond predominant erotic interest in one's own gender, it will be difficult to apply the term to the past, but no more difficult than it is to apply it to the present outside one or two narrow circles. Leaving aside the problem of "latent" or "closeted" homosexual desires, which might be predominant but unacknowledged or unrecognized, there are still a great many types of conscious "gay identities": single gay men vacationing in Key West or living on Castro Street may have very little in common with a lesbian couple on a farm in New Hampshire, with self-consciously lesbian nuns in Cameroun, with members of a gay fathers group in Des Moines, with a Mexican who prides himself on being "macho" because he takes only the active role and only with younger boys, with the *xanitha* of the Middle East who play only a passive role with older or richer men. Because all these people have erotic interactions primarily with their own gender, which is statistically less frequent in most human cultures, they have something interesting and important in common. It may not be a fundamental basis of identity in all cases (even on Castro Street), but it must play some role, as any noticeable and important divergence from the norm will. On the other hand, there is as much difference in "sexual identity" among them as there is between them and the characters in the Satyricon whose eroticism is focussed on their own gender. One might well argue that other issues are more important for some of these persons in defining their "sexuality" than the sex of their partner—gender roles, monogamy, politics, celibacy, preferred activity—but that does not efface what they have in common; it simply privileges another category for purposes of discussion.[15]

Some constructionists would, in fact, argue that only the first group (unmarried homosexual men or women in a subculture of such persons) meets their definition of 'gay,' and that some other term should be used for other categories of same-sex eroticism. It is obviously legitimate and potentially helpful for some scholars to employ terms like 'homosexual' or 'gay' with definitions different from or more specialized than others, and to criticize writing in which such categories are used imprecisely or inconsistently, although not writings in which they are used differently, as if such terms had a "natural" meaning. Equally obviously, such specialized use of language must be articulated and defended: a universal or self-evident meaning of words cannot be assumed, and if a default meaning of 'gay' can be claimed, it should probably be that of common parlance, where it is juxtaposed by the population at large with 'straight' to refer to (also using common parlance) "sexual preference." ('Homosexuality,' even more simply, has a nearly ubiquitous meaning in English of sexuality between persons of the same gender.) Gay people themselves will often remark of someone that he does not yet "realize" he is gay—a clear indication that the category is not necessarily a self-conscious one in their view. Specialists and scholars, of course, need not be confined to ordinary speech in technical writing, but can hardly afford to ignore it in communicating with the public.

---

[15] This would not be true, of course, if it were a question of constraint rather than interest: prisoners are not "gay" because they have recourse to their own gender for sexual outlets in the absence of any other, nor are young males who engage in sexual relations simply to earn money and not as the result of their own interest or desire. Nor would most English speakers regard a man as "straight" simply because he was married and a father if his sexual interest was directed principally to other men.

Political

This raises the third and most explosive underlying issue of constructionism. The controversy evokes, subtly, a wide range of political and emotional connotations without consciously addressing them. These create an emotional undertone to the arguments, and invest them with a force out of proportion to the ostensible intellectual differences. Although there may be no practicing essentialists, "essentialism" as a mode of thought is associated with generally conservative assumptions about positivist historiography, less than up-to-date views of sexuality, biological determinism, and a general failure to think critically about underlying assumptions. By contrast, constructionism seems a more empowering concept, affirming in some ways the interactive strength and control of the individual, and locating the essence of sexuality in mutable social structures rather than inexorable evolutionary processes. Constructionism also fits well with anthropology and contemporary literary theory and their intellectual forebears, structural linguistics and structuralism, which all emphasize the ultimate relativity and subjectivity of language and observation.

If there are essentialists who say they know that homosexuality and heterosexuality are constants in history, they are certainly proceeding on faith rather than empirical evidence, but the same must be said of constructionists who claim to know the opposite. Since it is perfectly unclear what factors—social, psychological, genetic, etc.—produce varieties of sexual interest, no one can claim to "know" that there were or were not such interests in the past. He could say that he has not or has seen evidence for their existence, but to start from a position of certainty about sexuality in the past is a stance of faith, not really appropriate for historical enquiry. This is different from raising questions about whether there are social "constructions" of sexuality which affect personal identity. Doubtless there are and they do, but the relationship of these to the existence of "gay people" in the past is extremely subtle and has barely been broached to date in the literature on this subject, which tends to imply that a positive answer to the first question necessarily implies a negative to the second.

An additional political fillip is contributed by the claim of some constructionists that essentialists are solipsistically seeking themselves in the past while the constructionists are more open-mindedly looking for differences. This unprovable (and probably fanciful) charge raises an interesting point: since every human being (is the category "human being" a social construct? no doubt) is both like others and different from them, there seems little reason *a priori* to assume that one strategy is better than another, unless there is a political reason to emphasize differences over similarities. A conscientious quest for either one will necessarily disclose the other as well.

There is also a more cogent political dimension to the controversy, ultimately related to the issue of "fundamental difference" addressed above. At one level it is simply a matter of convention to refer to the residents of the Italian peninsula in the fifth century—1400 years before the creation of the modern state of Italy—as "fifth-century Italians." But it could become a highly political issue if, for example, Mussolini wished to argue that something which happened in fifth-century Italy justified an act of aggression in the twentieth-century by the "heirs" or "descendants" of those "Italians." It is polite, in one way, to refer to persons who used to be called "Indians" as "native Americans"; but it is quite silly and inaccurate in another way, since they almost certainly originated on another continent just like the European settlers, and even were there *homines sapientes* indigenous to the continent, the appellation 'American' could only be applied to them after Mercator labelled the Western hemisphere "America" in 1538.[16]

We all use such terms, or do not use them, for political reasons, and if constructionists or essentialists wish to make political arguments for certain ways of conceptualizing or

---

[16] The name '*America*' had been proposed for Brazil by the German geographer Martin Waldenseemüller in 1507; see Jozef Ijsewijn, *Companion to Neo-Latin Studies* (Amsterdam: North Holland Publishing Company, 1977) p. 199.

writing about the mysteries of sexuality they have as much right as anyone else to introduce political considerations into semantic, philosophical, or historical discussions. It is more helpful, obviously, if such issues are carefully and honestly identified as such.

Empirical

In the last analysis the theoretical revisions of constructionism will be of little value if there is no empirical basis for them. Does the historical record in fact suggest that premodern patterns of sexuality were fundamentally different from modern ones? Yes and no. Public discourse about sexuality in ancient and medieval Europe was markedly different from its modern descendants and rarely directed attention to the issues subsumed under or implied by the rubrics 'orientation,' 'preference,' or 'identity.'[17]

For example, in the Mediterranean city-states of the ancient world (ca.400 BC-400 AD) both public and private "norms" for human conduct were largely social and behavioral (as opposed, e.g., to intentional, psychological, or spiritual), and based on codes of public conduct and behavior anyone could follow, regardless of (what modern writers would call) "sexual orientation."[18] Ideals of human action focused on the

---

[17] The terminology of sexual preference, identity and orientation is not uniform, and there are no standard definitions or distinctions to cite. 'Preference' and 'orientation' clearly could mean different things and either could be the basis of an "identity," but all three are often used interchangeably, even in scientific literature. Precise use of such words depends on premises about the will which have yet to be established and agreed upon.

[18] No study of sexuality in the ancient world addresses these issues in this context or can be recommended without reservation. Michel Foucault offered a superficial but challenging overview of Greek and Roman sexual constructs in his *Histoire de la Sexualité*, especially volumes 2: *L'Usage des plaisirs* (Paris: Gallimard, 1984) and 3: *Le Souci de soi* (Paris: Gallimard, 1984). For bibliography of other approaches (to 1979) see Chapters 1 and 3 of *CSTH*. It omitted Paul Veyne's "La
--->

fulfillment of social roles and expectations: being a good citizen by serving in the army or civil service or donating resources or labor to the state, or being a responsible family member by treating one's spouse properly and caring well for children. "Sexual identity" had little to do with any of these— including the roles of spouse and parent, since marriage and parenthood were not thought to depend on erotic attachment.

Opportunities for sexual expression also tended to obviate questions of orientation. Marriage was a duty for all Roman citizens, in the eyes of the family and the state, but was not

---

famille et l'amour sous le Haut-Empire romain," *Annales E.S.C.* 33 (1978), pp. 3-23 and J.P. Sullivan's excellent "Martial's Sexual Attitudes," *Philologus. Zeitschrift für klassische Philologie* 123 (1979), pp. 288-302. F. Buffière *Éros adolescent. La pédérastie dans la Grèce antique* (Paris: Les Belles Lettres, 1980); Jan Bremmer, "An Enigmatic Indo-European Rite: Paederasty," *Arethusa* 13:2, pp. 279-98; and Gerda Kempter, *Ganymed: Studien zur Typologie, Ikonographie und Ikonologie* (Cologne: Bohlau Verlag, 1980) all appeared in 1980; and in the next year, Paul Veyne, "L'Homosexualité à Rome," *L'Histoire* 30 (1981), pp. 76-78 and D.S. Barrett, "The Friendship of Achilles and Patroclus," *Classical Bulletin* 57 (1981), pp. 87-93, which includes a thorough review of the literature on homosexuality in Homer. See also J.N. Adam, *The Latin Sexual Vocabulary* (Baltimore: Johns Hopkins University Press, 1982), and Amy Richlin, *The Garden of Priapus: Sexuality and Aggression in Roman Humor* (New Haven: Yale University Press, 1983). None of these works takes into account the chapter on Roman homosexuality in *CSTH*; for criticism of it see Ramsay MacMullen, "Roman Attitudes to Greek Love," *Historia* 31:4 (1982), pp. 484-502; for general agreement, Saara Lilja, *Homosexuality in Republican and Augustan Rome* (Helsinki: Societas Scientiarum Fennica, 1982). Robin Scroggs, *The New Testament and Homosexuality* (Philadelphia: Fortress Press, 1983), although addressed to religious issues, provides a useful overview of sexual practices in the Mediterranean during the first centuries of the Christian Era. I disagree with some of his conclusions; I also find myself in disagreement with Bernard Sergent, *Homosexuality in Greek Myth*, Arthur Goldhammer, trans. (Boston: Beacon Press, 1986). For a preliminary statement of my own views, see Boswell, "Revolutions, Universals and Sexual Categories," in *Salmagundi* 58-59 (Fall 1982-Winter 1983), pp. 89-113 [hereafter *RUSC*].

generally supposed to fulfill erotic needs.[19] Every male was
expected to marry, as were most females, regardless of
whether conjugal relations afforded an opportunity for erotic
satisfaction or not. In the case of males, extramarital sexuality
was normal and accepted; in the case of married females, it
was not, but for the latter, erotic fulfillment was not a public
issue—fair treatment, affection and respect were the expected
rewards of being a good wife and mother.[20]

Ethical ideals (as opposed to ordinary behavior)[21] were
slightly more complicated, and can be distinguished according
to three general approaches, depending on whether they
emphasized (1) the responsibilities, (2) dangers or (3)
religious significance of human sexuality. (1) The moral
views on human sexuality of the "average Greco-Roman"
were rarely articulated and are difficult to reconstruct with
precision. They seem to have presupposed that sexuality is
good or neutral so long as it is responsible—i.e., does not
interfere with duties to the state or family, and does not
involve the abuse of freeborn children or married women (a

---

[19] This is not to say that there were not persons who insisted that
marriage *should* limit one's erotic focus, but they were manifestly
arguing against a neutral assumption about this on the part of the
general populace.

[20] Sexual fulfillment for women was appropriate only for courtesans,
who could, if they wished, have recourse to either males or females, as
could unmarried men, although there are hints, especially in sensational
contexts, that married women also had recourse to slaves or
masturbation for sexual needs, and there are famous instances of
adultery involving married women. It seems unlikely on the face of it
that male writers' lack of interest in the sexual fulfillment of married
women reflects a corresponding lack of interest on the part of the
women.

[21] I.e., standards proposed as to how people *should* behave, as opposed to
an empirical description of how they did. In some societies—e.g.,
among Orthodox Jews—rules for proper conduct (such as laws of
kashrut) may shape daily life, but among Greeks and Romans the ideals
of patrician philosophers probably had little impact on the lives even of
other members of their own class until Christian emperors began
legislating morality in the fourth century.

reminder that class and citizenship were real for Greco-Romans in a way we can no longer appreciate). This loose code is implicit in much of Greek and Roman literature, art, mythology and law, and it is against it that (2) a second, more ascetic approach began in the centuries before the beginning of the Christian Era to urge that sexuality was an inherently dangerous force and should be avoided as much as possible. Some adherents of this view would call their followers to celibacy, some would limit sexual expression to marriage, others to procreative acts within marriage. Although the latter two prescriptions would apply to homosexual and heterosexual acts differentially (since the former would be categorically precluded, while the latter would only be circumscribed), they were not aimed at homosexuality or predicated on any invidious distinction between homosexual or heterosexual: their objective was primarily to curtail promiscuous or pleasure-centered heterosexual activity. They excluded homosexual acts incidentally or along with activities—such as masturbation—which were not special to any group. (3) A few specific religions attached theological or ceremonial significance to particular aspects of sexuality: traditional Romans idealized the sacrifice of sexual pleasure made by Vestal Virgins, while others embraced mystery cults which incorporated sexual acts in religious observance. Jews had very detailed rules about licit sexuality. Such practices and proscriptions had little impact on popular views: both Jews and Vestal Virgins were considered distinctive precisely because the standards they followed were exceptional. Apart from Judaism, no religion of the ancient world categorically prohibited homosexual relations, although some preached celibacy.[22]

---

[22] It is easy to miss this point in an incident of Apuleius' *Metamorphoses* (8.29) and to project modern constructs onto ancient ones. A group of priests who have sex with a young man are accused of "execrable filthiness" (*execrandas foeditates*), but homosexuality is not at issue. The fact that they are sexually passive is even a minor aspect; the chief ground of criticism is that they have taken a public vow of celibacy (*insuper ridicule sacerdotum purissimam laudantes*

--->

There was thus relatively little reason for Romans to confront or pose questions of sexual orientation. Opportunities for erotic expression were organized around issues of class and age or marital status rather than gender; personal worth was measured in terms of public contributions and family responsibility, neither essentially related to personal erotic interest; private sexual behavior was not an arena of judgement or concern; and even ethical systems did not make the gender of sexual object choice a criterion of moral action.

This does not mean that everyone was at liberty to perform any sort of sexual act with anyone of either gender. Gender, age, class, social standing, and in some cases citizenship set limitations on the range of acceptable forms of sexual expression for each individual. With a few exceptions, the higher one's social status the more restrictions would apply to sexual acts, and the fewer to sexual partners. A wealthy and powerful adult male citizen, for example, at the top of the status hierarchy, could penetrate any other person without loss of social status (although a dispute might arise if the other party were the wife or child of another citizen). "What does it matter," Antony wrote to Augustus, "where or in whom you stick it?"[23] But for the same male to be penetrated—by anyone—would incur disrespect if it were known, and might even subject him to loss of civil privilege. By contrast, although a slave (or even a freedman) would lose no status for being penetrated by someone more powerful,[24] he might

---

castimoniam), which they are hypocritically violating. Lucius himself shrinks from becoming a priest at the end of the novel because he cannot face the requirement of celibacy.

23 "An refert, ubi et in qua arrigas?" Suetonius, *Augustus* 69. '*Qua*' may be feminine because Antony is thinking primarily of females, but it could also refer to parts of the body, male or female. Cf. Martial 11.20.

24 "Sexual service is an offense for the free born, a necessity for the slave, and a duty for the freedman" (*inpudicitiae in ingenuo crimen est, in servo necessitas, in liberto officium*) Seneca, *Controversiae* 4.

suffer greatly (a slave could forfeit his life) if he penetrated a citizen.[25]

The restrictions on the sexual behavior of adult male citizens were not the result of prejudice against homosexuality: the same man could penetrate as many other men as he wished without incurring any stigma. The code of propriety was related to gender—penetration and power were associated with the prerogatives of the ruling male elite; surrendering to penetration was a symbolic abrogation of power and authority—but in a way which posed a polarity of domination-subjection rather than of homosexual-heterosexual.[26] It was generally acceptable for a member of a less powerful group to submit to penetration by a member of a more powerful one: this was not thought to characterize any defect of personality or to indicate any special psychological constitution or status.

The urgent personal question for males in Augustan Rome was not the gender with which one did it but what one did. Martial titillated his audience by speculating on the possibility of "passive"[27] sexual behavior on the part of well-known Roman citizens, and a number of prominent Athenians and Romans were the butt of humor because they had performed

---

[25] Several aspects of this code are evident in the incident adduced by Seneca the Elder in a legal "controversy": a slave is prosecuted for adultery with his mistress, but the wife claims that the husband has so charged him only after she objected to the fact that he wanted the slave in their bed for his own purposes (*Controversiae* 2.1.34-35).

[26] "For a man to be penetrated by a richer and older man is good: for it is customary to receive from such men. To be penetrated by a younger and poorer is bad: for it is the custom to give to such persons. It is also bad if the penetrator is older and poorer. . ." Artemidorus Daldianus [second century, A.D.], *Onirocriticon libri quinque*, Roger Pack, ed. (Leipzig: In aedibus B.G. Teubneri, 1963) 1.78, pp. 88-89.

[27] As is standard usage, I employ 'passive' to mean receptive, orally or anally. I do not mean to imply anything about personality or degree of psychological involvement in the activity. 'Active' is its corollary, and describes only a physical role.

an activity inappropriate to their status;[28] conversely, Juvenal composed a long satire on the several inversions of the prevailing ethic involved in someone of low status (a male prostitute) taking the active role with male citizen clients.[29] The issue in all such cases was behavior, not gender preference: no citizen was ridiculed for having recourse to passive partners of either sex, nor were prostitutes or slaves— male or female—pilloried for receptivity.

Beginning around 400 AD, Christianity began to introduce a new sexual code, focussed on religious concepts of "holiness" and "purity." The origins and sources of its norms—the New Testament, Alexandrian Judaism, popular taboos, neo-Platonic philosophy, Roman legal principles—are imperfectly understood and too complex to penetrate here. For the most part its regulations, like their Greco-Roman predecessors, were conceptually unrelated to sexual "identity" or "orientation." But because Christianity, unlike ancient ethical systems, used obedience to sexual ethics as a primary symbol and test of human conduct, its code was both more detailed and more prominent, and in practice it laid the groundwork for distinctions based on "orientation."

Two general approaches to Christian sexuality can be discerned in the early church, distinct in their relation to "orientation." The earliest, evident in the New Testament, is similar to the "sex is dangerous" approach of pagan ethics: eroticism is a troublesome aspect of a fallen world; Christians should attempt to control it through responsible use. This approach would not, in itself, create distinctions based on gender object choice, because it focuses on the permanence and fidelity of erotic relationships, qualities that could be and were present in both heterosexual and homosexual relationships in the ancient world. Longlasting homosexual unions and even official marriages were known in Greece and Rome, and Christian ceremonies of union for males closely

---

[28] See discussion in Boswell, *CSTH*, pp. 74-76 and Sullivan, "Martial's Sexual Attitudes."

[29] Juvenal, *Satire* 9.

resembling, if not actually constituting, marriage were also common in parts of the Christian world throughout the Early Middle Ages; they invoked well known pairs of saints as models for permanent, erotic same-sex relationships.[30] Even in areas where such relationships were not recognized, there was through the end of the twelfth century a strong tradition in Christian thought which regarded homosexuality and heterosexuality as two sides of the same coin—either could be put to good or bad use, depending on the extent to which it was directed toward godly or ungodly ends. Any faithful and selfless passion subordinated to God's love, in this tradition, might be holy and sanctifying, just as any selfish lust was sinful.[31]

An opposing school of thought held that to be sinless a sexual act must be procreative. Even non-procreative sexual activity between husband and wife was sinful, since procreative purpose was the sole justification for any sexual act. This idea was almost certainly borrowed from strands of late antique pagan ethics, and was at first limited to ascetic Christian writers deeply imbued with Hellenistic philosophy, especially in Alexandria. (Other Christians opposed sexuality *especially* when it was procreative, because birth trapped good souls in evil matter.) But the procreative-purpose stance gradually spread throughout the Christian world and became the favored position of ascetics in the West, since it both limited sexuality to the smallest possible arena and appealed to

---

[30] For the ancient world, see *CSTH*, pp. 20-21, 26-27, 69, 82-84, 123, 225-26. No previous author, to my knowledge, has written about the Christian ceremony of union for males performed in Eastern churches from the fifth into the twentieth century and in the West at least into the sixteenth, when Montaigne mentions it at Rome, *Journal de Voyage en Italie par la Suisse et l'Allemagne en 1580 et 1581*, Charles Dédéyan, ed. (Paris: Société Les Belles lettes, 1946), p. 231. Manuscripts of the ceremony survive in many parts of the Christian world, from the Middle East to France. I am preparing a critical edition and study of the ceremony and its significance.

[31] See, e.g., discussion in *CSTH*, chapters 8 and 9.

an easily articulated and understood principle. Ultimately it became the standard of Catholic orthodoxy.

By the end of the Middle Ages, although in parts of the Catholic world the "separate but equal" tradition survived,[32] the majority of Catholic churchmen and states had accepted the principle of procreative justification, and as a result nonprocreative sexual behavior was considered a serious sin everywhere in Western Europe. Most civil law codes included penalties for "unnatural acts," which were, theologically, the discharge of semen in any non-procreative context: non-procreative heterosexual activity (i.e., oral or anal), masturbation, homosexual acts, bestiality.[33] At least from the time of Augustine influential theologians had argued that non-procreative acts within marriage were even more sinful than those outside, but public legal systems found them difficult to detect and punish, and civil codes and popular attitudes often reduced the distinction to extramarital versus marital sexuality, or heterosexual versus homosexual acts.

This created a kind of dichotomy loosely related to sexual object choice: although many forms of heterosexual activity (even within marriage) and masturbation suffered the same moral sanctions as homosexual acts, only the latter two were *categorically* prohibited, while forms of the first could be

---

[32] Madame, the Princess Palatine and sister-in-law of Louis XIV, for example, records that many of her contemporaries criticized in private the "biblical prejudice" against homosexuality, noting that heterosexuality was necessary in earlier times to populate the planet, but is no longer required, and she adds that it is regarded as a sign of good breeding ("une gentillesse") to observe that since Sodom and Gomorrha the Lord has not punished anyone for such misdeeds (letter of 13 Dec., 1701).

[33] The *locus classicus* for this is Thomas Aquinas, *Summa theologiae* 2a.2ae.154.11-12, but Thomas stands in the middle of a long, relatively consistent tradition. In addition to *CSTH*, pp. 202-4, 323-25, and *passim*, see John Noonan, *Contraception: A History of Its Treatment by the Catholic Theologians and Canonists* (Cambridge: Belknap Press, 1965), and studies of the penitential tradition, e.g., Pierre J. Payer, *Sex and the Penitentials* (Toronto: Toronto University Press, 1984).

entirely moral.[34] It is essential to note, nonetheless, that whereas this late medieval system placed homosexual activity generically in an inferior category, it did not create a concept of sexual dimorphism in which a homosexual "orientation" or erotic preference was stigmatized as characterizing a special category of person. Those who engaged in forbidden sexual activity—homosexual or heterosexual—were sinners, but everyone in Catholic Europe was a sinner. All humans in all times (except Adam and Eve before the fall and the Virgin Mary after) were sinners. The rationale which made homosexual acts morally reprehensible also condemned contraception, masturbation, sexual expression between husband and wife undertaken for reasons of affection or pleasure, divorce, lending at interest, and a host of other common, everyday activities, familiar to (if not practiced by) most Europeans. "Sinner" was a universal, not a special, category, and if the particular vice which placed someone in this category was unusual, the category itself was thoroughly familiar to his neighbors.

Moreover, being "sinful" was a temporary state, no matter how often or for how long one found oneself in it. Anyone could cease being "sinful" at any moment, through repentance and contrition, ideally but not necessarily solemnized in the sacrament of penance. In this regard the public discourse of Catholic Europe regarding sexual ethics was much like the public ethos of ancient city-states, despite the change from secular to religious justification. Both were predicated on norms of external, modifiable behavior, rather than on internal disposition or inclination; and the ethical codes of both either treated homosexuality and heterosexuality as morally indistinguishable or focused on elements of sexual behavior which usually affected all varieties of sexual expression.

The splintering of the Christian tradition during the Reformation rendered it increasingly difficult in Early Modern

---

[34] This fact sometimes justified considering homosexual sodomy as worse than other forms, although this position was not consistent, and was easily conflated with the personal prejudice of heterosexual writers against homosexual acts as revolting.

Europe to sustain public codes of conduct based on a particular set of transcendental values, and religious concepts of holy versus sinful behavior gradually ceased to be the defining terms of public discourse about sexual conduct, even in officially Catholic countries. By the early twentieth century scientific—especially medical—values had replaced the consensus once based on theological principles, and as public attention focused less and less on the salvation of the soul and more and more on the body and its well-being the paramount standard in both public and private codes came to be the norm of health, both physical and psychological. The desirability of persons, actions and things is generally assessed in modern industrial nations against the "norm" of "health": what is physically or mentally "normal" is what would be found in a "healthy" person. That this is tautological is not particularly unusual or striking; what is more interesting is that "normality" and "health" are characteristics rather than modes of behavior, and one generally has less control over them than over actions or conduct. Paradoxically, many individuals in modern liberal states have less control over their status than they would have had in ancient or medieval societies.

The medieval notion of the unholiness of homosexual acts was transformed by this change into the abnormality of the homosexual "condition." The "condition" has been variously conceptualized as a genetic "trait," a psychological "state," an "inclination," or a "preference"; though these terms vary in their implications of permanence and mutability, all suggest an essential, internal characteristic of a person rather than an external, voluntary activity.

The importance of the difference between the modern view and preceding systems of conceptualizing sexuality can scarcely be exaggerated. Contemporary concepts have drastically altered social views of sexual behavior and its significance by focusing on sexual object choice and correlating it with an inherent, defining personal characteristic. The majority supposes itself to have the trait, condition, or preference of heterosexuality, which is "healthy" and "normal," and believes that a minority of persons have the "opposite" trait, condition or preference, which is "unhealthy" and "not normal." The difference is rendered more profound and alienating by the fact that the "normal" or "healthy" state is generally considered, like all forms of sexuality in the past, to be primarily behavioral. Because "heterosexual" is conceived to be the norm, it is unmarked and unnoticed. 'Heterosexual person' is unnecessary: 'person' implies heterosexual without indication to the contrary. And yet the normal person is not "heterosexual" in any defining sense; he engages in heterosexual activity from time to time, but hardly any information about his or her character, behavior, lifestyle or interest is inferable from this fact. "Homosexual," on the other hand, is understood as a primary and permanent category, a constant and defining characteristic which implies a great deal beyond occasional sexual behavior about the person to whom the term is applied. Not only, it is imagined, does his or her sexuality define all other aspects of personality and lifestyle—which are implicitly subordinate to sex in the case of homosexuals but not heterosexuals—but the connotations of the term and its place in the modern construction of sexuality suggest that homosexuals are much more sexual than heterosexuals. The majority chooses sexual "orientation" or object-choice-based-identity as the key polarity in sexual discourse, marks certain people on the basis of this, and then imagines that its categorization corresponds to the actual importance in their lives of the characteristic so marked.

The conceptual distance between "homosexual" and "heterosexual" is vastly greater in modern understandings of sexuality than its nearest correlates in ancient or medieval systems. "Homosexual/heterosexual" is the major dialectical foundation of all modern discourse about sexuality—scientific, social and ethical—and it seems urgent, intuitive and profoundly important to most Americans. This greatly complicates analysis of either the discourse about or the reality of sexuality in premodern Europe, since these primary modern rubrics were of little import or interest to ancient and medieval writers, and the categories the latter employed (e.g., active/passive; sinful/holy) often filter or obscure information necessary to answer questions of interest to modern researchers about sexual "orientation."

While, as the constructionists rightly note, premodern societies did not employ categories fully comparable to the modern "homosexual/heterosexual" dichotomy, this does not demonstrate that the polarity is not *applicable* to those societies as a way of understanding the lives and experiences of their members. A common thread of constructionist argument at the empirical level is that no one in antiquity or the Middle Ages experienced homosexuality (or heterosexuality, in some versions) as an exclusive, permanent or defining mode of sexuality. This argument can be shown to be factually incorrect (or at least a misleading oversimplification) fairly easily once philosophical, semantic and political difficulties have been identified as separate issues. To keep them at some remove, it is most effective to address the question in terms of a self-consciously arbitrary organizational scheme, not claiming to represent or reflect either "natural" or "social" constructs or to make any implicit statements about etiology and identity; it is simply a research tool, designed to facilitate the collating and assessment of information. This is the seven-point scale for describing sexual *behavior* utilized by Alfred Kinsey.

According to Kinsey's scale, a person of exclusively heterosexual experience is denoted by a 0, a person of exclusively homosexual experience by a 6, a person of equal experience of both kinds a 3, and so on.[35] In regard to experience, 'heterosexual' and 'homosexual' have their most obvious meaning: sexual behavior with the opposite gender or one's own, respectively. In addition, Kinsey would apply 'heterosexual' and 'homosexual' as adjectives to persons who occupied the endpoints of the scale (0-1, heterosexual; 5-6 homosexual). For consistency I occasionally follow him in doing so in the discussion that follows, but it is not necessary to accept these terms as significant to appreciate the potential

---

[35] A Kinsey 1 is "predominantly heterosexual, only incidentally homosexual"; a 2, "predominantly heterosexual, more than incidentally homosexual"; 4 and 5 the obverse. Kinsey tried to account for fantasy and desire as well as actual experience, but this was often difficult: for his methods and the scale itself, see Alfred Kinsey, Wardell Pomeroy and Clyde Martin, *Sexual Behavior in the Human Male* (Philadelphia: W. D. Saunders and Company, 1948), pp. 638-641.

value of the scale itself as an approach to (and point of discussion for) the meaning of varieties of sexual experience in different cultures.

Despite differing public constructions of sexuality and preoccupation with other issues, most ancient and medieval writers other than theologians do in fact evince awareness of a basic dimorphism in sexual attraction, and often comment on it explicitly; even theologians do so when writing about something other than theology. In the famous explanation of the etiology of romantic attachment in Plato's *Symposium*, Aristophanes plainly postulates a sexual taxonomy in which all humans are either inherently and permanently homosexual, heterosexual or bisexual. He, indeed, seems to have in mind Kinsey 0s, 3s, and 6s, although the mythic character of his speech may have induced him to use extremes as symbols of a phenomenon he knew to be empirically more fluid and complex.[36] What is clear is that he does not imagine a populace undifferentiated in experience or desire, responding circumstantially to individuals of either gender, but persons with lifelong preferences arising from innate character (or a

---

[36] Among many complex aspects of this speech as an indication of contemporary sexual constructs, two are especially notable. (1) Although it is the sole Attic reference to lesbianism as a concept, male homosexuality is of much greater concern as an erotic disposition in the discussion than either female homosexuality or heterosexuality. (2) It is this, in my view, which accounts for the additional subtlety of age distinctions in male-male relations, suggesting a general pattern of older *erastes* and younger *eromenonos*. Age differential was unquestionably a part of the construct of sexuality among elements of the population in Athens, but it can easily be given more weight than it deserves. "Romantic love" of any sort was thought to be provoked by and directed toward the young, as is clearly demonstrated in Agathon's speech a little further on, where he uses the greater beauty of young males and females interchangeably to prove that Love is a young god. In fact, most Athenian males married women considerably younger than themselves, but since marriage was not imagined to follow upon romantic attachment, this discrepancy does not appear in dialogues on *eros*.

mythic prehistory).[37] Aristotle, too, clearly believed that at least *some* humans were *naturally* inclined to homosexual behavior.[38]

A ninth-century Arabic psychology text explains very concretely that "some are disposed towards women," some towards men, and some toward both.[39] In one of the *Arabian Nights* a woman remarks to a man that she perceives him to be "among those who prefer men to women."[40]

In his twelfth-century discussion of sexuality Alan of Lille says that "of those men who employ the grammar of Venus there are some who embrace the masculine, others who embrace the feminine, and some who embrace both. . . ."[41]

---

[37] David Halperin, "Sex before Sexuality" in *Hidden from History: Reclaiming the Gay and Lesbian Past*, Martin Duberman, Martha Vicinus and George Chauncey, Jr. (New York: New American Library, 1989), pp. 37-53, argues that the speech does not indicate a taxonomy comparable to modern ones, chiefly because of the age differential, although in fact the creatures described by Aristophanes must have been seeking a partner of the same age, since joined at birth, they were coeval; see preceding note for the general significance of age in Athenian sexual relations.

[38] Aristotle, *Nicomachean Ethics* 7.5.3-5.

[39] Qustâ ibn Luqâ, "Li Livre des caractères de Qostâ ibn Loûqâ," Paul Sbath, ed. and trans., *Bulletin de l'Institut d'Egypte* 23 (1940-41), pp. 103-39. Sbath's translation must be used with caution; the Arabic is unambiguous on this point, although Qustâ must circumlocute to express some of the concepts. What I have translated as "inclined towards men" is literally "inclined towards [*yamîlu ilâ*] sexual partners other than women." Bestiality is not mentioned in the treatise, and Arabic has many terms for "boys" as sexual objects, so it seems clear that Qustâ means "males" (i.e., of any age).

[40] *CSTH*, pp. 256-58.

[41] "The Plaint of Nature," Thomas Wright, ed., *The Anglo-Latin Satirical Poets and Epigrammatists* (London: Longman, 1872), 2:463; better edited in N.M. Häring, *Studi medievali*, 3 ser. 19.2 (1978), pp. 797-879. The late antique and medieval debates on the most desirable gender pose interesting problems in this regard, since they sometimes seem to be discussions of which gender one should *choose* to love, and

--->

Arnald of Vernhola, brought before the inquisition in France in the fourteenth century for homosexual acts and invited to repent of them, argued that his "nature" inclined him to sodomy.[42]   Avicenna's canon addresses the problem of "bisexuality" in men, and offers a remedy for this "constitutional problem."[43]   Albertus Magnus considered homosexuality to be a contagious disease especially common among the wealthy, and Thomas Aquinas believed, like Aristotle, that some men were *congenitally* homosexual.[44] Whether they had in mind 6s is not perfectly clear, but it is apparent that they were describing people beyond 3, and that they imagined this was a personal characteristic rather than simply a question of opportunistic behavior.

Kinsey 5s and 6s are common in ancient and medieval literature: "My heart feels no love for women, but burns with an unquenchable flame for males."[45]   An early medieval poem about an exclusively gay male concludes with the complaint that "although you are not a woman, you decline to be a man."[46]   Ganymede is the archetype of a male erotically involved only with another male from Athens through the Renaissance; he is both desired by and desirous of other males, but not females—in contrast to figures like Adonis who might provoke desire in either gender.[47]   The Latin word

---

at other times about whether it is better to be *inclined* to one gender or another. See discussion in *CSTH*, pp. 124-27, 255-65.

[42] His confession is translated in *CSTH*, pp. 401-402; for discussion, see ibid., p. 285 and E. Le Roy Ladurie, *Montaillou, village occitan de 1294 à 1324* (Paris: Gallimard, 1975), pp. 209-215.

[43] *Liber Canonis* (Venice 1507, reprinted Hildesheim, 1964) fol. 358.

[44] *CSTH*, pp. 316-29.

[45] *The Greek Anthology* , W.R. Paton, ed. (Cambridge: Harvard University Press, 1963) 12.17 (my translation).

[46] "Femina cum non sis, vir tamen esse nequis" *Anthologia latina* 1:137-38, #129. An almost exact female correlate is translated in *CSTH*, p.185.

[47] See *CSTH*, chapter 9, "The Triumph of Ganymede" and James Saslow, *Ganymede in the Renaissance. Homosexuality in Art and Society* (New Haven: Yale University Press, 1986). In the poem "Ganymede and

--->

catamitus for an exclusively passive male—necessarily a Kinsey 6[48]— is derived from his name. Although in several medieval poems his interest in men is related to the "sin of sodomy"—which is a behavioral construct—and efforts are made to interest him in women, these are generally futile, and at the outset of the most popular treatment of this subject he announces that he "will never marry" and despises the sexual attractions of females.[49] A thirteenth-century satire of a bishop accuses the prelate not only of interest in males but of having *no desire* for females.[50] Boccaccio describes a man as being "as fond of women as dogs are of beatings; but on the contrary he delighted more than any other miserable man," and tells a story about another man who marries to quell suspicion that he is homosexual; he is unable to satisfy his wife, and ends up having sex with the male lover she takes.[51] "Because I have never liked women or cunts," an eighteenth-century Frenchman asks, "does that mean I should not like passive men? Everyone has his preferences. . . . In nature everyone

---

Helen," discussed in Boswell, *ut supra*, Helen does desire Ganymede, but the narrator suggests that he is *unable* to respond to her. They are in fact married at the end of the poem, but only after the intervention of the gods. It is a kind of metamorphosis story: Ganymede is, explicitly, exclusively homosexual at the outset, but is changed into someone capable at least of marriage at the end.

[48] Because he could only be "passive" with other men. On the other hand, a male with a very low Kinsey rating (e.g., a 1 or 2) might also be exclusively passive in his relations with males. The correlation between preference for a given role and for a particular gender appears not to be predictable or regular.

[49] But in the medieval poem "Ganymede and Helen" he abandons an exclusively homosexual orientation to marry Helen at the behest of the gods; see discussion in *CSTH*, pp. 254-260.

[50] Translated *ibid.*, p. 217.

[51] Boccaccio, *Decameron* 1.1 and 5.10, respectively. If the second story is a reworking of a similar incident in Apuleius *Metamorphoses* 9, as some scholars claim, it is striking that in the earlier incident neither male was portrayed as particularly *given* to homosexual behavior. On the contrary, heterosexual interest is the driving mechanism of the events.

has an orientation."[52]   His contemporary, the Duc de Vendome, was noted among his contemporaries for attraction to men *as opposed to women*:[53] both men seem to have been 5 or 6 on the Kinsey scale.

In a few cases ancient writers depict women who are exclusively attracted to other women, but because the vast majority of premodern writings about sexuality are male compositions addressed to other men and dealing with male erotic interests, lesbianism is very rarely a lively concern.[54] Martial and Lucian describe women who seem to be by choice involved only in sexual activity with other women,[55] and the twelfth-century bishop Etienne de Fougères divides the women of his world into three categories: virtuous, adulterous, and lesbian.[56]

---

[52] "Moi qui n'ai jamais aimé la garce ni le con, faut-il pour cela que je n'aime point les bardaches? Chacun a son appétit. . . . Dans la nature chacun a son inclination." "L'Ombre de Deschauffours," cited in Claude Courouve, *Vocabulaire de l'Homosexualité masculine* (Paris: Payot, 1985), p.64.

[53] "Ce jeune monsieur n'aimait pas les femmes. . .; see "Le goût de Monsieur n'était pas celui des femmes. . . ." Courouve, pp. 47-49 and. Marc Daniel, *Hommes du grand siècle* (Paris: Arcadie, 1957).

[54] It is also significant that women in most societies have had less *choice* about sexuality, rendering discussion of their "preferences" or "interests" difficult or even moot.

[55] Martial (7.67) and Lucian (*Dialogues of the Courtesans*, 5.3); see also *CSTH*, pp. 82-84. Such women are posited in Aristophanes' myth, cited above.

[56] Etienne de Fougères, *Le Livre des manières*, Anthony Lodge, ed. (Geneva: Droz, 1979), especially pp. 97-98. (I am grateful to Jeri Guthrie for bringing this to my attention.) Etienne's contemporary, the "monk of Eynsham" in England, had a vision in which he saw a crowd of women guilty of lesbianism in purgatory, but it is less clear in this case that he conceives of them as a distinct "type"; see "Vision of the Monk of Eynsham," in *Eynsham Cartulary*, H.E. Salter, ed. (Oxford, 1908) pp. 257-371. See also Judith Brown, *Immodest Acts: The Life of a Lesbian Nun in Renaissance Italy* (Oxford: Oxford University Press, 1985).

Ironically, what is now considered the "norm" of human sexuality is the hardest preference to locate in records of the past: heterosexuality has very rarely elicited notice in the Western tradition, either because it is "normal" and "unmarked," as in the modern West, or because, as in the ancient world, orientation itself was generally not addressed. A few classical writers did consider it worthy of mention. Clodius Albinus was noted for his aversion to homosexual activity.[57] Martial warns a friend interested in the wife of another man that if the adultery is discovered the friend need not imagine he could mollify the husband with sexual favors: "Do you trust in your buns? The husband is not interested in fucking males"[58]—an apparent reference to a Kinsey 0, discernible even through the layers of linguistic filter.

By contrast, there are many ostensible Kinsey 3s—so many that some historians have inferred that the whole populace of the ancient world fell into this category, or that "orientation" was a concept irrelevant to antiquity.

> Zeus came as an eagle to god-like Ganymede, as a swan came he
> to the fair-haired mother of Helen.

---

[57] ". . . Aversa Veneris semper ignarus et talium persecutor"; Capitolinus 11.7.

[58] *Epigrams* 2.47: "confidis natibus? non est pedico maritus; quae faciat duo sunt; irrumat aut futuit." 'Irrumo' and 'futuo' are verbs for 'to get a blow job' and 'to fuck a woman.' For 'pedicare' see note 68, below. Apuleius specifically describes a case of a husband taking sexual revenge on his wife's lover (*Metamorphoses*, 9.27-28). It is conceivable that Martial's threat is subtler: he might be warning the potential adulterer that he will have to fellate the husband to placate him rather than rely on his buns, but this seems highly unlikely to me. Penetrating a male anally was (and is) such a common metaphor for dominating or humiliating him that it would be counterintuitive to suggest *irrumo* as a pejorative alternative. When Catullus threatens to humiliate someone sexually he mentions both as equally insulting ("Pedicabo ego vos et irrumabo. . ." 16: this poem is a subtle evocation of prejudices relating to male sexual roles with other males and their social implications).

> So there is no comparison between the two things: one person
> likes one, another likes the other; I like both.[59]

It is easy to miss the fact that the writer is specifically
identifying his bisexual interest as a point of note, and
contrasting it to homosexual or heterosexual preferences, all
clearly viewed as in some sense characteristic of the persons in
question.[60]

Much medieval poetry celebrates or satirizes bisexual
inclinations, and it is a topos of parody that someone spares
neither sex in his lechery. "Men and women please the pope;
boys and girls please the pope; old men and old women please
the pope; shame on him who refuses. . ."[61] Such literary
effusions presumably derive some of their effectiveness from
the fact that ambivalence of this sort is thought noteworthy
rather than typical.

The sister-in-law of Louis XIV describes the sexual
interests of men at the French court in terms almost exactly like
modern sexual taxonomies: some prefer women, some like
both men and women, some prefer men, some prefer children,
and some have little interest in sex at all.[62]

The intermediate ranges around the middle are harder to
quantify, both now and in the records of the past. Ovid says
that homosexual relations appealed to him "less".[63] In the
Ephesiaca, a romantic novel of late antiquity, sexual categories
are not discussed, but play a major role in the action.
Habrocomes is involved throughout only with women, and

---

[59] *The Greek Anthology*, 1.65. Cf. 5.19, which seems to suggest a
change from homosexual to heterosexual orientation.

[60] This is also true of Plutarch's discussion in his "Dialogue on Love"
(*Moralia* 767), discussed in *RUSC*, p. 98.

[61] Hilary the Englishman (first half of the twelfth century), "De papa
scolastico," in *Hilarii versus et ludi*, J.J. Champollion-Figeac, ed.
(Paris, 1838), no.14, pp. 41-42.

[62] Passim in her correspondence, *Briefe 1676-1706* (Stuttgart, 1867),
discussed in Daniel, *passim*, but see especially the letter of Dec. 1705,
cited in Courouve, p. 54.

[63] *Ars amatoria* 2.684: "hoc est quod pueri tangar amore minus."

when, after his long separation from his true love Anthia, she
desires to know if he has been faithful to her, she inquires
only as to whether he has slept with other women, although
she knows that men have been interested in him. Another
character, Hippothoos, had been married to an older woman
and attracted to Anthia, but the two great loves of his life are
males (Hyperanthes and Habrocomes); he left all to follow
each of these, and at the end of the story he erects a statue to
the former and establishes his residence near that of the latter.
No woman plays an important erotic role in his life, and his
marriage was presumably a question of duty, as discussed
above. The author tidies up all the couples at the end by
reuniting Anthia and Habrocomes and introducing a new male
lover (Clisthenes) for Hippothoos. In the twelfth-century
Roman d'Eneas, Aeneas, famous for his erotic relation to
Dido, is said nonetheless to prefer males: "This wretch is of
the sort who have hardly any interest in women. He prefers
the opposite trade: he will not eat hens, but he loves very much
the flesh of a cock. . . He does not know how to play with
women, and would not parley at the wicket-gate; but he loves
very much the breech of a young man."[64]

In addition to comments about preference or orientation,
discussions of particular sexual practices sometimes disclose
evidence relatable to sexual preference. As noted, the issue of
males being penetrated was problematic in some social
contexts, and discussions of men who prefer to be penetrated
provide indirect evidence that their preferred sexual activity
necessarily involved other males. Although slaves and boys
may have accepted rather than sought a passive role, there is
no reason to assume that some of them did not enjoy it,[65] and
adult males who preferred to be penetrated were common
enough not only to have special names (not derogatory for

---

[64] *Eneas: A Twelfth-Century French Romance*, John Yunck, trans. (New
York: Columbia University Press, 1974), p. 226.

[65] Petronius makes a great joke out of a man's wooing a boy with gifts
to persuade him to allow this favor, which the boy then enjoys so
much that he keeps the man awake all night asking for more: *Satyricon*
85-87.

anyone other than an adult male citizen), but also to provoke scientific speculation on the origin of their unusual "orientation."[66] Satirists depict passive adult citizens as hiring bisexual males to satisfy their needs and impregnate their wives.[67]

Both Greek and Latin, moreover, use verbs which primarily or exclusively denote a male's penetrating another male, as opposed to a female, suggesting that in addition to the most prominent distinctions between active and passive there were common and familiar distinctions about preferred object choice.[68]

Suppose, for the sake of discussion, that the rough proportions of Kinsey 0s, 1s, 5s, 6s, etc. were the same in most populations. How would one then explain the casual ubiquity of homosexual activity at Athens or Rome? Do the data from these cultures in and of themselves suggest a sexual topography profoundly different from that of twentieth-century democracies?[69] Actually, no. Kinsey and other researchers

---

[66] E.g., in the *Problems* attributed to Aristotle, 4.26 (880A). See *Nicomachean Ethics* 7.5.3ss, quoted by Aquinas in *Summa theologiae* 1a.2ae.31.7.

[67] E.g., Juvenal, *Satire* 9; Martial, *Epigrams* 12.91. On loss of civil privileges, Paulus, *Sententiae* 2.27.12; *Digest* 3.1.1.6—both discussed in *CSTH*, p.122.

[68] In Greek *'pugizein'* means 'fuck a male' and *'binein'* 'fuck a female'; in Latin the same distinction is reflected in *'pedico/futuo'*. Although *'pugizein'* could refer to anal intercourse with a female, this usage is extremely rare, and *'pedico'* is never used for females. A graffito such as 'volo piidicarii,' therefore (from Pompeii: *CSTH*, p. 57), although properly translated as 'I want to fuck someone,' is clear evidence of preference for male sexual partners. Arabic also has a verb (*lâta*) which usually refers to a male's penetrating another male.

[69] One advantage of employing the Kinsey scale in assessing the varieties of sexual behavior of other cultures is that it brings into relief elements of the sexual landscape that make it easier to compare different times and places, offsetting to some extent the disorientation occasioned by focusing attention solely on unique aspects of a given society (e.g., the importance of age or social class). Although the latter may be just as important, they do not necessarily preclude choices based on gender; but

--->

have found an incidence of homosexual behavior among males
even in the most highly repressive societies which shocked
and outraged contemporaries who had never suspected such a
thing was possible.[70] If 30%-50% of American males, in the
face of overwhelming social condemnation, have homosexual
experiences, it is hardly surprising that a large percentage of
males should do so in cultures where it is a morally neutral
activity, or that this should then cause the muniments of that
civilization to appear rather different from the records available
in highly repressive societies. If all of the American males
who indulged in homosexual behavior felt free to acknowledge
it, American erotic literature might well resemble that of
Athens or Rome. This same percentage of men might not,
however, consider themselves predominantly interested in
their own gender, any more than the majority of Athenians or
Romans did.

Cognizance of the social significance of sexual behavior in
given times and places is fundamental to understanding both
the reality and the perception of sexuality. These have varied
so widely in the Western tradition that the most basic
taxonomic distinctions of one age may seem almost entirely
irrelevant to those of another. Primary ancient and medieval
sexual constructs were unrelated to the modern differentiation
between homosexual and heterosexual "orientation,"
"identity," or "preference." This does not mean that there was
no awareness of specifically homosexual or heterosexual
"orientation" in earlier societies. Much evidence indicates that
these were common and familiar concepts, which received
little attention in the records of these cultures not because few
people recognized them, but because they had little social or
ethical impact.[71]

---

because they are alien to us, they attract our attention
disproportionately.

[70] See, e.g., C.A. Tripp, *The Homosexual Matrix* (New York: McGraw-
Hill, 1975), pp. 232-40.

[71] St Thomas Aquinas, for example, cautioned against eliminating
prostitution on the grounds that if it were suppressed the world would
be filled with "sodomy" ("Tolle meretrices de mundo et replebis ipsum
--->

Challenges to the received wisdom are a major fuel for the advance of scholarship, and all scholars on any side of a controversy benefit from the energy it generates. Just as revolutionary ideals, however, once in power, often shift from being an innovative solution to being part of the problem, radical critiques of established positions rapidly become established themselves, and then require the same sort of critical scrutiny they once offered to older approaches. Constructionism may have much to offer the history and analysis of human sexuality, but it will be more effective if it diverts some of the critical energy presently aimed at the scarce "essentialists" to refining and questioning more of its own assumptions and conclusions.

---

sodomia" *De regimine principum* 4.14; perhaps inspired by Augustine's warning, "Aufer meretrices, turbaveris omnia libidinibus"). A constructionist could infer from this either that St. Thomas had no concept of sexual orientation at all or that he believed all those who frequented prostitutes to be Kinsey 3s: denied access to the latter, they will naturally satisfy themselves with homosexual intercourse. But in fact it can be shown that Aquinas did not believe this, since elsewhere he discusses homosexuality as innate and predicates his analysis on Kinsey 6s. His point about prostitutes is actually a moral one, derived from the prevailing ethical construct of sexuality in his day: the broadest and most urgent dichotomy among sexual acts was the division between "moral" and "immoral," which depended on whether they were undertaken to produce legitimate offspring or not. Since both prostitution and homosexual acts fall in the "immoral" category, it is logical to suppose that if one is removed the other will take its place. Constructions and context shape the articulation of sexuality, but do not efface recognition of erotic preference as a potential category. Indeed, one reason Aquinas would posit *sodomia* as a greater evil than prostitution is that popular prejudice against homosexuality, on the rise in the thirteenth century, often made it seem worse than the theological case against it could justify.

CHAPTER 8:
Reality or Social Construction?
James Weinrich

Playboy: So a homosexual is not a homosexual until he commits a physical homosexual act?
Anita Bryant: That's what I consider a homosexual to be.[1]

Like berdaches, "drag queens" are known to dress like women, or with a mixture of male and female clothing, but they are still queens even if they dress like men.[2]

Both realists and nominalists must lower their voices. Reconstructing the monuments of the past from the rubble of the present requires quiet concentration.[3]

Are things like "homosexuality" and "transvestism" real entities that exist out there somewhere rather than just in the mind? Or are they made-up concepts that only have meaning within the boundaries of a society? Just what *is* a drag queen? Why do we make all these distinctions, anyway?

This chapter is about the hottest philosophical controversy to hit psychology in years: the social-constructionist/realist debate. Since 'the social-constructionist/realist debate' is a

---

[1] Ken Kelley, "Playboy Interview: Anita Bryant," *Playboy* 25:5 (May 1978), pp. 85.

[2] Walter Williams, *The Spirit and the Flesh: Sexual Diversity in American Indian Culture* (Boston: Beacon Press, 1986), p. 125

[3] John Boswell, "Revolutions, Universals and Sexual Categories," *Salmagundi* 58-59 (1982-83), p. 113.

Reprinted from James Weinrich, *Sexual Landscapes: Why We Are What We Are, Why We Love Who We Love* (New York: Charles Scribner's Sons, 1987), chapter 5, by permission of the author.

mouthful, for the rest of this chapter I'll just call it 'the Debate.'

The Debate is so important that I have included both sides of it, implicitly, in the subtitle of this book. "Why we are what we are" implies that an *identity* or an *essence* is important in the ups and downs, the ins and outs, that form the human sexual landscape. "Why we love whom we love" implies that it is the *people* we love and the *meanings* we assign to the *acts* we perform with them that are the important things to study. Social constructionists tend to argue that all that objectively exists are sexual acts and that identities are constructed by societies out of those acts. They argue, geographically speaking, that "Nevada" is a social construction; it exists only because our culture says it exists. Their opponents argue that sexual identities are not arbitrarily constructed out of sexual acts but are to some extent "really there" in the structure of the acts of the relationships themselves. They argue, geographically speaking, that "Mount Baldy" has a reality that transcends the name a society gives to it.

The Debate is important for several reasons. First, it's socially important. If gender transpositions aren't real entities, then laws dealing with them don't make sense. For example, "silliness" and "ghosts" are pure social constructions (or pure nonsense)—so laws against just acting silly or laws protecting the rights of ghosts are absurd. Likewise, if homosexuality is purely a social construction, then laws against it or laws protecting the rights of homosexuals might be absurd.

Second, the Debate is important to gender transposees themselves. Some gay people, for example, like the idea that homosexuality is "real" because it contributes to their feeling that their struggle to achieve a gay identity is necessary and productive. Other gay people like the idea that homosexuality is a social construction, because it suggests that people can change the boundaries of the construction and thereby change—or escape entirely—the social consequences of what it means to be gay. After all, "define and conquer" is a strategy used at least since the time of Adam; by taking for granted the existence of categories like "homosexual" and "heterosexual," people give power to those who made the definitions in the first place.

And third, the Debate is scientifically important, because some of the theories depend on particular answers to it. In biology, for example, if the Debaters conclude that homosexuality isn't a real entity, then it's hard to justify genetic theories about its origin, since genetic theories have to model objectively "real" traits, not ones like "silliness" or "Nevadaness."

The Debate has been hottest when applied to homosexuality, so that's the gender transposition I'll talk about in this chapter. But the Debate concerns all the gender transpositions. Indeed, it questions the whole idea of gender transpositions in the first place.

The Debate asks the following question: is each gender transposition an essential (or real) trait, or is each a social construction? Let me illustrate the question with one of my pet examples: cat-lovers and dog-lovers.

Cat-lovers and Dog-Lovers

The realist: Frankly, there are only two kinds of people in this world: cat-lovers and dog-lovers. Cat-lovers (the scientific term for them is *feliphiles*[4]) are, as we all know, an oppressed class. Since most people are dog-lovers (*caniphiles*), cat-hating (*feliphobia*) has become part of our culture. It's even part of our language: 'catty,' for example, not to mention 'filibuster' and 'philippic.' Some countries even have laws that make feliphiles felons!

Much as caniphiles would deny it, the only real difference between caniphiles and feliphiles is their *petual orientation*. Petual orientation is the preference, ownership and/or desire, for a particular kind of pet in one's petual relationships. No one knows what causes people to have particular petual

---

[4] Those of you up to date on your Latin and Greek will note that, like some other terms used in this book [*Sexual Landscapes*], 'feliphile' has a hybrid etymology. The *feli* part comes from the Latin for "cat," the *phile* part from the Greek for "love." This may rub you the wrong way—*feliphile* could be confused with *philiphile* or "lover of love"—but so be it. I find the term more felicitous.

orientations, although most specialists believe that it usually begins in childhood.[5] It is *not* a choice, and it is very difficult to change one's petual orientation. Although there are instances in which a feliphile has gone out and bought a dog, either the relationship doesn't last, or the person wasn't really a feliphile in the first place. In short, petual orientation reflects an underlying reality; a feliphile who owns a dog is still a feliphile, and a caniphile who owns a cat is just slumming.

The taboo surrounding petual orientation is so severe, incidentally, that many careers have been seriously hurt when people showed too much interest in human petuality. The usual reaction is to ignore it; failing that, to trivialize it. And it used to be much worse; some people interested in petual orientation have been hounded until they resign in disgrace.

The social constructionist: I agree that feliphiles are an oppressed class in our modern society, but they are not an objectively "real" category. Rather, the category is a social construction. All that exists objectively is pet ownership; what it means to a particular pet is socially constructed. There is lots of evidence from other cultures that proves this is so.

For example, there once was a society in which petual preference was no big deal. In the United States, back in the twentieth century, society was so accepting of human petual diversity that *they didn't even have words for petual orientation*. Words like 'feliphobia,' 'caniphilia,' and even 'fidophobia' were not listed in their dictionaries. Laws regulating pet ownership were few. Although there were rules (seldom enforced) about which kinds of pets could be kept in particular apartments and laws about registering and caring for pets, that was all. Most importantly, there were no words that specifically meant anything like what we now mean when we say 'feliphilia' or 'petual preference.'

I say 'petual preference' rather than 'petual orientation' because 'orientation' is too essentialistic. It implies that what one likes petually is an eternal—a given—and will never

---

[5] The theory that one becomes a feliphile by having overtly *sexual* relations with a cat, while perhaps true in certain tragic clinical cases, is no longer considered applicable to the vast majority of feliphiles.

change. But society makes a choice to participate in particular antifeliphilic actions. Likewise, even if it's true that some people have an unchangingly felic preference, that doesn't mean that others don't change. As I said, the only concrete, observable variable is pet ownership; everything else is an epiphenomenon of cultural interpretation.

For example, what about bipetuals—people who have both feliphilic and caniphilic feelings? It's true that some people who call themselves bipetual later come out openly as feliphiles, but everyone is at least a little bit bipetual. Think back to your childhood; can't you remember times when you played innocently both with cats *and* with dogs? It was just social conditioning that got you thinking that you had to choose between the two. The only reason you feliphiles are so insistent about this "petual orientation" stuff is that you think your profelic feelings mean you don't have any caniphilic ones!

The realist replies: Well, it's true that the twentieth century was the golden age for freedom of petual orientation and that cultures nowadays differ in the way they think about petual orientation. But that doesn't mean that petual orientation is just a figment of the imagination. If you look carefully enough, even people living in the golden age recognized the distinction.

I know it's hard to believe, but back in 1985 there was a book published entitled *Dogs Are Better than Cats*.[6] It's important to note that this was no scholarly tome; it was a popular book, illustrated with scurrilous cartoons and loaded with typically prejudiced comments like this:

> DOGS know that life is . . . Ruff, ruff!
> CATS don't think of life, only of themselves. That's why they say. . . ME-ow.

These lines have, of course, the familiar ring of feliphobia. But if I hadn't already told you where they came from, would

---

[6] Missy Dizick and Mary Bly, *Dogs Are Better than Cats* (New York: Dolphin/Doubleday, 1985).

you have guessed that they were written in an era that had no word for feliphobia? Of course not! Moreover, what about the possibility that Americans back then really did have such a term but that petual orientation was such a sensitive topic that it was discreetly edited out of the reference works of the time? Scholars have dug up the terms 'cat-lover' and 'cat fancier,' but there is no evidence that these terms meant anything like what we now mean by the term feliphilia. In fact, these phrases probably had an explicitly erotic orientation—referring to people who had sexual relations with their cats. Many people in the twentieth century did have strong aversions to sexual matters and coined all manner of terms to refer to their sexuality, but only indirectly, so it is not surprising that they would have refrained from defining these sexually embarrassing terms in their dictionaries. Sexual matters, believe it or not, were just about as taboo back then as petual matters are today.

The social constructionist replies: But that's exactly the point! Back then, they had 'homosexuals,' 'heterosexuals,' 'dog-lovers,' 'cat fanciers'—all those sexually loaded terms! They made a big deal about that sort of thing, and they had a separate word for every kind of socially deviant act. We don't. It's all a social construction. If there really was anyone back then who could be called a feliphile, it must have had entirely different consequences for the person in question. Back then, being a feliphile was perfectly okay. Nowadays it can land you in jail. Back then, catnip was openly for sale in local "pet shops"; now mere possession of catnip can get you twenty years. No, to talk of "feliphilia" in a culture like that is to talk of the ridiculous.

The realist, again: No, *this* is the point! Back then they didn't have words for petual orientation. True enough. But that doesn't mean they didn't know about it; it just means they didn't make a big deal about it. If they didn't know about it, they couldn't have written books like *Dogs Are Better than Cats*, right? Maybe they thought of the book as a joke, but joking about something means you know it's there to be joked about. Think of it this way. . . .

And here, dear reader, we will leave our two doggedly caterwauling debaters—because I expect by now that you've gotten the point.

Interactionism

The point is that both social constructionism and realism are correct in very important ways. It's not that something "in between" the two is correct; it's that both are true simultaneously. Moreover, they interact in a way that is fascinating and that deserves a name of its own: interactionism (see figure 1).

This might seem obvious, but to some of the Debators it's not. Another thing that's not obvious is that the Debate is *not* a replay of the infamous nature-nurture debate. Although social constructionists sometimes are more comfortable with nurture and realists with nature, this is a different debate. Social constructionists are not just people with a good point; they are *right*: the social construction of homosexuality in different societies adds a captivating and vital dimension that is more than just "part of the answer." Likewise, realists are not just people interested in reducing homosexuality to some essential oversimplification; they are *right*: the similarities linking homosexual behavior around the world and over time are as interesting as the differences are.

When it comes to the pure theories—pure social constructionism and pure realism—there are strong and weak forms. The *strong* forms say that a particular theory is the *only* one that's important; all the others can be safely be ignored. The *weak* forms say the particular theory is just *one of several* theories that are important. Obviously, only one strong form at a time can be true; they are mutually incompatible. But the weak forms are not. As I just suggested, I think that weak forms of both the social-constructionist and realist theories are correct.

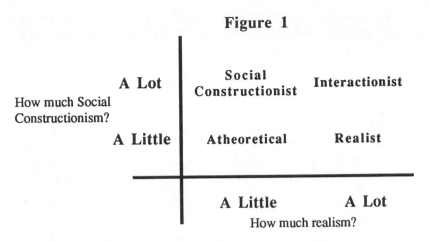

Figure 1

But interactionism goes further. Interactionism says not only that both factors are important but also that the two factors interact in a way that is more than the sum of their parts. Interactionism says that in order to understand the effect of one factor, you need to know how the other factor is operating and you need to know that in detail.

Here's a simple example of interaction. Your genes affect your skin color. Also, being in the sun affects your skin color—a statement that happens to be true no matter what your race and genetic background. *How much* effect being in the sun has on your skin color depends on your genes; *that's* the interaction. Some people are too dark skinned to tan very much. Some light-skinned people burn rather than tan. And some people tan deeply and quickly. So in order to predict a person's final skin color, you need to know (1) their genetic makeup, (2) their environment, *and* (3) how the two interact.

In theory, someone could even have genes that make their skin *lighter* after exposure to the sun. After all, sunlight bleaches out lots of pigments used in printing and painting, so why not skin pigments? In such a hypothetical person, you'd need to be especially careful to focus on the interaction rather than just the sum of independent factors.

So let's pretend for a moment that we don't know the importance of interaction in sexual orientation and look at the argument for each side.

Why "Homosexuality" Is a Social Construction

There is a lot of evidence suggesting that homosexuality is a social construction. The most important piece is that the pattern of homosexuality differs a lot from culture to culture; in particular, that "the same" acts are construed entirely differently in different cultures. Let me give you examples of three patterns, approximately as they were set out by anthropologist Gilbert Herdt.[7]

Age-Biased Homosexuality

One of the commonest forms homosexuality takes in other societies is the age-biased form, such as in ancient Greece.[8] In this pattern, sexual relationships conventionally or ideally take place between two partners rather different in age, experience, or power. Often, this is as true of heterosexual relationships as it is of homosexual ones. Different terms— usually translated as *lover* and *beloved*—are used to describe the two people participating in the partnership, and different things are expected of the two according to which role they are playing. In ancient Greece, for example, the lover was expected to be erotically aroused or obsessed by the beloved, to give him[9] gifts, to educate him (explicitly or by example),

---

[7] Herdt set out these three patterns in a speech given at the Kinsey Institute at Indiana University in 1986.

[8] Classical scholars know that the term 'ancient Greece' covers a staggering variety of cultural patterns, not all of them approving of this form of homosexuality. See for example, the discussion in John Boswell, *Christianity, Social Tolerance and Homosexuality* (Chicago: University of Chicago Press, 1980) and Kenneth Dover, *Greek Homosexuality* (Cambridge: Harvard University Press, 1975). So my discussions of ancient Greece in this book should be taken only to apply to particular Greek city-states (especially Athens) at particular times in their histories.

[9] As is common in classical sources, males are far more often described than females especially in detail. I will therefore use the male terms in

--->

and to be persistent (but not too pushy) when the beloved was reticent.   The beloved was expected to respond to the attentions paid to him by the lover, but not necessarily in kind—at least, not in public.

This pattern seems strange by modern standards in several respects.   For example, if you were someone's beloved in ancient Greece, you could be someone else's lover at the same time.   Parents would be concerned about the status of their son's lover and of the propriety of the relationship—not about whether their sons should be taking lovers in the first place—and they assumed as a matter of course that the lovers would be male.   Sometimes there were specific rules about what kinds of gifts a lover should give to his beloved as tokens of having reached particular stages in their relationship.   Rooster or hares, for example, show up often on Greek vase paintings as courtship gifts from lovers to beloveds.   There were also, at times, ceremonies of commitment that were at least as meaningful as heterosexual ones and that were described using the same terms used for heterosexual marriage.

Homosexuality in ancient Greece was so well integrated into the social structure that it is impossible to understand the culture without learning about homosexuality in detail.   It is true that there were no words for the generic 'homosexual' and 'heterosexual' as we now use them, but the Greeks had an extensive erotic vocabulary.   There *were* words for several specific sexual acts that would clearly be called "homosexual" in today's terms and for particular kinds of people who nowadays would be considered particular kinds of homosexual.[10]

---

this discussion, since it is not clear whether women's homosexual relationships were or mirror images of the men's or if they were quite different. That they existed is clear from Sappho's poetry, of course.

[10] Some of these facts are not well known because the more obviously homosexual passages in the classics were mistranslated or left untranslated in the English versions available to those who do not read Greek. Sensibilities were so tender on this topic just a few decades ago that the Loeb Classics edition—with the original language on the left-hand pages and the English translation on the right rendered "the good

--->

Many Greek vases show quite explicit sexual interactions—or earlier stages of courtship between older and younger males at various ages. These vases are some of the most valuable bits of information we have about Greek culture and are displayed in many museums around the world (although some of the more prudish museums don't display the obviously sexual ones or turn an offending scene against the wall, especially if another picture on the vase is more discreet by modern standards). Photographs of these scenes are now available in several books.[11]

In sum, Greek culture socially constructed homosexuality in a way totally different from the way ours does. They took it in stride, they put it on their artwork, and their literature is permeated with its influences. For people raised in modern Western culture, it is so hard to deal with these facts that they have been denied rather than understood.[12] After all, understanding them would be a bit like trying to make sense of Alice's Wonderland.

Inversion Homosexuality

A second common pattern for homosexuality is the *inversion* pattern, in which at least one of the participants in homosexual activity has officially taken up the role of the opposite sex. Or so it seems to the eyes of Western observers; as we'll see, their real status was far more complicated. According to a recent book by University of Southern California anthropologist Walter Williams, who has probably done more fieldwork with living berdaches (defined below)

---

stuff" not into English but into Latin. Good stuff in the Latin originals was left untranslated or translated into Italian.

[11] For example, *Greek Homosexuality* and John Boardman, *Athenian Black Figure Vases* (New York: Oxford University Press, 1974) and *Athenian Red Figure Vases: The Archaic Period* (New York: Oxford University Press, 1975) .

[12] The final chapter in *Greek Homosexuality* is an evenhanded discussion of why so many modern scholars have had trouble dealing with these issues.

than any other anthropologist, many tribes regarded these people differently.[13]

> How many genders are there? To a modern Anglo-American, nothing might seem more definite than the answer that there are two: men and women. But not all societies around the world agree. . . . The commonly accepted notion of "the opposite sex," based on anatomy, is itself an artifact of our society's rigid sex roles.

The name anthropologists use for members of this third sex is *berdache*. What particular roles berdaches play depend upon the roles their society allows them to play.

Among men in American Indian and Eskimo tribes, for example, berdaches often are (or were) *shamans*—healers or medicine men—who acquired their magic powers while dressing as women.[14]   One of the best-investigated cases occurred among the Chukchee Eskimo in Siberia.[15]   Among

---

[13] *The Spirit and the Flesh*, p. 1.   Williams and I have independently reached many similar conclusions about the berdache.   His book appeared just as the final versions of this chapter were being prepared.   I am delighted to report that he has documented, in far better detail than I could possibly have done alone, most of the major points I make here.

[14] Cases of females taking the role of males were known but are very little described, so I will again use male pronouns in my account.   The most comprehensive recent account of the male berdache in modern Indian tribes is the book by Williams [*The Spirit and the Flesh*], who reserves the term for genetic males only, using *amazons* for women taking up men's roles.   A detailed (but psychoanalytic) description of both female-to-male and male-to-female individuals is provided by George Devereux, "Institutionalized Homosexuality of the Mohave Indians," *Human Biology* 9 (1937), pp. 498-527, reprinted in *The Problem of Homosexuality in Modern Society*, M. Hendrik, ed. (New York: Dutton, 1963), pp. 183-226.

[15] The best account is by Waldemar Bogoras, "The Chukchee," *Memoirs of the American Museum of Natural History* 11 (1904), pp. 448-457; I have summarized the pattern in much less detail in my Ph.D. thesis, James Weinrich, "Human Reproductive Strategy" (doctoral dissertation, Harvard University, 1976), *Dissertation Abstracts International* 37:5339-B (1976), University Microfilms no. 77-8348.   Note that

--->

the Chukchee, there were three kinds of shaman, differing according to the strength of their powers, for which men were required to wear some sort of female clothing. The least powerful shamans wore women's clothes only every now and then—at the commands of the spirits or perhaps when they became ill. (Supposedly, this was to confuse an evil spirit and get it to think it was living in the wrong kind of body.) More powerful shamans dressed as women for longer stretches of time—days or weeks, perhaps. There are hints that these shamans did so sometimes after losing a spouse or after encountering some other difficulty. And the most powerful shamans were completely sexually transformed: they wore women's clothes all the time, did women's work, and married men. Usually these people became shamans after they had a vision telling them to do so; the vision came to them during a *vision quest*, which was a period of time spent away from the tribe, fasting, and usually in a state that Western psychologists would call sensory deprivation.[16]

Among American Indians, Williams noted that "shamans are not necessarily berdaches, but because of their spiritual connection, berdaches in many cultures are often considered to be powerful shamans."[17] Parents typically wanted to know which choice sons would make so that they could raise them appropriately. In some tribes, parents figured this out by putting the son through a specific test: they would put symbols

---

anthropologists consider Siberian cultures to be different from American ones in many important respects. However, humans first came to the Americas by way of a land bridge (now flooded by the Bering Strait), expanding first into North America and then into South America. So it should not be surprising that there would be similarities among the cultures of both Americas and Siberia.

[16] I once had the impression that a vision quest involved a physical journey, with the person involved in the quest traveling through the forests away from the tribe. *The Spirit and the Flesh* describes his own vision quest among the Lakota, and the journey is mental, not geographic although the spot where it takes place is away from the settlement.

[17] *The Spirit and the Flesh* , p. 35.

of masculinity and femininity (women's weaving versus a bow and arrow, say) outside a tent while the boy was sleeping inside, then set the tent on fire. The boy, awakening in terror, would flee. On his way out, supposedly he would grab one article or the other—thus symbolizing a masculine or feminine choice.[18]

The status of berdaches varied from tribe to tribe, but many tribes gave them a place of honor and power. In some tribes, only the most intelligent and promising men found themselves encouraged to take the berdache's path. In other tribes, there are hints that people with particular problems were more likely to pursue the role. Conversations with berdaches surviving today suggest that these men had sexual relations with many of the men in the tribe—perhaps while on hunting or war expeditions, perhaps when other taboos prevented the men from having sexual relations with their wives, or perhaps just when the two men felt like it. Often the nonberdache men were (and still are) quite open in their sexual approaches toward—indeed, competition for—the berdaches.[19] Again, these facts are disorienting to Western observers.

Perhaps the most important aspect of berdachism was its spiritual side, similar in a way to the decision to join a religious order today. It was the gods that told you to take up the role, the spirits who told you to cross-dress. The spiritual aspects are so important, in fact, that Williams covers them first in his book about the berdache. On the other hand, although it was the spirits who commanded you to transform yourself, it was you who took the time to seek their advice, and it was you who actually walked over, picked up the clothing, and put it on. Accordingly, both choices made by your society and choices made by you were important in the role.

---

[18] A version recounted by *The Spirit and the Flesh*, p. 24, among the Yuman placed the symbols inside an enclosure, made of brush, constructed especially for the test. Nor was the boy asleep.

[19] *The Spirit and the Flesh* is especially detailed on these points.

Role-Playing Homosexuality

A third pattern of homosexuality in other cultures is a variation on the inversion pattern: no one officially takes up the role of the other sex, but in any particular interaction one person takes a "receptive" role and the other an "active" role ("insertee" and "insertor," respectively, when penetration is involved). But neither participant pretends to be a member of the other sex.

This is the pattern[20] that exists in modern urban Mexico, according to the detailed descriptions by University of California anthropologist Joseph Carrier.[21] The insertor role is perceived as more masculine and hence more valued, so most Mexican homosexual men present themselves in this role. However, many of these men change their preferred role over time, or at least add aspects of the other role to their repertoire.

> A significant aspect of the behavior of those who change, however, is that they usually do not play both sex roles with the same partner. They *rank* prospective partners as to whether they are more masculine or more effeminate than themselves. If thought more masculine, the prospective partner is generally rated active sexually; if more effeminate, passive sexually.[22]

This flexibility to the contrary notwithstanding, the cultural insistence that one or the other role be presented and played is very strong in Mexico. For example, travel features directed at American gay men (who, as explained in chapter 2 [of *Sexual Landscapes*] often "play" both "roles" with the same person)

---

[20] Again, among men, because Carrier happened to study only men.

[21] See, for example, Joseph Carrier, "Participants in Urban Mexican Male Homosexual Encounters," *Archives of Sexual Behavior* 1 (1971), pp. 279-291 and "Cultural Factors Affecting Urban Mexican Male Homosexual Behavior," *Archives of Sexual Behavior* 5 (1976), pp. 103-124.

[22] "Cultural Factors Affecting Urban Mexican Male Homosexual Behavior," pp. 120-121.

warn them that in Mexico (and several other countries) Americans are valued by native homosexuals because the Americans are willing to play the insertee role more often than the native homosexuals are. The message is: as a guest, be accommodating—but remember, you'll probably be asked to accommodate the same way each time. Americans may find that the acts they perform at home seem to have an eerily unreal interpretation abroad.

Conclusion

This last example of culture clash makes the social-constructionist point very well. What homosexuality "is" in a given culture is crucially dependent on the way that culture constructs its categories of sexual acts. To the typical Mexican homosexual described by Carrier, an American willing to be inserted into has declared himself to "be" the insertee and to play a particular role, but the American may think nothing of the sort. In fact, gay Americans feel, when they look into "gay life" in other countries, that people that seem familiar act strangely. Presumably, foreign gays visiting the United States feel the same way. Seen in this light, definitions of 'homosexuality' like the one I presented in chapter 2 [of *Sexual Landscapes*] seem culturally shortsighted.

Likewise, my very ability to refer to "the other sex" throughout this book presumes that there is only one other sex to refer to in any given context. If there is a third or a fourth sex, then I really ought to revise my definitions in chapter 2 [of *Sexual Landscapes*] to reflect this point of view. Examples like these are what Mary McIntosh, a British sociologist who was the first proponent of the social-constructionist viewpoint in sexual-preference matters, had in mind when she wrote:

> The current conceptualization of homosexuality as a medical condition is a false one, resulting from ethnocentric bias. Homosexuality should be seen rather as a social role.[23]

---

[23] Mary McIntosh, "The Homosexual Role," *Social Problems* 16 (1968), pp. 182-192, reprinted this volume.

Notice that McIntosh endorses the strong social-constructionist model: she uses the word 'rather' to indicate not only that social constructionism is correct but also that realism is wrong. McIntosh's views are widely admired, and her paper on homosexuality and social constructionism is probably the most widely cited one in the field. But her views are incomplete, as I will now show.

Why Homosexuality Is Essentially Real

There is also a lot of evidence suggesting that homosexuality is a real[24] category—even in the examples I gave you in the previous section. In particular, there are cross-cultural similarities between them and the situations of corresponding groups in modern societies that are hard to explain if social customs are the only factors involved. These similarities are admittedly more striking in some cases than in others, but they exist in each case.

The *age-biased* form of homosexuality survives today but—with the exception of homosexual rape—is the most frowned-upon type of homosexuality in the United States.[25] Of course, this role comes in heterosexual as well as homosexual varieties, but the belief that it is characteristic of homosexual men forms part of the American stereotype of homosexuality. (I'll have more to say about this stereotype in a later chapter [of *Sexual Landscapes*].) Scientists single out this "type" of homosexual when they coin terms (for the older partners) such as 'pedophile,' 'hebephile,' and 'ephebephile,' depending on the age group the older partners find attractive. The validity (scientific "reality," if you will) of the categories these terms describe can be scientifically validated using penile

---

24 'Realist' is the term applied to this school of thought by Boswell, "Revolutions." The term the social constructionists use is 'essentialist'; they criticize realists for assuming an essence in homosexuality that crosses cultural boundaries and for reducing complicated phenomena to simplistic equations.

25 Other Western culture including many Western European nations— do not frown upon age bias quite as much.

plethysmography (of the sort explained in chapter 8 [of *Sexual Landscapes*]). Likewise, many of the participants in these acts see themselves as particular types of people and use words to describe these types themselves. For example, the term used by men involved in such relationships is 'boy-lover.' Scientists lack a term for the younger partners (unless they are adults, in which case their partners are much older and the term is 'gerontophile'). As far as I know, boys involved in relationships with older men do not have a term for themselves.

The terminologies can make some fine distinctions. Some boy-lovers do not consider themselves homosexual and tend to seek out boys they consider to be ordinarily boyish. These boys often grow up to lead conventionally heterosexual lives.[26] Other boy-lovers do consider themselves homosexual and often seek as sex partners teenagers who already identify themselves as gay (while understanding that this age preference sets them apart from other kinds of homosexuals). Homosexuals, for their part, also make distinctions, albeit not always the same ones; boy-love organizations are permitted to march in some gay-pride marches but are excluded from others. Yet boy-lovers and homosexuals alike see their emotions reflected in the more accurate modern translations of the Greek classics.

All this suggests that there is an underlying reality in the categorizations of same-sex love that has outlasted the cultural changes of the past two thousand years. There did seem to be "men who loved boys" in ancient Greece as well as "men who loved girls." And nowadays there do seem to be "men who love men," "men who love boys," "men who love women," and "men who love girls."

The inversion model of homosexuality is also alive and kicking today. First and foremost, it survives in the stereotype of homosexual men as effeminate and homosexual women as

---

26 Two examples are given in John Money and James Weinrich, "Juvenile, Pedophile, Heterophile: Hermeneutics of Science, Medicine and Law in Two Outcome Studies," *Medicine and Law* 2 (1983), pp. 39-54.

mannish. There is a grain of truth in this stereotype, too, but mostly in the childhoods of lesbians and homosexual men— the childhood gender nonconformity discussed in chapter 2 [of *Sexual Landscapes*]—and in the results of some masculinity-femininity questionnaires I'll describe in a later chapter [of *Sexual Landscapes*].

But more convincing than this stereotype is that the inversion pattern gives some of the spookiest examples of cross-cultural similarity I know. "Bitchiness"—being bad-tempered, complaining frequently—is one of these, even though some people might consider it a trivial trait. Let me review the evidence on this (during which you should keep in mind that heterosexual transvestites have no such reputation).

Drag queens are widely viewed as bitchy in the U.S., and apparently also in all Western societies. Moreover, drag-queen-like behavior is not difficult to find in non-Western cultures, and bitchiness shows up in most if not all of them.

The *hijras*—a Hindu caste in India consisting of males who dress as females—are one example. Hijras leave their families in their teen years, run away to a group of adult hijras living in a large city, and eventually may undergo a castration operation that finalizes their status in the caste. They entertain at weddings and other festivals, sometimes uninvited, but they always expect to get paid. If they are not, they have a habit of lifting their skirts in their disgust to show what they (no longer) have underneath.[27] Hijras are as a rule bitchy and insistent, and have been known to demand (rather than politely request) donations of used women's clothes from Indian women who are well off.[28]

---

[27] A rule of the sect, believe it or not, forbids hijras to wear underwear, so this display is one that fathers of the bride presumably wish to avoid.

[28] The best modern account of hijras is Serenà Nanda, "The Hijras of India: A Preliminary Report," *Medicine and Law* 3 (1954), pp. 59-75. The skirt-lifting and underwear details are not mentioned in this paper; they come from a speech Nanda gave at a conference I attended. The dress-demanding incident was told to me by an American woman who had been a foreign exchange student in India.

Chukchee berdaches even have an argument that *requires* them to be bitchy or bossy. The Chukchee berdache, married to an ordinary male, had a spirit who, according to Bogoras, "is supposed to be the real head of the family, and to communicate his orders by means of his transformed [berdache] wife. The human husband, of course, has to execute these orders faithfully under fear of prompt punishment."[29] Just about every drag queen I know would kill to have *that* weapon in her arsenal.

And then there are some American Indian berdaches who insist in the strongest possible terms that they really *are* women in a physiological sense. If they are doubted, they will scratch their thighs to simulate menstruation, claim to "get pregnant" and insist the baby was stillborn. These carryings-on fool no one but are engaged in dead seriously, sometimes literally so. One American Indian man had jokingly questioned whether a berdache was really a woman; that berdache then "picked up a club and for one or two weeks tried to assault the man whenever he saw him."[30]

This suspiciously strong insistence that role-inverted males be treated as physiologically real women is not limited to berdaches. There are some black drag queens in the United States who claim they can get pregnant and proceed a few months later to deliver a so-called blood baby (described as stillborn, just as in the berdache example).[31] And, as I described in chapter 2 [of *Sexual Landscapes*], there are male-to-female transsexuals who insist that their surgeons perform uterus transplantation operations to make them capable of

---

[29] *The Spirit and the Flesh*, p. 254, reminded me of this quotation, which is taken from Bogoras, "The Chukchee," pp. 452-454. Incidentally, in his brief discussion of *castrati* (men castrated before puberty, in order to keep their soprano voices), *The Spirit and the Flesh*, p. 261 notes that they became "the prima donnas of the high culture of their time"—and we all know how bossy prima donnas are.

[30] Devereux, "Institutionalized Homosexuality of the Mohave Indians," pp. 510-513.

[31] See John Money and Geoffrey Hosta, "Negro Folklore of Male Pregnancy," *Journal of Sex Research* 4 (1968), pp. 34-50.

bearing children.   In striking contrast, heterosexual transvestites are rarely or never described as bitchy. I am not aware of any such description of them in scientific papers, and the ones I have met I would not call bitchy. In preparing this chapter, I asked a heterosexual transvestite I know about this. Significantly, she not only had an answer; the question had already occurred to her, because she had obviously thought about her answer. She pointed out that when transvestites want to act forcefully, vindictively, or pushily, they can do so in their masculine persona—and she added that many of them do.[32]

This is, then, another example of a generalization I made in chapter 2 [of *Sexual Landscapes*]: that drag queens combine masculine and feminine qualities in a single androgynous personality, whereas transvestites prefer to express these two facets by way of two separate personalities.

What about the possibility that bitchiness is simply learned as part of the drag queen (or hijra, or whatever) role? That's conceivable but unconvincing. Why would so many culturally diverse groups have the same trait? Moreover, there are indications that bitchiness shows up long before the drag queens themselves know they're supposed to be bitchy. For example, sissy boys typically have a "bossy" personality that could easily be viewed as the childhood antecedent of adult bitchiness.[33] Sissy boys are disliked by their peers not merely because they're sissy; typically, they also boss kids around in a way that is resented by their playmates.

Aside from bitchiness and envy of women's roles, there are other similarities between various gender-mixing institutions and the gender-inversion pattern of homosexuality in our own culture. In nearly every case, cultures with the inversion pattern of homosexuality believe that the signs of inversion

---

[32] I thank Ariadne Kane for her suggestions and insight on this topic.

[33] Richard Green, *Sexual Identity Conflict in Children and Adults* (New York: Basic Books, 1974) is the now-classic reference on sissy boys, and it was Green who pointed out the bossy trait without seeing the cross-cultural parallel or suggesting (as far as I know) that this bossiness develops into adult bitchiness.

show up in childhood or, at the very latest, in the teen years. (Recall that hijras usually join hijra groups at that age.) The inversion is not just of sexual acts but also of gender role. That is, it's not just that these males enjoy being penetrated rather than penetrating but, rather, that they enjoy taking up weaving, child rearing, or some other aspect of the other sex's *gender* role not specifically involving sexual relations. And the inversion is usually lifelong, or at the very least viewed as being long-term, with entry into the status being beyond the control of the individuals in question.

Another remarkable similarity—related to the gender-role inversion itself is that drag queens around the world use feminine terms and pronouns to refer to each other, even when the gender crossing is incomplete.[34] But when females take up the roles of males, it is scarcely ever mentioned whether they are referred to as 'he'—in fact, I cannot recall any instances in which they are.[35] Some feminine homosexual men use 'she' or 'her' when talking about other homosexual men, but I have never heard of lesbian women referring to each other as 'he' or 'him.'

The playing-model of homosexuality is also eerily echoed in other accounts. Walter Williams, again, reported:

> A Hupa berdache says of his partners, "As far as it was publicly known, he [the nonberdache] was the man. But in bed there was

---

[34] Examples here are too numerous to cite in their entirety. Frederick Whitam and Robin Mathy, *Male Homosexuality in Four Societies: Brazil, Guatemala, the Philippines, and the United States* (New York: Praeger Scientific, 1986) give examples from the United States, Guatemala, Brazil, and the Philippines. Two examples from American Indians are on pp. 52-53 and 62 of *The Spirit and the Flesh.* In my experience, American drag queens frequently or always refer to each other as "she," whether the queen in question is dressed as a woman or not.

[35] Nor, in a conversation, was Walter Williams able to recall any anthropological account of masculine women being referred to as 'he.'

an exchange of roles. They have to keep an image as masculine, so they always ask me not to tell anybody.[36]

Many other openly gay men have tracked down berdaches and found that they nowadays identify themselves as gay.[37]

Even the "third-sex" status of the berdache may be overstated. Here is what anthropologist Elsie Clews Parsons had to say about the Zuñi berdache way back in 1916. She was trying to figure out whether the berdaches (*la'mana*) in that tribe were "really" considered male or female by the other members of the tribe. After she made a number of observations about a *la'mana*'s position in dances and rituals, she admitted to herself that she was confused and turned to the question of burial:

> When prepared for burial the corpse of a *la'mana* is dressed in the usual woman's outfit, with one exception, under the woman's skirt a pair of trousers are put on. "And on which side of the graveyard will he be buried?" I asked, with eagerness of heart if not of voice, for here at last was a test of the sex status of the *la'mana*. "On the south side, the men's side, of course. *Kwash lu itse teame* [Is this man not]?" And my old friend smiled the peculiarly gentle smile he reserved for my particularly unintelligent questions.[38]

Notice that this final question—"Is this man not?"—embodies a realist point of view.

So although there are few if any gay bars in Chukchee Siberia and few if any American fathers of the bride who permit drag queens to sing and dance at the wedding reception, there are nevertheless some aspects of the gender transpositions that appear cross-culturally far more often than would be expected by chance.

---

[36] *The Spirit and the Flesh*, p. 97.

[37] For one example from the earliest days of gay liberation, see Bob Waltrip, "Elmer Gage: American Indian," *ONE: The Homosexual Point of View* 13 (March 1965), pp. 6-10.

[38] See Elsie Clews Parsons, "The Zuñi la'mana," *American Anthropologist* 18 (1916), pp. 521-528.

If this is so, then why hasn't it been observed by previous workers?   Sue-Ellen Jacobs, an anthropologist at the University of Washington, suggested that different members of the Tewa tribe gave anthropologists different answers. The village elders gave one definition, but

> [g]oing on accounts given by others, the characterizations of *quethos* [Tewa berdaches] begin to look more like characterizations of contemporary gay males, particularly.[39]

Indeed, if anthropologists don't know contemporary gay males, how can they be expected to recognize similarities to them?

Examples like these are what Arizona sociologist Fred Whitam had in mind when he studied the inversion of form of homosexuality in several countries (specifically the United States, Guatemala, Brazil, and the Philippines). He found many similarities, among them the very important one that children typically are not socialized into becoming homosexuals.

> While a role, as it is ordinarily understood, may be ascribed or achieved, children are neither socialized into the "homosexual role" nor do they rationally chooses it. . . . Homosexuality is neither a [medical] "condition" nor a role but rather a sexual orientation and no useful theoretical purpose is served by regarding it as role behavior.[40]

---

[39] Sue-Ellen Jacobs, "Comments," *Current Anthropology* 24 (1983), p. 460.

[40] The quotation is from Frederick Whitam, "The Homosexual Role: A Reconsideration," *Journal of Sex Research* 13 (1977), pp. 1-11. Other works are Whitam, "The Prehomosexual Male Child in Three Societies: The United States, Guatemala, Brazil," *Archives of Sexual Behavior* 9 (1980), pp. 87-99 and "Culturally Invariable Properties of Male Homosexuality: Tentative Conclusions from Cross-cultural Research," *Archives of Sexual Behavior* 12 (1983), pp. 207-226. Whitam and Mathy, *Male Homosexuality in Four Societies*, is the most detailed.

Notice that Whitam, too, endorses a strong model—the realist one—in the phrase beginning "no useful theoretical purpose . . ."

An Interactionist Approach

Hiding among these examples, of course, is evidence that both realist and social-constructionist approaches are required if we want to understand sexual orientation fully. Below is an excerpt from a story written by Plato; it shows that even though the ancient Greeks did not attach moral significance to homosexuality as opposed to heterosexuality, they still seemed to understand the distinction between the two.

The situation is a dinner party at which each guest gives a speech on love. It is assumed as a matter of course by all participants that they will talk of the love of males by males. One guest—Aristophanes—describes the mythical origins of what can only be described as preferential homosexuality. The Aristophanes character says that there were at first three sexes—male, female, and hermaphrodite. Every human had two faces, four arms and four legs, two sets of genitalia—double the usual number of everything. They were so powerful they attacked the gods, and of course the gods struck back: Zeus sent his thunderbolts to chop each of them in half. Here was the result:

> Each of us when separated is but the indenture [half] of a man, . . . like a flat fish, and he is always looking for his other half. Men who are a section of that double nature which was once called Androgynous are lascivious [for women]. . . : the women who are a section of the [former] woman don't care for men, but have female attachments. . . . But the men who are a section of the [ancient] male follow the male. . . . And when one of them finds his other half, . . . the pair are lost in an amazement of love and friendship and intimacy, and one will not be out of the other's sight, as I may say, even for a moment.[41]

---

[41] B. Jowett, *The Republic and Other Works by Plato* (Garden City, NY: Anchor Books, 1973).

One colleague of mine, reading between the lines in other works, tells me that the real Aristophanes was probably interested in women (in modern terms, 'was heterosexual')— and was widely known as such. If so, then his character's stirring defense of homosexual love in "The Symposium" would have been interpreted as a bit of dry humor. Another colleague believes the entire story was intended by Plato to be taken as a joke. Neither suggestion changes the bottom line: that in ancient Greece one could talk and write about homosexuality and heterosexuality lightheartedly, *at the same time as* one talked as if they were unchangeable sexual orientations.

This conclusion shows how a realist factor interacts with a social constructionist factor in a way equal to more than just the sum of the parts. Yes, ancient Greece clearly had a social construction of "homosexuality" that is very different from the one we have today. But yes, even ancient Greeks realized that people could have a lifelong trait that meant they would search for lovers among one sex only. In order to understand the sociology, you need the realistic "given," and in order to understand the biology, you need the socially constructed "given."

Moreover, ancient Greece was not as committed to the age-biased ideal as it may seem. Some documents imply that because of appearance or personality a particular person would be a beloved his entire life, while another would be a lover throughout his. Some of the famous lover/beloveds of the time were of the same age, and some couples were so well reciprocally bonded to each other that their friends never could figure out which of the two was "the lover" and which "the beloved." Indeed, recall the story told by Aristophanes above, which explained why each man seeks his "other half" erotically. There's an aspect of this story that I have never seen discussed. If indeed people search for a life partner because they were split off from the partner physically, then it follows that both partners must be the same age. Yet Greek literature records an ideal that the partners be quite different in age. I don't know what to make of this: nor does any classicist with whom I've discussed it.[42]

The berdache-burial matter among the Zuñi is also more complicated than a purely realist point of view would admit. True, the berdache was buried among the men. But the phrase "Is this man not?" is ambiguous; it suggests that the informant viewed the berdache as both essentially male (as shown by the burial on the men's side) *and* essentially a mixture of the male and female sexes (as shown by the burial clothing). Tellingly, Parsons included a footnote to the word '*lu*,' explaining that "personal pronouns showing sex are lacking in Zuñi"—which is presumably why she translated '*lu*' as 'this' instead of 'he' or 'she.' It's our Westerner dualism, remember, that insists that a particular Zuñi would have only one point of view on that matter.

Jacobs likewise demonstrated how we have to get rid of our Western dualism to understand these other cultures; she asked her informants

> if women are ever *quethos*. The answer was no. Then I asked if men were the only ones who were *quethos*. Again, the answer was no. In trying to force a categorization of *quethos* as women or men (or female or male), I only exasperated my Tewa friends. . . [43]

And Williams himself pointed out:

> If those [American Indian] languages are intentionally vague on this matter [whether berdaches are a third gender or a mixture of male and female], perhaps we should not split hairs. Manwoman, halfman-halfwoman, notman-notwoman—all convey the same idea.[44]

---

[42] John Boswell, the noted Yale historian, however, suggested in a recent conversation that this aspect of the story told by Aristophanes means just what it appears to mean: that male-male relationships without significant age differences were taken in stride by the ancient Greeks.

[43] Jacobs, "Comments," p. 460.

[44] *The Spirit and the Flesh*, p. 83.

The late anthropologist Margaret Mead was interested in the light anthropology could shed on gender roles, and her work is often cited to demonstrate that human sex differences have cultural roots. Few people know she studied the berdache, however, and fewer still have run across the following passage:

> During our stay in the field [among the Omaha Indians], we were visited by a male friend who had been living an avowed homoerotic life in Japan, who was not a transvestite but who had a complete repertoire of homosexual postures. Within an hour of his arrival, the single berdache in the tribe turned up and tried to make contact with him.[45]

I'm not exactly sure what Mead meant by the phrase 'homosexual postures,' but the point is that this berdache clearly recognized a kinship with, and perhaps also a sexual attraction to, the visitor. Indeed, according to Williams, "All of the berdaches I have interviewed eventually specified their sexual activities with men, but only after I had gained their confidence."[46]

This instant recognition is one that many gay people say they have when they recognize homosexuality in others—sometimes even before admitting that they have homosexual desires. Compare Mead's story with the following passage from the autobiography of Robert Bauman, the conservative ex-congressperson from Maryland who lost his seat when his attraction to men became public in 1980. Bauman was nineteen or twenty when, one evening about dusk, a young sailor in navy whites approached him.

> I cannot to this day explain what happened next. Something occurred between this young sailor and me, some undefined

---

[45] Margaret Mead, "Cultural Determinants of Sexual Behavior," in *Sex and Internal Secretions*, third edition, William C. Young, ed. (Baltimore: Williams and Wilkins, 1961), p. 1452.

[46] *The Spirit and the Flesh*, p. 105.

> understanding we both accepted. Without words, we knew what
> was going to happen. . . . It was a couple of hours later before I
> let him out of the car at the entrance to the Baltimore-
> Washington Parkway.[47]

It is very difficult to explain things like this purely with social constructionism. The existence of such desires, and the fact that they can be acted upon with no explicit recognition of their meaning, strongly suggests that some underlying substrate is coming to the fore.

Children learn that "playing doctor" is a way of taking off clothes and examining each other's bodies; they don't need anyone to teach them that they enjoy playing doctor. I suspect that they'd invent something like playing doctor even if no one socialized them into its quasi-acceptability. Likewise, people like Bauman *act* as if they know exactly what they want to do even when they and their society conspire to keep them from thinking about it consciously.

Yet whatever that substrate may consist of, it is clearly not enough to explain the full range of variation from the berdache's bitchiness to sex between congressmen and sailors. The social constructions through which the substrates are interpreted are amazing in and of themselves and become positively dizzying when you think out their interactions—just as dizzying as Alice's experiences in Wonderland were. On the other hand, the substrates themselves must be pretty amazing in order to survive repression by the powerful forces of culture and socialization.

In fact, when someone studies a culture in enough detail, *it turns out again and again that the range of gender transpositions in the culture is amazingly similar to the range in our own.* Even the barriers between the three types of homosexuality (age-biased, inversion, and role-playing) become fuzzy when you get to know individual people and

---

[47] See Robert Bauman, "The Secret Life of Bob Bauman," *The Washingtonian* 21 (1986), pp. 98-148, or *The Gentleman from Maryland: The Conscience of a Gay Conservative* (New York: Arbor House, 1986).

cultures well enough. Serena Nanda, professor of anthropology at John Jay College of Criminal Justice, in studying the hijras, privately classified each one as "transsexual," "homosexual cross-dresser," and "heterosexual transvestite," because these terms seemed to accurately describe important variations in their personalities. Williams reports a teenaged effeminate American Indian boy who ran away to a city and was picked up by two Sioux Indian drag queens, who let him stay with them and introduced him to the drag scene[48]—just as the hijras do in their own way. In modern American drag pageants, participants learn their best techniques from older and wiser drag queens who have taken them under their wing after winning the pageants themselves in previous years. Many American Indian berdaches were highly cross-gendered and insisted that they "really" were women (e.g., by faking menstruation; see above)—just as many male-to-female transsexuals today insist that they are physical hermaphrodites even in the absence of medical confirmation. These berdaches find their genitals so inconsistent with their preferred sex role that they resist touching their own erect penis and insist that their partners do the same[49] (i.e., refrain from touching the berdache's penis)— just as many transsexuals find their genitals repulsive, say that they do not touch them when (and if) they masturbate, and insist that their sexual partners likewise refrain from touching these parts of the body (the transsexual's body). On the other hand, other berdaches seemed perpetually surrounded by teenaged males, with whom it was assumed they were having sexual relations,[50] while other berdaches report that they have always been attracted to men much older than themselves,[51]

---

[48] *The Spirit and the Flesh*, p. 213.

[49] *Ibid.*, pp. 97-98, quoting Devereux.

[50] *Ibid.*, p. 100. See also the passage from Catlin that Williams quotes on pp. 107-108.

[51] *Ibid.*, pp. 99-100. The largest age discrepancy he happens to report involves a relationship between a feminine boy of eight and a man over forty.

and yet others report behavior and attractions to boys and men their own age. Sexual relations or no, many berdaches adopt teenagers no longer willing or able to live with their biological parents[52]—and act, as the ancient Greeks did, as mentors and confidants to them. Some berdaches confined their cross-dressing to articles of women's *under*clothing and seemed to have fetishistic attachments to such clothing and to women's jewelry,[53] which closely resembles the behavior of heterosexual transvestites.

Williams, who reported many of these instances, describes certain berdaches in terms that suggest that they resemble modern transsexuals. He has, apparently, independently discovered among modern working-class whites a category John Money calls "gynemimetic" and which I classify as a subtype of drag queen (a man who so effectively mimics a woman's behavior patterns that otherwise ordinary heterosexual men can be sexually attracted to him even when they know the gynemimetic is "really" a man). Since Williams approached the spectrum of the gender transpositions with a different set of assumptions than Money and I do, it is remarkable—and very important—that he nevertheless ended up with the same conclusion about the similarities between berdaches and the various gender transpositions as classified by Western scientists.[54]

And finally, consider a conservative culture like Saudi Arabia, where traditional women are still veiled, where no woman is ever left alone with a man not a close relative, and where what little homosexuality manages to escape severe suppression is supposedly satisfied with boys or with Western gay tourists willing to play a receptive role. But in such a

---

[52] *Ibid.*, pp. 54-55 and passim.

[53] *Ibid.*, p. 72, cites an example from Margaret Mead's work among the Omaha; on p. 73, a modern example from the same tribe.

[54] Since so many of these points depend on *The Spirit and the Flesh*, let me stress that his observations are widely confirmed by other observers. Note also that Williams does not endorse the concept of transsexualism (pp. 79-80), which makes his agreement on other points all the more striking. A gynemimetic is described on pp. 116-117.

society, there exist men quite like the openly gay men of the United States in all respects except their openness.

> I was more curious than ever about this man who challenged all the myths about sex with an Arab. . . . Once, in response to one of my personal questions, he shook his head disgustedly, grabbing my mustache and then his own. "You are a man. See? I am a man. See? No problem. We like fucking. That's all. OK?" But as he dropped me off a few minutes later, he said with the moon in his eyes, "Oh, Habibi, I will dream of us making love all night." And then he kissed me.[55]

Moreover, a formal berdachelike institution does exist in neighboring Oman.[56] The *xaniths*, as they're called, mix freely with women no matter what the rules of male-female contact would otherwise require. They wear an article of clothing called the *dishdasha*—typical for men, but they wrap it in a feminine way and dye it any of several pastel colors. (Ordinary men always wear white dishdashas.) Hairstyles and jewelry are (as a rule) intermediate between what would be considered ordinary for men and for women. So once again Arabic culture expresses the full range of homosexuality seen in the West: the cross-gendered, the age-biased, and the urban gay male buddy.

In short, *the better we know the cultures involved, the more the various gender-transposition patterns merge into and overlap each other.* Social constructionists say that's just the point—this incredible mishmash of gender patterns is organized by particular cultures into particular discrete categories: berdache versus nonberdache; ordinary homosexual versus drag queen versus transsexual versus ordinary heterosexual; hijra versus nonhijra. And they're right. The realists are also right; they argue that the similarity

---

[55] Vincent Traughber, "Arabian Nights: Gay Sex in the Heart of Islam," *The Advocate* 416 (March 19, 1985), p. 36.

[56] Unni Wikan, *Behind the Veil in Arabia: Women in Oman* (Baltimore: Johns Hopkins University Press, 1982).

of this mishmash from culture to culture is very strong evidence that it is not constructed from culture alone.

Conclusions

There is more than one kind of homosexuality in the world. Most societies have most types and encourage them in different proportions. It is likely—as we will see in later chapters [of *Sexual Landscapes*]—that some of these types exist ultimately because of genetic factors that go at least as far back as our hunter-gatherer ancestors (which is where the human race spent most of its time evolving away from other primates). This means that we need to gather data on genetic factors in order to explain *why we are what we are.* But it is also clear that each society has its own way of socially constructing and emphasizing these types—constructions that can change and that have enormously important influences on individual people's lives. These behaviors are constructed so drastically differently that people from one society trying to find themselves in another might just as well be looking for the Mad Hatter and the March Hare. These different constructions perhaps depend in part on the genetic distributions prevalent in a given society, but if so, they are certainly not completely determined by such distributions. In order to understand *why we love whom we love*, we need to know how society has constructed particular sexual classifications, because the effects of having particular genetic predispositions can be entirely different, depending on the social constructions of the society possessing those genes.

In short, genes and societies don't just add; they interact. Was it all right for me, back in chapter 2 [of *Sexual Landscapes*], to give definitions of transvestite, drag queen, transsexual, and homosexual—as if they constituted real categories? Yes. Was it culturally biased for me to give these definitions rather than others? Yes.

So: are the gender transpositions social constructions of particular societies, or are they essential realities transcending particular cultures? The answer, of course, is yes—which is obvious, once you've transcended your own Western dualism.[57]

If you are a native speaker of English, you don't really comprehend its complexities and limitations unless you know at least one foreign language. You cannot imagine how varied the English language can be until you seek out the languages that are most extremely unlike it. And, of course, these variations are due to cultural factors, not genetic ones.

But neither can you arrive at a complete understanding of language without understanding the uniquely human adaptation that language constitutes biologically. We speak because others around us speak, but we also speak because we have circuits built into our brains that seem designed to understand speech. Accordingly, as I construct my theory of the gender transpositions in the chapters [of *Sexual Landscapes*] that follow, I will have to pay close attention to the interaction between genetic predispositions and the society in which those predispositions have their effects. I will have to explain not only why we are what we are but also why we love whom we love. It's time to start constructing human sexual desire socially and biologically: in both heterosexual and homosexual varieties, for both females and males. That is the job of chapter 6 [of *Sexual Landscapes*].

---

[57]Once you've solved this problem, you can start dealing with the sound of one hand clapping.

CHAPTER 9:
Wayne R. Dynes
Wrestling with the
Social Boa Constructor

The 1980s saw the rise of a new approach to the history of same-sex behavior, Social Construction (SC). Looking beyond both psychiatric and gay liberation perspectives, advocates of SC believe that they have achieved an exciting new synthesis. The key to this synthesis is the conviction that the history of sexual conduct must be framed in terms of cultural malleability. "[T]he various possibilities of same sex behaviour are variously constructed in different cultures as an aspect of wider gender and sexual regulation. The physical acts might be similar, but their social implications are often profoundly different."[1]

The persuasiveness of this assertion of Jeffrey Weeks stems from its seeming accord with the findings of anthropologists, who have found that some areas of human culture, notably language and religion, are luxuriantly diverse. Field work and historical study have isolated some 5000 distinct human cultures, each with its own language. Yet what we have learned of the sexual arrangements of these cultures demonstrates that each does not possess its very own "construction" of same-sex behavior. In fact, six categories suffice to classify those in which the sexual configuration is

---

[1] Jeffrey Weeks, *Sex, Politics and Society: The Regulation of Sexuality Since 1800* (London: Longman, 1981), p. 97.

An earlier version of the essay was written for private circulation at the Amsterdam Conference "Homosexuality, Which Homosexuality?" held in December 1987 and was published in *Out in Academia* 2 (1988), pp. 18-29.

known.[2] This contrast between a handful of sexual categories vs. 5000 different languages is surely a striking fact. To appreciate, say, the oral literature of a tribal culture the anthropologist must batten down to the hard work of learning the vocabulary and syntax of a language radically different from his own, and this laborious task must be repeated with each new culture. But sexual arrangements may be readily coded because only a tiny "vocabulary" is needed. Thus the strong version of the diversitarian hypothesis, which meets the case for human languages, does not suit the study of sexual arrangements. In short, assumptions of variety must not be overgeneralized.

Those who subscribe to the SC program reject any historically transcendent category such as "the homosexual"; at most one can apply this concept to a few recent generations, for it seems to have originated at some point in the nineteenth century. As Stephen O. Murray, a critic of SC, has pointed out, this "nativity legend" stems from a single paragraph of Michel Foucault, which states (in part):

> The nineteenth-century homosexual became a personage, a past, a case history, and a childhood, in addition to being a type of life, a life form, and a morphology, with an indiscreet anatomy and possibly a mysterious physiology; . . . the homosexual was now a species.[3]

This foundation document, which Foucault first published in French in 1976, has engendered a towering edifice—but one of uncertain stability. By contrast, Mary McIntosh, in an earlier contribution much admired by SC scholars, dates the

---

2 For a history and explanation of classification schemes, see "Typology," *Encyclopedia of Homosexuality* (New York: Garland Publishing, 1990), pp. 1332-37.

3 *The History of Sexuality: Volume I: Introduction* (New York: Random House, 1978), p. 42; the relevant chapter of Foucault is reprinted in this volume. Murray's trenchant remarks appear in "Homosexual Acts and Selves in Early Modern Europe," *Journal of Homosexuality* 16 (1988), pp. 457-77.

crystallization of the modern homosexual to the early *eighteenth* century.[4] SC advocates have rarely tarried to address this contradiction in fixing the birth date of the modern homosexual; what they stress is that there was a time—not many generations ago—when the modern homosexual did not exist. Taking this point as given, Weeks insists that "it is no longer possible to talk of the possibility of a universalistic history of homosexuality."[5]

Some would go farther still in their assertion of malleability, holding that even within a specific historical era no claims of stable orientation can be supported, for identities are always in flux. This view sometimes takes the form of a syntactic commandment: the word 'homosexual' may only be used as an adjective referring to acts, never a noun.[6] In this light even the expression "modern homosexual" is a misnomer that circulates only provisionally, for convenience' sake. Thus, in this extreme SC formulation, there are homosexual acts but no homosexual actors.

These nuances aside, Social Construction boosters insinuate that its superiority has been conclusively established: to resist its triumphant progress is a confession of intellectual backwardness—and may also be "politically incorrect." As will be seen, there are no compelling grounds for endorsing any of these claims. In view of its uncertain logical status, this paper generally treats SC as an "approach" or "project" rather than a method.

In the current division of academic labor SC finds its happiest affinities neither in the humanities nor the natural sciences. Instead SC taps traditions of sociology that focus on the synchronic analysis of living societies. In so doing, it

---

[4] "The Homosexual Role," *Social Problems* 16 (1968), pp. 182-92; reprinted, with postscript, in Kenneth Plummer, ed., *The Making of the Modern Homosexual* (Totowa, NJ: Barnes and Noble, 1981), pp. 30-49; reprinted (without postscript) in this volume.

[5] Weeks, *Sex, Politics and Society*, p. 97.

[6] See recently Gore Vidal, in *Times Literary Supplement* (October 3-8, 1987), and letter in following issue.

seeks to endow these sociological precipitates with a dynamic, temporal dimension.

While the chief pioneers of SC, including Mary McIntosh, Kenneth Plummer, Diane Richardson, and Jeffrey Weeks, have been English, its main sources are the labeling theory and symbolic interactionism of American sociology and French post-structuralism and deconstructionism, especially the work of the late Michel Foucault. In this way Britain, geographically poised between the two, has served as an intellectual crucible. It is possible to hazard an explanation for this leading role. During the first half of the twentieth century England lagged behind other advanced industrial countries in the movement for sexual enlightenment. However, the Wolfenden Report of 1957 and the decriminalization that followed ten years later changed the climate and set the stage for the rise of an ebullient gay liberation movement. During those halcyon days the British scholars who were to develop Social Construction attained maturity. With the economic downturn of the mid-1970s, however, the British gay movement declined in comparison with other Western nations, where the AIDS crisis challenged, but did not cripple, gay political activity. Scholarly reassessment often flourishes in the lull that follows vigorous activity: the owl of Minerva flies only at dusk. For its admirers, SC is a kind of "silver lining" produced by today's British exceptionalism, when a faltering social movement nonetheless yielded a theoretical dividend. And in fact SC did attract many adherents elsewhere, notably in North America, Australia, the Netherlands (where a large scholarly conference on the subject was held in December 1987), and Scandinavia. Yet Germany, Italy, and Latin America remained largely aloof. This contrasted pattern of reception and resistance may reflect the tendency to relative cohesion of the Anglophone intellectual community (with the Netherlands and Scandinavia, where English is the second language) as distinct from the Latin and Germanic worlds.[7]

---

[7] Compare the well-known split in academic philosophy where the analytic tradition has dominated the English-speaking world and

--->

Giovanni Dall'Orto, who has concluded that Social Constructionist ideas are ill-suited to explain sexual arrangements in the circum-Mediterranean cultural area, holds that SC is an outgrowth of northwest European chauvinism, created by scholars who have an insufficient comprehension of differing sexual paradigms found in other areas and periods.[8]

Another suggested source is the widely read book of an American and a German sociologist: Peter L. Berger and Thomas Luckmann, *The Social Construction of Reality: A Treatise in the Sociology of Knowledge,*[9] which reflects the ideas of such continental thinkers as Karl Mannheim, Alfred Schutz, and Sigmund Freud. Influential as it was for a time in sociology, this book impacted SC mainly by its catchy title. Berger and Luckmann's theory is too schematic, too ahistorical, and too anti-empirical to serve historians. And in fact SC writings rarely cite the book.

SC also has ramifications or consequences in the realms of politics, law, and psychotherapy. The encroachment of the project into these domains is not without its costs. Abandonment of the idea that homosexuals constitute a discrete social entity or minority will make it difficult to persuade already skeptical lawmakers that we deserve civil rights protections.[10] This problem has led some to conclude

---

Scandinavia, while the idealist-existentialist amalgam has generally been dominant on the European continent and in Latin America.

[8] Dall'Orto will explore these views in a series of articles to be published in *Babilonia* (Milan).

[9] Peter L. Berger and Thomas Luckmann, *The Social Construction of Reality: A Treatise in the Sociology of Knowledge*, (New York: Anchor Books, 1966).

[10] This problem is discussed with some frankness by a scholar sympathetic to SC: John D'Emilio, "Making and Unmaking Minorities: The Tensions between Gay Politics and History," *New York University Review of Law and Social Change* 14 (1986), pp. 915-22. Astute comments in a broader framework appear in Steven Epstein, "Gay Politics, Ethnic Identity: The Limits of Social Constructionism," *Socialist Review* 93/94 (1987), pp. 9-54, reprinted this volume, though

--->

that if SC provides a pretext for rejecting political reform, that defect alone should scuttle it. Rejecting this instrumental view, the present writer takes a different stance. If SC does in fact offer the most satisfactory account of sexual/social reality, then we must courageously embrace it—and take our lumps. Acknowledging the truth can, at times, be inconvenient. But SC has not in fact succeeded in attaining the intellectual hegemony to which it aspires, and politicians—if they are interested—may be reassured that it remains but one approach among several that are current. Speculative theories, however promising they may seem to some, offer no firm ground for the making (or unmaking) of laws.

One wing of the SC school narrows the principle of malleability to the time frame of the individual lifetime. In the mental health field, reception of the notion of the plasticity of sexuality opens the door to a revival of "cure" therapies that claim to be able to change clients from a homosexual orientation to a heterosexual one, a problem that does not seem to dampen the enthusiasm of Diane Richardson.[11] But again there are no present grounds for heroic efforts at damage control. The mountain of evidence that has accumulated on the extreme difficulty—the virtual impossibility—of changing an established sexual orientation through therapeutic intervention should give the supporters of SC-inspired plasticity pause. The failure rate of "cure" attempts is massive not only in coercive situations—as in prisons and mental hospitals—but also when the "patient" voluntarily and valiantly participates in the attempted restructuring of sexual orientation. In fact this pattern of failure, well documented before the rise of SC, constitutes one of the most impressive empirical counterconfirmations of at least this wing of Social Construction.

---

this paper fails to distinguish carefully the epistemological/empirical problem, on the one hand, from the political/strategic one, on the other.
[11] Diane Richardson, "Recent Challenges to Traditional Assumptions about Homosexuality: Some Implications for Practice," *Journal of Homosexuality* 13 (Summer 1987), pp. 1-12.

Disregarding these interesting, but still inchoate developments from the premises of Social Construction, this essay concentrates on its effects on the study of history, for it is here that the most extensive discussion and application have taken place.

Historiography, Lay and Professional

Interest in the historical dimensions of homosexual behavior is not limited to professional historians. In the body of lay writing and protoscholarship on homosexuality that began to emerge in English-speaking countries after World War II, a prime concern was with "affectional ancestors," men and women of past eras who had been homosexual. Writings of this kind met an eager response from gay people who smarted under the accusation that homosexuality was a "perversion" of recent origin, caused by certain decadent conditions of modern urban life and likely to pass away once the "underlying social pathology" had been treated. In short, homosexuals felt that they needed role models—not just a few contemporaries, but a full range of stalwart individuals who would attest the enduring value of homosexual feeling and expression in the great tapestry of human experience.

The works that appeared to satisfy these longings, such as Noel I. Garde's *Jonathan to Gide* [12] and W. H. Kayy's *The Gay Geniuses*,[13] were not very sophisticated. Readers with professional historical training noted that such books were anachronistic through and through, presupposing a homosexual type invariant through all times and climes with which one could immediately identify. According to this popular genre homosexuals have a vast "hidden history," which, once the mists of censorship have been dispelled, turns out to be populated by individuals much like ourselves.

---

[12] Noel I. Garde, pseud., *Jonathan to Gide: The Homosexual in History* (New York: Vantage, 1964).

[13] W. H. Kayy, pseud., *The Gay Geniuses: Psychiatric and Literary Studies of Famous Homosexuals* (Glendale, CA: Marvin Miller, 1965).

A major goal of the SC project is to combat and correct the well-intentioned but naïve anachronism propagated by these writings. It is the thesis of the present paper, however, that the SC movement constitutes an *overcorrection*, which either greatly exaggerates historical differences or simply claims that the homosexual feelings and acts of men and women of earlier eras are of no concern to us. The first approach may be provisionally termed "diversitarian exoticism"; the second "presentist chauvinism."

The Bogeyman of "Essentialism"

The roots of SC are of prime importance. Yet before they can be traced, one must consider the possibility that the approach can be defined or at least bolstered by contrasting it with its proclaimed opposite. Although SC assumes a number of guises, most adherents agree that it stands starkly opposed to an "essentialism" rooted in biological constants which hold human action everywhere in a vice-like grip. "For the essentialist, homosexuality is a universal, a form found across cultures and throughout history: and the 'homosexual' of ancient Greece is directly comparable to the 'homosexual' of modern London."[14] What is an essentialist? The creature had supposedly been heard from before: others had previously sought to banish it.[15] As conceived by the SC party, the essentialist is a straw man, an adversary necessary for

---

[14] Kenneth Plummer, "Going Gay: Identities, Life Cycles and Lifestyles in the Male Gay World," in *The Theory and Practice of Homosexuality*, John Hart and Diane Richardson, eds. (London: Routledge & Kegan Paul, 1981), p. 94.

[15] Earlier, existentialists had, without offering much specificity, contrasted their own views with those of "essentialism." Writing from a very different standpoint, Sir Karl Popper, in *The Poverty of Historicism*, (London: Routledge & Kegan Paul, 1957), p. 27, states: "This 'realist' theory has also been called 'idealist.' I therefore propose to rename this antinominalist theory 'essentialism.'" Popper subsumes the idealism of classical antiquity and modern Europe, together with the realism of medieval philosophy, under the umbrella of essentialism.

symmetry's sake. After uttering a brief warning, the SC adherent generally disengages, leaving the impression that the essentialist is some kind of intellectual Neanderthal, not fitting company for the modern scholar's salon.[16] But the unwelcome intruder is strangely elusive.

To employ a military metaphor, the odd thing is that this is a battle in which only one army is engaged.[17] And beyond the field of combat the turrets of the wicked city of Essence lie deserted and undefended. Hence the unreality of the Solomonic solution proposed by some earnest bystanders: a compromise in which each side gets part of what it wants. There is no mirror symmetry of sides.[18] This lack of

---

[16] Occasionally, that brave sociologist Frederick Whitam is exhibited to the multitudes as a living specimen of this atavistic type, but it is not certain that he fits the bill. There are of course those who doubt, as I do, the viability of the SC program, and other scholars who are simply oblivious of it. But our detachment does not make any of us doubters an "essentialist," a straw man if there ever was one.

[17] It has been said that John Boswell heads an opposing contingent. While it is true that he incautiously used the word 'gay' throughout his magnum opus *Christianity, Social Tolerance and Homosexuality* (Chicago: Chicago University Press, 1980), in a later theoretical paper, discussed below, he effectively distanced himself from any strong version of essentialism. While such psychoanalytically oriented writers as Arno Karlen seem to be essentialists, they do not deserve serious consideration as historians.

[18] As has been noted, there is an analogy between the contrast of SC and essentialism, on the one hand, and the antithesis between nature and nurture, on the other. Significantly, while the environmentalists (nurture) are inclined to claim the whole pie for themselves, excluding or at least limiting biological factors as much as possible, the advocates of sociobiology and allied trends (nature), readily concede that environmental elements may account for as much as 40 to 60% of the phenomena. Some SC adherents are vigilant against any concessions towards "biologism," while others lend fleeting lip service to the biological substrate, but show a marked distaste for exploring its interaction with the environmental. For examples of the insights that accrue from integrating the biological perspective, see now James

--->

symmetry notwithstanding, it would be unwise to concede the game to SC, for it is not a new method, but rather an old one spruced up.[19] We may readily grant that time-honored theories may be better than newfangled ones, but it is deceptive practice to market a venerable nostrum as a new breakthrough. Moreover, as will be demonstrated below, SC fails to capitalize on the best features of its heritage, because it remains largely unaware of its own lineage.   SC has reinvented the wheel, but the new model fails to reflect the improvements that several generations of sophisticated historians had made in the old one.

The Intellectual Lineage of Social Construction

If SC is not the absolute novelty its enthusiasts claim, we must attempt to trace its position in the history of ideas and methodologies.   The Yale historian John Boswell has attempted to clarify the SC/"essentialist" clash by tracing it to the medieval dispute regarding universals, as conducted by the opposing parties of the realists and the nominalists.

> Realists consider categories to be the footprints of reality ("universals"): they exist because humans perceive a real order in the universe and name it. . . .[By contrast, nominalism]. . . is the belief that categories are only the names (Latin: *nomina*) of things agreed upon by humans, and the "order" people see is their creation rather than their perception.[20]

Weinrich, *Sexual Landscapes* (New York: Scribner, 1987); chapter five of this book is reprinted in this volume.

[19] Some significant critiques of SC: Stephen O. Murray, *Social Theory, Homosexual Realities* (New York: Gay Academic Union, 1984), Will Roscoe, "Making History: The Challenge of Gay and Lesbian Studies," *Journal of Homosexuality*, 15 (1988), pp. 1-40, and Gary Simes, "History and Sexual Categories," *Gay Information* 13 (Autumn 1983), pp. 15-22. See also Wayne R. Dynes in *Sociologist Gay Caucus Newsletter* 45 (1985), and discussion in the following issue.

[20] John Boswell, "Revolutions, Universals and Sexual Categories," *Salmagundi* 58-59 (1982-83), p. 91.

It is true that under various guises this controversy has been of continuing significance in the history of Western thought. But as Boswell himself concedes later in his essay, SC proponents cannot be simply equated with nominalists, since substantial residues of "realism" inform their writings. One need only glance at a few pages of any SC text to see that it abounds in reifications and abstractions—except of course where sexual categories are in question. And to its credit, SC tackles a problem that the disputants in the realist-nominalist controversy did not have to face: historical change. The recognition that we are all immersed in a dynamic process of cultural evolution is surely the key insight of SC.

In order better to understand what is valuable in SC we must look back at the history of historiography itself. Two themes call for special attention: the rise of Historicism and the crystallization of schemes of historical periodization.

Historicism

Some SC views revive ideas that came to the fore in the historiographic revolution that occurred in Germany during the second half of the eighteenth century with such writers as Justus Möser, Johann Gottfried Herder, and J. W. Goethe. These writers are usually regarded as reacting against the Enlightenment, but what they supplanted was broader and more pervasive: the Exemplar Theory of History. This last trend was the dominant (though not the only) model of historiographic practice from ca. 1550 to 1750.[21] The Exemplar Theory stressed great figures, some of them deserving emulation and veneration, others meriting only scorn. History is the *magistra vitae*, the great compass of how we should live, linking the experiences of the student with those of exemplary protagonists. This then was preeminently a judgmental view of the past, which was not only usable but peremptory.

---

[21] See George H. Nagel, "Philosophy of History before Historicism," in George H. Nagel, ed., *Studies in the Philosophy of History* (New York: Harper Torchbooks, 1965), pp. 49-73.

Moreover, as there have been good and bad people, there have been good and bad eras. Outstanding among the happy eras of human history were Periclean Athens, Augustan Rome, and Medici Florence. The supreme instance of a bad era was, of course, the Middle Ages, dubbed the "Dark Ages."

When the standard bearers of the new view appeared in the second half of the eighteenth century, the Exemplar Theory was already fading—though it never completely died out, exacting tribute even today in journalistic treatments of "Great Men" of the past.[22] The new view sometimes receives the term Historicism—though some prefer the rarer form Historism, modeled on the German *Historismus*.[23] The approach stresses the fundamental difference between the phenomena of nature and those of history. Nature, in this perspective, is the theater of the stable and eternally recurring, while history comprises unique and unduplicable human acts.

> The world of man is in a state of incessant flux, although within it there are centers of stability (personalities, institutions, nations, epochs), each possessing an inner structure, a character, and each in constant metamorphosis in accord with its own internal principles of development. . . . There is no constant human nature; rather the character of each man reveals itself only in his development.[24]

---

[22] A special department of this journalism is made up of compilations of the *Jonathan to Gide* type, in which the gay/lesbian reader encounters a pageant of famous homosexuals and lesbians abstracted from historical context and flattened into a kind of eternal present.

[23] In *The Open Society and Its Enemies* (London: Routledge and Sons, 1945) and other works Sir Karl Popper has used "historicism" in a broader sense than the one meant here.

[24] George G. Iggers, *The German Concept of History* (Middletown: Wesleyan University Press, 1968), p. 5. The classic account of the emergence of this approach is Friedrich Meinecke, *Historism: The Rise of a New Historical Outlook*, J. E. Anderson, trans. (London: Routledge & Kegan Paul, 1972).

In its emphasis on subjective uniqueness the new orientation of Historicism accorded in part with romanticism. Yet the individual was not seen as alienated and atomic, but was rather immersed in that ongoing stream that is Process. With regard to epochs it insisted that sympathetic understanding must always precede judgment. As Leopold von Ranke put it, "Before God all generations of mankind are equal."

Periodization

Stressing the harmony of thought, expression, and endeavor that reigned in any given time, the eighteenth-century writers tended to presuppose the self-contained character of each era. In fact the term 'epoch' in its historical sense was introduced in the eighteenth century.[25] Yet the idea is older, stemming from the Christian conception of discrete eras each cordoned off from the previous one by a striking event or crisis reflecting divine judgment.[26] As the concept underwent secularization, disagreements about working out the historical patterns led to an overall problematic of periodization. Another zone of dispute lay in the character of the breaks—were they indeed sharp and distinct or did history rather proceed by a series of short incremental steps with but slight rifts between them? Both sides of the dispute gained unexpected support from eighteenth-century geologists embroiled in the quarrel between the uniformitarians and the catastrophists.[27] The former stressed gradual evolutionary change, the latter sudden revolutionary shifts. It is the

---

[25] M. Riedel, "Epoche, Epochenbewusstsein," *Historisches Wörterbuch der Philosophie* II (1972), pp. 596-98.

[26] The most recent account of this broad development is Robert Nisbet, *History of the Idea of Progress* (New York: Basic Books, 1980).

[27] See Stephen Toulmin and June Goodfield, *The Discovery of Time* (London: Penguin Books, 1967), 200ff., and, more generally, I. Bernard Cohen, *Revolution in Science* (Cambridge: Harvard University Press, 1985).

catastrophist heritage that lives on today in those who emphasize sharp breaks between historical eras.

Visions of Cultural History

With a growing consensus on periodization, the two major elements fell into place: the assumption of pervasive harmony of thought and feeling, and the distinctness of each historical epoch. The joining of these two themes—those of consonance and periodization—yielded the grand principle of the Spirit of the Age or Zeitgeist, the "vital unity of individual epochs." To capture the distinctive character of epochs, mere nominalist or proto-positivist description would not suffice; rather one must work with general concepts, the Renaissance being suffused by one set of characteristics, the Baroque age which succeeded it by another. These examples point up the boundary problem. Where should we set the customs lines, the historical divides between self-contained epochs? And more important, why do epochs occur in the sequences that they do? The problem of boundaries is sometimes held to be the outgrowth of a mere didactic stratagem, a set of pigeonholes for History 101, which the more advanced student can easily discard. In some sense this may be true: Florentines of five centuries ago didn't go to sleep one night in the Middle Ages and wake up the next morning in the Renaissance. Yet it seems clear that when we posit unitary epochs succeeding one another in an orderly fashion we require criteria for defining and understanding the partitions that separate them.[28]

Why then does one epoch yield to another? Some historians have appealed explicitly to a biological metaphor; world views get old and doddering, and are then shoved aside by new ones.[29] But this concept would not explain why some eras such as the Middle Ages last much longer than others.

---

[28] For some sharp criticisms of Zeitgeist theories, see E. H. Gombrich, *In Search of Cultural History* (Oxford: Clarendon Press, 1969).

[29] The exhaustion hypothesis was explored by the anthropologist Alfred Kroeber in a number of works.

No: in the light of the postulates examined thus far the rotations of the great historical Wheel of Fortune can only be explained by an external agent: Hegel's Geist, itself only a stand-in for God. It was to solve this problem and give Historicism a truly secular character that Karl Marx sought to explain the changes in the "superstructure"—the realm of culture and noneconomic behavior—by saying that the source of the changes lies in the economic base, with its evolving relations of production. The changing configuration of the base can in turn be considered purely in technological terms, or rather in the interaction of technology with the human factor which is always needed to deploy it. But all was not thereby solved. As the sociologist Max Weber and many others after him have pointed out (and Engels grudgingly admitted), ideas do have their own power. Even disregarding this complication, Marxists continue to worry about the vexing problem of transitions: when and how did humanity go from feudalism to capitalism? The length of time that Marxists have been grappling, with scant success, with these key problems suggests that no simple return to a "historical materialist" perspective will suffice.

At this point in the debate the spotlight shifts to Michel Foucault, with his hegemonic epistemes separated by *coupures* or breaks.[30] The epistemes are epochs governed by uniform cultural climates; the *coupures* are the partitions that separate

---

[30] For bibliography through 1982, see Michael Clark, *Michael Foucault: An Annotated Bibliography* (New York: Garland Publishing, 1983). A sharply critical account, emphasizing cultural history and problems of verification, is J. G. Merquior, *Foucault* (London: Collins, 1985). Biographical details appear in Didier Eribon, *Michel Foucault* (Paris: Flammarion, 1989). Foucault's influential concepts of cultural history stem from his earlier phase, produced under the sign of the "archaeology of knowledge," rather than his later focus on "genealogy." The concept of the *coupure*, characteristic of the earlier work, is generally ascribed to the influence of the older French scholars Gaston Bachelard and Georges Canguilhem. These may well be the immediate sources but (as has been shown above), the idea of breaks stems from Christian historiography and the eighteenth-century catastrophists.

the epochs. To make a long story short, Foucault and his
disciples have reinvented the basic premises of Historicism,
vesting the ideas in an oracular new terminology. Foucault
and company seem blissfully unaware that the job had been
done before. The key problem is monoglot or monocultural
parochialism. Foucault was schooled in French history, and
his anglophone followers treat mainly the history of their own
countries. These limited perspectives block any in-depth
understanding of intracultural variance from nation to nation.
A genuine rebirth of Grand Theory, grounded in a large body
of empirical data, might provide a solid foundation for
progress. But no recovery of the fertility of Historicism is
feasible as long as we cling to historiographic amnesia.

In short there is much, derived from the explorations of
historicism, that is persuasive in SC, but it is not new. Indeed
the viable methods that it has managed to convey are stunted,
because they imperfectly recapture the sophistication of its
great predecessor. For progress to occur what is needed is a
sustained grappling with the question of historical change per
se. And candor requires that we acknowledge that progress in
solving this overarching problem may do little to solve the
more specific puzzle: why is there historical change in the
patterns of sexual behavior? To be sure, any advance towards
resolving these conundrums, which are among the thorniest
bequeathed to us by the European historical tradition, far
transcends the relatively parochial matter of the fate of SC.
But it is to this that we must return.

Difficulties of SC Practice

In its quest for historical data regarding human sexuality,
SC necessarily relies—as do the rest of us—mainly on written
records produced by the ruling sectors of society. It is true
that a certain amount of manuscript evidence from diaries and
letters is becoming available, but even here the authors tend to
censor themselves, or to be unconsciously in the grip of ideas
generated by the forces of social control. The biases that seep
in from this Establishment-generated and Establishment-
monitored body of evidence tend to remain uncorrected in SC.
The reason for this neglect is the SC commitment to seeing

things in terms of hegemonic ideologies imposed by ruling circles. A telltale marker of this approach is the ubiquitous term "discourse," which is almost always learned discourse, not the conversation the ordinary people—those having sex. In this way, SC opts for a "top-down" concept of idea formation, neglecting sources in folklore and popular imagery. In reality ordinary folk did not just take over the ideas as they were handed to them, but translated them into terms belonging to their own mindset and language habits.[31] Moreover, homosexual subcultures, sites of this creativity, can be traced back to the central Middle Ages.[32] Homosexual actors were neither mute nor isolated. The highly placed purveyors of such concepts as "inversion" and "contrary sexual feeling" could not simply impose them on men and women who had no parallel way of describing themselves.

If SC researchers, most of whom are anglophone, have any acquaintance with a foreign language, it is French. This affinity shines forth from perusal of almost any SC text which bristles with "franglais" neologisms. What has been less noticed is the tendency of French scholars to discover the historical "invention" of ideas and sentiments that had been thought to be historical universals. Nearly half a century ago Denis de Rougemont announced that romantic love, unknown to the ancient peoples, had been created only in the Provence of the eleventh and twelfth centuries. More famously, Philippe Ariès held that childhood as a distinct stage of human

---

[31] Stephen O. Murray, in private communication, notes: "This point is vitally important. I sometimes get the impression that particular sodomites are being tried a second time to see if they were really guilty of sodomy. There is no warrant for supposing that only the historian, like the inquisitors and the Paris police, recognized patterned sexual behavior, and that those who were congregating in 'notorious' locales were engaging in random homosexual acts."

[32] For a revealing glimpse, see [Wayne Dynes and] Warren Johansson, "London's Medieval Sodomites," *Cabirion* 10 (1984), pp. 5-7, 34. A methodological overview is provided by Stephen O. Murray and Kent Gerard, "Renaissance Sodomite Subcultures?" in *Among Men, Among Women* (Amsterdam: University, 1983), 183-96.

life was a creation of the early modern period in Europe. Roland Barthes insisted that there was no concept of the author before the sixteenth century. And Foucault once shocked his admirers by claiming that "man" is a historically circumscribed concept, one that is probably now doomed. As these "inventions" begin (and perhaps end?) at different dates, it is hard to see how they can be reconciled with an overarching system of epistemes understood in the sense of climates of discourse which regulate the component elements. This "reconciliation problem" tends to get sidestepped, for cultural relativists operate with one set of assumptions when trying to show that unit-ideas are culturally dependent and another when positing the epistemes, each of which should rule absolutely in its sphere. For it looks very much as if the developments isolated by Rougemont, Ariès, Barthes, and Foucault have the power to cross from one epistemic jurisdiction to another— that they are (*horresco referens*) "transhistorical." The difficulty, episteme-dependent formations that transcend their epistemic moorings, points up the fact that SC, unlike classical Marxism, has no serious and principled concept of the relation of base to superstructure. In any event, the nostalgic claim of some SCers that they remain "historical materialists," good followers of Marx, cannot be sustained.

What is the appeal of the "inventions?" Although much counterevidence has come to light, brandishing them has the attractions of a daredevil iconoclasm. More seriously, suggesting that a seeming cultural given is really a time-bound fashion may clear (or so the iconoclasts hope) the way for its demolition. It is this utopian desire to sweep away some parts of our inherited cultural amalgam that is, so to speak, the hidden agenda of SC. The selection of which categories are to be demolished and which ones to be left in peace reflects motives that are not explicitly justified—and may be obscure to SC adherents themselves. (There seems to be a tacit agreement that such categories as poverty and oppression must remain untouched, presumably because of their "emancipatory" potential.)

A major element in the SC reconstruction of the "modern homosexual" is its belief that a powerful and unprecedented intervention of the medical profession took place at the end of the nineteenth century.[33] The physicians are held to have seized control, imposing their own concepts on everyone else. This view has something to recommend it, for such medical experts as K.F.O. Westphal and Richard von Krafft-Ebing did have a major impact on the subject. Yet medical preoccupation with homosexual behavior is scarcely an innovation of late Victorian times. It can be traced to the formation of the Hippocratic Corpus in the fourth century B.C., a tradition continued by such ancient authorities as Soranus and Caelius Aurelianus. Reviving in the Renaissance, the matter received an influential reformulation at the hands of the forensic physician Paolo Zacchia (1584-1659).[34]

One revealing mistake appears over and over. The coinage of the word "homosexual," triumphantly proffered as encapsulating the process of medicalization, does no such thing. Károly Mária Kertbeny (a.k.a. Benkert), who created the word in 1869, was not—as often alleged—a medical doctor, but a translator and littérateur.[35] Moreover, the term owes its spread, in the first instance, to Gustav Jaeger, a zoologist and lifestyle advocate, and then to the nascent German gay movement. The physicians took up the neologism only slowly and in some instances reluctantly.[36]

---

[33] Jeffrey Weeks, *Coming Out: Homosexual Politics in Britain from the Nineteenth Century to the Present* (London: Quartet Books, 1977).

[34] For bibliographical details, see Wayne R. Dynes, *Homosexuality: A Research Guide* (New York: Garland Publishing, 1987), pp. 725-31. A monograph surveying medical ideas about same-sex behavior from Greco-Roman antiquity to the present is sorely needed. The empirical material ably marshalled by Gert Hekma, *Homosexualiteit, een medische reputatie: De uitdoktering van de homoseksueel in negentiende-eeuws Nederland* (Amsterdam: Sua, 1987) does not alter the overall picture of change within continuity.

[35] See Manfred Herzer, "Kertbeny and the Nameless Love," *Journal of Homosexuality* 12 (1985), pp. 1-26.

[36] See Jean-Claude Feray, "Une histoire critique du mot homosexualité," *Arcadie* no. 325 (January 1981), pp. 11-21, with continuation in the following three issues.

Not only does the SC medicalization hypothesis tend towards monothematism—the reduction of a constellation of causes to a single overriding one—it illustrates the fixation on "top-down" explanations. This point is aptly made by one student of the problem:

> [I]t would be wrong to assume . . . that doctors created and defined the identities of "inverts" and "homosexuals" at the turn of the century, that people uncritically internalized the new medical models, or even that homosexuality emerged as a fully defined category in the medical discourse of the 1870s. Such assumptions attribute inordinate power to ideology as an autonomous social force; they oversimplify the complex dialectic between social conditions, ideology, and consciousness which produced gay identities, and they belie the evidence of preexisting subcultures and identities contained in the literature itself.[37]

Much of the SC discussion has been focused on the last 130 years (or less) in Western Europe and North America. Yet even in this relatively recent slice of history a major shift, that from pederasty (man-boy relations) to mutual androphilia (adult-adult relations) as dominant modes of homosexual desire, has been occluded. It is sometimes said that SC can equip one for the study of earlier epochs in Western society and also for other societies; the methodology is fully transferable. Why then has this so rarely been done? Uncharitably perhaps, it has been suggested that the reason SCers are largely unwilling to study ancient Greece or medieval Islam is their reluctance to learn languages. Yet this is surely not the only explanation. SC, as a product of our own era, seems unsuited to scan other periods. Its temporal parochialism forfeits the corrective of a comparative perspective.

Many SC writings, especially those with a programmatic emphasis, betray an inorganic relation between data and

---

37 George Chauncey, Jr., "From Sexual Inversion to Homosexuality: Medicine and the Changing Conceptualization of Female Deviance," *Salmagundi* 58-59 (1982-83), p. 115.

theory. When concrete data are offered, their evidentiary value is often moot, because the information is presented selectively or merely emblematically. Here Foucault has set a bad example: as J. G. Merquior has shown, commonly the facts he adduces are either too thin on the ground or poorly suited to support the argument. To be sure, modern philosophers of science hold that the positing of theories often precedes the concrete exemplification that will determine whether they are viable or not. With touching faith, however, SC proponents revert to certain key statements of Foucault—one has been cited at the beginning of this essay—as if they were mantras efficacious by mere recitation. But proclamation must yield to proof. And in the phase of testing that is now required taboos are unacceptable; Social Construction must undergo global examination.

Stephen O. Murray has noted the reluctance of SCers to place the historically demarcated category of race under their microscopes.[38] Why is it that homosexuals should be told that their sense of identity is a mere illusion foisted on them by a passing convention, while blacks are not? One could in fact list a whole series of currently accepted categories, such as egalitarianism, freedom of speech, contraception, and ecology, which SC adherents conspicuously refrain from dissecting. Probably for political reasons, SCers are not keen on highlighting the relatively recent origins of the equation of lesbianism and male homosexuality. There seems a tacit understanding that concepts one endorses, regarded as inherently progressive and emancipatory, are to be left alone, while more ambivalent ones such as family, childhood, human nature, masculinity, and homosexuality must bear the full brunt of deconstruction.[39] As has been noted, SC is not consistently nominalist since it freely resorts to such

---

[38] Stephen O. Murray, "Fuzzy Sets and Abominations," *Man* 18 (1983), pp. 396-99.

[39] This group of terms suggests that one of the latent features of the SC enterprise may be a disguised manifestation of being uncomfortable about one's own homosexuality.

abstractions as capitalism, medicalization, subculture, and the like. There is the ultimate protected category of Social Construction itself: as a trend that is characteristic of its era, but scarcely an immutable part of the natural order, it too must submit to the knife.

Carefully inspected, most intellectual fashions harbor two key constituents. The first component is truistic, a set of principles about which there is little to disagree since they have long been accepted. The other component in the alloy is what makes it saleable: a series of modish propositions that garner temporary acclaim, but which time is likely to expose as tinsel. The first, the truistic part, allows the purveyors of the theory to fend off opponents by saying, in effect: "How can you disagree with something that all serious researchers have long accepted?" This point granted, they covertly shift the consensus attached to the first aspect to the other. The solidity of the truistic component serves to anchor the second, where the glitter of novelty beckons. Or so it seems for a time. One is reminded of the anecdote of the young scholar and the old scholar. Having confidently presented the manuscript of his dissertation to his mentor, the eager neophyte returns for the verdict. "There is much that is true and much that is new in your work," the master avers. "But that which is true is not new, and that which is new is not true."

As we have seen, the persuasive side of SC stems from its unacknowledged debt to Historicism. To this heritage it has added a triad of less plausible adjuncts: antibiologism, radical discontinuity, and selective nominalism. First, the matter of biology. SC adherents insist that homosexuality is not a transhistorical concept. Yet the capacity for homosexual response is found among so many cultures that one must at least entertain the possibility that it has a broad substratum. Moreover, if the "modern homosexual" is recent and culture-bound, the practice of pederasty is not; it is found among many, many unrelated cultures. The aversion to even positing a biological dimension—granted that this is not the only dimension—seems intellectually irresponsible.

As regards radical discontinuities, the legitimate question of where to make divisions in periodization has been transformed into a series of impermeable barriers.[40] No aspiring "transhistorical" ideas need apply for passports. Yet within the boundaries of a single episteme one can travel as much one likes; in fact circulation is obligatory, since paradigms are assumed to be hegemonic within the episteme, but not viable outside it.[41]

SC is selectively nominalist in that, as has just been noted, it holds that some categories, such as family, childhood, and homosexuality, must be deconstructed. They must be shown not to be a part of nature but a part of culture, with only a temporary validity. Yet other abstractions, cherished by the investigator, are shielded from such deconstruction (feudalism, capitalism, patriarchy, sexism, etc.).

Few critics would be so hostile as to deny SC any genuine insights. These, however, stem from a historiographic revolution of the eighteenth century. That the proponents of SC are the victims of a methodological amnesia not of their own making in no way exempts them from the obligation to own up to this debt, and to cease vaunting their purported innovations. The tragic flaw of SC is that it elevates its own partial and derivative perspective into a universal one, attempting to disarm critics by alleging that they are out of date.

The Appeal of SC

Scrutiny of a popular intellectual trend must not stop with the arguments themselves. For even when these are wanting, the task of specifying its appeal remains. For theories, even misguided ones, spread because they answer human needs.

---

[40] Substantial problems persist, in many instances, as to where even the break should be made. See, e.g., the case studies in Paul Egon Hübinger, ed., *Zur Frage der Periodengrenze zwischen Altertum und Mittelalter* (Darmstadt: Wissenschaftliche Buchgesellschaft, 1969).

[41] Here again there arises the conundrum that is inseparable from this kind of relativism. Since we too, the observers, are embedded in our own epistemic paradigms, how can we claim a suprahistorical objectivity?

More than a fad, the SC trend has secured the allegiance of some of our most earnest and energetic scholars. Wherein lies the attraction?

First, SC seems to avoid the temptation to regard persons as automata commanded by some general principle (economic man; the assertive competitor; the neurotic), perceiving them as capable of shaping their own consciousness. Since human beings have made the world, they can remake it. The recognition that traditional cultural arrangements, previously taken to be "natural" and unalterable, are only the impositions of ideological structures whose reign is doomed to pass away, seems empowering. This view of individuals responsible for their own destiny, paralleling Jean-Paul Sartre's existentialist ethics, can easily be pushed to an extreme: we can do or be almost anything we want, a notion that Michel Foucault sometimes espoused towards the end of his life. For most SC adherents awareness of overarching social determinants bars any wholehearted embrace of such romantic voluntarism. But it cannot be denied that a new sense of flexibility and openness is something to which SC recruits respond.

Over against the previous theme, which emphasizes agency and empowerment, another strand of SC tends to see the sexual actor as object, a passive recipient of "definitions" imposed on him or her from the top of the social pyramid, as the sodomite (decreed by the medieval church) and the invert (decreed by nineteenth-century physicians). How can these two opposed views, that of this paragraph and the preceding one, be reconciled? Of course they cannot be. Their coexistence may be taken either as a token of the dialectical subtlety of SC or of its philosophical confusion. The term dialectical reminds one that some of the SC adherents have had Marxist leanings, and both sides—voluntarism and determinism—may find succor in passages of Marx's writings. SC is generally, but vaguely assigned a position "on the left," but this perception is largely an expression of sentimental loyalties: the inherent adaptability of the project permits right, center, or politically neutral versions.

Another element of appeal is that of disinterested objectivity. In joining SC, which is not programmatically "gay scholarship," one no longer seems to be conducting a partisan or parochial search for mirror images of oneself ("Jonathan to Gide") through history,[42] but instead seeking to understand individuals who are fundamentally different. The contemplation of difference seems to attest a largeness of spirit. But here there is a risk of overestimating contrasts: just as the identificationist approach, which finds "gay people" throughout history, exaggerates similarity, the SC diversitarian one augments difference.

Several decades of discussion have made us familiar with the social-science thesis of human plasticity or malleability, which downgrades the sense of abiding character or core personality. Practitioners of the social sciences have a professional interest in human variability as a function of the social matrix; hence they are tempted to see people as mirrors reflecting contents projected on them. Thus while malleability offers a promise of openness, it does so at the cost of a reductive portrayal of the individual as a mere puppet jerked about by collective forces.

For those in the universities, there is the lure of participating in a prestigious academic fashion: the wave of "theory" generally of French origin as the names of Foucault, Derrida, Lacan, Deleuze and Guattari attest. The most common label for this bundle of trends, "deconstruction," complements (though less exactly than would be ideally desirable) Social

---

[42] The reference is to Noel I. Garde, *Jonathan to Gide: The Homosexual in History*, which is only the longest of a series of works providing potted biographies of famous homosexuals and lesbians, detaching them from their historical context and exhibiting them as forebears to be admired and emulated. The cherishing of such rosters seems to be a defensive stratagem of minorities in general. With the coming of gay liberation, this "our hidden history" approach shifted to a less elitist but still ahistorical mode; the representative work is Jonathan Katz, *Gay American History* (New York: Crowell, 1974), which presents a veritable pageant of "lesbians" and "gay men" in North America from 1566 onwards. (In his later work, Katz reversed himself 180 degrees, becoming an enthusiastic SCer.) Overcoming these potted biographical works would rank as a major service of SC—were it not for the fact that they were never espoused by serious historians.

Construction. These continental approaches first took root in French, English, and other humanities departments of universities as an insurgents' credo, the battle cry of graduate students and younger professors reacting against the entrenched old fogies of the establishment. Adhesion to "theory" thus bears the double cachet of meritorious service in class struggle (hence the bizarre notion that adepts of the elaborate jargon of these trends are somehow aiding the revolution) and also of rallying to modernity—or rather post-modernity (which is even better)—against creaky traditionalism.

In the background hovers the concept of scientific revolutions advocated by Professor Thomas Kuhn in his pivotal book *The Structure of Scientific Revolutions* .[43] Kuhn's thinking regards the history of science as a succession of "paradigms," which eventually play themselves out and are supplanted by radically different ones (the breaks in this uneven pattern are clearly avatars of Foucault's ruptures or *coupures*). Each of the ruling scientific paradigms, though it *may* represent an advance on its predecessor, comes to the fore through its imaginative, or if you will, ideological power. Without Kuhn the "discontinuous" Foucault would not have loomed so large in the anglophone countries that have welcomed him so generously. But while Kuhn and Foucault posit schemata with many paradigm shifts, SC has isolated only one rupture in its bailiwick: that which separates "modern homosexuality" from what preceded it. Repetition has given this break virtually the status of a B.C.-A.D. separation.

In view of the Marxist background of some SCers, Antonio Gramsci's notion of hegemony may be relevant. According to Gramsci (1891-1937), each ruling class strives to prevail not only through force but by promulgating an ideology that simplifies its task of domination. The "modern homosexual" would rank as one component of such an ideology. The influence of the Italian Marxist theorist, pervasive in the

---

[43] Thomas Kuhn, *The Structure of Scientific Revolutions*, (Chicago: University of Chicago Press, 1962).

1970s, may help to account for the "top-down" indoctrination posited by SC. Getting new sexual paradigms off the ground is the job of theologians, physicians, and scholars, rather than of ordinary people guided by folklore, popular religion, and social practice.

Concluding Reflections

Once its various facets have been viewed, the intellectual genealogy of SC brands it as no dazzling innovation, but in its modest core a tried-and-true specific against historical anachronism. It has succeeded in replacing a seventeenth-century theory—the Exemplar gambit surviving in popular gay writings—with an anemic and adulterated version of an eighteenth-century theory—Historicism. Some reasons have been offered above as to why some have yearned to erect the partial, often banal truths purveyed by SC into a dogmatic, and sometimes intolerant system.

One final line of defense remains. When all is said and done, does not SC still possess inherent heuristic value? Its flaws notwithstanding, can SC not boast a catalytic power of generating new research? The history of science shows many instances of theories that were "wrong" but still productive. For example, despite its enshrinement of the geocentric principle, Ptolemaic astronomy led to many observations that ultimately supplied data for a new interpretation. Thus we must not foreclose the potential of SC to generate important new work, apart from reservations we may have about its ultimate standing as a theory. The story of the project goes back now a decade with the publications of Jeffrey Weeks and Kenneth Plummer. Formerly a decade's work was not much, but in today's intense world of scholarship it seems a fair trial. And the jury's verdict is, at best, "not proven."[44]

---

[44] There is still no adequate comprehensive bibliography of the SC controversy. Surveys and lists produced by SC adherents tend to be restricted to one side, their own.

Social Construction shares with the other "post-modern" projects a bracing sense that it has embarked on uncharted seas, setting a course that is completely unprecedented. Future historians will probably subject such assertions to the glaring light of intellectual history, pitilessly exposing their propounders' debt to earlier thinking. Space forbids further pursuit of these lines of inquiry. However, our discovery of the Historicist precedents of Social Construction suggests that its claims of absolute novelty are at best public relations, at worst willful ignorance. SC constitutes part—though an imperfectly realized part—of a *methodologia perennis*. But herein may lie a consolation: if SC can come to terms with its own "hidden heritage" it may yet contribute to the advance of knowledge. Recently, the sociologist David F. Greenberg has shown that a much-modified SC approach can, in combination with research stemming from other sources, offer some useful pointers to deepening our understanding of non-Western and non-recent societies.[45]

A New Template

Further empirical research is badly needed, and its results are sure to bring forth surprises. Yet it may be helpful to ponder a five-level model for the investigations of sexual meanings and behaviors in historical context.

1) The universal horizon grounded in biology. This most general level recognizes that in human beings the libido emerges forcefully in adolescence and is capable of direction to a single gender, though such narrowing is not universal. Further investigation of biological parameters is not to be discouraged but encouraged. There is also the possibility of detection of universals that are not, in any obvious sense, biological, as some universals of language reflect principles of logic also observed by thinking machines, which are not biological. Such principles appear to be suprabiological.

---

[45] David Greenberg, *The Construction of Homosexuality* (Chicago: Chicago University Press, 1988).

2) *Kulturkreise* (supraregional cultural entities). As employed by some Central European ethnologists, the *Kulturkreis* is a large complex of societies in which certain cultural constants can be observed. Examples are the Bantu-speaking peoples of southern Africa and the Subarctic peoples. The berdache phenomenon, which is historically recorded not only in North America but also in Western Siberia and Madagascar, would be a good instance of a same-sex *Kulturkreis*. Another is the *kedeshim* (cult prostitutes) who are found in many cultures of classical antiquity. The possibility of "submerged *Kulturkreise*," where only a few islands survive of once much larger complexes, must be entertained. If Bernard Sergent is right, the institution of pederasty, known from the record for only a few Indo-European peoples, is the relict of a once-vast family.[46]

3) Migration of individual motifs across cultural boundaries. For example, the category of the "unnatural" was first applied to same-sex behavior by the philosopher Plato and his circle in classical Greece. It found its way into the Pauline corpus of the New Testament, and then permeated medieval Scholasticism which transmitted it to the present, when it has achieved some global penetration.[47] Of course such "unit-ideas" undergo modification according to context, but continuity must also be recognized. If one is studying the unnatural in, say, nineteenth-century texts, it does not suffice to limit one's horizon to that century, especially since widespread reading of the classics linked the era to antiquity. The history-of-ideas methodology developed many years ago by the philosopher Arthur O. Lovejoy offers guidance in this approach.[48]

------

[46] Bernard Sergent, *Homosexuality in Greek Myth* (Boston: Beacon Press, 1986).

[47] See Wayne R. Dynes, "Nature and the Unnatural," *Encyclopedia of Homosexuality*, pp. 879-81.

[48] See Arthur Lovejoy, *Essays in the History of Ideas* (Baltimore: Johns Hopkins University Press, 1948).

4) Cultural epochs. There are attitudes that are specific to the later Western Middle Ages and the early Renaissance, to cite but two examples. In investigating these, care must be taken not to overinsulate them in the manner of Foucault's epistemes. One must also be wary of a too-easy acceptance of economic and social determinism, where "superstructure" attitudes simply mimic the structure of the all-determining *Unterbau* or base. The fixing of a pervasive pattern of such determinisms is the Holy Grail of the historical materialists. Without denying such dependent relationships in this or that case, one must be skeptical of positing any universal validity for the scheme, especially in view of levels 1-3.

5) Temporary fashions lasting only one or two generations. The "hippie" organization of sexuality of the 1960s and 70s (though it has roots and successors like anything else) seems a relatively limited phenomenon. So may be the molly subculture of early eighteenth-century England, which was snuffed out before it had much chance to develop.[49]

The advantage of this template (1-5) is that it favors investigations in all time frames, from the longest (humanity itself) to the shortest (a single generation). Given its general character, the template does not anticipate constants, but allows one to correlate those that seem to be emerging, however tentatively. Investigation of the full range of same-sex behavior remains at an early stage. For scholars the ongoing imperative is twofold: to find more data and to fashion better lenses for their interpretation.

---

[49] Documented in Randolph Trumbach, "London's Sodomites: Homosexual Behavior in the Eighteenth Century," *Journal of Social History* 11 (1977), pp. 1-33.

CHAPTER 10:
Steven Epstein
Gay Politics, Ethnic Identity:
The Limits of Social Constructionism

I seem to be surrounded at all times in all ways by who I am. . .
It goes with me wherever I go. . . and my life is gay and where I
go I take my gay life with me. I don't consciously sit and think
while I'm eating soup that I'm eating this "gayly," but, you
know, it surrounds me.

To me being gay is like having a tan. When you are in a gay
relationship, you're gay. When you're not in a gay relationship,
you're not gay.

As I sit at a concert or engage volubly in a conversation in the
office or at home, or as I look up from my newspaper and glance
at the people occupying the seats of the bus, my mind will
suddenly jump from the words, the thoughts, or the music
around me, and with horrible impact I will hear, pounding within
myself, the fateful words: *I am different.* I am different from
these people, and I must always be different from them. I do not
belong to them, nor they to me.

There's nothing in me that is not in everybody else, and nothing
in everybody else that is not in me. We're trapped in language,
of course. But homosexual is not a noun. At least not in my
book.

What does it mean to be gay? Do lesbians and gay men
constitute a "deviant subculture"? A "sexual minority"? A
privileged "revolutionary subject"? Is homosexuality a

This essay originally appeared in *Socialist Review* 93/94
(May-August 1987), pp. 9-54 and is reprinted with
permission.

"preference" (like a taste for chocolate ice cream)? Or perhaps an "orientation" (a fixed position relative to the points of a compass)? Or maybe it's a "lifestyle," like being a "yuppie" or a surfer? Is being gay something that has some importance? Or is it a relatively inconsequential difference?

The gay men and women quoted above are undoubtedly not a representative sample, but the range of contradictory opinions certainly testifies to the difficulties involved in answering these questions.[1] And the types of disagreements observed in these quotes are present not only between individuals, but also within them. Most people who identify as gay or practice homosexuality adopt some variety of relatively inconsistent positions regarding their identity over the course of time, often depending on the needs of the moment. These contradictions are paralleled by the attitudes of homophobic opponents of the gay movement, which are typically even less consistent; for example, one frequently hears the belief that homosexuality is an "illness" combined with a simultaneous concern that youngsters can be "seduced" into it. The whole issue, it seems, is a terminological and conceptual minefield. Yet given the startling newness of the idea of there being such a thing as a "gay identity"—neither that term, nor "lesbian identity," nor "homosexual identity" appeared in writing by or about gays and lesbians before the mid-1970's—the confusion is hardly surprising.[2]

This article does not address the question of what "causes" homosexuality, or what "causes" heterosexuality. Instead,

---

[1] The four quotes are, in order, (1) an unnamed lesbian, interviewed by Barbara Ponse in *Identities in the Lesbian World: The Social Construction of Self* (Westport, Conn.: Greenwood Press, 1978), p. 178; (2) a different lesbian interview subject, quoted Ponse, p. 189; (3) Donald Webster Cory, pseud., *The Homosexual in America* (New York: Castle Books, 1951), p. 9; (4) James Baldwin, interviewed by Richard Goldstein, "Go the Way Your Blood Beats: An Interview with James Baldwin," *Village Voice*, June 26, 1984, p. 14.

[2] Vivienne C. Cass, "Homosexual Identity: A Concept in Need of a Definition," *Journal of Homosexuality* 9 (Winter 1983/Spring 1984), p. 105.

what I seek to explore is how lesbians and gay men, on a day-to-day basis, interpret their sexual desires and practices so as to situate themselves in the world; how these self-understandings relate to social theories about homosexuals; and how both the theories and the self-understandings can shape—or block—different varieties of political activism by gays.[3] I take as given that power inheres in the ability to name, and that what we call ourselves has implications for political practice. An additional assumption is that lesbians and gay men in our society consciously seek, in a wide variety of ways, to *legitimate* their forms of sexual expression, by developing explanations, strategies, and defenses. These legitimations are articulated both on an individual level ("This is who I am, and this is why I am that way") and on a collective level ("This is what we are, and here is what we should do"). Legitimation strategies play a mediating function between self-understanding and political programs, and between groups and their individual members.

Existing theories of sexuality fail to address these concerns adequately. For some time now, sexual theory has been preoccupied with a debate between "essentialism" and "constructionism"—a debate which, despite its importance in reorienting our thinking about sexuality, may well have outlived its usefulness. "Essentialists" treat sexuality as a biological force and consider sexual identities to be cognitive realizations of genuine, underlying differences; "constructionists," on the other hand, stress that sexuality, and

---

[3] This analysis does not systematically explore the self-understandings or politics of people who identify as bisexuals, though the category "bisexual" itself is important to the discussion. For an analysis of bisexuality that touches on many of the issues explored here, see Lisa Orlando, "Bisexuality: Loving Whom We Chose," *Gay Community News*, February 25, 1984, p. 6. At times, I will discuss gay men separately from lesbians; at other points, the analysis will refer to both at the same time. While this may be confusing from an analytic standpoint, it seems unavoidable if one wants to avoid simplistic assumptions of parallelism between experiences of gay men and women.

sexual identities, are social constructions, and belong to the world of culture and meaning, not biology. In the first case, there is considered to be some "essence" within homosexuals that makes them homosexual—some gay "core" of their being, or their psyche, or their genetic make-up. In the second case, 'homosexual,' 'gay,' and 'lesbian' are just labels, created by cultures and applied to the self.

Both essentialist and constructionist views are ingrained in the folk understandings of homosexuality in our society— often in a highly contradictory fashion. In a recent letter to Ann Landers, "Worried in Montana" expresses concern that her fourteen-year-old son may be "seduced" into homosexuality (folk constructionism) by the boy's friend, who she has "no question" is gay, because of his "feminine mannerisms" (folk essentialism). Ann reassures the mother that the only way her son would turn out to be gay is if "the seeds of homosexuality were already present" (folk essentialism). At the same time, she questions the mother's certainty about the sexual orientation of the friend, claiming that it is "presumptuous" to label a fourteen-year-old as "gay" (folk constructionism).[4] But if such inconsistent views can at times exist side by side, it is equally true that at other times they clash violently. Homosexuals who are advised to "change" and become straight, for example, might have more than a passing investment in the claim that they've "always been that way"—that their gayness is a fundamental part of who they "really are."

This debate is not restricted to the field of sexuality; it parallels similar ones that have taken place in many other domains, including gender, race, and class. For example, while some feminists have proposed that qualities such as nurturance constitute a feminine "essence," others have insisted that any differences between men and women, beyond the strictly biological, are the products of culture and history:

---

[4] *Oakland Tribune*, March 6, 1987, p. F-7.

men and women have no essential "nature."[5] But while the issues may be generalizable, they have a special salience for contemporary gay politics, because of a peculiar historical irony. With regard to sexuality, the constructionist critique of essentialism has become the received wisdom in left academic circles. And yet, curiously, the historical ascendancy of the new constructionist orthodoxy has paralleled a growing inclination within the gay movement in the United States to understand itself and project an image of itself in ever more "essentialist" terms.

As many observers have noted, gays in the 1970's increasingly came to conceptualize themselves as a legitimate minority group, having a certain quasi-"ethnic" status, and deserving the same protections against discrimination that are claimed by other groups in our society.[6] To be gay, then, became something like being Italian, black, or Jewish. The "politics of identity" have crystallized around a notion of "gayness" as a real, and not arbitrary, difference. So while constructionist theorists have been preaching the gospel that the hetero/homosexual distinction is a social fiction, gays and lesbians, in everyday life and in political action, have been busy hardening the categories. Theory, it seems, has not been informing practice. Perhaps the practitioners are misguided; or perhaps there is something about the strict constructionist

---

[5] See Nancy Chodorow, "Feminism and Difference: Gender, Relation, and Difference in Psychoanalytic Perspective," *Socialist Review* 46 (July-August 1979), pp. 51-69. For an analogous discussion in the domain of race, see Michael Omi and Howard Winant, *Racial Formation in the United States: From the 1960s to the 1980s* (New York: Routledge and Kegan Paul, 1986), p. 68 and *passim*. For class, see Ernesto Laclau and Chantal Mouffe, *Hegemony and Socialist Strategy: Towards a Radical Democratic Theory of Politics* (London: Verso, 1985) or Pierre Bourdieu, "The Social Space and the Genesis of Groups," *Theory and Society* 14:6 (November 1985), pp. 723-744. Similar arguments have taken place with regard to mental illness, alcoholism, and drug addiction.

[6] See, in particular, Dennis Altman, *The Homosexualization of America* (Boston: Beacon Press, 1982).

perspective which neither adequately describes the experiences of gays and lesbians nor speaks to their need to understand and legitimate their places in the world.[7]

To address these questions, my analysis will proceed as follows. First, I will recapitulate the constructionist-essentialist debate and discuss why neither side proves altogether useful in understanding or guiding contemporary gay politics. Then, I will argue that other theoretical perspectives on identity and ethnicity can provide valuable help in understanding recent political trends and in defending some version of an "ethnic/minority group model." In the process, I will return to the theoretical debate, examine some more subtle expressions of it, and show that the "ethnic"model is congruent with a modified constructionist position. Finally, I will explore the implications of this analysis for the future directions of gay politics.

The Debate

At heart, the theoretical debate is located on the all-too-familiar terrain of nature vs. nurture. As against the essentialist position that sexuality is a biological force seeking expression in ways that are preordained, constructionists treat sexuality as a blank slate, capable of bearing whatever meanings are generated by the society in question. In addition, the debaters line up on opposite sides of an old

---

[7] I do not mean to suggest that constructionism is the *only* theoretical perspective on homosexuality proposed by left academics. Clearly, feminist theory has played a significant role in informing debates on sexual politics. However, feminism has often been guilty of "gender reduction" by treating questions of sexual identity as epiphenomena of gender debates. To the extent that there is a coherent theoretical perspective on homosexuality *as* homosexuality, it is constructionism. For a discussion of the contributions and limitation of feminist theory (and, somewhat analogously, Marxism) to the study of sex, see Gayle Rubin, "Thinking Sex: Notes for a Radical Theory of the Politics of Sexuality," in *Pleasure and Danger: Exploring Female Sexuality*, Carol Vance, ed. (Boston: Routledge and Kegan Paul, 1974), pp. 300-309.

epistemological argument concerning categorization.[8] Essentialists are "realists" in their insistence that social categories (e.g., "homosexual," "heterosexual," "bisexual") reflect an underlying reality of difference; constructionists are "nominalists" in their contrary assertion that such categories are arbitrary, human-imposed divisions of the continuum of experience—categories create social types, rather than revealing them.

"Essentialism" is often equated with "traditional" views on sexuality in general, but can be linked specifically to the work of nineteenth-century "sexologists," such as Havelock Ellis and Krafft-Ebing; to certain aspects of Freud's work; and to deterministic theories such as sociobiology.[9] Essentialist views stress the "natural" dimensions of sex; and essentialist conceptions of homosexuality seek to account for such persons on the basis of some core of difference, whether that difference be hormonal, or medical, or a consequence of early child-rearing, or "just the way we are."

The constructionist critique of sexual essentialism has played an important role in debunking this traditional view. Much like essentialism, though, constructionism should not be thought of as a specific school, but rather as a broader tendency of thinking that has found representations in a number of disciplines. At the risk of oversimplifying, it can be said that recent historical and sociological work on gays and

---

[8] This argument about "nominalism" and "realism" is taken from John Boswell, "Revolutions, Universals and Sexual Categories," *Salmagundi* 58-59 (1982-83), pp. 89-113. See also Ian Hacking, "Making Up People," in *Reconstructing Individualism: Autonomy, Individuality, and the Self in Western Thought*, Thomas Heller, Morton Sosna, and David Wellbery, eds. (Stanford: Stanford University Press, 1986), pp. 222-36, reprinted in this volume.

[9] Gay and lesbian exponents of essentialist positions include John Boswell, *Christianity, Social Tolerance and Homosexuality* (Chicago: University of Chicago Press, 1980) and Adrienne Rich, "Compulsory Heterosexuality and Lesbian Existence," in *Powers of Desire: The Politics of Sexuality*, Ann Snitow, et al., eds. (New York: Monthly Review Press, 1983), pp. 177-206.

lesbians in Western societies[10] traces its roots to two schools of sociology: *symbolic interactionists*, particularly the pathbreaking work of John Gagnon and William Simon on "sexual conduct"; and *labeling theorists*, especially Mary McIntosh's analysis of the "homosexual role" and Kenneth Plummer on "sexual stigma."[11] To a lesser degree, analyses of sexual constructionism in Western societies have also been influenced by the cross-cultural work of constructionist anthropology; these studies of "sex/gender systems" trace a somewhat different history from the mid-century cultural anthropology of Boas, Benedict, and Mead.[12] Finally, in the 1980's, the work of Michel Foucault has become a new

---

[10] Prime examples of this recent scholarship would be Jeffrey Weeks, *Coming Out: Homosexual Politics in Britain from the Nineteenth Century to the Present* (London: Quartet Books, 1977), John D'Emilio, *Sexual Politics, Sexual Communities: The Making of a Homosexual Minority in the United States, 1940-1970* (Chicago: University of Chicago Press, 1983) and the essays in Kenneth Plummer, ed., *The Making of the Modern Homosexual*, (Totowa, NJ: Barnes and Noble, 1981). Many other examples could be added. In the bibliography to *Coming Out*, Weeks identifies the main influences on his thinking as Plummer, McIntosh, and Gagnon and Simon (p. 239); in later essays, he has testified to the importance of Foucault. D'Emilio, p. 4n, cites the same casts of characters, with a few additions, such as Jonathan Katz and Estelle Freedman.

[11] John Gagnon and William Simon, *Sexual Conduct* (Chicago: Aldine, 1973), Mary McIntosh, "The Homosexual Role," *Social Problems* 17 (Fall 1968), pp. 262-270, reprinted this volume, and Ken Plummer, *Sexual Stigma* (London: Routledge and Kegan Paul, 1975).

[12] The phrase 'sex/gender system' is from Gayle Rubin, "The Traffic in Women: Notes on the 'Political Economy' of Sex," in *Towards an Anthropology of Women*, Rayna Reiter, ed. (New York, Monthly Review, 1975), pp. 157-210. Good examples of anthropological studies in this vein include the essays in Sherry B. Ortner and Harriet Whitehead, eds., *Sexual Meanings: The Cultural Construction of Gender and Sexuality* (Cambridge: Cambridge University Press, 1981). Anthropological constructionism escapes some, but not all of the problems I identify in the sociological and historical forms, for reasons I return to in the conclusion.

rallying point for sexual constructionism, and has served as the impetus for further investigations.[13] I will briefly discuss some of these sources of constructionism, in order to describe the main contours of the perspective as it has evolved.

In keeping with the central thrust of symbolic interactionism, constructionists propose that sexuality be investigated on the level of subjective meaning. Sexual acts have no inherent meaning, and in fact, no act is inherently sexual. Rather, in the course of interactions and over the course of time, individuals and societies spin webs of significance around the realm designated as "sexual." People *learn* to be sexual, Gagnon and Simon stress, in the same way they learn everything else: "Without much reflection, they pick up directions from their social environment."[14] As actors attribute subjective meanings to their interactions with others, they begin to develop "sexual scripts" which guide them in their future sexual interactions. Unlike "drives," which are understood as fixed essences destined to seek a particular expression, "scripts" are highly variable and fluid, subject to constant revision and editing.[15]

Central to the constructionist critique of essentialist "drive theory" is a repudiation of the popular imagery of sex. In this view we tend to see sex as

> an overpowering, instinctual force, whose characteristics are built into the biology of the human animal, which shapes human institutions and whose will will out, either in the form of direct sexual expression, or if blocked, in the form of perversion or neuroses.[16]

---

[13] Michel Foucault, *The History of Sexuality, Volume I: An Introduction*, Robert Hurley, trans., (New York: Pantheon, 1978).

[14] John Gagnon, *Human Sexualities* (Chicago: Scott, Foresman and Co., 1977), p. 2, quoted in Kenneth Plummer, "Symbolic Interactionism and Sexual Conduct," in *Human Sexual Relations*, Mike Brake, ed. (New York, Pantheon, 1982), p. 226.

[15] Gagnon and Simon, *Sexual Conduct*, p. 19.

[16] Jeffrey Weeks, "The Development of Sexual Theory and Sexual Politics," in *Human Sexual Relations*, p. 294.

In this view, which preceded but was popularized by Freud, "society" must restrain "sexuality," and social order depends on the proper channeling of sexual energy. In the left-wing version of the same ideology, "sex radicals" such as Willhelm Reich and Herbert Marcuse have treated sexual repression as the liberator from bondage.[17] More generally, in the popularizations of this imagery, the sex drive is treated as some sort of magical energy; hence the idea that athletes shouldn't have sex before the big game, or that masturbation constitutes a waste of one's potency. In all these views the sex drive is credited "with enormous—almost mystical—power."[18]

While symbolic interactionists debunked the notion of a "natural" sexuality, it was labeling theory that first provided the means to challenge essentialist views of "the homosexual" as a natural, transhistorical category. This challenge, which lies at the very crux of the constructionist argument about homosexuality, can be expressed in the following claim: although every known society has examples of homosexual *behavior*, only recently has there arisen a conception of "the homosexual" as a distinct type of *person*. In Mary McIntosh's important essay on the modern "homosexual role," her immediate target was the medical conception of the homosexual person. McIntosh argued vehemently against the prevailing medical logic:

> Many scientists and ordinary people assume that there are two kinds of people in the world: homosexuals and heterosexuals. Some of them recognize that homosexual feelings and behaviour are not confined to the persons they would like to call "homosexuals" and that some of these persons do not actually engage in homosexual behaviour. This should pose a crucial problem, but they evade the crux by retaining their assumption

---

[17] Wilhelm Reich, *The Sexual Revolution* (New York: Farrar, Straus and Giroux, 1969) and Herbert Marcuse, *Eros and Civilization* (Boston: Beacon Press, 1966).

[18] Weeks, "Development of Sexual Theory," p. 295.

and puzzling over the question of how to tell whether someone is "really" homosexual or not. Lay people too will discuss whether a certain person is "queer" in much the same way as they might question whether a certain pain indicated cancer. And in much the same way they will often turn to scientists or to medical men for a surer diagnosis.[19]

In place of this essentialism, McIntosh argues that "the homosexual" has come to occupy a distinct "social role" in modern societies. Since homosexual *practices* are widespread but socially threatening, a special, stigmatized category of *individuals* is created so as to keep the rest of society pure. By this means, a "clear-cut, publicized and recognizable threshold between permissible and impermissible behaviour" is constructed; anyone who begins to approach that threshold is immediately threatened with being labeled a full-fledged deviant: one of "them."[20] A homosexual identity, then, is created not so much through homosexual activity per se (what labeling theorists would call "primary deviance"), but through the reactions of the deviant individual to being so described, and through the internalization of the imposed categorization ("secondary deviance").

These sociological theories were employed by historians who, in empirical studies, have traced the genesis of the modern homosexual.[21] More recently, the work of Foucault has helped us to theorize a historical dimension to the constructionist arguments. According to Foucault, sexuality in the modern Western world has been the site of an explosion of discourses of power and knowledge; sexual meanings, sexual doctrines, and sexual beings have been generated incessantly by a culture that has come to be obsessed with the significance of the sexual, has elevated it to unprecedented dimensions, and has sought in it "the truth of our being."[22]

---

[19] McIntosh, "Homosexual Role," p. 182.

[20] *Ibid.*, pp. 183-184.

[21] The first and most influential of these was Weeks's study of Britain, *Coming Out.*

[22] Foucault, *History of Sexuality.*

Foucault has tried to use this perspective to account for the origin of "the homosexual." In Foucault's view, the transformation from sexual behavior to sexual personhood is attributable to three factors: the increasing importance attached to sexuality in general; a more widespread transformation in structures of social control, from control that operates through sanctions against specific acts to control based on highly individualized discipline; and the growing power of professionals, and especially doctors, to define social problems and enforce social norms. In an oft-cited passage, Foucault argues:

> As defined by the ancient civil or canonical codes, sodomy was a category of forbidden acts; their perpetrator was nothing more than the juridical subject of them. The nineteenth-century homosexual became a personage, a past, a case history, and a childhood, in addition to being a type of life, a life form, and a morphology. . . Homosexuality appeared as one of the forms of sexuality when it was transposed from the practice of sodomy onto a kind of interior androgyny, a hermaphrodism of the soul. The sodomite has been a temporary aberration; the homosexual was now a species.[23]

As summarized in this brief sketch, constructionism posed a serious challenge to the prevailing essentialist orthodoxy concerning homosexuality. Where essentialism took for granted that all societies consist of people who are either heterosexuals or homosexuals (with perhaps some bisexuals), constructionists demonstrated that the notion of "the homosexual" is a sociohistorical product, not universally applicable, and worthy of explanation in its own right. And where essentialism would treat the self-attribution of a "homosexual identity" as unproblematic—as simply the conscious recognition of a true, underlying "orientation"—constructionism focused attention on identity as a complex developmental outcome, the consequence of an interactive

---

[23] *Ibid.*, p. 43, the chapter containing this passage is reprinted in this volume.

process of social labeling and self-identification. Finally, by refusing to privilege any particular expression of sexuality as "natural," constructionism shifted the whole framework of debate on the question of homosexuality: instead of asking, why is there homosexuality? the constructionists took variation for granted and asked, why is there homophobia?[24]

Unfortunately, while constituting a significant advance in our understanding of sexuality and homosexuality, constructionism also posed some inherent difficulties. However, before attempting a critique of constructionism, it is important to situate the debate within a social and political context. Rather than juxtaposing ideas in the abstract, we need to examine the politics of gay communities during the postwar period and the connection between those politics and the evolving theoretical stances.

The Political Context

As Foucault notes, the labeling practices of the nineteenth-century doctors who invented the term "homosexual" created the possibility for a "reverse affirmation," by which the stigmatized could gradually begin to organize around their label and assert the legitimacy of that identity.[25] Foucault, however, neglects the material bases for these practices. As Jeffrey Weeks and John D'Emilio have argued, the medical categorization itself presupposed certain social conditions, including changes in family structure that were linked to the Industrial Revolution, and urbanization, which provided the social space for a homosexual subculture to develop.[26] By mid-century, such subcultures were firmly established in most major cities in the United States.

---

[24] Tomás Almaguer, "Conceptualizing Sexual Stratification: Notes Toward a Sociology of Sexuality" (unpublished essay, 1986), p. 8.

[25] *History of Sexuality*, p. 101.

[26] Weeks, *Coming Out*, p. 2 and parts I-III, D'Emilio, *Sexual Politics*, pp. 9-22; also D'Emilio, "Capitalism and Gay Identity," in *Powers of Desire*, pp. 100-113.

Homosexual politics in the 1950's and early 1960's preached liberal tolerance and stressed the goal of integration into the larger society.[27]   The birth of the gay liberation movement marked a radical break with these accommodationist politics.   When American gay liberation burst out of quiescence with the Stonewall riot in Greenwich Village in 1969, the politics that were espoused represented a mixture of the new-left ideology and the left Freudian arguments that anticipated constructionism.[28] Activists with groups such as the Gay Liberation Front portrayed homosexuals as revolutionary subjects who were uniquely situated to advance the cause of sexual liberation for society as a whole. However, the notion of "the homosexual" as a distinct type of person was specifically repudiated, in favor of a left Freudian view of human sexuality as "polymorphously perverse."   In utopian fashion, activists prophesied the disappearance of both "the homosexual" and "the heterosexual" through the abolition of constraining categories:

> The reason so few of us are bisexual is because society made such a big stink about homosexuality that we got forced into seeing ourselves as either straight or nonstraight. . . We'll be gay until everyone has forgotten that it's an issue. Then we'll begin to be complete people.[29]

Or in the words of a lesbian activist:

> I will tell you what we want, we radical homosexuals: not for you to tolerate us, to accept us, but to understand us. And this you can do only by becoming one of us. We want to reach the

---

[27] Jeffrey Escoffier, "Sexual Revolutions and the Politics of Gay Identity," *Socialist Review* 82-83 (July-October 1985), pp. 119-153 and *Sexual Politics*, chapters 5-7.

[28] The most influential of the left Freudians was Herbert Marcuse, *Eros and Civilization*.

[29] Carl Wittman, "Refugees from Amerika: A Gay Manifesto," in *The Homosexual Dialectic*, Joseph A. McCaffrey, ed. (Englewood Cliffs, NJ: Prentice-Hall, 1972), p. 159.

homosexuals entombed in you, to liberate our brothers and sisters, locked in the prisons of your skulls. . . We will never go straight until you go gay. As long as you divide yourselves, we will be divided from you—separated by a mirror trick of your mind.[30]

Perhaps the most sophisticated expression of this ideology is Dennis Altman's, whose *Homosexual: Oppression and Liberation* (1971) remains the classic statement of early post-Stonewall gay male politics. In the final chapter, entitled "The End of the Homosexual?", Altman looks forward to not only the abolition of sexual categorization but also the elimination of "masculinity" and "femininity," along with the creation of a "new human" for whom such distinctions would simply be irrelevant.[31]

While such arguments are not exactly "constructionist"— Gagnon and Simon, after all, would criticize the lingering essentialism of the left Freudians such as Marcuse—they resonated fairly closely with the gay and lesbian constructionist history that began to be written soon afterward; this history, in fact, was inspired by the events of the early gay liberation movement, and many of the historians had been active in it from the start. What the liberationist position shared with the constructionist arguments was an insistence that sexual typologies are social, rather than natural facts; that these categories are highly fluid; and that they need to be transcended. Both shared a sense of the openness of historical possibilities that was inspired by the political climate of the day.

Needless to say, the radical liberationist politics did not achieve its goals. However, the greater irony is that, to the extent that the activists did succeed in advancing the situation of gays and lesbians, they undermined the logical supports for their own arguments. That is, simply by advancing the cause

---

[30] Quoted in Ponse, *Identities*, p. 95.

[31] Dennis Altman, *Homosexual: Oppression and Liberation* (New York: Avon, 1971). Altman's radical Freudian views can be seen in the frequent references to Marcuse.

of gay liberation, the liberationists helped to further the notion, among both gays and straights, that gays constitute a distinct social group with their own political and social interests. This is a familiar dilemma, and one that is by no means peculiar to the gay movement: How do you protest a socially imposed categorization, except by organizing around the category? Just as blacks cannot fight the arbitrariness of racial classification without organizing *as blacks*, so gays could not advocate the overthrow of the sexual order without making their gayness the very basis of their claims.

The 1970's witnessed a phenomenal growth in the institutionalization of a gay identity, as "deviant subcultures" gave way to "gay communities." And contrary to the "proto-constructionist" perspective that had been espoused by the early liberationists, the next generation of gay activists embraced a conception of gay identity that was significantly essentialist. To some extent, these essentialist notions had been around from the start; and in the political climate of the late 1970's, one can imagine why they would have more appeal than the utopian vision of the early liberationism, with its focus on historical openness. What this meant, however, is that a disjuncture developed between theory and practice: in place of the rough congruence between early gay liberation politics and evolving constructionist theory, we now find a growing tension between an evolving essentialist politics and a constructionist theory that is firmly in place.

Each variant of essentialism is based on some sort of legitimation strategy. In some cases, activists have legitimated their claims with reference to the trans-historical unity of homosexuals or their trans-cultural functional role. Perhaps most prominently, Adrienne Rich has proposed the existence of a "lesbian continuum" which links the resisters of heterosexist patriarchy across cultures and throughout history.[32] In a somewhat analogous vein, a male activist

---

[32] Rich, "Compulsory Heterosexuality." Other forms of lesbian essentialism are actually gender essentialism, stressing the superiority of the intrinsic qualities of women. For a striking example, see Karla
--->

claimed: "We look forward to regaining our ancient historical role as medicine people, healers, prophets, shamans, and sorcerers."[33] Others have sought legitimations of a more "scientific" sort, making reference to a biological or genetic basis for homosexuality. Most typically, and far more usefully, gays and lesbians have adopted what Altman has in recent writings characterized as an "ethnic" identification.[34]

This "ethnic" self-characterization by gays and lesbians has a clear political utility, for it has permitted a form of group organizing that is particularly suited to the American experience, with its history of civil-rights struggles and ethnic-based, interest-group competition. In fact, an irony that Altman points out is that, by appealing to civil rights, gays as a group have been able to claim a legitimacy that homosexuals as individuals are often denied:

> One of the paradoxes of the present situation is that even where the old laws defining homosexual behavior as a major crime remain, there is a growing de facto recognition of a gay minority, deserving of full civil and political rights *as* a minority. Thus for years the mayor of New York could proclaim an official Gay Pride Week while the very people being honored remained criminals under state law.[35]

Gay people's sense of themselves as belonging to a "minority group" was not altogether new; this view had been stated publicly at least as early 1951, when Donald Webster Cory discussed the "invisible minority" in *The Homosexual in*

Jay, "No Man's Land," in *Lavender Culture*, Karla Jay and Allen Young, eds. (New York: Jove, 1978), pp. 48-68.

[33] Quoted in Altman, *Homosexualization of America*, p. 161.

[34] This is one of the prime arguments made by Altman in *Homosexualization of America*, written a decade after his earlier "liberationist" book.

[35] Altman, *Homosexualization of America*, p. 9.

America.[36] However, this self-conception could not really take root at a time when the institutional and cultural content of the gay subculture was so relatively impoverished. By the late 1970's, however, the "ethnic" self-understanding truly seemed to correspond to the reality of the burgeoning gay male communities, which had become, at least in New York and San Francisco, wholly contained cities-within-cities (or "ghettoes," as they were not infrequently called). Inhabitants of these "urban villages" need never leave them to satisfy their desires, whether those desires be sexual, recreational, cultural, or commercial. There were gay churches, gay banks, gay theaters, gay hiking clubs, gay bookstores, and gay yellow pages listing hundreds of gay-owned businesses. While lesbian communities were neither as visible nor as territorially based, they, too, provided a variety of cultural supports and institutions, fostering a sense of minority-group identity that was furthered by separatist tendencies. Little wonder, then, that lesbians and gay men began to be seen as, and to think of themselves as, almost a distinct type of being, on an ontological par with "Irish-Americans" or "Japanese-Americans."[37] Gone were the dreams of liberating society by releasing "the homosexual in everyone." Instead, homosexuals concentrated their energies on social advancement *as homosexuals.*

It should be noted that the "ethnic" self-understanding is a much looser form of essentialism than, say, a strict genetic or

---

[36] Cory, *The Homosexual in America.* It is interesting to note that while the term 'minority' is indexed frequently, 'identity' does not appear.

[37] Granted, the majority of self-identified gays and lesbians did not live in these communities, but many of them did make their pilgrimages to the "Gay Mecca" or were exposed to it through the mass media. And beyond that, to use a different religious metaphor, San Francisco came to symbolize for gays around the United States what Israel represents for Jews around the world: a focal point for cultural identity, that functions even for those who are not firmly integrated into the culture. It should be clear, of course, that there is no *single* gay or lesbian "culture," but rather a variety of them that are loosely integrated.

hormonal theory of homosexuality. Based on an analogy that is not necessarily intended literally, this form of group identification is peculiarly vague about where the essential "core" of gayness resides. Nonetheless, the notion does tend toward a reification of the category "homosexual," implying that lesbians and gay men are in some fundamental sense different from heterosexuals. Such viewpoints can be quite dangerous: they can lend support to eugenicist arguments and are also disturbingly compatible with the contemporary understanding of AIDS as a "gay disease."

Moreover, there are a number of questions that can be raised, from a progressive standpoint, about the political manifestations of "ethnicity." It would be unfortunate to reduce the politics of gay liberation to nothing more than the self-interested actions of an interest group, in competition with other such groups for various resources; such a model would imply that gays have no interests in common with other oppressed groups, and would almost entirely abandon any notion of a broader role for the gay movement in radical politics. In addition, such a move would further separate gay men from gay women, by questioning whether even they have sufficient common interests to overcome their senses of difference. Finally, as many critics have noted, the politics of gay "ethnicity" have tended to foster the hegemonic role in community-building played by white males within the gay movement,[38] and have been articulated to an uncomfortable extent through capitalist enterprise and the commodification of sexual desire.[39]

Given the problems posed by "ethnic" essentialism, one might think that the role of gay and lesbian theorists should be to continue promotion a constructionist critique. In a certain sense, I think this is true; but it is a project that needs some

[38] Almaguer, "Conceptualizing Sexual Stratification," p. 25, and Frances Fitzgerald, *Cities on a Hill: A Journey through Contemporary American Cultures* (New York: Simon and Schuster, 1986), p. 58.

[39] Jeffrey Weeks, *Sexuality and Its Discontents: Meanings, Myths and Modern Sexuality* (London: Routledge and Kegan Paul, 1985), pp. 21-25 and Altman, *Homosexualization of America*, chapter 3.

rethinking. Is constructionism to be defended unproblematically? If so, the defenders must grapple with the problem that their theoretical perspective is "out of sync" with the self-understandings of many gay people. From the standpoint of the defenders of constructionism, lesbians and gay men must be seen as victims of "false consciousness," unaware of the constructedness of their identities. Moreover, we might predict that constructionists would experience considerable difficulties in leading the gay masses to a state of "true consciousness," given that constructionism poses a real and direct threat to the ethnic legitimation: people who base their claims to social rights on the basis of a group identity will not appreciate being told that that identity is just a social construct; and people who see their sexual desires as fixed—as "just the way we are"—are unlikely to adopt a viewpoint that presents "sexual scripting" as a fluid, changeable process open to intentional redefinition. Altman has recognized this dilemma:

> Few arguments have caused as much controversy among gay audiences as the assertion of a universal bisexual potential. I was once interrupted during a taping of a gay radio program in Los Angeles by a producer very concerned by this position, which he said justified Anita Bryant's claim that all homosexuals could be "cured." He was only partially mollified by my pointing out that the reverse was equally true.[40]

While it is important to challenge essentialism, particularly in its most insidious forms, we need not do so by reverting to a dogmatic constructionism. A strict constructionist position of the kind outlined above not only poses a threat to contemporary legitimations of lesbians and gay men: it is also theoretically unsound and analytically incomplete. Having situated the essentialist-constructionist debate within contemporary politics, I would now like to return to the examination of constructionism and spell out its shortcomings.

---

[40] *Homosexualization of America*, p. 45.

Constructionist Pitfalls

For all its radical potential, constructionism has trapped itself in the basic dualisms of classic liberalism. Liberal discourse goes back and forth between two extreme views of the relation between the individual and society: either it asserts that individuals are free to create themselves, rise above their environments, and take control over their lives; or it sees individuals as simply the product of their environment (or their genes, or what have you), molded like clay into various shapes.[41] Similarly, constructionism vacillates between a certain type of libertarian individualism (the left Freudian variant is the best example here)[42] in which sexual categories may be appropriated, transcended, and deconstructed at will; and just the opposite conception of the individual's sexual identity as created for him or her by the social and historical context (a strand of thinking best represented by Foucault). In either case, the "individual" is pitted against "Society"; and what is missing is any dynamic sense of how society comes to dwell within individuals or how individuality comes to be socially constituted.

Put more simply, constructionism is unable to theorize the issue of determination. This is true both on the societal level and on the level of individual lives. As Jeffrey Weeks has acknowledged, though constructionism would predict an infinite variety of sexual identities, sexual acts, and sexual scripts, practical experience indicates that only the tiniest fraction of these possibilities are realized.[43] Stephen Murray

---

[41] On the dualism of liberal thought, see Roberto M. Unger, *Knowledge and Politics* (New York: Free Press, 1975), esp. chapter 5. I want to thank Steve McMahon for pointing out this argument to me.

[42] For a discussion of the underlying asocial individualism in Marcuse, see Nancy Chodorow, "Beyond Drive Theory: Object Relations and the Limits of Radical Individualism," *Theory and Society* 14:3 (May 1985), pp. 271-319.

[43] Jeffrey Weeks, "Discourse, Desire and Sexual Deviance: Some Problems in a History of Homosexuality," in *The Making of the Modern Homosexual*, pp. 94-95.

points out that if we take the constructionist assumption that gender identity, gender roles, sexual identity, sex roles, and object choice can all vary independently of each other, and if we assume that each feature might take on one of three possible values (e.g., "masculine," "feminine," and neither/both), then there are 243 potential permutations of sexual beings. Needless to say, even if we combed through the entire history of human civilization, we would not find anywhere near that many variations.[44] Each society seems to have a limited range of potential storylines for its sexual scripts—and constructionists have surprisingly little to say about how that limiting process takes place. Moreover, strict constructionism implies a lack of determination in the sexual histories of *individuals* as well: their scripts are assumed to be in a constant state of revision. While this is no doubt true to a point, it would seem to belie most people's experiences of a relatively fixed sexual identity. It may be that we're all acting out scripts—but most of us seem to be typecast.

It is precisely this perceived non-voluntary component of identity that cannot be accounted for within a strict constructionist perspective. Constructionism has no theory of the intrapsychic; it is unable to specify the ways in which desire comes to be structured over the course of people's lives. While it asserts that people are social products, it has no way of explaining how it is that social meaning come to resonate with the core of who people are.[45] Falling into the dualistic

---

[44] Stephen O. Murray, *Social Theory, Homosexual Realities* (New York: Gay Academic Union, 1984), pp. 19-20.

[45] In a more recent revision that deserves attention, Gagnon and Simon speak of three levels of scripting: "cultural scenarios," "interpersonal scripts," and "intrapsychic scripts." While this is a drastic improvement over the original definition of scripts, it still does not go far enough. The intrapsychic is conceptualized primarily as the realm in which the self "rehearses" for interpersonal experience; there is no real dynamic theory of intrapsychic processes in relation to actions in the external world. Also, a conception of unconscious mental processes, as opposed to conscious ones, is missing from their version

--->

traps of liberal theory, constructionism then lends itself to further misunderstanding on the part of those who encounter the theory.   A "folk constructionism" comes to be disseminated: the view that sexual identities are willful self-creations. And in reaction against this folk constructionism, which denies the experience of a non-voluntary component to identity, lesbians and gays operating within the liberal discourse slide to the opposite extreme: they assert that there is something "real" about their identity, and then try to locate that felt reality in their gènes, or their earliest experiences, or their mystical nature. In this way, constructionism becomes its own worst enemy, driving its potential converts into the enemy camp.

A final point can be made about the theoretical inadequacies of constructionism as well as essentialism. If such theories are to be politically useful, then they should provide some means of evaluating concrete political strategies. In fact, the debate can at times appear quite beside the point, for there are many gay political strategies which cannot be cleanly conceptualized as either "essentialist" or "constructionist." For example, consider the situation of "political lesbians" living in separatist communities of women. Such women have consolidated an (essentialist) conception of group difference to a significant extent—but the emphasis on identity as a conscious political choice would seem to place them squarely within the constructionist camp. Alternately, we might examine the politics of the pre-Stonewall homophile movement in the United States in the 1950's and '60's. The leaders of this integrationist movement stressed in no uncertain terms that homosexuality was not a consequential difference, and that homosexuals were really just the same as straights and wanted to be treated as such. But this more-or-less constructionist viewpoint was mixed with an equally rigid essentialist insistence that homosexuals could not help being the way they

---

of intrapsychic scripts. See Simon and Gagnon, "Sexual Scripts," *Society* 22:1 (November-December 1984), pp. 53-60.

were, and should therefore not be asked or forced to "change."[46]

It seems that when we scrutinize the essentialist-constructionist debate closely, it immediately unravels into two underlying dualisms: "sameness" vs. "difference," and "choice" vs. "constraint." Constructionism insists that homosexuals and heterosexuals are basically the same, and not fundamentally distinct types of beings; and it emphasizes the possibilities for the self-conscious creation of sexual identities ("choice"). Essentialism, conversely, stresses the politics of difference and presumes the existence of constraint on one's sexual identity: sexual desires are not a "preference" but a fixed "orientation."

However, when we separate out the two dimensions, we find that there are four logical possibilities (chart 1), rather

Chart 1:
Political Embodiments of a Deconstructed Debate

	CHOICE	CONSTRAINT
SAMENESS	Post-Stonewall (transformative) Gay Liberation Civil Libertarianism	Integrationism (e.g., 1950s-60s homophile movements)
DIFFERENCE	Political Lesbians Cultural Radicalism	Civil Rights Minority/Ethnicity Cultural Radicalism

---

[46] On the politics of the homophile movement, see D'Emilio, *Sexual Politics*, chapter 5-7 and Escoffier, "Sexual Revolution."

than the two presumed by the constructionist-essentialist debate. First, there is *sameness-choice*, which is exemplified by the early 1970's gay liberationist perspective, as well as by certain civil-libertarian arguments. Gay liberationists of the early seventies, for example, thought that all people were bisexual and hence fundamentally similar; and they stressed the role of volition in identity-formation. Next, there is *sameness-constraint*, the position of the pre-Stonewall homophile movements. Then, there is *difference-constraint*, best exemplified by the ethnic/civil rights model. Actors within such a model possess a strong sense of group difference and a notion of sexual identity as a fixed orientation. Finally, there is *difference-choice*, which would characterize "political lesbians" as well as certain expressions of cultural radicalism within the gay male community.[47] Each box, then, has its political embodiments, and each box also implies specific legitimating strategies which would need to confront specific ideological challenges (chart 2). The problem, though, is that the politics of only two of the boxes (sameness-choice and difference-constraint) are explicable within the context of the constructionist-essentialist debate. That is, sameness-choice can be seen as pure constructionist, while difference-constraint is pure essentialist. The other two boxes would seem to indiscriminately criss-cross the bounds of the argument—and yet they are no less logically defensible or worthy of theoretical attention. It follows that to explore systematically the essentialist-constructionist debate, we really need to delve more deeply into these two oppositions—choice vs. constraint, and sameness vs. difference—and see if they are really so opposing.

---

[47] It should be clear that groups or individuals can be "located" within these boxes only in a highly ideal-typical fashion. In the real world, at some point or another, most of us are all over the map.

Chart 2:
Corresponding Legitimation
Strategies and Deligitimating Threats

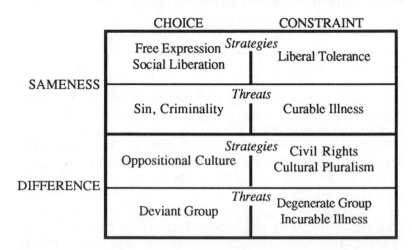

	CHOICE	CONSTRAINT
SAMENESS	Free Expression *Strategies* Social Liberation	Liberal Tolerance
	Threats Sin, Criminality	Curable Illness
DIFFERENCE	*Strategies* Oppositional Culture	Civil Rights Cultural Pluralism
	Threats Deviant Group	Degenerate Group Incurable Illness

In order to build up a stronger constructionist position, my strategy will be as follows. First, I will examine more closely the idea of a gay "ethnic identity," exploring, from the standpoint of theories of identity and of ethnicity, the historical conjuncture in which this idea appeared. I will argue that the debates on identity and ethnicity have been bogged down by certain polar oppositions that parallel the essentialism-constructionism divide. By staking out an alternative position in these debates, I will further argue that it is reasonable, with certain qualifications, to accept the "ethnic" model—both as a relatively accurate characterization of contemporary gay identity formation, and as a politically defensible starting point from which the gay movement can evolve in a progressive direction. In the course of this analysis, I will return to the oppositions that undergird the essentialism-constructionism debate—choice vs. constraint, and sameness vs. difference—and once again seek some way of transcending the dualisms, in a way that helps sexual theory to resonate more closely with the politics of gay "ethnic" identity.

Identity

The concept of "homosexual identity," as mentioned earlier, is a surprisingly new one; though the term is now ubiquitous, it first appeared in the relevant literature little more than a decade ago.[48] Perhaps it is not so surprising, then, that the term has been used in a consistently haphazard fashion. In her survey of the literature on homosexual identity, Vivienne Cass has found that

> in these articles it is possible to infer diverse meanings such as (1) defining oneself as gay, (2) a sense of self as gay, (3) image of self as homosexual, (4) the way a homosexual person *is*, and (5) consistent behavior in relation to homosexual-related activity.[49]

General definitions of identity are equally problematic. In an interesting "semantic history" of the term, Philip Gleason notes that it, too, is a new concept, having entered the general social-science literature only in the 1950's. Popularized initially by psychoanalyst Erik Erikson, "identity" then wound its way through various sociological "feeder streams," including role theory, reference-group theory, and symbolic interactionism. By the mid-1960's, the term "was used so widely and so loosely that to determine its provenance in every context would be impossible."[50]

Nevertheless, Gleason observes that most definitions tend to fall toward one or the other pole of an opposition between

---

[48] Cass, "Homosexual Identity," pp. 107-108. A comparison of the indexes of Altman's *Homosexual: Oppression and Liberation* (1971) and *The Homosexualization of American* (1982) is instructive. In the earlier book, the term 'identity' does not appear in any form in the index. In the more recent book, 'Identity, homosexual' has eleven direct page references, and six subheadings with further page references.

[49] Cass, "Homosexual Identity," p. 108.

[50] Philip Gleason, "Identifying Identity: A Semantic History, " *Journal of American History* 69:4 (March 1983), pp. 910-931. The quote is from p. 918.

two conceptions of identity, one a psychological reductionism, the other a sociological reductionism. The first conception of identity—which might be called "intrapsychic"—treats identity as a relatively fixed and stable characteristic of a person, which, from a developmental standpoint, more or less unwinds from within. In a word, this sense of identity is essentialist: it is the type of "identity" that we mean when we speak of identity as describing who someone *really is*. Quite distinct is the sense of "identity" which I will call "acquired" (although the term 'constructionist' would not be inappropriate). In this sense, identity is the internalization or conscious adoption of socially imposed or socially constructed labels or roles. According to the "acquired" definition, identity is not so deeply entrenched in the psyche of the individual, and can vary considerably over the course of one's life. This is the type of "identity" that we have in mind when we say that someone "identifies as" a such-and-such.[51]

It should be clear that not all psychologists adopt a simplistic intrapsychic definition, nor do all sociologists see identity as purely acquired. Erikson, for example, was quite specific on the point that identity emerged through an interactive developmental process between self and others.[52] Conversely, the symbolic interactionsts Berger and Luckmann argue that "identity is a phenomenon that emerges from the dialectic between individual and society."[53] Nonetheless, these two polar senses have each become prevalent, and it is not uncommon to encounter fairly pure expression of either type.[54]

---

[51] *Ibid.*, pp. 918-919.

[52] *Ibid.*

[53] Peter Berger and Thomas Luckmann, *The Social Construction of Reality* (New York: Anchor Books, 1967), p. 174.

[54] Lee Rainwater, for example, has used a definition of identity as something completely acquired, treating identities as things that people "try on," like hats: "Individuals are led to announce a particular identity when they feel it is congruent with their needs, and the society influences these needs by its willingness to validate such announcements by a congruent placement. . . . Each individual tries on

--->

Mediating between the poles of intrapsychic and acquired identity is Habermas's useful discussion of identity:

> [Ego] identity is produced through *socialization,* that is, through the fact that the growing child first of all integrates itself into a specific social system by appropriating symbolic generalities; it is later secured and developed through *individuation,* that is, precisely through a growing independence in relation to social systems.[55]

Ego identity, then, is a *socialized sense of individuality,* an internal organization of self-perceptions concerning one's relationship to social categories, that also incorporates views of the self perceived to be held by others. At its core, identity is constituted relationally, through involvement with—and incorporation of—significant others and integration into communities. The relationship of ego identity to subsidiary identities (such as occupational, class, racial, gender, or sexual identities) is an interactive one, in which all subsidiary identities are integrated into a relatively coherent and unique life history.[56]

Where then do these subsidiary identities come from, and in what circumstances can they be appropriated and incorporated? As Berger and Luckmann maintain, it is important to recognize that such identities are, at the same time, both human self-creations and constraining structures. To paraphrase Marx,

---

identities that emerge from the cultural material available to him and tests them by making appropriate announcements." See Lee Rainwater, *Behind Ghetto Walls: Black Families in a Federal Slum* (Chicago: Aldine, 1970), p. 375; quoted in Laud Humphreys, "Exodus and Identity: The Emerging Gay Culture," in *Gay Men: The Sociology of Male Homosexuality,* Martin Levine, ed. (New York: Harper and Row, 1979), p. 144.

[55] Jürgen Habermas, "Moral Development and Ego Identity," in *Communication and the Evolution of Society* (Boston: Beacon Press, 1979), p. 74.

[56] *Ibid.,* pp. 90-91, Cass, "Homosexual Identity," p. 110, Unger, *Knowledge and Politics,* p. 195, and Chodorow, "Feminism and Difference," p. 60.

people make their own identities, but they do not make them just as they please. Identities are phenomena that permit people to become acting "subjects" who define who they are in the world, but at the same time identities "subject" those people to the controlling power of external categorization.[57]

In this regard, it is vital to note that identity has increasingly come to be seen as something quite important. In modern, fluid, "mass" society, the relationship of the individual to the social whole is rendered problematic; as part of a continual "quest for identity," we go through "identity crises"; we seek to "find ourselves." It is not surprising that group identities— occupational, racial, ethnic, sexual—become increasingly attractive, since they provide an intermediate link between the individual and the mass.[58] As we accept more and more identities, it does indeed begin to seem that they are all somewhat arbitrary, tried on like hats and discarded for next year's style. And yet the fundamental irony of this apparent freedom to define ourselves is that in a world where identity has been transformed into a problem—where identity "crises" must be resolved, and where we all search for our identities— external cues and definitions become increasingly authoritative. The more we feel impelled to discover our "true" identity, the more we are likely to grasp at the reassurance provided by the adoption of available identity types.

The pressure to define oneself *sexually* is particularly keenly felt. This is true in part because labels such as "homosexual" are powerfully charged, carrying with them the risk of strong social disapproval. But beyond that, a Foucaultian argument can be made about the increasing importance of sex, in general, to the constitution of identity. As Dennis Altman notes,

---

[57] Louis Althusser, "Ideology and Ideological State Apparatuses," in *Lenin and Philosophy* (New York: Monthly Review, 1971), p. 183.

[58] Kenneth Plummer, "Homosexual Categories: Some Research Problems in the Labelling Perspective of Homosexuality," in *Making of the Modern Homosexual*, pp. 60-61.

sex remains one of the few areas of life where we feel able to be more than passive spectators. It is a feature of modern society that we increasingly define achievement in terms of immediate gratification, and the move to burden sexuality with greater expectations is closely related to the stress on ideas of "self-fulfillment" and "personal actualization."[59]

In a similar vein, Jeffrey Weeks observes:

As divorce rates rise, fertility declines, and the distinction between married and unmarried tends to blur, "the couple" rather than marriage emerges as the one seeming constant of western life. But sex becomes even more central to its success. . . Sex has become the cement that binds people together.[60]

Gay, lesbian, and bisexual identities must be understood as arising out of this historical conjuncture.[61] Their emergence reflects a world in which group identity has assumed paramount importance, and where sexuality has become a central dimension of identity formation in general. In addition, as already suggested, these identities constitute "reverse affirmations" of social labels, adoptive contestations of imposed stigma categories. As labeling theory indicates, deviant identities are particularly likely to assume totalizing dimensions: *all* behavior of persons so categorized becomes interpreted by others through the prism of the perceived

---

[59] *Homosexualization of America*, p. 82.

[60] Weeks, *Sexuality and Its Discontents*, p. 28. See also Simon and Gagnon, "Sexual Scripts," a recent discussion of how "the erotic" historically has come to be separated out as a distinct realm of human experience.

[61] In a somewhat different, though clearly related sense, the notion of "straight" identity emerges out of the same historical conjuncture. The idea of a "heterosexual" person is also quite new, and has been created in some sense by its opposite. See Michael Omi and Howard Winant, "By the Rivers of Babylon: Race in the United States (Part 2)," *Socialist Review* 72 (November-December 1983), p. 45, for a discussion of the changing concepts of "white" identity through redefinitions of "black" identity.

difference: "One will be identified as a deviant first, before other identifications are made."[62] And as Erving Goffman points out, the need for the stigmatized to "manage" their stigma in social situations—to tell or not to tell, to confront or to excuse—causes the stigma-identity to assume substantial proportions within the overall ego identity—to become, in some cases, an all-consuming preoccupation.[63] Attempts to assert the legitimacy of one's position and claim that one's stigma is not grounds for social exclusion tend to have the ironic effect, also noted by Goffman, of furthering the process by which the particular identity consumes the overall ego.[64]

Finally, the emergence of various types of sexual identity as important components of ego identity presumes the existence of individuals who are in some loose sense qualified to fill the categories—people who are capable of interpreting their erotic and emotional desires and actions as corresponding to their understanding of the meaning of these social terms.[65] This is the point at which both labeling theory and symbolic interactionism falter, for they have nothing to say about how such people come to exist. The rigid temporal sequence laid down by labeling theory is particularly inadequate. In that model, the individual commits an act of "primary" deviance (in this case, a homosexual act), is in consequence met with a stigmatizing label ("You're a queer"), and by internalizing this label becomes fixed in a "secondary" deviant identity ("I'm a homosexual").[66] But in the real world, the developmental

---

[62] Howard Becker, *Outsiders: Studies in the Sociology of Deviance* (New York: Free Press, 1963), pp. 33-34.

[63] Erving Goffman, *Stigma: Notes on the Management of Spoiled Identity* (Englewood Cliffs, NJ: Prentice-Hall, 1963), pp. 14,88.

[64] *Ibid.*, p. 114.

[65] Cass, "Homosexual Identity," pp. 10, 114.

[66] See, for example, Becker, *Outsiders*. A notable exception to this presumption of a standard sequence of deviant identity-formation is Goffman's discussion of the "moral career" of the stigmatized individual, which can unfold in several distinctive fashions, depending upon the relative timing of (1) developing of stigma and (2) learning

--->

sequences vary tremendously. Interview data suggest, in fact, the relationship among the processes of engaging in homosexual identity, being labeled a homosexual, and having suspicions that one is a homosexual can come in various orders; typical patterns seem to include "engaged, suspicious, labeled," "engaged, labeled," "suspicious, engaged, labeled," "suspicious, labeled, engaged." As Plummer has pointed out in his review of several studies, some gay men and lesbians report a fixity and clarity of sexual preferences dating to early childhood; others experience several shifts in sexual identity and the structure of desire over the course of their lives.[67] Research into the lives of homosexuals increasingly suggests that there is no "homosexuality," but rather "homosexualities."[68]

A theory of sexual identity formation, therefore, must be able to identify a wide range of potential developmental strategies by which individuals, in relation with significant others, compare (or fail to compare) their experiences and feelings against their comprehension (or lack of comprehension) of existing sexual and gender typologies.[69] As a result of these processes, individuals arrive (or fail to arrive) at consistent or variable interpretations of their sexual identity.[70] This is a complex and never-ending activity,

---

that the world considers this to *be* a "stigma." Goffman, *Stigma*, pp. 32-34.

[67] Plummer, "Homosexual Categories," pp. 66-72. See also the critique of the "stages" theory in labeling theory as applied to homosexual identity development, in Murray, *Social Theory*, p. 17.

[68] Alan Bell and Martin Weinberg, *Homosexualities: A Study of Diversity Among Men and Women* (New York: Simon and Schuster, 1978).

[69] I would like to thank Ellyn Kestenbaum for substantially helping me to clarify and rethink the discussion that follows.

[70] To complicate the above discussion even further, it should probably be added that, to the extent that sexual identity and gender identity are ideologically linked, the individual's perception of his or her relationship to the gender categories (e.g., gender "conformity" or

--->

involving both conscious and unconscious dimensions. Consciously, people perform what Barbara Ponse has called "identity work": they actively seek to organize into a coherent whole their thoughts, motivations, and experiences with others—to create a consistent biography which legitimates their places in the world.[71]   Critical phases, such as the "coming out" process, may represent cognitive strategies for handling breaks and discontinuities in these biographies. To the extent that such processes remain unconscious, people are often subject to constraints that they but dimly perceive; their needs, desires, actions, cognitions and self-concepts may all be out of sync with one another, and a consistent biography may not be achieved.

This discussion sheds new light on the polarity between "choice" and "constraint," which was observed to be one dimension underlying the essentialist-constructionist debate. If the question is, "Are sexual identities the outcome of choice or constraint?", then the whole thrust of the preceding argument is to suggest that the only possible answer is "neither and both." Choice and constraint constitute a false opposition; and the way to transcend this dualism, I think, is with some form of psychoanalytic theory. Such a perspective can account for the ways that sexual and emotional desires can be structured, developmentally, into relatively well-defined directions. In particular, the "object relations" school of psychoanalysis, with its focus on relational experience, and with its theory of the ego as possessing a "relational core,"

"nonconformity") can influence the developmental understanding of sexual identity.

[71] Ponse, *Identities*. This much underrated book may be the best symbolic interactionist study of identity and legitimacy; the discussion of methods of biographical reconstruction, drawing on Berger and Luckmann, is particularly excellent. Still, the notion of identity never really sneaks beneath the level of "roles"; Ponse has no conception of the intrapsychic, or of conscious processes. Also, she focuses almost exclusively on adult life, to the exclusion of childhood.

might be usefully applied to an analysis of sexual identity.[72] Object relations theory describes, in a vivid way, how from a child's earliest moments onward a sense of self is constituted through "introjections" of significant others. The child's needs and desires, which can only be satisfied externally, come to be mediated and shaped through these encounters; while aspects of these desires may remain highly fluid and subject to what constructionists want to call scripting, other dimensions may be sharply structured and come to comprise fundamental parts of the ego core.[73] Without displacing the symbolic interactionist focus on conscious, adult experience, psychoanalysis also permits us to conceptualize the unconscious and to appreciate the formative element of early childhood experiences. From such a perspective, identity becomes more than just a serial enactment of roles; it takes on a socially constituted reality.

In light of this discussion, the organization of the gay community around the "politics of identity" would seem to have strong social roots. Once we abandon both the strict

---

[72] See Nancy Chodorow, *The Reproduction of Mothering: Psychoanalysis and the Sociology of Gender* (Berkeley: University of California Press, 1978); also Chodorow, "Feminism and Difference," pp. 54-60. For differences between the object-relations school and the appropriation of Freud by Marcuse that has influenced gay liberation so far, see Chodorow, "Beyond Drive Theory."

[73] It may even be useful to reintroduce a concept of "drives"—stripped of its essentialist Freudian baggage. Rather than treat drives as pre-social and biological, Chodorow (following Edith Jacobson) suggests that "the infant is born with undifferentiated drive potentials, which are transformed and used in the process of development, in the interest of internal and external relationships, to become aggressive and libidinal drives." Chodorow, "Beyond Drive Theory," p. 308. From this perspective, it might be possible to conceptualize a developmental organization of drives that results in a homosexual "object choice." However, it could be argued that the term 'drive' has been so contaminated by Freud's biologism, ahistoricism, prescriptive claims about "normality," and assumptions that drives serve to "channel" sexuality in order to stabilize the moral and social order, that it would be best to avoid the term altogether.

essentialist notion of identity as forever fixed within the psyche, as well as the strict constructionist conception of identity as an arbitrary acquisition, we can recognize that a gay or lesbian identity might have a clear resonance for individuals without necessarily binding them to any specific definition of what that identity "means." An intermediate position between the poles of intrapsychic and acquired identity allows us to recognize that these sexual identities are *both inescapable and transformable*, and are capable of giving rise to a variety of political expressions. The question that must now be asked is why the contemporary gay identity in the United States has particularly assumed an "ethnic" dimension, and what this implies for gay politics.

Ethnicity

How can we speak seriously of gays and lesbians as an "ethnic" group—or even a minority group? After all, there would seem to be some rather fundamental differences between gays and the other groups that we normally associate with these terms. In the first place, ethnic or racial identifications are normally conferred at birth and transmitted through the family. In place of this "primary socialization" into a racial or ethnic identity, the entrance into a gay community constitutes a "secondary socialization," occurring later in life.

A process of secondary socialization is typically seen as less formative than primary socialization, because "it must deal with an already formed self and an already internalized world. It cannot construct subjective reality *ex nihilo*."[74] In particular, it is unclear what sort of coherent cultural content can be transmitted through a secondary socialization into a gay community, and whether this cultural distinctiveness corresponds with the kinds of cultural differences that we normally consider to be ethnic. Ethnic culture is presumed to be handed down through the generations; gay "culture" lacks

[74] Berger and Luckmann, *Social Construction of Reality*, p. 140 and Escoffier, "Sexual Revolution," p. 127.

both the historical roots and the standard transmission devices. This problem is compounded by the fact that individuals being socialized into a gay community will already possess a variety of cross-cutting identities—ethnic, racial, class, gender, religious, occupational, and so on—which may claim much greater allegiance and inhibit the secondary socialization process.[75]

The treatment of these objections rest ultimately on the particular definition of "ethnicity" that is adopted. And once again, an investigation into the existing definitional possibilities reveals a debate between two polar opposite conceptions. Lining up on one side are the "primordialists," who treat ethnicity as an inescapable given, an absolute ascription. And in opposition to this traditional view has arisen the "optionalist" (a.k.a. "circumstantialist") critique, which in its most vulgar manifestations argues that "ethnicity may be shed, resurrected, or adopted as the situation warrants."[76] It should be clear that a "primordialist" conception of ethnicity implies an "intrapsychic" notion of ethnic identity; while conversely, an understanding of ethnicity in the "optionalist" sense is quite compatible with a definition of ethnic identity as "acquired."[77]

Once again, we need to transcend a false dualism: on the one hand, it seems ridiculous to claim that we can shed or adopt ethnicities as we please. Clearly, there are major constraints on this process. But on the other hand, it is quite true that racial and ethnic categories are historical products that are subject to extensive redefinition over time. Omi and Winant give an interesting example of the definitional crisis

---

[75] Almaguer, "Conceptualizing Sexual Stratification," p. 27.

[76] Peter K. Eisenger, "Ethnicity as a Strategic Option: An Emerging View," *Public Administration Review* 38 (January-February 1978). The terms 'primordialist' and 'circumstantialist' are used by Nathan Glazer and Daniel P. Moynihan in their introduction to *Ethnicity: Theory and Experience* (Cambridge: Harvard University Press, 1975), pp. 19-20. 'Optionalist' is used in place of 'circumstantialist' by Eisenger and Gleason.

[77] This point is made by Gleason, "Identifying Identity," pp. 919-920.

surrounding the influx of Mexicans and Chinese into the United States in the mid-nineteenth century. Confused over what sort of racial/legal status to accord these groups, courts eventually ruled that Mexicans were "white" but that Chinese were "Indian."[78] Even in the lives of individuals, racial designations can change. In South Africa, where race, of course, is of paramount importance, there is a special government agency responsible for adjudicating claims about one's racial classification; and each year many people officially "upgrade" their racial identity.[79]

Donald Horowitz strikes a good intermediate note between primordialism and optionalism:

> Ascription is, of course, the key characteristic that distinguishes ethnicity from voluntary affiliation. *Ethnic identity is generally acquired at birth. But this is a matter of degree.* In the first place, in greater or lesser measure, there are possibilities for changing individual identity. Linguistic or religious conversion will suffice in some cases, but in others the changes may require a generation or more to accomplish by means of intermarriage and procreation. In the second place, collective action, in the sense of conscious modification of group behavior and identification, may effect shifts of boundaries. . . It is, therefore, a putative ascription, rather than an absolute one, that we are dealing with. . . Ethnicity thus differs from voluntary affiliation, not because the two are dichotomous, but because they occupy *different positions on a continuum.*[80]

This definition brings us a step closer to feeling comfortable with the idea that the ethnic analogy is a reasonable one for gays and lesbians. If ethnicity does not necessarily begin at birth, and if ethnicity involves some combination of external ascription and chosen affiliation, then a gay identity as described above seems not wholly unlike an ethnic identity.

---

[78] Omi and Winant, "By the Rivers of Babylon: Race in the United States (Part 1)," *Socialist Review* 71 (September-October 1983), p. 52.

[79] *Ibid.*, p. 47.

[80] Donald L. Horowitz, "Ethnic Identity," in *Ethnicity*, pp. 113-114, emphasis added.

But we can better understand the adoption of the ethnic model by gays and lesbians if we spell out the particular ways in which ethnicity has come to be understood in the contemporary United States.

In the 1970's, social scientists announced that the United States was in the throes of an "ethnic revival"—a "resurgence" of ethnicity.[81] Though heavily influenced by the cultural and political assertiveness of racial minorities in the late 1960's, the revival was essentially a phenomenon of white European ethnic groups, manifesting a rediscovered pride in their heritage.[82] It was quickly observed that, despite the implications of a turn toward the past, there was something quite new about this form of ethnicity. As Frank Parkin notes,

> the nature of collective action mounted by ethnic groups has undergone a significant change in recent times. Originally dedicated to fighting rearguard actions of cultural preservation, they have now adopted more combative forms of activity expressly designed to alter the distribution of rewards in their members' favour.[83]

The "new ethnicity" differs from traditional ethnicity in a variety of respects. First, as Daniel Bell points out, the new ethnicity combines an affective tie with the pursuit of explicitly sociopolitical goals in "interest group" form: ethnic groups

---

[81] *Ethnicity.*

[82] This occurrence posed a bit of a puzzle to social scientists, many of whom had previously adopted the assumptions of the "melting pot" theory, or who, following the predictions of classical social theorists such as Karl Marx and Max Weber, had assumed that "irrational," "communal" ties such as ethnicity would be progressively swept away by the advance of capitalism and the inexorable process of rationalization. See Stephen Steinberg, *The Ethnic Myth: Race, Ethnicity, and Class in America* (Boston: Beacon Press, 1981), pp. 3-4; also Frank Parkin, *Marxism and Class Theory: A Bourgeois Critique* (New York: Columbia University Press, 1979), pp. 32.

[83] Parkin, *Marxism and Class Theory*, pp. 33-34.

become "instrumental" and not just "expressive."[84] Second, the new ethnicity places ethnic-group activity firmly on the terrain of the state.[85]   Third, and as a corollary to the preceding arguments, the new ethnicity is "forward-looking," seeking to expand the group's social position, while the old ethnicity was "backward-looking," aimed at "preserv[ing] the past against the encroachments of centralization and 'modernization.'"[86]   Fourth, as a reaction against "mass society," the new ethnicity is not so much a new form of aggregation as a "disaggregation" or "de-assimilation" from the mass.[87]   Fifth, lacking the type of structural power possessed by subordinate social classes (i.e., the ability to disrupt production), the new ethnic groups are increasingly inclined to press their demands by appealing to, and manipulating, hegemonic ideologies (such as "equal rights").[88] And finally, neo-ethnic politics frequently take on a localist character, organized around specific geographic space or community, leading to a distinctively ethnic involvement in urban political affairs.[89] While to some extent a general feature of contemporary Western politics, the "new ethnicity" manifested itself most prominently in the United States, where the political possibilities for organizing around ethnicity were the greatest (and, conversely, class-based organizing had proven relatively ineffective).[90]

---

[84] Daniel Bell, "Ethnicity and Social Change," in *Ethnicity*, pp. 169-170.

[85] *Ethnicity*, pp. 9-10 and Marxism *and Class Theory*, p. 95.

[86] Eisenger, "Ethnicity as a Strategic Option," p. 90. The quote is from Altman, *Homosexualization in America*, p. 223.

[87] Glazer and Moynihan discuss ethnic "disaggregation," *Ethnicity*, p. 9. Murray makes a parallel argument about gay "de-assimilation," *Social Theory*, p. 38.

[88] *Marxism and Class Theory*, pp. 85-86.

[89] Ira Katznelson, *City Trenches: Urban Politics and the Patterning of Class in the United States* (New York: Pantheon, 1981).

[90] *Ibid.*

Of course, it would be a mistake to exaggerate the changes that have occurred and ignore either the continuities between the "old" and the "new" ethnicity, or the extent to which both varieties have always been present. Nonetheless, it seems that a somewhat new understanding of what ethnicity is all about emerged in the United States in the 1970's—that is to say, at the very same time that gay and lesbian identity was taking on an ethnic cast.[91] And indeed, on the basis of the preceding discussion, this notion of gay ethnic identity seems increasingly comprehensible and plausible. Like the archetypal "new ethnicity," gay ethnicity is a "future-oriented" identity linking an affective bond with an instrumental goal of influencing state policy and securing social rewards on behalf of the group. Like the other ethnic groups, gay ethnicity functions typically through appeals to the professed beliefs of the dominant culture, emphasizing traditional American values such as equality, fairness, and freedom from persecution. And finally, in neo-ethnic fashion, gay identity (in this case, gay *male* identity in particular) operates by using the control of a specific geographic space to influence urban political decision-making.[92]

The final question that must be addressed, to understand and assess the gay community's adoption of an ethnic self-understanding, has to do with the issue of culture and tradition. No matter how much ethnicity may now be articulated in the sociopolitical realm, most conceptions of ethnicity would certainly still include some sense of a unique ethnic culture heritage; indeed, one manifestation of the new ethnicity that was frequently alluded to in the 1970's was the

---

[91] Other countries that have gay political movements have failed to develop gay "ethnicity." French activist Guy Hocquenghem, for example, has commented that France does not have a "gay community." Mark Blasius, "Interview with Guy Hocquenghem," *Christopher Street*, April 1980, p. 36. This would tend to support the argument that the United States has structural spaces for "ethnic" organizing that other countries lack.

[92] On the last point, see Manuel Castells, *The City and the Grassroots* (Berkeley: University of California Press, 1983), chapter 14.

resurgence of pride in one's ethnic cuisine, ethnic costume, and so on. And no matter how much ethnic groups may now be "forward looking," many of the legitimations for group allegiance are focused on the past and argue for the preservation of traditional forms. Can the lesbian and gay communities claim to be ethnic, given these considerations?

The answer is that the analogy holds. On the one hand, gay communities have developed a variety of cultural forms which, despite the considerable internal variation, serve to unify those communities.[93] And on the other hand, the cultural potency of at least the European ethnic groups would seem to be much less than it's often cracked up to be. In an interesting twist on the "new ethnicity" argument, Stephen Steinberg has characterized the recent "ethnic fever" as sort of a Freudian reaction-formation: an assertion that ethnicity is still culturally and psychologically meaningful, voiced with such rigid insistence as to imply that even the proponents themselves are not convinced. He quotes Irving Howe to this effect:

> These ethnic groups now turn back—and as they nervously insist, "with pride"—to look for fragments of a racial or national or religious identity that moves them to the extent that it is no longer available. Perhaps, also, *because* it is no longer available.[94]

Because ethnicity no longer provides the institutional supports capable of integrating individuals into the community and providing them with a sense of belonging, individuals futilely attempt to re-create that sense of belonging by grasping at a *psychological* affiliation. In the process, they fail to observe that the ground has fallen away beneath their feet:

> Indeed, it is precisely because the real and objective basis for ethnic culture is rapidly disappearing that identity has been

---

93 Michael Bronski, *Culture Clash: The Making of Gay Sensibility* (Boston: South End Press, 1984).

94 Irving Howe, "The Limits of Ethnicity," *New Republic*, June 25, 1977, p. 18; quoted in Steinberg, *Ethnic Myth*, p. 73.

elevated to a "symbolic" plane and a premium is placed on the subjective dimensions of ethnicity. People desperately wish to "feel" ethnic precisely because they have all but lost the prerequisites for "being" ethnic.[95]

Steinberg's analysis would lead one to characterize the gay community's adoption of an ethnic identity as profoundly ironic. It would seem to be precisely the fact that ethnic culture has been *evacuated of content* that has permitted the transposition of the category of "ethnicity" onto a group that, in the traditional sense of the term, clearly would not qualify for the designation. Thus it is true that lesbians and gay men don't really fit the original definition of what an ethnic group is: but then, neither really, do contemporary Jews, or Italian-Americans, or anyone else. In this way, the decline of the old ethnicity permits and encourages new groups to adopt the mantle and revive the phenomenon. Indeed, to the extent that the gay community has succeeded in creating new institutional supports that link individuals into the community and provide their lives with a sense of meaning, gays may now be more "ethnic" than the original ethnic groups.[96] And in any event, as the term progressively loses its original significations and acquires a more future-oriented, sociopolitical connotation, there is a diminishing tendency to assume that an ethnic group needs to provide those original functions anyway.

Now that we have explored the historical conjuncture in which the idea of a "gay ethnicity" made its appearance, we can see that the term is more than a simple catch-phrase, as it appears in Altman's analysis. Rather, it is at the very least a compelling analogy, and perhaps even the most accurate designation we can come up with.[97]

---

[95] Steinberg, *Ethnic Myth*, p. 63.

[96] This process is limited, of course, by the extensive variation within and among the gay communities and the fact that integration of individuals into those "communities" is often extremely partial.

[97] Purists who wish to preserve a more conventional sense of the term 'ethnicity' that would be applicable outside of the contemporary American context might instead prefer to call the gay community a

--->

This discussion of the particular sense in which "gay identity" has come to resemble an "ethnic" identity also sheds light on the "sameness-difference" dichotomy that underlies the essentialism-constructionism debate. Just as "choice" and "constraint" proved to be a false polarity with regard to gay *identity*, so are "sameness" and "difference" an unhelpful analytical distinction with regard to gay *ethnicity*: it makes little sense to quarrel over whether homosexuals and heterosexuals are fundamentally the same or fundamentally different. First, we need to rethink what we mean by the terms, and escape a sense of "sameness" as meaning a coercive uniformity, or "difference" as the clash of opposites. As Chodorow argues in the analogous case of gender difference, a rigid assertion of differentness reflects a defensive need to separate: it stems from anxieties about one's sense of self that are manifested in a refusal to recognize the other as also a "self"—as an active subject. It is possible to be differentiated, she argues, "without turning the cognitive fact into an emotional, moral, or political one."[98]

In this regard, it may be useful to talk about the relationship between gay "ethnic" communities and the larger society in terms of varying combinations of "sameness-in-difference," or "difference-in-sameness." This is true in several senses. First, the adoption of a neo-ethnic form of social closure combined with a civil-rights political strategy implies that gays are asserting their difference partly as a way of gaining entry into the system. By consolidating as a group, they are essentially following the rules of the modern American pluralist myth, which portrays a harmonious competition among distinct social groups. Neither "sameness" nor

---

"status group" of a "communal" character, organized around sexual expression. While Parkin does not discuss sexual minorities, it would not be hard to incorporate them into his neo-Weberian argument on "communal" forms of usurpationary social closure. See Parkin, *Marxism and Class Theory*, p. 67 and Almaguer "Conceptualizing Sexual Stratification."

[98] Chodorow, "Feminism and Difference," p. 57.

"difference" would seem to capture the peculiar ambiguity of this political expression.

Second, as many commentators have noted, the more coherent an ethnic group in the United States becomes, the greater its cultural influence upon the larger society. That is, at the time when Jews, or blacks, have been most "separatist," the diffusion of those cultures has also been the greatest. In the areas of sexual practices and urban lifestyles, lesbians and gays have indeed had an influence on the general culture in opening up possibilities for new forms of sexual and aesthetic expressions.[99]

This leads to another point, which is that the "lifestyles" of homosexuals and heterosexuals (at least among the white middle class) would seem in some ways to be moving closer together, even as the identity categories congeal. Once again, neither "sameness" nor "difference" seems to adequately characterize the phenomenon. As D'Emilio indicates, the conventional nuclear family is less and less the norm; the variety of living arrangements has multiplied; and sexuality has been increasingly divorced from a procreative intent: "As the life cycle of heterosexuals exhibits greater variety and less predictability, they have come to face many of the choices and experiences that gay men and women confront."[100] And conversely, D'Emilio argues that homosexuals are moving closer to heterosexuals:

> The gay liberation movement allowed many lesbians and homosexuals to break out of the ideological prison that confined them to a sexual self-definition. It also began the transformation of a sexual subculture into an urban community. The group life of gay men and women came to encompass not only erotic interaction but also political, religious, and cultural activity. Homosexuality and lesbianism have become less of a sexual category and more of a human identity.[101]

---

[99] *Homosexualization of America*, pp. 223-224.
[100] D'Emilio, *Sexual Politics*, p. 248.
[101] *Ibid.*

D'Emilio would seem to be exaggerating somewhat the convergence that has taken place; moreover, his endorsement of a "desexualized" lesbian and gay identity is certainly controversial.[102] Nonetheless, to the extent that there is some truth in the argument, it would seem that gays are becoming "the same" as straights to the extent that they are "different."

A final point in this regard relates to the potency of sexual classification itself. Jeffrey Weeks points out that the consolidation of typologies of sexual "persons" can have the paradoxical effect of challenging the whole system of categorization. Initially, labels such as "homosexual" were applied by doctors and sex researchers to describe deviations from a presumed norm. But once the people so labeled, in a "reverse" affirmation, began to assert the legitimacy of their sexual identity—and once that legitimacy began to be more widely recognized—then the whole classificatory schema began to lose its cultural force:

> For the elaborate taxonomies and distinctions existed in the end
> only to explain the variations in relationship to an assumed

---

[102] Much of the early panic surrounding AIDS within the gay male community would seem to cast doubts on the viability of a "desexualized" notion of gay identity. The view was frequently expressed that if gay men couldn't have sex with each other, they would lose their identity altogether and the community would fall apart. Clearly, sex is unlikely ever to become an incidental part of gay male sexuality. Conversely, the general public seems unprepared to grant gays a "desexualized" gay identity, even if gays want it. Here again, AIDS is a good example: much of the "moral panic" surrounding AIDS can be interpreted as an attempt to "re-sexualize" gay (male) identity, by asserting that "the homosexual" (as a person) is inherently diseased, due to the diseased nature of his sexuality. Similarly, for lesbians, the issue of a "desexualized" identity has been controversial. While some lesbian-feminists have proposed "desexualized" definitions of 'lesbian' that would be more inclusive of feminists in general, others have protested against these "'women-loving-women' definitions, which too often hide the genital homophobia of an otherwise purified and cleansed reconstruction of the term." Jacquelyn Zita, "Historical Amnesia and the Lesbian Continuum," *Signs* 7 (Autumn 1981), p. 173.

norm. Once the norm itself was challenged, then the category of the perverse became redundant, and with them the whole elaborate edifice of "sexuality"—the belief that the erotic is a unified domain, governed by its own laws, organized around a norm and its variations—began to crumble.[103]

Week's argument is misleading because it presumes that categorization can be abolished—that the elimination of one set of norms somehow precludes the installation of others. In fact, as Weeks himself has noted elsewhere, not only is categorization a never ending process, but gays and lesbians have increasingly become the new catergorizers, subdividing and stratifying their communities into a variety of new types.[104] But clearly Weeks has a point. By consolidating their sense of difference *and* asserting their legitimacy, lesbians and gays may be helping to usher in a world where they no longer seem to be different. But neither an essentialist claim of basic difference, nor a constructionist insistence on fundamental similitude, alone seems adequate to capture this ambiguous process.

Conclusion

In making sense of the notion of "gay 'ethnic' identity," I have deliberately steered clear of both the strict essentialist and the strict constructionist understandings of ethnicity as well as identity. The constitution of a gay identity is not something that simply unwinds from within, nor is it just an amalgam of roles that proceed according to scripts; only an intermediate, and dialectical, definition makes sense in this case. Similarly, if "ethnicity" is to serve even as an analogy for comprehending gay and lesbian group identity, then ethnicity must be understood as something that is neither an absolutely inescapable ascription nor something chosen and discarded at

---

[103] Weeks, *Sexuality and Its Discontents*, p. 244.

[104] Weeks, "Development of Sexual Theory," pp. 305-307. See also Plummer, "Homosexual Categories," pp. 55-57 and Jacquelyn N. Zita, "Historical Amnesia," p. 173.

will; as something neither there from birth, nor something one joins like a club; as something that makes one neither fundamentally different from others, nor fundamentally the same. It is in the dialectics between choice and constraint, and between the individual, the group, and the larger society, that "identities," "ethnic identities," and "gay and lesbian identities" emerge.

Neither strict constructionism nor strict essentialism are capable of explaining what it means to be gay. The fact that contemporary gay self-understandings and political expressions are inexplicable within the bounds of these theoretical perspectives therefore should come as no surprise. No sexual theory can inform sexual practice without transcending the limitations imposed by aligning oneself on either fringe of a bootless philosophical argument between "nature" and "society." This whole discussion so far has really been a series of variations on that theme, since all the oppositions that have been described can be located at one or the other pole of what is basically the same debate:

essentialist	constructionist
realist	nominalist
constraint	choice
difference	sameness
intrapsychic	acquired
primordialist	optionalist
nature	society
internal	external
real	fictive

The fact that, in seeking to transcend these oppositions, I have ended up quoting the arguments of many constructionists, is not incidental. Constructionists have become increasingly aware of the complexities of these debates, and have continued to provide the most insightful analyses of the changing character of the gay community and gay identity. But what constructionists have failed to acknowledge are the ways in which their own observations are increasingly at odds with the basic premises of the theoretical perspective. Plummer, in an interesting article aimed at a "synthetic" position, has gone so far as to embrace the possibility of the existence of fixed sexual "orientations"— while carefully skirting the question of how such a concept accords with his general theoretical stance.[105] Altman, one of the most subtle chroniclers of the gay ethnic experience, can never seem to quite escape his own suspicion that ethnicity rests on an illusion that is also a trap. Weeks, who is perhaps the most sensitive to the theoretical limitations of strict constructionism, and who provides the most insightful discussions of both the limitations and the possibilities inherent in gay identities, is also capable of lapsing into the most utopian constructionist arguments about the abolition of sexual categories. The hold of strict constructionism remains tenacious; and its expositors seem unwilling to clarify their relationship to the doctrine.[106]

Clarification would require a number of modifications to strict constructionism, yet would in no way amount to an endorsement of essentialism. First, there is a need to understand the issue of determination: out of the range of potential forms of sexual expression, how are limitations created on that expression, both socially and within the individual psyche? On the individual level, this implies the systematic introduction of psychoanalytic conceptions of needs and desires and of the development of the self in relation to others. On the social level, it implies a more comprehensive understanding of power, and of the dialectical relationship between identities as self-expressions and identities as ascriptive impositions. Anthropological analyses of "sex/gender systems" in kinship-based societies have something to offer here. As Harriet Whitehead has pointed out, "To say that gender definitions and concepts pertaining to sex and gender are culturally variable is not necessarily to say that they can vary infinitely or along any old axis." Analyses

---

[105] Plummer, "Homosexual Categories," pp. 71-72.

[106] And on the other side of the divide are scholars such as John Boswell, who rightly claim the need to develop some sort of middle ground, but continue to conceive of "gay history" in fundamentally essentialist terms. See Boswell, "Revolutions."

such as hers have attempted to connect cultural meanings about gender and sexuality with specific social-structural relations, so as to show how culture can structure the possibilities for personhood in distinctive ways.[107]

An example of how such an analysis might proceed for Western societies is offered by Michael Omi and Howard Winant's analysis of a different domain, "racial formation."

> Racial formation. . . should be understood as a *process*: (1) through which an unstable and contradictory set of social practices and beliefs are articulated in an ideology based fundamentally on race; (2) through which the particular ideology thus generated is enforced by a system of racial subjection having both institutional and individual means of reproduction at its disposal; and (3) through which new instabilities and contradictions emerge at a subsequent historical point and challenge the pre-existing system once more.[108]

Substitute "sexuality" for "race" in the above quote, and its relevance to the present discussion would be apparent. It is important to note, however, that Omi and Winant also intend "subjection" to be understood in the dual sense discussed earlier: both the creation of political *subjects*, and their simultaneous *subjection* to structural and ideological controls. For as Omi and Winant point out in their evaluation of the black movement:

> Probably the greatest triumph of the movement was not its legislative accomplishments or even the extent of this mass mobilization. The social movement for racial equality had its

---

[107] Harriet Whitehead, "The Bow and the Burden Strap: A New Look at Institutionalized Homosexuality in Native America," in *Sexual Meanings*, pp. 80-115 (quote is from p. 110). The idea that culture structures the possibilities of personhood is developed more generally in Clifford Geertz, *The Interpretation of Cultures* (New York: Basic Books, 1973), chapter 2. See the analogous argument by Hacking, "Making Up People."

[108] Omi and Winant, "By the Rivers of Babylon: Race in the United States (Part 1)," p. 50. See also their *Racial Formation*.

greatest success in its ability to create new racial "subjects," in its ability to *redefine the meaning of racial identity*, and consequently, of race *itself*, in American society.[109]

Similarly, the creation of a positive identity, and the simultaneous redefinition of legitimate sexual and affectional possibilities, is the overriding accomplishment of the lesbian and gay movements to date.

Beyond the issue of determination, a second requirement for the reinvigoration of constructionism is a better understanding of the "collectivization of subjectivity." We must be able to speak of sexually based group identities without assuming *either* that the group has some mystical or biological unity, *or* that the "group" doesn't exist and that its "members" are indulging in a dangerous mystification. "Ethnicity" is a metaphor; but the relationships that it entails can come to be internalized as a fundamental part of the self. To the extent that this is consciously recognized—to the extent that "ethnicity" can be seen as both strategy and reality—then the dangers of it being misunderstood in a rigidly essentialist sense become greatly reduced. Furthermore, this sense of what it means to be part of a distinctive community can rescue us from investing "difference" with moral implications. Rather than reifying difference into a defensive separatism or dissolving it into a false vision of homogeneity, we need to acquire an appreciation for difference as harmless, perhaps synergistic.[110]

A modified constructionist perspective of this sort would address the deficiencies of constructionism that were noted earlier in this paper. Not only would it permit a fuller description of the complex experiences of being homosexual, but it might also permit lesbians and gay men to feel that constructionism described the world and themselves as they

---

[109] Omi and Winant, "By the Rivers of Babylon: Race in the United States (Part 2)," p. 35, emphasis in the original.

[110] This implies a greater degree of acceptance among the gay community of those who stand at the "boundary," namely, bisexuals. See Lisa Orlando, "Bisexuality: Loving Whom We Chose."

experience it, rather than inducing them to flee from constructionism and into the arms of essentialism.

A modified constructionism could also allow theory to play a more helpful role in the analysis of the contemporary political expressions of gays and lesbians. In fact, the preceding analysis of the complexities and ironies of gay identity and ethnicity raises several important political dilemmas. The first of these has to do with the political manifestations of ethnicity. As I indicated, the gay movement's (and in this case, particularly the gay male movement's) subscription to the tenets of pluralism—its attempt to simply get its "piece of the pie" by appealing to hegemonic ideologies—raises questions about its potential (or desire) to mount a serious challenge to the structural roots of inequality—whether that be sexual inequality or any other kind. However, we might be better off avoiding facile distinctions between "reformist" and "revolutionary" strategies. As Omi and Winant note, civil-rights movements have an inherently radical dimension:

> By asserting that society denied minorities their rights as *groups*, they challenged the overall legitimacy of a hegemonic social order whose political logic and cultural coherence was based fundamentally in ideologies of competitive individualism.[111]

Moreover, rights movements that are organized around the politics of identity tend, by their nature, to imbue political actors with the capacity to make radical demands that they may not even intend. When the leader of the New York Gay Men's Chorus proclaims: "We show the straight community that we're just as normal as they are,"[112] this would seem on the face of it to be a rather conservative proposition, reminiscent of the accommodationist politics of the 1950's homophile movements. And yet in fact the comparison is inappropriate. When the members of homophile organizations stressed their "normality," they meant: We're the same as you, so please stop excluding us. But the sense of the above quote is quite

---

[111] "By the Rivers of Babylon," p. 53.
[112] Altman, *Homosexualization of America*, p. viii.

different; it is saying: We're different from you, and that doesn't make us any less human. In this sense, it would seem that the modern adherents of identity politics are engaged, willy-nilly, in a process of changing the very bounds of the normal.

Gay "ethnic" politics, therefore, certainly have capacities for moving in a more radical direction. Part of what would be required, however, is a recognition that the freedom from discrimination of homosexual *persons* is an insufficient goal, if homosexuality as a *practice* retains its inferior status. The disjuncture that Altman has noted between "homosexuality" and "the homosexual"—whereby the former remains stigmatized while the latter increasingly is awarded civil rights and civil liberties—presents an opportunity, in the short run, and a hurdle to be leaped, in the long run. Overcoming this obstacle would entail the adoption of political methods beyond those appropriate for electoral and established institutional politics.

But part of what may determine the political direction in which gays move is the particular model of minority-group organizing and political consciousness that is employed. Despite the adoption of a goal of civil rights, gay collective identity is at present closer in form to that of the white ethnic groups than to those of racial minorities. Movement away from a political consciousness based on white "ethnicity" and toward a "sexual minority" self-understanding might increase the gay movement's capacity to pose a more fundamental challenge to the socio-sexual order.

This, however, raises other dilemmas, regarding both the internal composition of the gay movement and its leadership, and the relationship of the gay movement to other social movements. The adoption of a "white ethnic" model, in other words, is not unexpected in a movement dominated by white, middle-class males. An adequate discussion of these issues is beyond the scope of this essay; however, it seems clear enough that the gay movement will never be able to forge effective alliances with other social movements unless it can address the inequalities that plague its internal organization. In this light it is worth noting a peculiar paradox of identity politics: while affirming a distinctive group identity that legitimately differs from the larger society, this form of political expression simultaneously imposes a "totalizing" sameness *within* the group: it says, this is who we "really are."[113]   A greater appreciation for internal diversity—on racial, gender, class, and even sexual dimensions—is a prerequisite if the gay movement is to move beyond "ethnic" insularity and join with other progressive causes.[114] The obvious first step in that direction would be improved understandings between lesbians and gay men—and a better articulation of feminist theory with theoretical perspectives on sexuality.

Finally, in considering the political dilemmas confronting lesbians and gays, it is vital to discuss the most serious crisis that the movement has yet faced, namely, AIDS. The "moral panic" surrounding AIDS demonstrates some of the inherent fragility of identity politics. By hardening a notion of group difference, identity politics present a highly visible target. Those social groups who see their understandings of the world as called into question by changing conceptions of sexuality, gender, and morality more broadly defined, have found in the consolidated notion of "gayness" a potent and available symbol upon which they can easily discharge their anxieties— and vent their wrath. And if there is perceived to be such a thing as a "homosexual person," then it is only a small step to the conclusion that there is such a thing as a "homosexual disease," itself the peculiar consequence of the "homosexual lifestyle."[115]

Thus the ideological and practical consequences of a complete solidification of identity into a reified notion of "the gay person" would seem to be quite grave. But to reiterate, this is not an argument for the maintenance of a strict-

---

[113] Escoffier, "Sexual Revolution," pp. 148-149 and Weeks, *Sexuality and Its Discontents*, p. 187.

[114] On sexual intolerance *within* the gay community, see Rubin, "Thinking Sex."

[115] See Steven Epstein, "Moral Contagion and the Medicalizing of Gay Identity: AIDS in Historical Perspective," *Research in Law, Deviance, and Social Control* 9 (1987).

constructionist pose; for both the "politics of constructionism" and the "politics of essentialism" present legitimating possibilities as well as dangers of delegitimation. The task of melding theory with practice will involve creatively capitalizing on the most effective legitimations of the moment, while still remaining true both to theoretical insights and to the contemporary self-understandings of the women and men who populate the movement.[116]

[116] This paper could not have been written without the encouragement, advice, and criticisms offered by a good number of people (many of whom, it should be said, do not agree with aspects of my argument). I would particularly like to thank Jeffrey Escoffier for a series of inspiring conversations on these topics. I also owe a debt to the following people for their comments on an earlier version of this essay: Tomás Almaguer, Jeanne Bergman, Alan Bérubé, Ellyn Kestnbaum, David Kirp, Lisa Orlando, Gayle Rubin, Arlene Stein, Indi Talwani, Jackie Urla, Carole Vance, Chris Waters, Jeff Weintraub, and the members of the Bay Area *Socialist Review* collective.

CHAPTER 11:
Leonore Tiefer
Social Constructionism and
the Study of Human Sexuality

In the last 10 years, a radical transformation has been taking place in scholarship on human sexuality, but only within certain disciplines. New theories "potentially explosive in their implications for our future understanding and behavior in regard to sex"[1] have been proposed, but psychology seems not to have noticed. The need for new ideas and research in the psychology of sexuality comes with some real-world urgency; the study of sexual discourses is no mere intellectual enterprise. As feminist anthropologist Gayle Rubin puts it,

> There are historical periods in which sexuality is more sharply contested and more overtly politicized. In such periods, the domain of erotic life is, in effect, renegotiated. . . Periods such as the 1880s in England and the 1950s in the United States recodify the relations of human sexuality. The struggles that were fought leave a residue in the form of laws, social practices, and ideologies which then affect the way sexuality is experienced long after the immediate conflicts have faded. All signs indicate that the present era is another of those watersheds.[2]

---

[1] Martha Vicinus, "Sexuality and Power: A Review of Current Work in the History of Sexuality," *Feminist Studies* 8 (1982), p. 137.

[2] Gayle Rubin, "Thinking Sex: Notes for a Radical Theory of the Politics of Sexuality," in *Pleasure and Danger: Exploring Female Sexuality*,

--->

Reprinted from *Review of Personality and Social Psychology,* volume 7, P. Shaver and C. Hendrick, eds. (1987), pp. 77-94, with permission of the author.

Since *Brown v. Board of Education*, the 1954 U.S. Supreme Court decision outlawing school segregation, social scientists have contributed their theories and data to the public debate over momentous social issues. As I write, public places of sexual activity are being closed "for health reasons" because of AIDS and quarantine is being discussed; censorship statutes are being passed to limit the production and dissemination of explicit sexual images to "protect" women and children; penal codes specify in ever greater detail illegal sexual activities between adults and children; and the U.S. Attorney General's Commission on Pornography (the Meese Commission) is conducting hearings on the causes of sexual violence in our society.

History may show that the academic community did not, and perhaps could not, take a leadership role in these great sociosexual issues. Perhaps academia speaks with too fragmented a voice or on too slow a time scale. Most recent histories of sexuality (e.g., Weeks, *Sex, Politics and Society*[3]), however, agree that social scientists, physicians, mental health professionals, and other sexuality "experts" are increasingly relied on for advice and authority regarding social sexual policy. Whether this represents part of the problem or part of the solution need not concern us at the moment. It provides sufficient reason to be aware of the range of scholarship concerning sexuality.

In this chapter I will present some key elements in the social constructionist approach and indicate how and why current psychological writing and research about human sexuality is dominated by a limiting, medicalized perspective. I hope to show how a transformed perspective offers social and personality psychologists exciting opportunities for scholarship on issues already familiar to them as these pertain to human sexuality.

Carole Vance, ed. (Boston, Routledge and Kegan Paul, 1984), pp. 267, 274

[3] Jeffrey Weeks, *Sex, Politics and Society: The Regulation of Sexuality since 1800*, (London: Longman, 1981).

The Social Constructionist Approach

In a recent essay, Gergen[4] defined the social constructionist approach as a form of inquiry indebted to intellectual trends such as symbolic interactionism, symbolic anthropology, ethnomethodology, literary deconstructionism, existentialism, phenomenology, and, to some degree, conventional social psychological theories. What these disciplines have in common is an emphasis on the person's active role, guided by his or her culture, in structuring reality. This "endogenic" perspective is to be contrasted with empiricism and positivism, which emphasize the objective existence and reality of topics of scientific inquiry, an "exogenic" perspective.

Gergen identified four assumptions made by social constructionists:

(1) The way we go about studying the world is determined by available concepts, categories, and methods. Our concepts often incline us toward or even dictate certain lines of inquiry while precluding others, making our results the products more of our language than of empirical discovery. For example, the assumption that there are two and only two genders is taken for granted. We don't ask where gender conceptions come from, and gender, then, becomes only an independent variable.[5]

(2) The concepts and categories we use vary considerably in their meaning and connotations over time and across cultures. Scholars without sufficient historical or cultural awareness

---

[4] K.J. Gergen, "The Social Constructionist Movement in Modern Psychology," *American Psychologist* 40 (1985), pp. 266-275.

[5] S.J. Kessler and W. McKenna, *Gender: An Ethnomethodological Approach* (Chicago: University of Chicago Press, 1985), J.G. Morawski, "The Troubled Quest for Masculinity, Femininity and Androgyny" *Review of Personality and Social Psychology*, volume 7, P. Shaver and C. Hendrick, eds. (1987), pp. 44-69, and Leonore Tiefer, "A Political Perspective on the Use of Gender as Independent Variable," paper presented at the meeting of the International Academy of Sex Research, November 1983, Harriman, NY.

may not realize this. Gergen lists concepts such as romantic love, childhood, mother's love, the self, and emotion, which have meant very different things at different points historically and culturally. Insofar as these concepts are often uncritically assumed to relate to permanent human experiences or functions, their relativity is an important limitation on theory and method.

(3) The popularity or persistence of a particular concept, category, or method depends more on its usefulness (particularly its political usefulness for social influence and control) than on its validity. For example, the "hard" science, positivist-empiricist model of psychological research has been criticized for its limitations and omissions, yet it persists because of prestige, tradition, and unexamined congruence with cultural values.[6]

(4) Descriptions and explanations of the world are themselves forms of social action and have consequences. Gergen cites Gilligan's discussion[7] of the consequences of prominent theories of moral development to show how theoretical concepts and categories have systematically ignored and denied certain (in this case, women's) ethical values and processes.

Social Constructionism and Sexuality Scholarship

Many scholars credit French philosopher Michel Foucault's 1976 essay with first showing how the modern idea of sexuality has been constructed in a particular social-historical

---

[6] C.W. Sherif, "Bias in Psychology," in *The Prism of Sex*, J.A. Sherman and E.T. Beck, eds. (Madison: University of Wisconsin Press, 1979), pp. 93-133, and R. K. Unger, "Through the Looking-glass: No Wonderland Yet! (The Reciprocal Relationship between Methodology and Models of Reality)," *Psychology of Women Quarterly* 8 (1983), pp. 9-32.

[7] C. Gilligan, *In a Different Voice* (Cambridge: Harvard University Press, 1982).

context.[8] Foucault argues that, contrary to popular belief, sexuality has not been repressed and suppressed during a long, Victorian era only to gradually reawaken under the warming influence of twentieth-century permissiveness. In fact, he argues, there is no essential human quality or inner drive, sexuality, that can be repressed in one era and liberated in another. Rather, there is a human potential for consciousness, behavior, and physical experience available ("incited") by social forces of definition, regulation, organization, and categorization. Sexualities, he argued, are constantly produced, changed, and modified, and the nature of sexual discourse and experience changes accordingly.

In one of the most accessible explication of this approach, Plummer contrasts, point by point, the conventional drive-based sexologic view of the sources of human sexuality with a social constructionist (here, symbolic interactionist) position.[9] Is sexuality "really" a powerful universal biological drive that can be shaped by sociocultural forces and individual learning, or is it more akin to a learned "script," expressed in physical performance, fundamentally created, not just shaped, by the sociocultural moment?

Plummer shows how the dramaturgic metaphor of sexual script introduced and elaborated by Gagnon and Simon[10] leads to a vision of sexuality (1) as emergent in relationships and situations rather than as universal essence; (2) as needing to be constricted rather than as needing to be controlled; (3) as a shaper of conduct (as when sex is used to satisfy needs for affection, protection, and gender-validation); (4) as a contingent (depending on particular lives) rather than a necessary (mandated by some inevitable internal energy) form

---

[8] Michel Foucault, *The History of Sexuality*, volume 1 (New York: Pantheon, 1978).

[9] Kenneth Plummer, "Symbolic Interactionism and Sexual Conduct: An Emergent Perspective," in *Human Sexual Relations: Towards a Redefinition of Sexual Politics*, K. Howells, ed. (Oxford: Basil Blackwell, 1982), pp. 223-241.

[10] J.H. Gagnon and William Simon, *Sexual Conduct: The Social Sources of Human Sexuality* (Chicago: Aldine, 1973).

of human behavior; and (5) as an aspect of life that is qualitatively different for children and adults.

Histories and anthropologies of sexuality are being altered by the new constructionist emphases. If intercourse has always and everywhere felt, meant, and been the same, if a kiss is just a kiss, a sigh just a sigh, then it doesn't matter whether you are Roman or Barbarian, ancient or modern, 5 or 55, in love or just earning a living. This, of course, is counterintuitive, and indicates the fallacy of universal assumptions.[11] Whereas earlier scholarship merely reviewed cultural and historical variations in acts and attitudes,[12] newer history[13] and anthropology[14] trace the variations of the categories and concepts themselves. "In any approach that takes as predetermined and universal the categories of sexuality, real history disappears."[15]

Most sexologists appear unaware of these developments. Weeks points out that "even in the case of writers like Kinsey, whose work radically demystified sexuality, and whose taxonomic efforts undermined the notions of "normality," the [naturalistic] concept is still traceable in the emphasis on sexual 'outlet' as opposed to beliefs or identities."[16] Naturalistic assumptions are often related to belief in an evolution-related universal sex drive. Kinsey, whose biological background and fundamental allegiance have been described by

---

[11] Leonore Tiefer, "The Kiss," *Human Nature* (July 1978), pp. 149-158.

[12] For example, C.S. Ford and F.A. Beach, *Patterns of Sexual Behavior* (New York: Harper and Row, 1951) and R. Lewinsohn, *A History of Sexual Customs* (New York: Harper and Row, 1958).

[13] For example, Weeks, *Sex, Politics and Society.*

[14] For example, S.B. Ortner and H. Whitehead, eds., *Sexual Meanings: The Cultural Construction of Gender and Sexuality* (Cambridge: Cambridge University Press, 1981).

[15] Robert Padgug, "On Conceptualizing Sexuality in History," *Radical History Review* 20 (1979), p. 5, reprinted this volume.

[16] Jeffrey Weeks, "The Development of Sexual Theory and Sexual Politics," in *Human Sexual Relations: Towards a Redefinition of Sexual Politics*, M. Brake, ed. (New York: Pantheon, 1982), p. 295.

Robinson,[17] ultimately assumed a hydraulic model of sexual drive not unlike Freud's despite their differences concerning the source of sexual energy.

Why this universalization? Although all human conduct, from eating to dancing to thinking, is expressed through the body, scholars of these subjects do not see the role of anatomy and physiology as primary for understanding human experience. Hastrup, in analyzing the concepts of virginity and abortion, for example, contrasts the limited role of physiological realities with the multiple social and symbolic meanings, obvious cultural and historical variations, and so on.[18] Yet this emphasis is reversed in the case of erotic sexuality.

Miller and Fowlkes, among others, have suggested that the sociological perspective on sexuality has been limited because the few sociologists who are interested in sex have focused on deviance and social control, and have studied prostitutes, nudists, transvestites, and homosexuals much more than conventional patterns and populations.[19] Deviations became the subject, rather than the problematic nature of psychological sexuality itself. Although occasional social scientists, such as Simon,[20] have argued that it is an "illusion" that the body is a source of compelling sexual messages, controls sexual conduct, or is universal in its sexual expressions, the symbolic interactionist message has remained a minor voice in sexuality scholarship. It has taken the recent burst of publication from constructionist historians to make a noise loud enough to disturb the prevailing naturalism:

---

[17] P. Robinson, *The Modernization of Sex* (New York: Harper and Row, 1976).

[18] K. Hastrup, "The Semantics of Biology: Virginity," in *Defining Females: The Nature of Women in Society* (New York: John Wiley, 1978), pp. 49-65.

[19] P.Y. Miller and M.R. Fowlkes, "Social and Behavioral Construction of Female Sexuality," *Signs* 5 (1980), pp. 783-800.

[20] William Simon, "The Social, the Erotic, and the Sensual: The Complexities of Sexual Scripts," *Nebraska Symposium on Motivation* 21 (1973), pp. 61-82.

> Biological sexuality is the necessary precondition for human
> sexuality. But biological sexuality is only a precondition, a set
> of potentialities, which is never unmediated by human reality,
> and which becomes transformed in qualitatively new ways in
> human society.[21]

Aspects of the Social Constructionist Approach

It may be useful to outline some elements of a social
constructionist approach to the psychology of human sexuality
that builds on the platform introduced above.

- Analysis and challenge of categories and concepts

The most basic, and also most difficult, aspect of the study
of sexuality is defining the subject matter. Any study must
begin with an attempt to say both what is and what is not to be
included. How much of the body is relevant? How much of
the life span? How much of human behavior is to be
considered sexual? How much of thought and feeling? Which
interpersonal activities are sexual? Which group activities?
Can we use similar language for animals and people? How do
we deal with historical change and cultural variation?

The challenge, obviously, is to be inclusive enough to
capture a meaningful amount of human variation while being
selective enough not to study everything and its relation to
everything else! As Kinsey plaintively wrote in describing his
method,

> In spite of the long list of items included in the present
> [interview] study, [anywhere from 300 to 521 items per
> interview] and in spite of the fact that each history has covered
> five times as much material as in any previous study, numerous
> students have suggested, and undoubtedly will continue to
> suggest after the publication of the present volume, that we
> should have secured more data in the fields of their special

---

[21] Padgug, "On Conceptualizing Sexuality in History," p. 9.

interests. Specifically it has been suggested that the following matters should have had more thorough investigation: racial ancestry. . . somatotypes. . . hormonal assays. . . physical examination of the genitalia. . . marital adjustment. . . early childhood and parental relations. . . motivations and attitudes. . . cultural and community backgrounds. . . sperm counts.[22]

Sexologists have occasionally addressed issues of "terminology," but the assumptions of essentialism and naturalism prevent their seeing that the discussion of language is not a search for the "real" or "best" or "clearest" terms and definitions, but an exercise in boundary legitimation. What will we choose to see as sexual?

During a 1977 interdisciplinary conference, Katchadourian, a psychiatrist, made an unusual effort to discuss "the many meanings of sex."[23] His list included the fact of being male or female ("biological" sex), sexual behavior (including "internal" behavior such as fantasy), sexual experience (private feelings and thoughts), sex as behavior leading to orgasm (Kinsey's definition), sex as whatever is sexually motivated (Freud's definition), sexuality (the quality of being sexual, possessing of sexual capacity, or being capable of sexual feelings), sexual identity (including partner preference and sex-role identity), and core gender identity (the sense of being a man or woman). However, the entire discussion was a superficial review of terminological diversity, with no critical analysis. Had his discussion taken a constructionist turn, Katchadourian might have observed that almost all the terms relate to individuals and to functions. Is that what the many meaning of sex boil down to? If so, why? And, are we satisfied with that vocabulary?

Contrast this discussion with the one offered in a dialogue between Foucault and Sennett on the modern vocabulary of

---

[22] A.C. Kinsey, W.B. Pomeroy, and C.E. Martin, *Sexual Behavior in the Human Male* (Philadelphia: W. B. Saunders, 1948), p. 56

[23] H.A. Katchadourian, "The Terminology of Sex and Gender," in *Human Sexuality: A Comparative and Developmental Perspective* (Berkeley: University of California Press, 1979), pp. 8-34.

sexology.[24] They explicitly wonder where the individualized focus of the language (e.g., libido, desire, fantasy) comes from, and their study takes them to the contributions of early Christian theology and nineteenth-century medicine. Both theology, preoccupied at that time with sexual purity and personal obedience, and medicine, preoccupied at that time with sexual excess and insanity, emphasized sexuality as an individual matter. Sexuality fit into the domains of personal responsibility and personal medical disorder. The modern vocabulary has inherited this focus, in contrast to an emphasis on sexuality as a domain of interpersonal relations. Foucault and Sennett's historical discussion of terminology construes concepts as fluid, responsive, and constructed within a particular context, rather than as objectively valid. In such a discussion, there is no expectation that "the" definition of sexuality will ever emerge.

Another illuminating conceptual analysis is Robinson's discussion[25] of how Masters and Johnson's commitment to equal sexual rights for women led them to force their physiological findings to fit a procrustean bed of uniform human function, the "human sexual response cycle."[26] After selecting a homogeneous sample and testing subjects in an environment where the definition of sexual behavior was physical arousal and orgasm, Master and Johnson "found" similar physical patterns between men and women, which they described in terms of a fixed four-stage "cycle." The persistence of this concept is due to its political and professional usefulness, an example of one of Gergen's fundamental points about social constructions in science.

For the social constructionist, categories and concepts (such as gender, orgasm, homosexuality, genitals, desire, sexual offender, and sexual response-cycle) organize our personal

---

[24] Michel Foucault and R. Sennett, "Sexuality and Solitude," *Humanities in Review* 1 (1982), pp. 3-21.

[25] Robinson, *The Modernization of Sex.*

[26] W.H. Masters and V.E. Johnson, *Human Sexual Response* (Boston: Little, Brown, 1966).

and professional approach to sexuality. These concepts cannot simply be taken as objectively valid or given brief "factual" definitions.

- Imagery and Metaphor

As significant from a social constructionist point of view as terminology is the question of metaphor: What kinds of things is sexuality like? What metaphors are useful?

As mentioned above, Gagnon and Simon have found the language of dramatic scripts helpful for discussing sexuality.[27] Such a metaphor directs our attention to learned, planned, external sources of sexual behavior. Person, a psychoanalyst, shifts the metaphor to sexuality as a "sex print. . . in the sense of a fingerprint, unchangeable and unique. . . an individualized script that elicits erotic desire."[28] She wants to focus on the learned sources of eroticism, but also to retain a Freudian early-life determinism. By using "script," Simon had explicitly wanted to reject psychoanalytic ideas of irreversibility with a metaphor that would underscore

> a continuing potential for reordering of meanings, . . . a reordering that has permanent consequences in the sense that later changes are at the very least as significant in informing current behavior as were the original or earlier meanings and, in many instances, more significant.[29]

Metaphors such as "script" and "fingerprint" carry significantly different implications that relate in important ways to their originators' assumptions.

In one of the earliest social-constructionist papers, McIntosh contrasted the models of homosexuality as a

---

[27] J.H. Gagnon, "Scripts and the Coordination of Sexual Conduct," *Nebraska Symposium on Motivation* 21 (1973), pp. 27-60, and Simon, "The Social, the Erotic, and the Sensual."

[28] E.S. Person, "Sexuality as the Mainstay of Identity: Psychoanalytic Perspective," *Signs* 5 (1980), p. 620.

[29] "The Social, the Erotic, and the Sensual," p. 70.

"condition" and as a "role," and concluded that "role" imagery was more conducive to examining social, historic, and individual sexual variability, aspects that seemed central to her.[30]

The 1973 struggle over diagnostic nomenclature within the American Psychiatric Association provided a dramatic illustration of the power of imagery in sexual discourse.[31] Should homosexuality continue to be listed in the official APA manual of psychiatric disorders? Bayer describes how both proponents and opponents of "declassification" argued that the presence of homosexuality in the manual carries a powerful message to young people, parents, legislators, patients, teachers, and homosexuals. Decades of research on the effects of labeling (both halo and stigma effects) validate the impression that, in many cases, the metaphor is the message.

Poets have favored the language and imagery of sexual "pleasure" and "appetite" to emphasize the rich diversity of personal meaning and experience. Social scientists, however, have limited their discussions of sexual appetite and pleasure only to learned expectations that result from the reinforcing effects of "innate" enjoyment of genital stimulation.[32] Perhaps this is to distinguish learned human anticipation of sexuality from the primarily innate appetitive patterns of animals that indicate arousal and predict imminent mating.[33] Even psychoanalytic usage seems to restrict discussion to the acquisition of sexual appetites based on the experiences of early childhood. But the metaphor of appetite could also lend itself to exploring personal connections among appetites for sex, food, beauty, power, and so on. Similarly, a social constructionist approach could analyze the relationships among

---

[30] Mary McIntosh, "The Homosexual Role," *Social Problems* 16 (1968), pp. 182-192, reprinted this volume.

[31] R. Bayer, *Homosexuality and American Psychiatry* (New York: Basic Books, 1981).

[32] K.R. Hardy, "An Appetitional Theory of Sexual Motivation," *Psychology Review* 71 (1964), pp. 1-18.

[33] F.A. Beach, "Sexual Attractivity, Proceptivity, and Receptivity in Female Mammals," *Hormones and Behavior* 4 (1976), pp. 421-431.

various pleasures for an individual or a cultural group. So they feel the same? Can they be substituted? What effect does one type of enjoyment have on others? Once learned, can they be lost or forgotten?

The metaphors of work and play offer many images of individual and interpersonal activity and expression. The sex therapy literature seems to favor the work language of skills, practice, scheduling, technique, and mastery even as it stresses the importance of a playful attitude.[34] There may be interesting connections between an individual's values and models of work and play and how she or he perceives sexuality.

Images, as much as technical terms, organize our thinking, and are not to be taken lightly. They provide a fertile field for analysis, and the choice of metaphor in one's own communication about sexuality offers an opportunity to persuade at a level different from the factual.

- Historical Dimensions of Sexuality Languages

Historical analysis is especially effective in disputing essentialist biases. Social constructionism is attentive to the appearance, disappearance, and changes of many sexological concepts. Plummer's recent collection, *The Making of the Modern Homosexual*, for example, contains extended discussions of how the modern terms for describing physical and emotional closeness between two men or two women has evolved, and, furthermore, how the actors themselves have been affected by the linguistic changes.[35]

Recently, Elliott counted the prevalence of the terms "impotence" and "frigidity" in the psychological literature

---

[34] L.S. Lewis and D. Brissett, "Sex as Work: A Study of Avocational Counseling," *Social Problems* 15 (1967), pp. 8-18.
[35] Kenneth Plummer, ed., *The Making of the Modern Homosexual* (Totowa, NJ: Barnes and Noble, 1981).

between 1940 and 1983.[36] He found that each term appeared in titles indexed in *Psychological Abstracts* between two and eight times per year until 1970, when titles including "impotence" escalated dramatically. Despite numerous calls in the 1970s sexological literature for the elimination of both terms because of imprecision and pejorative connotations, "impotence" continued to flourish whereas "frigidity" almost disappeared. These observations open the door to a variety of constructionist analyses, and I have elsewhere suggested some social and economic explanations.[37]

Methods for Studying Sexuality

Feminists have examined the limitations and biases in traditional scholarship that prevent appreciation of the personal and social impact of gender. Many believe that the overwhelming emphasis on positivist-empiricist truth criteria in social science thwarts full understanding, a restriction not found in the interpretive traditions of history, anthropology, and literature.[38]

The social scientific study of human sexuality is similarly fettered by professional standards and reward systems that value only "experimentally rigorous" research in the most "objective" tradition.[39] The prestige hierarchy in psychology, with applied, correlational, descriptive work at the bottom and experimental, controlled, highly quantitative methods at the

---

[36] M. Elliott, "The Use of 'Impotence' and 'Frigidity': Why Has 'Impotence' Survived?" *Journal of Sex and Marital Therapy* 11 (1985), pp. 51-56.

[37] Leonore Tiefer, "In Pursuit of the Perfect Penis: The Medicalization of Male Sexuality," *American Behavioral Scientist* 29 (1986), pp. 579-600.

[38] J. Stacey and B. Thorne, "The Missing Feminist Revolution in Sociology," *Social Problems* 32 (1985), pp. 301-316.

[39] Leonore Tiefer, "The Context and Consequences of Contemporary Sex Research: A Feminist Perspective," in *Sex and Behavior: Status and Prospectus*, T.E. McGill, D.A. Dewsbury and B.D. Sachs, eds. (New York: Plenum, 1978), pp. 363-385.

top, holds true in sexuality research.[40] The small, prestigious, admission-by-election-only International Academy of Sex Research, for example, will not elect anyone to associate membership, much less full membership, without a suitable number of "empirical" sexuality publications. Annual arguments occur at the business meeting over the suitability of work in history or anthropology (to my knowledge, no literary expert in sexuality has applied for admission), but thus far the gates hold fast. It is not that such work is not worthy, the argument goes, it's just not science!

Contrast this position with Gergen's assertion that a constructionist analysis must

> eschew the empiricist account of scientific knowledge. . . the traditional Western conception of objective, individualistic, ahistorical knowledge. . . [and embrace criteria such as] the analyst's capacity to invite, compel, stimulate, or delight the audience. . . virtually any methodology can be employed so long as it enables the analyst to develop a more compelling case.[41]

To understand human sexuality fully, we need to see experimental, correlational, and clinical methods as complementary, not competing.[42] The popularity of sexual surveys[43] lies in their combination of quantitative and qualitative methods, generalizations derived from data together with personal stories and vignettes. Individual constructions of sexuality involve an interplay of social and psychological factors, and cannot be explored with only one method. When and how does a person construe a situation as sexual? How do people negotiate a sexual script? How does this change

---

[40] Sherif, "Bias in Psychology," pp. 93-133.

[41] Gergen, "The Social Constructionist Movement in Modern Psychology," pp. 271, 272, 273.

[42] R. Carlson, "Where Is the Person in Personality Research?" *Psychological Bulletin* 75 (1971), pp. 203-219.

[43] For example, S. Hite, *The Hite Report: A Nationwide Survey on Female Sexuality* (New York: Macmillan, 1976).

over the history of a relationship, a lifetime, a social generation?

Bell has recommended that researchers interested in homosexuality need to involve themselves more in the lives of their research subjects in order to appreciate fully the meanings of sexuality for their subjects.[44] Carlson called for new methods bridging former categories: short-term longitudinal studies, anonymous accounts of subjects' experiences during experimental research (wouldn't these have added a great deal to Masters and Johnson's physiological report?), and the publication of "incidental" phenomenological information that now rarely appears in the social science literatures.[45]

Suppose we were to start with a speculation such as the following:

> It is the recollection rather than the anticipation of the act that assumes a primary importance in homosexual relations. That is why the great homosexual writers of our culture can write so elegantly about the sexual act itself, because the homosexual imagination is for the most part concerned with reminiscing about the act rather than anticipating it. . . this is all due to concrete and practical considerations and says nothing about the intrinsic nature of homosexuality.[46]

Following Gergen's lead, our reaction would not merely be to formulate empirical research to decide whether and under what circumstances it is "true" that homosexuals feel and behave this way (although that agenda would be a welcome part of the exploratory enterprise), but rather to use a variety of avenues to explore and understand the who, what, when, where, and why of this speculation. What does clinical work on the nature of fantasy have to say? What about theories on the nature of artistic and literary representation? How might

---

[44] A.P. Bell, "Research in Homosexuality: Back to the Drawing Board, *Archives of Sexual Behavior* 4 (1975), pp. 421-431.
[45] Carlson, "Where Is the Person in Personality Research?"
[46] Michel Foucault, "An Interview with Michel Foucault," *Salmagundi* 58-59 (1982/1983), p. 19.

this change in an era with mass availability of erotic images? What differences do cultural variations in the encouragement of myth, fantasy, and individual imagination make?

Vance, analyzing a two-week sexology workshop, pointed out that "though sex research is inevitably based on theoretical and conceptual models, researchers and therapists alike maintain that they have no theory, no basic assumptions, no axe to grind. They are just collecting the facts."[47] This Mr. Clean image is in part a reaction against centuries of sexuality authorities' axes, but it serves to isolate and impoverish scholarship. A recent conference on sex research methodology sponsored by the National Institute of Mental Health underscored the field's commitment—at least that of the people who were invited—to "unambiguous concepts," "objective measurement," "operationalism," and "control" of many sorts.[48] Nevertheless, there were occasional suggestions for more constructionist scholarship, including life histories, analyses of the role of sex in diverse relationships, and the choice of real situations to study over laboratory analogs.

The Medicalization of Sexuality

The major obstacle to a social constructionist approach to sexuality is the domination of theory and research by the biomedical model.

The term medicalization refers to two interrelated processes. First, certain behaviors or conditions are given medical meaning—that is, defined in terms of health and illness. Second,

---

[47] Carole Vance, "Gender Systems, Ideology, and Sex Research," in *Powers of Desire: The Politics of Sexuality*, A. Snitow, C. Stansell and S. Thompson, eds. (New York: Monthly Review Press, 1983), p. 376.

[48] R. Green and J. Wiener, *Methodology in Sex Research*, report number 80-1502 (Washington, DC: Department of Health and Human Services, 1980)

medical practice becomes a vehicle for eliminating or controlling problemative experiences that are defined as deviant.[49]

The central ideological support for the medicalization of sexuality is essentialist, naturalist, biological thinking. The major constructionist project is to define and locate sexuality primarily in personal and relational, rather than physical, terms.

Analyzing the Privileged Position of Biology in Sexuality

Take a typical example of writing about sexuality:

> The scientific picture of sexual behavior has become so distorted that we must make a serious attempt to rediscover the obvious. In any attempt of this kind, it is always well to begin again at the beginning, in this case with a brief reexamination of the evolutionary differentiation of the sexes, and the physiologic basis of sexual activity. . . . In the most primitive protozoa, the individual propagates by its lone self.[50]

Even in a psychoanalytic article about sexuality we hear the familiar intonation: In the beginning were the birds and the bees. . . and the genes and the genitals and the protozoa. Every sexuality textbook gives the same testimony. The privileged position of biology in sexual discourse is based on the assumption that the body comes before everything else; it is the original source of action, experience, knowledge, and meaning for the species and the individual.

But isn't this just biological determinism and reductionism? Hasn't this fight already been successfully fought? Why is sexuality still so beholden to the body when other aspects of human conduct have long since been disengaged? The answer

---

[49] C.K. Riessman, "Women and Medicalization: A New Perspective," *Social Policy* 14 (1983), p. 4.

[50] S. Rado, "An Adaptational View of Sexual Behavior," in *Psychosexual Development in Health and Disease*, P. Hoch and J. Zubin, eds. (New York: Grune and Stratton, 1949), p. 159.

is complex, and will take far more unraveling than I can do here. I can touch on a bit of the answer, involving an analysis of the special position of sex in our Western Judeo-Christian sociocultural history, wherein sexual desire came to be located in the body, and spirit and reason in the mind.[51]

In his dialogue with Foucault, Sennett credits Tissot, the French-Swiss physician who believed masturbation was powerful and addictive, with translating the Christian moral agenda of sexuality (self-purification through sexual self-knowledge) to the biomedical idea that sexual desire exists in the individual, prior to any sexual attraction or relationship. The role of science became to examine sexuality as an individual phenomenon, and, incidentally, to support the hidden moral agenda.[52]

Weeks has traced the deep faith of early sexologists that in the struggle between sexual ignorance and enlightenment, the surest weapon would be biological science. He tells how German sexologist Magnus Hirschfeld, founder of sexology journals, research institutes, and international congresses, saw his Berlin Institute seized and its papers burned by the Nazis in 1933, yet could still write,

> I believe in Science, and I am convinced that Science, and above all the natural Sciences, must bring to mankind, not only truth, but with truth Justice, Liberty, and Peace.[53]

The hope that science would overcome prejudice and bring morality was widely shared.

---

[51] J.W. Petras, *Sexuality in Society* (Boston: Allyn and Bacon, 1973).

[52] Foucault and Sennett, "Sexuality and Solitude."

[53] Jeffrey Weeks, *Sexuality and Its Discontents* (London: Routledge and Kegan Paul, 1985), p. 71, citing Hirschfeld (1935).

> The laws which Science was uncovering would turn out to be the
> expression of the will of God—revelations of the divine Plan.
> Thus, science could provide moral guidelines for living.[54]

Sexual biology, at first the study of instincts, later the study of brain centers, germ plasm, hormones, genes, biochemical reactions, and fetal development, and most recently the study of vaginal blood flow, anal orgasm contractions, and clitoral histochemistry, would provide nature's direction for human sexual conduct. Set free from religious orthodoxy, science would allow what *is* to dictate what *ought to be*. Sexual biology would reveal true human sexual nature.

Biology's privileged position within contemporary sexuality discourse thus descends from the early researchers' hope that "objective science" would free us from the orthodoxies of the past. Yet the choice of biological variables limits our construction of sexuality even as empirical results do correct old prejudices. An example of this is the impact of Masters and Johnson's research on female sexuality, already mentioned. At the same time that their description and measurement of female orgasm documented some women's physical capacities, their focus on sexual desire and pleasure as measurable bodily states has mechanized, trivialized, and perhaps even further mystified the social and psychological aspects of sexuality.[55] Their work "corrected" past inaccuracy, but its sociological impact may ultimately be measured in terms of its effect on the social construction of sexual choices. The belief that a "true" understanding of biology must precede all other work is an assumption that requires detailed critical analysis.

Increasing Importance of Sexual "Adequacy"

---

[54] B. Ehrenreich and D. English, *For Her Own Good: 150 Years of the Experts' Advice to Women* (Garden City, NY: Anchor Press, 1978), p. 66.

[55] L. Segal, "Sensual Uncertainty, or Why the Clitoris Is not Enough," in *Sex and Love: New Thoughts on Old Contradictions*, J.A. Sherman and E.T. Beck, eds. (Madison: University of Wisconsin Press, 1983).

The social support for sexual medicalization arises in part from the increasing importance of sexuality itself in modern life. Like fitness, sexuality seems to gain importance as part of society's glorification of youth and health, its "denial of death." German sexologist Gunther Schmidt identifies three "compensatory" functions that sexuality serves in our time:

> [Sexuality] is supposed to hold marriages and relationships together because they scarcely fulfill material functions any longer; it is supposed to promote self-realization and self-esteem in a society that makes it more and more difficult to feel worth something and needed as an individual; it is supposed to drive out coldness and powerlessness in a world bureaucratized by administration, a world walled-up in concrete landscapes and a world of disrupted relationships at home and in the community. . . . All discontent—political, social, and personal—is meant to be deflected into the social and relationship sector in order to be compensated.[56]

In a world where gender remains important while the proofs of gender adequacy become more elusive, sexual knowledge and performance, for both men and women, need to serve that function, too.

Media and the Hegemony of Sexual Medicine

As sexual interest and adequacy gain in social importance, weaknesses in one's preparation become more significant. The major source of information for the young has become mass media, both because of parents' shyness and because of the dearth of sex education in the current conservative climate.[57] We know little of the impact of such dependence on commercial media.

---

[56] Gunther Schmidt, "Foreword," in *Human Sexuality and Its Problems*, J. Bancroft, ed. (Edinburgh: Churchill-Livingstine, 1983), pp. vii-viii.

[57] J.H. Gagnon, "Attitudes and Responses of Parents to Pre-Adolescent Masturbation," *Archives of Sexual Behavior* 14 (1985), pp. 451-466. I wrote sexual advice columns in the popular magazines *Playgirl* and

--->

In the twentieth century, mass media shape popular consciousness by providing language, experts, information, and fictional scripts. Nonfiction media are dominated by a health model of sexuality, with physicians, psychologists, or other health specialists the authorities. Sex enters the print media either because of a newsworthy event ("new" research or technology, sexual crimes, escapades of celebrities) or a feature article in which authorities give their opinions on issues of "normal" people's adjustment[58] or deviance.[59] Perhaps because of the history of obscenity censorship, media are more comfortable with the aspects of sexuality that seem most proper, that is, closer to medicine and public health than to pornography. The media use this health-model emphasis with little regard for scientific accuracy. A recent example is the promotion of a "new" sexual finding, "the 'G' spot," in 1981/1982.[60]

A trade book, based on skimpy research that even prior to publication had been contradicted in professional journals and scientific meetings, became a bestseller in 1982.[61] Its authors had appeared on national television a year earlier, drawing thousands of letters of interest from viewers. Newslike reports of a scientific "discovery," an area of unusual erotic sensitivity on the anterior wall of the vagina that appeared related in some way to the ability of women to ejaculate fluid at orgasm, had appeared in numerous women's magazines,

---

Playgirl Advisor in 1975-1976, as well as a series of essays about sex in *The New York Daily News* in 1980-1981. I still have hundreds of desperate and ignorance-filled letters I received at those times.

[58] L. Sarrel and P. Sarrel, "How to Have Great New Sex with Your Same Old Spouse," *Redbook* (March 1983), pp. 75-77, 172.

[59] S. Churcher, "The Anguish of the Transsexuals," *New York* (June 16, 1980), pp. 40-49.

[60] This discussion is based on an unpublished manuscript by Carol Tavris and Leonore Tiefer, "The 'G' Spot, the Media and Science," 1983.

[61] A.K. Ladas, B. Whipple, and J.D. Perry, *The G Spot and Other Recent Discoveries about Human Sexuality* (New York: Holt, Rinehart and Winston, 1982).

newspapers, and sex-oriented magazines. Seven book clubs purchased the book before publication. The insatiability of the media for the commercial potential of sexual topics results in an endless search for news and advice whereas disconfirming evidence receives little or no publicity.

The romantic and passion-filled portrayals of sexuality in the fiction media increase the public's expectations. If sex can provide such power, meaning, and material rewards, if it can make or break relationships, if it is such a large part of people's lives, then the public's dependence on experts and authorities for guidance in this maelstrom increases. A constructionist approach to sexuality can elucidate how individuals, couples, and social groups are affected by the media's various messages.

Political and Economic Aspects of Professional Expansion

Cultural authority in the area of sexuality is not passively conferred on health authorities; it is actively sought and consolidated. Through individual and group efforts, professionals act to ensure their autonomy, promote economic opportunities, and increase their public status.[62] Dominance is maintained through licensure (creating a monopoly by making it a crime for others to practice a particular craft), shaping service-providing institutions, multiplying subspecialities with high rates of cross-referral, eliminating "quacks" and other competitors through adverse publicity and legislation, controlling professional education, maintaining solidarity through professional conferences, journals, and jargon, and increasing the need for services in the eyes of the public.[63]

---

[62] M.S. Larson, *The Rise of Professionalism: A Sociological Analysis* (Berkeley: University of California Press, 1977).

[63] E.G. Mishler, "The Health-care System: Social Contexts and Consequences," in *Social Contexts of Health, Illness and Patient Care*, E.G. Mishler et al., eds. (Cambridge: Cambridge University Press, 1981) and P. Starr, *The Social Transformation of American Medicine* (New York: Basic Books, 1982).

In sexology, professional expansion and control have been promoted through specialty organizations with restricted memberships, locating "approved" service providers in medical institutions, using institutional public relations to advertise new services and disseminate research findings, holding frequent congresses and conferences open to the press, giving awards and other forms of recognition, and publishing numerous specialized technical journals and newsletters. The development of impotence treatment as a subspecialty within urology illustrates some of these processes.[64] The male gender role constructs potency narrowly as regular, resilient, rigid penile erections. In recent years, physicians (and the media) have challenged earlier claims that most erectile difficulties were not caused by medical problems, although this challenge is made without reliable data. At the same time, a surgical "cure" for erectile difficulties (the intrapenile implanting of a prosthesis) has been widely publicized through the media and patient education materials developed by prosthesis manufacturers. Social constructionist methods can analyze the ways such problems develop, solutions are provided, and individual men choose courses of action.

The recent establishment of female "anorgasmia" as a psychiatric disorder provides another example of medicalization.[65] Based on her wide familiarity with sexual patterns around the world, Margaret Mead had observed some decades ago,

---

[64] Tiefer, "In Pursuit of the Perfect Penis."

[65] American Psychiatric Association, *Diagnostic and Statistical Manual of Disorders*, (Washington DC: American Psychiatric Association, 1980). There were no sexual dysfunctions per se listed in the previous editions of the APA's *Diagnostic and Statistical Manual of Disorders* (1955, 1968), although "impotence" and "dyspareunia" (pain during intercourse) were mentioned as "psychophysiological genito-urinary disorders" in the 1968 edition. There are eight "psychosexual dysfunctions" listed in the 1980 (third) edition of the Manual, including "Inhibited Female Orgasm" (and "Inhibited Male Orgasm").

> There seems to be a reasonable basis to assuming that the human
> female's capacity for orgasm is to be viewed much more as a
> potentiality that may or may not be developed by a given
> culture, or in the specific life history of an individual, than as an
> inherent part of her full humanity.[66]

Just like playing the piano or grinding corn for tortillas,
having an orgasm is probably a universal human potential the
development of which depends on opportunity, training, and
goals. But rather than making orgasms a matter of talent and
predilection, our medicalized era has made them a matter of
health (and their absence a matter of disorder). The impact of
this on women's experience remains to be studied—a gold
mine for social constructionism.

The Public's Role in the Medicalization of Sexuality

The last factor to be acknowledged is the desiring public
itself. The public is no tabula rasa, passively responding to
the proselytizing of health experts and insatiable media.
Rather, for various personal and political reasons, medicalized
discourse about sexuality is actively sought.

The public's need for information and guidance has been
established by centuries of indoctrination on the centrality of
sexuality in judgments of sin and salvation. As sexual
performance assumes a more conspicuous role in personal life
satisfaction, the need for authoritative direction and self-
protective attributions increases. A medicalized discourse,
with its locus of explanation in the involuntary universe of
hormones and blood vessels, allows face-saving for
inadequacy the way "the Devil made me do it" permitted
exoneration from sin.

In addition, the public's desire for expert advice is fueled by
an eager and abiding interest in erotic pleasure. The "true"
human nature the public expects to be revealed by research on
sexual biology will include the capacity for sensual enjoyment,

---

[66] Margaret Mead, *Male and Female: A Study of the Sexes in a Changing
World* (New York: Mentor, 1955), p. 166.

and the public looks to scientific research for elucidation of that assumed basic capacity.

Politically, groups stigmatized or oppressed because of their sexuality welcome the morally neutral, biologically authoritative discourse of "objective medical science" to promote their own ends. Feminists, for example, embraced Masters and Johnson's medical model of sexuality because those authors insisted that their research "proved" women were entitled by their biology to sexual activity, pleasure, and orgasm. The American Psychiatric Association's battle over the classification of homosexuality as a disorder found both sides of the question citing medical research as evidence. And the gay community has gone on to cite their APA "victory" as evidence of the biological normalcy of homosexuality.

The assumption that the "bedrock" of biology will define and direct our choices as sexual beings provided the justification for the medicalization of sexuality and the major obstacle for social constructionism. The variety of political, economic, and personal motives for maintaining a medicalized discourse makes it a formidable obstacle, indeed.

Sexuality and Social-Personality Psychology

Throughout this chapter, I have made suggestions as to research topics and directions for a social-constructionist approach to human sexuality. Let me conclude, however, by focusing more directly on several areas where social-personality psychology can have an important impact.

Refocusing on Social Personality Dimensions of Sexuality

Personality and social psychologists could contribute to the social constructionist, rather than the medical, model. Any research that emphasizes individual and social group variations in sexual meaning and experience will undermine the assumptions of universalism that are so important to the medical mode.

Major issues that need to be addressed include: (1) How, from the universe of possible physical and mental activities, do people come to call certain ones sexual and conduct them in particular ways? (2) What are the personal meanings with which people invest these sexual activities? (3) How do these individual constructions change over the lifetime of a person or of a relationship?

We know very little for example, about the social and psychological meanings of words used very often in sexology: pleasure and intimacy. Young people, at least, rate pleasure as the most important element of sexual satisfaction;[67] yet if we cease assuming a universal inborn experience, what do we know of how people acquire the label 'pleasure' for what they do and feel in sexual relations? How does sexual "pleasure" relate to other activities also labeled 'pleasure?' The sex therapy literature is full of claims about the importance of intimacy to adequate sexual performance and experience,[68] although it is safe to assume that the vast majority of genital unions over the centuries have occurred without the presence of anything remotely like our modern idea of intimacy! Again, we know very little about the ways in which people feel intimate in sexual relations, or about how this can change. How does power imbalance between lovers affect their feelings of intimacy? What images do people have of their own bodies and those of their sexual partners, and what connections occur between those images and perceptions of intimacy? How do personality and social influences on self-disclosure and interpersonal trust affect sexual intimacy?[69]

---

[67] S.D. Perlman and P.R. Abramson, "Sexual Satisfaction among Married and Cohabitating Individuals," *Journal of Clinical and Consulting Psychology* 50 (1982), pp. 458-460.

[68] For example, A.N. Levay and A. Kagel, "Ego Deficiencies in the Areas of Pleasure, Intimacy, and Cooperation: Guidelines in the Diagnosis and Treatment of Sexual Dysfunctions," *Journal of Sex and Marital Therapy* 3 (1977), pp. 10-18.

[69] J.D. Cunningham, "Self-Disclosure Intimacy: Sex, Sex of Target, Cross-national and 'Generational' Differences," *Personality and Social Psychology Bulletin* 7 (1981), pp. 314-319, and C. Johnson-George and W.C. Swap, "Measurement of Specific Interpersonal Trust: Construction and Validation of a Scale to Assess Trust in a Specific

--->

Medicalized discourse with its smooth, unanalyzed prescriptions for what sexual experience ought ideally to be assumes that deviations from the ideal are pathological and the result of conflict or deficiency. But this position has been defined without real exploration of the ways sexuality develops, and the range of variations. In contrast to the individualized, physicalized focus of the medical model, it is particularly important that we develop ways to construe the relational aspects of sexuality.   Unfortunately, as psychologists, our tendency is to look at individual variables, which leads inevitably to an emphasis on the body as source and focus. If there is one central image in our efforts to refocus our thinking about sexuality, it should be to see sexuality as a construct that emerges in interaction as a result of expectations and negotiation, not something "inside" each of us.

Sexual Attributions

A rich area for social-personality psychologists at the moment is the study of sexual attributions. When we speak of the social construction of sexuality, we are literally referring to attributional processes, something that social and personality psychologists have studied extensively in recent years. How do people select attributions for sexual behavior (for themselves and others)? How many motives for sexual feelings and activities do people find plausible? How do the patterns of sexual attribution relate to gender, age, social class, sexual history—and to other patterns of attribution?

In my work in a hospital urology department with men who are complaining of erectile difficulties, I am aware of the extraordinary range of attributions they make for their problem, at least in the medical office setting. Other attributions emerge during interviews conducted separately

Other," *Journal of Personality and Social Psychology* 43, (1982), pp. 1306-1317.

with their primary sexual partners.[70] The use of physical attributions for sexual dysfunction seems a prime example of the "self-handicapping" strategy to maintain self-esteem and competency that Snyder and Smith have discussed in relation to other labels and symptoms.[71] I wonder to what extent self-enhancing and self-protecting attributions for sexual "success" and "failure" follow the same rules as for other forms of performance.[72]

Concluding Comments

John Gagnon, who has been one of the very few social-constructionist voices in sexology, believes that

> people become sexual in the same way they become everything else. Without much reflection, they pick up directions from their social environment. They acquire and assemble meanings, skills and values from the people around them. . . . The study of sex is best realized not through the creation of a special discipline called sexology and special scientists called sexologists, but rather by using the same theories and methods that are used to study other aspects of human conduct.[73]

Any social-personality psychologist who becomes interested in sex research will rapidly realize that, although Gagnon may theoretically be right in saying that sexual behavior is "just like" any other form of human conduct in its

---

[70] Leonore Tiefer and A. Melman, "Interview of Wives: A Necessary Adjunct in the Evaluation of Impotence," *Sexuality and Disability* 6 (1983), pp. 167-175.

[71] C.R. Snyder and T.W. Smith, "Symptoms of Self-Handicapping Strategies: The Virtues of Old Wine in a New Bottle," in *Integration of Clinical and Social Psychology*, G. Weary and H.L. Mirels, eds. (New York: Oxford University Press: 1982), pp. 104-127.

[72] D.T. Miller and M. Ross, "Self-Serving Biases in the Attribution of Causality: Fact or Fiction?" *Psychological Bulletin* 82 (1975), pp. 213-225.

[73] J.H. Gagnon, *Human Sexualities* (Glenview, IL: Scott, Foresman, 1977), p. 2.

acquisition, it is emphatically not just like any other form of human conduct in the public mind. By seeing how sexuality concepts and metaphors have been the subject of struggle over the centuries, I hope the reader will be in a better position to appreciate why sexuality scholarship has had and continues to have a hard time achieving legitimacy, not to mention funding.

Sexology as a discipline developed as much for the mutual protection of those interested in the subject as in any deliberate effort to create a dominant ideology and expand cultural authority. Because a major function of the medical cloak has been that of respectability for the sexologist,[74] engaging in nonbiomedical sexuality research will almost certainly be controversial. Nevertheless, the social constructionist agenda offers the social and personality psychologist some support and camaraderie in challenging the biomedical monolith, and the encouragement that beyond lies a form of human conduct rich, fascinating, and only barely understood.

---

[74] Weeks, *Sexuality and Its Discontents.*

CHAPTER 12:
Edward Stein
Conclusion: The Essentials of Constructionism and the Construction of Essentialism

The essays in this anthology cover a wide range of perspectives and points of view. As a supplement and complement to them, I will endeavor to look at the core of the debate between social constructionists and essentialists. First, I will distinguish the social constructionist controversy from other issues with which it is often confused. Second, I will consider some social constructionist arguments against essentialism; I will show that these arguments miss their mark by focusing on inessential details of essentialism. Third, I will sketch a more sophisticated version of essentialism and briefly consider some arguments for it. Fourth, I will turn to social constructionism and differentiate among various claims of social constructionists that are commonly conflated. Finally, I will turn to some arguments for social constructionism.

I.

Essentialists hold that a person's sexual orientation[1] is a culture-independent, objective and intrinsic property while social constructionists think it is culture-dependent, relational and, perhaps, not objective. (Roughly, an objective property is one a person has from a "god's eye" point of view, while an intrinsic property is one that a person has non-relationally, i.e., "inside" him or her; in other words, an intrinsic property

---

[1] See my introductory essay for an explanation of what I mean by 'sexual orientation.'

is one that a person could have even if she were the only person or thing in the world.) Essentialists think that being a heterosexual or homosexual is like having a certain blood type or being a person taller than six feet. The essentialist would have no problem saying that there were heterosexuals and homosexuals in Ancient Greece; it is just a matter of whether or not a person has the relevant properties (such as a certain gene, hormone, psychological condition, etc. or some combination of these). Even though people in past cultures may have had no idea what constitutes a gene, a hormone, an Oedipal complex or whatever the relevant properties are, they either did or did not have such properties, and thus the essentialist would claim that they were thereby either heterosexual or homosexual (or whatever the appropriate categories of sexual orientation are). In contrast, while social constructionists agree that people in all cultures engaged in sexual acts, they think that only in some cultures (e.g., our culture) are there people who have sexual orientations.

Some critics of social constructionism claim that the version of essentialism with which some people contrast social constructionism is a straw man;[2] essentialism, these critics say, is really a construction of the social constructionists.[3] Although there is a sense in which this is right, there is a viable position against which social constructionism can be contrasted that is appropriately called essentialism. What this position involves, however, is not exactly what many social constructionists or their critics think it is. Both often conflate

---

[2] See, for example, Wayne R. Dynes, "Wrestling with the Social Boa Constructor," this volume, pp. 216-18. See also John Boswell, "Concepts, Experiences and Sexuality," this volume, his "Revolutions, Universal and Sexual Categories," *Salmagundi* 58-59 (1982-83), pp. 89-113, the postscript to "Revolutions" which appeared in *Hidden from History*, Martin Duberman, et al., eds. (New York: New American Library, 1989), pp. 34-36, and his "Gay History," *Atlantic Monthly* (February 1989), pp. 74-78, which is a review of David Greenberg, *The Construction of Homosexuality* (Chicago: University of Chicago Press, 1988).

[3] Thanks to Charley Shively for this felicitous turn of phrase.

the social constructionist/essentialist debate variously with the nature/nurture debate as applied to sexual orientation and with the voluntarism/determinism debate as applied to sexual orientation.[4] While there are no doubt some connections among whether or not the property of being a homosexual is an objective property and whether or not a person can choose his or her sexual orientation and whether or not sexual orientation is learned or innate, these various claims do not amount to the same thing.

An interesting question about the categories of sexual orientation is whether or not people decide which category they fit. Voluntarists think that people can and do choose to be heterosexual or homosexual while determinists think that sexual orientation is determined. Many people (social constructionists and essentialists alike) think that all social constructionists are voluntarists and all essentialists are determinists. While it may turn out that many social constructionists are voluntarists and many essentialists are determinists, it is certainly *not* true that the pairings are universal. One could be both a social constructionist and a determinist; in fact, some social constructionists do think that sexual orientation is not at all a matter of an individual's

---

[4] Padgug, "Sexual Matters," this volume, p. 50, says that essentialists are committed to determinism and implies that social constructionists are committed to voluntarism. See also Steven Epstein, "Gay Politics, Gay Identity," this volume, pp. 241-42, for his definitions of essentialism and social constructionism which involve nature/nurture and voluntarism/determinism. Also see pp. 244-51, 261-62, and his "Nature vs. Nurture and the Politics of AIDS Organizing," *Out/Look* (Fall 1988), pp. 46-53. To his credit, Epstein, in the conclusion to his "Gay Politics" essay, pp. 285-293, does try to see beyond the rather impoverished version of social constructionism which he considered earlier (but he fails to consider an unimpoverished version of essentialism). See also, Carol Vance, "Social Construction Theory: Problems in the History of Sexuality," in *Homosexuality, Which Homosexuality?*, Dennis Altman, et al., eds. (London: GMP Publishers, 1989), pp. 13-34, especially pp. 13-14.

choice.[5] To see how it is possible for some property to be both constructed and determined, consider the property of being a peasant. This is surely a paradigmatic example of a socially constructed property, but it might very well be determined that someone has this property and will continue to have it whether or not she likes it since something about it is determined for her even though she has no choice in the matter. Just as one might not be able to choose to be a member of any social or economic class even though membership in such a class is a cultural artifact, so too it might be that sexual orientation is determined even though sexual orientation is a social construct.

Similarly, one could be both an essentialist and a voluntarist; some essentialists think that one can in effect choose one's own sexual orientation. To see how something can be an objective, transcultural property and yet be chosen, consider the property of being a biological mother. There are transcultural, objective facts about whether a particular person is a mother, yet it is possible to choose to be a mother. Just as someone could choose to be a mother even though being a mother is an objective, transcultural property, it might be possible to choose to be a homosexual even if being a homosexual was an objective, transcultural property. An example of a theory about the origin of sexual orientations which is essentialist and voluntarist is the so-called "first encounter" theory.[6] According to one version of this theory,

---

[5] David M. Halperin, "'Homosexuality': A Cultural Construct (An Exchange with Richard Schneider)," *One Hundred Years of Homosexuality and Other Essays on Greek Love* (New York: Routledge, 1990), pp. 41-53, explicitly defends such a view.

[6] See, for example, R.J. McGuire, J.M. Carlisle, and B.G. Young, "Sexual Deviations as Conditioned Behavior: a Hypothesis," *Behavior Research and Therapy* 2 (1965), pp. 185-190. See also Roger Brown, *Social Psychology: The Second Edition*, chapter 10, "Sources of Erotic Orientation" (New York: Free Press, 1986), pp. 344-373, and Michael Ruse, *Homosexuality: A Philosophical Inquiry* (New York: Basil Blackwell, 1988), chapter 4, "Freud: Extensions and Replacements," pp. 63-83, for discussions of this view. For a review of Ruse, see Paul

--->

one's sexual orientation is fixed by one's first pleasurable sexual experience. On such a view, being a heterosexual or homosexual is an objective, transcultural property, but one can have a choice in what his or her sexual orientation is by appropriately choosing the person with whom to have sexual contact for the first time. Despite the fact that this view has been shown to be empirically false,[7] it provides an example of a theory which is both essentialist and voluntarist. Since one can be a social constructionist and a determinist and since one can be an essentialist and a voluntarist, it is thus a mistake to collapse the distinction between social constructionism and essentialism into the distinction between determinism and voluntarism or *vice versa*.

A similar situation obtains with respect to the nature/nurture issue. Some people think that all essentialists hold that sexual orientation is innate and all social constructionists hold that sexual orientation is learned. Once again, this simple pairing does not work—one could be an essentialist and think sexual orientation is learned;[8] in fact, some essentialists hold such a view. As an example, consider again the first encounter theory. This theory of the origin of sexual orientations is essentialist (since on this theory there is an objective, transcultural, intrinsic fact about what one's sexual orientation is—this fact was determined by one's first sexual encounter) and yet this theory sees sexual orientation as learned, not innate. This example shows that essentialism does not necessarily imply that sexual orientation is innate.

Bloom and Edward Stein, "Reasonig Why?," *American Scholar* (Spring 1991), pp. 315-320. For further references, see Wayne R. Dynes, *Homosexuality: A Research Guide* (New York: Garland Publishing Company, 1987), chapter XVI, "Psychology," section A, pp. 511-514.

[7] For example, the data reported in Alan Bell, Martin Weinberg and Sue Hammersmith, *Sexual Preference* (Bloomington: Indiana University Press, 1981), chapter 9, pp. 96-113, refute at least this naïve version of the "first encounter" theory.

[8] James Weinrich, this volume, p. 181, makes a similar point. See also Boswell, this volume, pp. 135-36.

However, one cannot be a social constructionist and still think that sexual orientation is innate.[9] I need not, however, show that this is a possibility in order to show that the essentialist/social constructionist dichotomy is a quite different dichotomy from the innate/learned dichotomy.[10] Showing that essentialism is compatible either with sexual orientation being learned or with sexual orientation being innate is enough to show that it is a mistake to collapse the distinction between social constructionism and essentialism into the distinction between something being innate and something being learned (and *vice versa*). In sum, the essentialism/social constructionism question is not to be conflated with the question of the source of sexual orientations and the question of the voluntariness of sexual orientations.

So far, I have said that an essentialist does not have to think that homosexuality is innate or that heterosexuals have no choice but to be heterosexuals. An essentialist, however, *is* committed to there being transcultural law-like generalizations that can be made about the nature and origins of sexual orientation. An example of an essentialist theory is a hormonal theory of sexual orientation.[11] On a simplistic version of such

---

[9] Halperin, *One Hundred Years*, p. 49, admits that his constructionist theory would be proven false if sexual orientation were innate. See also Boswell, this volume, p. 138; Boswell's footnote 10 discusses a previous comment by Halperin on this same point.

[10] One might think that it is possible to be a constructionist *just* about the properties of being heterosexual and homosexual and yet think that sexual orientation is innate. This is possible if one thinks some other categories of sexual orientation are properly used to characterize sexual orientation and the relevant properties relating to these categories are innate. Such a theory is social constructionist only in a narrow sense (that is, only in relation to two categories) and is properly thought of as essentialist. I discuss this type of sophisticated essentialism below.

[11] For a recent example of a hormonal theory, see Lee Ellis and M. Ashley Ames, "Neurohormonal Functioning and Sexual Orientation: A Theory of Homosexuality-Heterosexuality," *Psychological Bulletin* 101 (1987), pp. 233-258. Also, see any of the many relevant books by John Money, e.g., most recently, his *Gay, Straight and In-Between: The Sexology of Erotic Orientation* (New York: Oxford University

--->

a theory, the level of certain hormones a person has in her system at some time determines her future sexual orientation. If this theory is true, the categories of sexual orientation are transcultural because a person's hormone level is what it is independent of culture; and the categories involve law-like generalizations because the theory claims, for example, that if a biologically female fetus is exposed to more than a certain level of testosterone, then this fetus will be strongly inclined to develop into a lesbian. Another example of an essentialist theory is a psychoanalytic theory.[12] On such a theory, a person's sexual orientation is the result of the nature of his childhood interactions with his primary adult contacts, usually his parents. If this theory is true, the categories of sexual orientation are transcultural in that the theory explains sexual orientations in all cultures and it makes law-like generalizations in that it predicts that a male child who has a dominant father and a passive mother will be inclined to develop into a heterosexual adult.

Press, 1988). For a critical review of this literature, see Ruse, *Homosexuality*, chapter 5, "Hormones and Homosexuality," pp. 84-129. For further references, see *Homosexuality: A Research Guide*, chapter XXIV, "Biology," section A, pp. 732-738.

[12]Sigmund Freud, *Three Essays on the Theory of Sexuality*, James Strachey, trans. (London: Imago, 1949). For more recent (essentialist) versions of psychoanalytic theories of sexual orientation, see Irving Bieber and T.B. Bieber, "Male Homosexuality," *Canadian Journal of Psychiatry* 24 (1979), pp. 409-421 and C.W. Socarides, "A Provisional Theory of Aetiology in Male Homosexuality," *International Journal of Psychoanalysis* 49 (1968), pp. 27-37. See Ronald Bayer, *Homosexuality and American Psychiatry* (New York: Basic Books, 1981) and Kenneth Lewes, *The Psychoanalytic Theory of Homosexuality* (New York: Simon and Schuster, 1988) for longer discussions. For more references, see *Homosexuality: A Research Guide*, chapter XVII, "Psychiatry," pp. 553-590. Interestingly, social constructionists also claim Freud's work supports their view.

II.

Having spelled out what essentialism is, I now turn to how the social constructionists see essentialism and to evaluating the claim that they have constructed a straw man version of it. When social constructionists make their anti-essentialist arguments, they usually direct them against specific versions of essentialism rather than against essentialism in general. The versions of essentialism they attack have one or more of the following attributes:

1. The essentialist theory is (at least primarily) a theory of homosexuality rather than of sexual orientation in general.
2. The essentialist theory uses naïve categories of sexual orientation.
3. The essentialist theory explains the origin of sexual orientations using a single theory (i.e., hormonal, psychoanalytic, etc.).

I will have more to say about each of these characteristics commonly attributed to essentialism, but first note that by arguing only against versions of essentialism that involve any or all of these attributes, social constructionists fail to attack the core of essentialism (i.e., that there are objective, transcultural categories of sexual orientation). Merely arguing against a naïve version of essentialism does not constitute an argument against essentialism in general. This is an instance of a common, yet fallacious, argument strategy: attack a general position by way of particular versions of it, or, more specifically, criticize a position by focusing on inessential features of it. If this is what anti-constructionists mean when they say that constructionists are attacking a straw man, then I think they are guilty of a misnomer. Essentialists who hold theories with these attributes hold false versions of essentialism; the social constructionists are right in arguing against theories which have the three aforementioned features. In other words, flogging a dead horse is fine as long as there are people who are trying to ride it. The social constructionists are wrong, however, in thinking that these arguments are *general* anti-essentialist arguments; they need to remember that the horse they are beating really is a dead one even though some essentialists are trying to ride it. The conceptual issue may seem a trivial one, but the way that some social constructionists mistake *some* essentialist theories for *all* essentialist theories is worth examining.

I will now return to the three features of essentialism commonly but wrongly thought to be necessary features of the view. The first feature is that essentialist theories often assume that we either do not require an explanation of heterosexuality or that we already have an explanation of heterosexuality and that all we need to do is explain homosexuality. Such essentialist theories are thereby only theories of the origin of homosexuality. But from the standpoint of scientific inquiry, it is mistaken simply to ask why some people are homosexuals. What requires explanation is the origin of sexual orientations of any (and every) sort. This is more than a plea for equal time for heterosexuals and bisexuals; any serious discussion of theories of homosexuality must evaluate these theories in terms of how well they can explain *all* sexual orientations. It is a mistake to assume that heterosexuality needs no explanation; explaining why a man wants to engage in vaginal intercourse with women is no easier than explaining why a man wants to engage in anal intercourse with men. Any version of essentialism that only offers a theory of homosexuality is woefully incomplete (not to mention heterosexist)—a *viable* version of essentialism will explain the origins of *all* sexual orientations. Social constructionists who argue against versions of essentialism that deal only with homosexuality are thus right in so doing but they are mistaken if they think they are thereby arguing against all forms of essentialism.

A brief caveat is in order. Some social constructionists go too far in reacting to this common mistake of essentialists. They say that since it is a mistake to try solely to explain homosexuality, the whole project of trying to discover the origins of sexual orientation is mistaken.[13] This is wrong.

---

13 Epstein, this volume, p. 251, points to the tendency of social constructionists to encourage a shift from questions about the origins of

--->

Just because homosexuality is no more mysterious than heterosexuality does not mean that neither is a mystery. Instead of asking why there is homosexuality, we should ask why there is homosexuality, heterosexuality, bisexuality, etc. It *is* heterosexist to search only for an explanation of homosexuality; it is *not* heterosexist to try to discover the origins of sexual orientation in general.

The second feature which many versions of essentialism have is an assumption that the categories of sexual orientation which are currently used by most people will be the same categories which will appear in an advanced theory of sexual orientation. In particular, they assume either a bipolar or binary view of sexual orientation.[14] A binary view of sexual orientation is one that assumes that a person's sexual orientation is one of two mutually exclusive sexual types— namely heterosexual and homosexual—while a bipolar view is one that assumes that a person's sexual orientation lies somewhere on a one-dimensional scale between two extreme poles, exclusive homosexuality and exclusive heterosexuality. Most essentialist theories are bipolar; they are based on the Kinsey scale, a sociological tool for describing human sexual behavior and the standard diagnostic for sexual orientation used by researchers working in the field of human sexuality.[15] The Kinsey scale assigns every person a number from zero to six according to how they respond to a series of questions about their sexual desires, fantasies and practices. Zero stands

---

homosexuality to those about the origins of homophobia. A recent example can be found in Halperin, *One Hundred Years*, p. 49: ". . . the search for a 'scientific' etiology of sexual orientation is itself a homophobic project, and needs to be more clearly seen as such."

[14] Epstein, this volume, p. 250, seems to think that all essentialist theories are committed to a binary or bipolar view of sexual orientation. See also Jan Schippers, "Homosexual Identity: Essentialism and Constructionism," in *Homosexuality, Which Homosexuality?*, pp. 139-147, especially pp. 142-143.

[15] A.C. Kinsey, W.B. Pomeroy, and C.E. Martin, *Sexual Behavior in the Human Male* (Philadelphia: W.B. Saunders, 1948) and *Sexual Behavior in the Human Female* (Philadelphia: W.B. Saunders, 1953).

for exclusive heterosexual fantasies, etc., and six stands for exclusive homosexual ones. This scale is useful for certain empirical studies. Adopting this scale leads, however, to a striking problem with respect to bisexuality.[16] Categorizing people who rate between two and four as bisexuals results in lumping together people who are erotically inclined to both men and women with a variety of other people including primarily heterosexual people who on one occasion engaged in same-sex[17] sexual activity,[18] primarily homosexual people who engaged in an isolated instance of other-sex sexual activity and people who are not very sexually attracted to either sex.[19]

---

[16] Neither essentialists or social constructionists have had much to say about bisexuality (as an objective or constructed category, respectively). For example, Greenberg, *Construction of Homosexuality*, has no entry for 'bisexual' or 'bisexuality' in its twenty page index (though 'heterosexuality' has sixteen page references to its credit). What has been written on the topic is referenced either in *Homosexuality: A Research Guide*, pp. 441-444 (though there are only twenty references here), or in the much more substantial bibliography by Charles Steir in *Two Lives to Lead: Bisexuality in Men and Women*, Fritz Klein and Timothy Wolf, eds. (New York: Harrington Park Press, 1985), pp. 235-248.

[17] I use the word 'sex' here to refer to a person's biological sex and 'gender' to a person's masculinity or femininity. To put in terms of a slogan, sex is between the legs and gender is between the ears—in other words, gender is socially constructed while sex is not. This slogan is an expanded version of a comment made by Roger Brown in *Social Psychology*, pp. 313-14. For a discussion of social constructionism about gender including an attempt to connect it to constructionism about sexual orientation and race, see Diana Fuss, *Essentially Speaking: Feminism, Nature and Difference* (New York: Routledge, 1989).

[18] The somewhat awkward locutions 'same-sex sexual activities' and 'other-sex sexual activities' are used to avoid the potentially question-begging move of calling such activities homosexual and heterosexual.

[19] Kinsey, et al. use an additional (non-numbered) category, the "X" category, for those who have "no social-sexual contacts or reactions," (*Sexual Behavior in the Human Male*, p. 656). This category, for

--->

A bipolar or binary view of sexual orientation cannot just be assumed. What reason have we to think that the categories homosexual, heterosexual, and (perhaps) bisexual will turn out to be the categories explained by an advanced theory of sexual orientation? This scheme of categorization may seem quite natural, but seemingly natural ways of looking at things are frequently rejected in emerging fields of knowledge; contrary to what we first thought, whales are mammals, not fish, and glass is a liquid, not a solid. Looked at in this light, it would be very surprising if our commonsense categories of sexuality get used in an advanced theory of sexual orientation.

Bipolar and binary views of sexual orientation have more going against them than that they are mere commonsense categories which act as unargued assumptions; there is good reason to believe they are false. This idea was developed from an analogy with the project of developing accurate measures of masculinity and femininity. Working independently, psychologists Sandra Bem[20] and Janet Spence[21] have pointed out that there is something seriously wrong with viewing masculinity and femininity, defined in terms of conformity to gender stereotypes, as opposite sides of a scale. They suggest that masculinity and femininity should be viewed as independent sets of traits; somebody can have a high (or low)

---

example, includes about fifteen percent of twenty-five year old, single females (*Sexual Behavior in the Human Female*, p. 473). Presumably, many people who fit in the category of people who are not sexually attracted to either sex (i.e., people who might be called asexuals) would be placed in the X category.

[20] Sandra Bem, "The Measurement of Psychological Androgyny," *Journal of Consulting and Clinical Psychology* 42 (1974), pp. 155-162, and "On the Utility of Alternative Procedures for Assessing Psychological Androgyny," *Journal of Consulting and Clinical Psychology* 46 (1977), pp. 195-205, as well as other articles by Bem.

[21] Janet Spence, R.L. Helmreich and J. Stapp, "The Personal Attributes Questionnaire: A Measure of Sex-role Stereotypes and Masculinity and Femininity," *JSAS Catalog of Selected Documents in Psychology* 4 (1974), p. 43, and "Ratings of Self and Peers on Sex Role Stereotypes and Masculinity-Femininity" *Journal of Personality and Social Psychology* 32 (1975), pp. 29-39, as well as other articles by Spence.

degree of masculinity and at the same time have a high (or low) degree of femininity. This conflicts with a bipolar (Kinsey-style) view of gender characteristics, where high masculinity entails low femininity, and high femininity entails low masculinity. The Bem-Spence critique extends naturally to the issue of sexual orientation; contrary to the Kinsey scale, human sexuality might not be unidimensional. That a person is highly attracted to members of his or her own sex does not necessarily imply that the same person is not attracted to members of the opposite sex and *vice versa*. In fact, psychologist Michael Storms has found that, on average, bisexuals are as attracted to their own sex as exclusive homosexuals are and as attracted to the opposite sex as exclusive heterosexuals are.[22] Storms argues for a two-dimensional view of sexual orientation—with one dimension representing degree of attraction to the same sex and the other representing degree of attraction to the opposite sex—in order to characterize accurately the variety of sexual orientations. Our commonsense categories of sexual orientation may well be inadequate for scientific theories dealing with the origin of sexual orientation. For this reason, a viable version of essentialism should not assume our standard categories of sexual orientation. Anti-essentialist arguments which assume that essentialism must involve such categories are thus impotent against essentialism in general.

The remaining feature commonly and wrongly thought to be essential to essentialism is that there is a single explanation for the development of sexual orientations. Freudian theories claim that homosexuality is due to unresolved Oedipal complexes and heterosexuality is due to resolved ones; hormonal theories claim that homosexuality is due to an imbalance of sex-linked hormones, while heterosexuality is

---

[22] Michael Storms, "Theories of Sexual Orientation," *Journal of Personality and Social Psychology* 38 (1980), pp. 783-792. See also his "Sex-Role Identity and Its Relationship to Sex-Role Attributes and Sex-Role Stereotypes," *Journal of Personality and Social Psychology* 37 (1979), pp. 1779-1789, and "A Theory of Erotic Orientation Development," *Psychological Review* 88 (1981), pp. 340-353.

due to a balance of them, etc. Clearly, things need not be so simple. A person's sexual orientation might be caused by a combination of a variety of factors—genetic, hormonal, environmental, psychological, etc.—and different people's sexual orientations might have developed out of different sets of factors.[23]   Thus, an anti-essentialist argument which assumes that essentialism must involve only a single explanatory theory will fail. A sophisticated essentialism will be a theory of all sexual orientations, will not use our naïve categories of sexual orientation, and will not be committed to explaining the origins of sexual orientations using a single theory. Such an essentialist theory will look for culture-independent, objective and intrinsic properties—what might be called "deep" properties—which are involved in sexual orientation.

III.

Briefly, I will turn to the arguments for essentialism. Most of these arguments proceed as follows: a particular theory of the origin of sexual orientation is offered, evidence is given for this theory, and the theory is then used as support for essentialism. For example, a sociobiological theory for the origins of sexual orientation might be sketched and some evidence given for it; this, in turn, is taken as evidence for the truth of essentialism. This is not the place to evaluate the details of such arguments—I only have room to point to their structure.[24]

---

[23] For an attempt to combine several theories, see Ruse, *Homosexuality*, chapter 7, "Reductionism and Determinism." See Bloom and Stein, "Philosophy of Sexual Orientation" for a brief evaluation of this attempt.

[24] For a general discussion of particular scientific theories, see, for example, Ruse, *Homosexuality*, and Roger Brown, *Social Psychology*, pp. 344-373. For sociobiological theories, see Ruse, chapter 6, "The Sociobiology of Homosexuality" and Donald Symonds, *The Evolution of Human Sexuality* (New York: Oxford University Press, 1979). For critiques of sociobiological theories, see Douglas Futuyma and Stephen

--->

Another type argument for essentialism worth mentioning is the one I call the argument from Ockham's razor. Ockham's razor (also known as the principle of parsimony) says that, all else being equal, the simplest of the candidate explanations for something should be accepted. The argument for essentialism based on Ockham's razor goes as follows: either we explain the various forms of same-sex and other-sex sexual behaviors in various cultures by appealing to the different social situations in each culture which give rise to these sexual behaviors, or we explain the various forms of same-sex and other-sex sexual behaviors by appealing to a single essential feature of people which is culture independent; the second explanation is simpler, therefore, by Ockham's razor, it should be accepted.[25]

This argument, though interesting, fails. Although social constructionism does have to tell more stories in order to explain same-sex and other-sex sexual activities, it is able to give such an explanation by using a more familiar (i.e., observable and commonly understood), and hence, by one standard, a simpler mechanism. In other words, the social constructionist can respond that using a variety of what might be loosely described as "social factors" to explain sexual activities is simpler than using genes, hormones, or the like to explain such behaviors. The social constructionists' point can be made even stronger by noting that any theory of sexual orientation (even an essentialist one) will admit *some* learning mechanism in the development of a particular sexual preference. Thus social constructionist theories are simpler in that they have a theory of the origin of sexual orientation that appeals *only* to such learning mechanisms. More generally, Ockham's razor cannot decide between these two candidate explanations. There are various metrics of simplicity (no one

---

Risch, "Sexual Orientation, Sociobiology and Evolution," *Journal of Homosexuality* 9 (1983-84), pp. 157-168, and Bloom and Stein, "Philosophy of Sexual Orientation." For further references, see *Homosexuality: A Reference Guide*, chapter XXIV, "Biology," section B.

[25] Boswell, "Gay History," p. 75.

of which is sufficient) and one explanation may fare better with respect to one metric but not with respect to another. In the case at hand, essentialism fares better when the metric is the number of independent hypotheses required, while social constructionism fares better when the metric is the complexity of the mechanism involved in the explanation. The appeal to Ockham's razor is at best inconclusive.

There is another type of argument for essentialism, which I call the "good for gays" argument. "Good for gays" type of arguments take the following form: essentialism, if true, would be good for gay rights and/or writing social criticism, literary criticism, or history; therefore, essentialism is true.[26] These arguments fail because their conclusions about the truth of essentialism do not follow logically from (or, more bluntly, are simply irrelevant to) their premises.[27]

IV.

Having spelled out the central thesis of essentialism and argued that many features commonly attributed to essentialism are not necessary features of it, I now turn to social constructionism. I have characterized the central thesis of social constructionism as negative; social constructionism is the view that there are no objective, culture-independent categories of sexual orientation—no one is, independent of a culture, a heterosexual or homosexual. In part, social constructionism is defined negatively because, historically, essentialism has been dominant. But there is another part to a

---

[26] For example, see Boswell, "Revolutions," p. 93, and his "Gay History," especially pp. 74-75.

[27] Essentialists are not alone in making "good for gays" arguments; social constructionists make them as well. See, for example, Halperin, *One Hundred Years*, p. 42. Also, Schippers, "Homosexual Identity," p. 143, makes what sounds like the "good for gays" argument when he says that essentialism is "repressive and limiting." See Epstein, this volume, for a discussion of the politics of the social constructionist controversy. Also, see Fuss, *Essentially Speaking*, chapter 6, pp. 97-112.

complete social constructionist theory: the social constructionist owes an account of how sexual desires are constructed and produced. This account involves a "conceptual history" of why we use the terms 'heterosexual' and 'homosexual' in our cultural vocabulary, where they come from, what they are supposed to refer, etc.[28] There are thus two parts to social constructionism—a negative claim and a positive claim. The negative claim is the anti-essentialist claim while the positive claim tries to explain how we have the sexual desires that we do and, as part of this, to explain why people think that the categories heterosexual and homosexual are objective, transcultural and refer to particular groups of people.

There are, however, two types of social constructionism. While both types share the negative and positive claims sketched above, they diverge over the issue of whether there are actually heterosexuals and homosexuals in our society today. One version of social constructionism has its roots in Hegel and comes to us via Foucault. It holds that there *are* heterosexuals and homosexuals in today's society but that there have been such people only since the homosexual emerged as a type of person sometime in the nineteenth century.[29] On this version of social constructionism, sexual orientation is an objective property, but it is not a culture-independent or intrinsic one. Social constructionists of this stripe need to explain the process whereby homosexuals and heterosexuals emerged as types of people or forms of life. The other version, which I shall call the "empty-category"

---

[28] This sort of account is offered by Foucault, this volume, and Davidson, this volume. Padgug, this volume, does so as well.

[29] See the essays of Foucault, Hacking and Davidson in this volume. See also Jeffrey Weeks, *Coming Out: Homosexual Politics in Britain from the Nineteenth Century to the Present* (New York: Horizon Press, 1977), *Sexuality and Its Discontents: Meanings, Myths and Modern Sexuality* (London: Routledge and Kegan Paul, 1985) and Halperin, *One Hundred Years.*

version of constructionism,[30] (which has some roots in "labeling theory" in sociology and comes to us via the "social interactionist" school[31]), holds that, although we have the categories heterosexual and homosexual, there are no people who actually fit into these categories. On such a view, as characterized by Gore Vidal

> [t]here is no such thing as a homosexual, no such thing as a heterosexual. Everyone has homosexual and heterosexual desires and impulses and responses. . . [T]rust a nitwit society like this one to think that there are only two categories [for men]—fag and straight and if you are the first, you want to be a woman and if you're the second, you're a pretty damned wonderful guy.

The empty-category social constructionist thinks that the categories heterosexual and homosexual are like the category witch. There were people in the 17th century who were claimed (sometimes by others and sometimes by themselves) to be witches but we now know that there were no witches (i.e., there were no women with supernatural powers who had sex with the devil) and that the category witch (in the specific sense of the term I have indicated) just did not and does not properly apply to any person. Similarly, that many people in the 20th century are claimed (by themselves and others) to be homosexual or heterosexual does not prove that these categories properly apply to people. According to the empty-category constructionists, these categories do not, in fact, apply to anyone. In contrast, the Foucault-style social constructionists think that the category homosexual is more like the category yuppie. The term 'yuppie' is a recent creation, yuppies have only come into being recently, yuppie

---

30 See Boswell, "Revolutions," p. 97, for a discussion of what he calls "type A" theories. Although neither embraces empty-category constructionism in the bald form I sketch it here, see McIntosh, this volume, and the works of Jeffrey Weeks.

31 See Epstein, this volume, pp. 245-51, for a discussion of the sociological origins of social constructionism. For a more detailed discussion, see Stephen O. Murray, *Social Theory, Homosexual Reality* (New York: Gay Academic Union, 1984).

is not a transcultural category, (e.g., there were no yuppies in Ancient Greece), but there clearly are yuppies here and now.

Note that these two versions of social constructionism are related. A Foucault-style social constructionist would have been an empty-category social constructionist before that seminal moment in the 19th century which gave rise to the term 'homosexual' and with it the homosexual as a type of person. Both types of social constructionists would agree, for example, that there were no homosexuals in Ancient Greece (although both would accept that there were people in Ancient Greece who engaged in sexual activities with people of the same sex). The point of disagreement is whether anybody in this culture is properly claimed to be homosexual or heterosexual. The Foucault types say "yes," while the empty-category types say "no."

Although all social constructionists think that there were no homosexuals in Ancient Greece, they would accept that people were engaging in same-sex sexual activities then. This may seem confusing because having sex with a person of the same sex might seem to be just what it means to be a homosexual. This, however, is not what being a homosexual (or heterosexual) means. To see this, note that a person could die without ever having engaged in any sexual acts with any person of either sex and still be considered a homosexual (or heterosexual) and that a person does not instantly become a homosexual (or heterosexual) simply by engaging in his or her first sexual act.[32] This shows that behavior alone does not determine sexual orientation,[33] which in turn leaves the door

---

[32] That this is true is suggested both by common usage of 'homosexual' and 'heterosexual' as well as empirical inquiry. See my discussion of the "first encounter theory" and footnote 6, above.

[33] This discussion of what having a sexual orientation amounts to is rather quick. The idea is that certain behavior is not necessary (I also do not think it is sufficient) for having a certain sexual orientation; rather, fantasies, desires, dispositions and the like determine sexual orientation. In terms of a slogan, sexual orientation is in the head, not in the bed. Looked at in this way, the debate between essentialists and social

--->

open for the social constructionist to admit that Ancient Greeks engaged in same-sex sexual acts while denying that there were any homosexuals in Ancient Greece.

That there are two parts to social constructionism—the negative and the positive—holds for both empty-category constructionism and Foucault-style constructionism. So far, however, I have said very little about the positive part which attempts to account for why we use the terms 'heterosexual' and 'homosexual' in our culture. The other essays in this volume discuss the details of the social constructionists' positive claims; I will thus limit myself to one general comment. The positive claims of social constructionism are independent of its negative (anti-essentialist) claims, and, are therefore perfectly compatible with essentialism. Simply put, a theory of the origins of sexual orientations of people is independent of a history of currently used categories of sexual orientation or a history of the emergence of "different forms of life." For example, that the word 'homosexual' signifying a type of person entered the human vocabulary in the nineteenth century is compatible with almost every essentialist theory. In fact, most essentialist theories do not even try to explain where our current concepts come from[34]—they are concerned with how people have the *sexual orientations* they do, not how people have the *concepts* they do.[35] This is not to say that the

---

constructionist is over the status of these dispositions and the categories that they determine.

[34] Schippers, "Homosexual Identity," p. 143, for example, seems to overlook this when he says that it is a drawback of essentialism that it cannot account for cross-cultural differences. Essentialism needs to be (and is) *consistent* with there being many cross-cultural differences; it need not offer a theory of such differences, it just needs to posit an adequate degree of flexibility to allow for them.

[35] I think this is implicit in Weinrich's "interactionist" theory of sexual orientation as discussed in his contribution to this anthology, pp. 181-82 and *passim*. His view is that the proper theory of sexual orientation will have essentialist *and* constructionist components. In the sense he means, this is true but also trivial. Only a naïve essentialist would have thought that social factors play no role at all in the development

--->

way people conceptualize the categories of sexual orientation has nothing to do with the origins of sexual orientations in people—in fact, social constructionists think that the two are intimately connected. My point is that simply telling tales (even true ones) about where concepts come from is not enough to establish social constructionism.

But if story telling is insufficient to establish social constructionism, what sort of arguments can social constructionists make for their view? One argument frequently given for social constructionism is based on the observation that different cultures have various ways of categorizing sexual orientation and that only recently has it become common practice to group people on the basis of which biological sex they are attracted to. Examples from Ancient Greece and Medieval times are frequently cited as historical evidence for social constructionism.[36] Two other frequently cited examples involve the Native American berdache and certain cultures of the Pacific.

In many Native American tribes, there are certain men and women who assume the gender role of the opposite sex. These people, called berdaches, often dress and behave in the traditional manner of the opposite sex and engage in sexual and marital relations with members of the same sex.[37] In some

---

of a person's sexual orientation and preferences. Weinrich suggests otherwise when he calls his interactionist theory a mix between essentialism (realism) and social constructionism. Interactionism only involves social constructionism in a minimal sense; no good constructionist would embrace the tenets of Weinrich's interactionism and most good essentialists already do.

[36] See *The Construction of Homosexuality* for a survey of the historical and anthropological evidence. See Kenneth Dover, *Greek Homosexuality* (Cambridge: Harvard University Press, 1975), for the classic discussion of Ancient Greece and *One Hundred Years* for a recent (and constructionist) discussion of Ancient Greece. For more references, see *Homosexuality: A Research Guide*, chapter IV, "Anthropology," pp. 198-235.

[37] See *The Construction of Homosexuality*, pp. 40- 56 and *passim*, as well as Walter Williams, *The Spirit and the Flesh: Sexual Diversity in*

--->

cultures of New Guinea and Melanesia, a more general institutionalized role for same-sex behavior exists. Males and females of certain ages live separately and communally in these cultures. Until they reach marriage age, men participate in primarily same-sex sexual activities. Engaging in age-asymmetrical, same-sex sexual behaviors is traditionally practiced in these cultures—it is viewed as part of the maturational process of pubescent boys to play the receptor role in anal or oral intercourse with older men.[38] These examples demonstrate that most cultures do not share our culture's way of categorizing people on the basis of the sex they are primarily attracted to.

These sorts of examples can be multiplied and the results are quite interesting, but what does this evidence prove? Some social constructionists take it to show that since the categories of homosexual and heterosexual are culture specific, any general theory which makes use of these terms will necessarily be false. I will call this argument for social constructionism the "no concept" argument, because the premise of the argument is that other cultures do not have the words or concepts for heterosexuals and homosexuals.

For the "no concept" argument to be successful it has to give good reasons for thinking that the categories heterosexual and homosexual are like the categories witch or yuppie (depending on which type of social constructionism is being advanced). But it does not do so. Merely demonstrating that previous cultures used different categories is not enough; if it were, the same technique could be used to disprove much of our current knowledge. To see this point, consider the example of color blindness. Color blindness (as a particular

---

American Indian Culture (Boston: Beacon Press, 1986) and Weinrich, this volume.

[38] See The Construction of Homosexuality, pp. 26-40 and passim, and G.H. Herdt, ed., Ritualized Homosexuality in Melanesia (Berkeley: University of California Press, 1984) as well as Herdt, Guardians of the Flutes: Idioms of Masculinity (New York: McGraw Hill, 1981) and The Sambia: Ritual and Gender in New Guinea (New York: Holt, 1987).

physiological condition) wasn't discovered (that is, no one knew about it, not even people who had it) until relatively recently. This does not mean that no one before the nineteenth century had genes that coded for color blindness and that everyone could distinguish colors; there were of course color blind people regardless of whether or not any one knew about color blindness. If this were not the case, it would be easy to cure color blindness in 100 years: simply wipe out all discussion of color blindness from textbooks and never tell our children about it. Then, after we all die out, there would be no one left who would know about color blindness and the condition would simply disappear. The point of this example is that just showing that many other cultures did not have categories for a certain sort of person (a color blind person or a homosexual) does not show that these concepts fail to pick out intrinsic properties, that they cannot properly be applied transculturally or that such concepts are not objective and about the world; to use a term I introduced above, it does not show that there are no relevant deep properties. The "no concept" argument thus fails.[39]

But the "no concept" argument is not the only one that social constructionists make. Foucault-type social constructionists also argue that different cultures produce different forms of sexual desire and different types of people and this difference shows that essentialism is false. I call this the "different forms of life" argument. Social constructionists who make this argument again appeal to anthropological and historical evidence but in a different way. These examples are supposed to show that different cultures *produce* different sorts of sexuality and sexual desires.[40] The sorts of sexual

---

[39] Will Roscoe, "Making History: The Challenge of Lesbian and Gay Scholarship," *Journal of Homosexuality* 15 (1988), p. 12, makes a brief comment which seems similar to my response to the "no concept" argument. Roscoe's article is a very nice attempt to provide a foundation for lesbian and gay studies without committing either to essentialism or social constructionism.

[40] See the essays of Foucault, Hacking and Davidson in this volume, as well as the works of Weeks and *One Hundred Years*, "'Homosexuality':

--->

lives that people live in some other cultures are so dramatically different from ours that the way we describe sexual activities in our culture cannot possibly describe their cultures. The fact of varying "forms of life" prevents transcultural application of the terms 'heterosexual' and 'homosexual' and thus constitutes an argument against essentialism.

No doubt it is true that such examples provide very strong evidence that people in different cultures have radically different ways of looking at sex as well as sexual relationships and different ways of expressing and experiencing sexual desire and pleasure. However, only the most extreme essentialist would disagree with this. What most essentialists *would* disagree with is whether the fact that different societies have different ways of experiencing and looking at sex and sexual relationships has anything to do with whether or not there are homosexuals or heterosexuals in such societies.[41]

To show that the "different forms of life" argument also fails, consider a (contrived) example involving epilepsy. Suppose that an anthropologist studying various societies' conceptions of epilepsy showed that different cultures had vastly different views of this condition and thereby constructed it differently. Ancient Greeks, let us say, thought that epileptic fits were blessings from a deity. In Medieval times, epileptics were thought to be possessed by the devil. In certain Native American cultures, epileptics were thought to have special powers and to be able to cause rainstorms. Some cultures might construct institutions and attitudes around the epileptic condition as a disease (as our society does), whereas others might construct institutions and attitudes around epilepsy as a spiritual phenomenon. A great diversity of social constructions around this condition is perfectly compatible with the fact that epilepsy involves irregularities in neurotransmitters which is caused by a certain genetic

---

A Cultural Construct." Numerous conversations with David Halperin have helped me to formulate my gloss of and take on the "different forms of life" argument (neither of which he necessarily accepts).

[41] Boswell, "Gay History," p. 76, makes what I take to be a similar point against Greenberg's constructionism.

configuration, with the associated fact that being an epileptic is a paradigmatic essential property. That historians and anthropologists tell such stories about the way societies conceived and constructed epilepsy does not change the fact that being an epileptic is an essential property. The mere fact that there are different ways of producing social forms of life around a property (such as epilepsy or heterosexuality) does not mean that the property cannot appropriately be applied across cultures or that the property is not an objective one. The "different forms of life" argument thus fails as well.

Perhaps I am being a bit unfair to social constructionists by watering down their arguments. Some social constructionists make more radical arguments for their view by appealing to quite general relativistic arguments.[42] If metaphysical relativism is true and there is no mind- or culture-independent world, then social constructionism will turn out to be correct about heterosexuals and homosexuals. If there are no objective, culture-independent categories of any sort in the world, then there are no objective, culture-independent categories of sexual orientation. But such radical social constructionism, at best, amounts to throwing the baby out with the bath water. The bath water is the categories heterosexual and homosexual which the social constructionist wants to say are not objective and not culture-independent, while the baby is the rest of our (possibly) objective, culture-independent categories.

The project of social constructionism about sexual orientation is to distinguish the property of being a heterosexual (which is claimed to be not objective and culture-independent) from properties like being a proton or having a Y-chromosome (which are supposed to be objective and culture-independent). But if metaphysical relativism is true, then there is nothing special about the property of being a

---

[42] Boswell, "Revolutions," p. 92, points out that *most* social constructionists "would be willing to admit that some aspects of sexuality are present, and might be distinguished, without direction from society." Either such constructionists do not embrace general relativistic arguments or they blatantly contradict themselves.

homosexual; sexual orientation would be a social construct, but so would everything else (that is, having a Y-chromosome or being a proton would be a construct as well). The point here is that social constructionism is an interesting position *about sexual orientation* only if the relativism involved in it is limited. Extreme social constructionism just collapses into metaphysical relativism, a position which may be interesting for metaphysics but which has nothing particular to say about sexual orientation; using metaphysical relativism as an argument for social constructionism is like using an atomic bomb to kill a fly.

Part of the problem with seeing what would count as a good argument for social constructionism is that the view may still seem hard to understand. In an attempt to explain the position in another way, I offer a parable. Consider a society which I shall call Zomnia, a society that is very much like the one we live in, but where the society's members are all very interested in the details of sleep habits. In particular, Zomnians are concerned with whether a person sleeps on her back or on her stomach: people who sleep on their backs are called "backers" and people who sleep on their stomachs are called "fronters." The majority of people in Zomnia are thought to be fronters, and until recently there was explicit and prevalent discrimination against people known or suspected to be backers. I say "suspected," because most Zomnians think that they can tell a backer by sight. Backers, so the folk wisdom goes, have very rigid posture and tan skin. They are also typically quick-tempered and have aggressive personalities. Scientists and psychiatrists in Zomnia are interested in what makes some people backers. Some think that whether or not you are a backer is genetically determined, others think it is due to your relationship with your parents, and others think it has to do with your diet during puberty. Recently, some self-identified backers in Zomnia have started forming underground groups designed to combat discrimination against them, dispel myths about them and form a community of kindred spirits; they have been partially successful. This community-organizing has had an effect on academic research; some historians in Zomnia have become concerned about the sleep positions of historical figures and (claim to) have evidence that certain important figures in Zomnian history were backers. It has also had the political effect of helping backers to attain "ethnic minority" status.[43]

Now imagine that you were a visitor to Zomnia: what would you have to say about the importance which Zomnians place on sleep positions? My first reaction would be to tell them that at best their practice of grouping people into backers and fronters is laughable, their practice of discriminating against people on the basis of their sleep habits is morally wrong, and their scientific theories which concern the "etiology" of "backerhood" are pseudo-scientific. Of course, I can imagine that my anti-Zomnian position *might* be wrong. It is *possible* that their scientific theories are right, that their categories are objective and transcultural, but, given what we know about humans, it seems highly unlikely that they are.

The point of this parable is to offer an intuitive analogy for social constructionism. My complaint against grouping people into backers and fronters is much like the complaint that social constructionists make about categorizing people as heterosexuals and homosexuals. The only reason why groupings based on sleep positions seem silly while the groupings by sexual orientation seem sensible is, according to the social constructionist, because we are used to the latter but not to the former.

Several points about this parable are important to note. My claim that the use of the fronter/backer categories is a mistaken way to group people is an *empirical* claim—it is true or false depending on contingent facts about the world and the people who inhabit it. If it were to turn out that it is genetically determined that particular people sleep on their backs while

---

[43] While this parable has some of the same motives and morals as does Weinrich's example of "petual orientation" in his essay in this volume, pp. 177-81, the Zomnian example serves my purposes better since sleep, like sex and unlike the preference for cats as pets, is an important physiological function of humans. For this reason (and others), sleep habits, like sexual behavior and unlike behavior towards pets, are more controversial in terms of the nature/nurture and the voluntarism/determinism questions.

others do not or that there are interesting historical or scientific generalizations that can be made about backers (beyond their sleep habits), then the Zomnians' theories would be right and I would be wrong. The social constructionist should be seen as making the same sort of empirical claim—if one's sexual orientation is caused by having a certain gene, then social constructionism is wrong.[44] This point also reiterates what is wrong with the "no concept" and the "different forms of life" arguments. Suppose, as is empirically possible, that the Zomnian theories about sleep position are right, not just about Zomnians, but about all humans. The fact that we have no concepts backer or fronter and the fact that there are different forms of life (or types of people) in Zomnia and in our culture would not constitute a disproof of the Zomnian theories. What anti-Zomnian theorists (such as me) need to do is give good reasons for thinking that there are no deep properties having to do with sleep positions.

Also, note that my anti-Zomnian claim does not involve rejecting that some people tend to sleep on their backs and others tend to sleep on their stomachs. My claim had better not involve anything of the sort because of course people do have such tendencies—I, for one, usually sleep on my stomach, but some people do sleep on their backs (not to mention the insidious group consisting of those that sleep on their sides, who, no doubt, would be rated between 2 and 4 on the sleep habit version of the Kinsey scale[45]). Much the same

---

[44] Halperin, *One Hundred Years*, p. 49, is one of the few social constructionists who admits this explicitly, though he goes on to express a variety of reservations (which I think are provocative and highly contentious) about scientific research. See note 13 above.

[45] A bipolar scale is better suited to representing the varieties of people grouped by sleep positions, once sleeping on one's side is included as a possibility, than it is to for representing the varieties of people grouped by sexual orientation. If '0' represents some one who sleeps exclusively on her stomach and '6' represents some one who sleep exclusively on her back, then '3' could represent some one who sleeps exclusively on her side at a position perpendicular to the ground while the remaining numbers could represent the various sleep positions in
--->

is true for the social constructionists: they are not denying that there are men who have sex with men, women who have sex with women and women and men who have sex with members of the opposite sex, nor are they denying that such varieties of sexual behavior occur in other cultures and have occurred in many or all previous cultures. Further, an anti-Zomnian theory, to be complete, would both have to argue that backers and fronters are mistaken categories and have to explain how these categories came to be entrenched, how people came to see themselves as either backers or fronters, etc. This is analogous to the positive claim of social constructionism.

In this parable, just as in this concluding essay in general, I have tried to clarify what exactly is at issue between social constructionists and essentialists. The disagreement is over the nature of the categories of sexual orientation. Is it possible to develop a theory of sexual orientation which involves transcultural, objective categories (like being color blind or being six feet tall) or are the categories merely culture-dependent ones (like being a witch and yuppie)? This is both an interesting and important question which requires an empirical answer; such an empirical answer will, if found, begin to settle the controversy between social constructionists and essentialists.[46]

---

between. (Even this use of the bipolar scale is imperfect, however, since the information of whether a '3' sleeps on her right side or her left side is lost.) This point was brought to my attention by Gene Buckley.

[46]Many people have helped me on this essay. In particular, discussion with and comments from Michael Antony, Alyssa Bernstein, Paul Bloom, Gene Buckley, Ron Caldwell, Wayne Dynes, Keith Green, David Halperin, Michael Inman, Morris Kaplan, Peter Lipton, Eric Lormand, Bonnie McElhinny, Richard Mohr, Georges Rey, Eugene Rice, Sean Walter, and Rob Wilson have been useful. Various versions of this paper were read at M.I.T., at Brown University for the "Perspectives and Lesbian and Gay Studies" conference, at SUNY-Purchase, at the University of Maryland-College Park, and at Boston University.

BIBLIOGRAPHY

Adam, Barry, "Structural Foundations of the Gay World," *Comparative Study of Society and History* 27:4 (October 1985), pp. 658-71.

Altman, Dennis, *The Homosexualization of America*, Boston: Beacon Press, 1982.

Altman, Dennis, et al., *Homosexuality, Which Homosexuality?: Essays for the International Scientific Conference on Lesbian and Gay Studies*, London: GMP Publishers, 1989.

Ariès, Philippe and André Béjin, eds., *Western Sexuality: Practice and Perception in Past and Present Times*, Oxford: Basil Blackwell, 1985.

Bayer, Ronald, *Homosexuality and American Psychiatry*, New York: Basic Books, 1981.

Bell, Alan and Martin Weinberg, *Homosexualities: A Study of Diversity Among Men and Women*, New York: Simon and Schuster, 1978.

Bell, Alan, Martin Weinberg and Sue Hammersmith, *Sexual Preference: Its Development in Men and Women*, Bloomington: Indiana University Press, 1981.

Bem, Sandra, "The Measurement of Psychological Androgyny," *Journal of Consulting and Clinical Psychology* 42 (1974), pp. 155-162.

————, "On the Utility of Alternative Procedures for Assessing Psychological Androgyny," *Journal of Consulting and Clinical Psychology* 46 (1977), pp. 195-205.

Bieber, Irving, "Clinical Aspects of Male Homosexuality," in *Sexual Inversion: The Multiple Roots of Homosexuality*, J. Marmor, ed., New York: Basic Books, 1965.

Bieber, Irving, and T.B. Bieber, "Male Homosexuality," *Canadian Journal of Psychiatry* 24, (1979), pp. 409-421.

Bloom, Paul, and Edward Stein, "Reasoning Why?," *American Scholar* (Spring 1990), pp. 351-320.

Boswell, John, *Christianity, Social Tolerance and Homosexuality*, Chicago: University of Chicago Press, 1980.

————, "Gay History," *Atlantic Monthly* (February 1989), pp. 74-78.

————, "Revolutions, Universals and Sexual Categories," *Salmagundi* 58-59 (1982-83), pp. 89-114.

Brown, Roger, *Social Psychology: The Second Edition*, chapter 10, "Sources of Erotic Orientation," New York: Free Press, 1986, pp. 344-373.

Bullough, Vern, *Homosexuality: A History*, New York: New American Library, 1979.

Butler, Judith, *Gender Trouble: Feminism and the Subversion of Identity*, New York: Routledge, 1990.

Cass, Vivienne C., "Homosexual Identity: A Concept in Need of a Definition," *Journal of Homosexuality* 9 (Winter 1983/Spring 1984), pp. 105-126.

Chauncey, George, Jr., "From Gender Roles to Sexual Desire," *Salmagundi* 58-59 (1982-83), pp. 114-146.

Davidson, Arnold, "Closing Up the Corpses: Diseases of Sexuality and the Emergence of the Psychiatric Style of Reasoning," in *Meaning and Method: Essays in Honor of Hilary Putnam*, George Boolos, ed., Cambridge: Cambridge University Press, 1990.

————, "Sex and the Emergence of Sexuality," *Critical Inquiry* 14 (Autumn 1987), pp. 16-48, reprinted this volume.

D'Emilio, John, "Making and Unmaking Minorities: The Tensions between Gay Politics and History," *New York University Review of Law and Social Change* 14 (1986), pp. 915-22.

————, *Sexual Politics, Sexual Communities: The Making of a Homosexual Minority in the United States, 1940-1970*, Chicago: University of Chicago Press, 1983.

D'Emilio, John and Estelle Freedman, *Intimate Matters: A History of Sexuality in America*, New York: Harper and Row, 1988.

Dover, K.J., *Greek Homosexuality*, Cambridge: Harvard University Press, 1975.

Duberman, Martin, Martha Vicinus, and George Chauncey, Jr., eds., *Hidden from History: Reclaiming the Gay and Lesbian Past*, New York: New American Library, 1989.

Dynes, Wayne, *Homosexuality: A Research Guide*, New York: Garland Publishing, 1987.

————, "Wrestling with the Social Boa Constructor," *Out in Academia* 2 (1988), pp. 18-29; a substantially revised version appears in this volume.

Dynes, Wayne R., et al., eds., *Encyclopedia of Homosexuality*, two volumes, New York: Garland Publishing, 1990.

Ellis, Havelock, *Studies in the Psychology of Sex*, 4 volumes, New York: Random House, 1936.

Ellis, Lee, and M. Ashley Ames, "Neurohormonal Functioning and Sexual Orientation: A Theory of Homosexuality-Heterosexuality," *Psychological Bulletin* 101 (1987), pp. 233-258.

Epstein, Steven, "Gay Politics, Ethnic Identity: The Limits of Social Constructionism," *Socialist Review* 93/94 (May/August 1987), pp. 9-54, reprinted this volume.

————, "Nature vs. Nurture and the Politics of AIDS Organizing," *Out/Look* (Fall 1988), pp. 46-53.

Faraday, Annabel, "Liberating Lesbian Research," in *The Making of the Modern Homosexual*, Kenneth Plummer, ed., Totowa, NJ: Barnes and Noble, 1981, pp. 112-29, pp. 93-110.

Ferguson, Ann, "Patriarchy, Identity, and the Sexual Revolution," *Signs* 7:1 (Autumn 1981), pp. 159-71.

Ford, C.S. and F.A. Beach, *Patterns of Sexual Behavior*, New York: Harper, 1951.

Foucault, Michel, *The History of Sexuality, Volume I: An Introduction*, Robert Hurley, trans., New York: Pantheon, 1978, part two, chapter 2, "The Perverse Implantation," reprinted this volume.

————, "An Interview with Michel Foucault," *Salmagundi* 58-59 (1982/1983), pp. 10-24.

Foucault, Michel, and Richard Sennett, "Sexuality and Solitude," *Humanities in Review* 1 (1982), pp. 3-21.

Freud, Sigmund, *Three Essays on the Theory of Sexuality*, James Strachey, trans., London: Imago, 1949.

Fuss, Diana, *Essentially Speaking: Feminism, Nature and Difference*, New York: Routledge, 1989.

Futuyma, Douglas and Stephen Risch, "Sexual Orientation, Sociobiology and Evolution," *Journal of Homosexuality* 9 (1983-84), pp. 157-168.

Gagnon, John, *Human Sexualities*, Glenview, IL: Scott, Foresman, 1977.

Gagnon, John, and William Simon, *Sexual Conduct*, Chicago: Aldine, 1973.

Garde, N.I., pseud., *Jonathan to Gide: The Homosexual in History*, New York: Vantage, 1964.

Gergen, K.J. "The Social Constructionist Movement in Modern Psychology," *American Psychologist* 40 (1985), pp. 266-275.

Greenberg, David, *The Construction of Homosexuality*, Chicago: University of Chicago Press, 1988.

Hacking, Ian, "Five Parables," in *Philosophy in History: Essays on the Historiography of Philosophy*, R. Rorty, et al., eds., Cambridge: Cambridge University Press, 1984, pp. 103-124.

———, "The Invention of Split Personalities," in *Human Nature and Natural Knowledge*, Alan Donagan, Anthony Perovich, Jr., and Michael Wedin, eds., Dordrecht: D. Reidel, 1986, pp. 63-85.

————, "Making Up People," in *Reconstructing Individualism: Autonomy, Individuality, and the Self in Western Thought*, Thomas Heller, Morton Sosna, and David Wellbery, eds., Stanford: Stanford University Press, 1986, pp. 222-36, reprinted in this volume.

Halperin, David, *One Hundred Years of Homosexuality and Other Essays on Greek Love*, New York: Routledge, 1990.

Hart, John, and Diane Richardson, eds., *The Theory and Practice of Homosexuality*, Boston: Routledge and Kegan Paul, 1981.

Herdt, G.H., *Guardians of the Flutes: Idioms of Masculinity*, New York: McGraw Hill, 1981.

Herdt, G.H., ed., *Rituals of Manhood*, Berkeley: University of California Press, 1982.

Herdt, G.H., ed., *Ritualized Homosexuality in Melanesia*, Berkeley: University of California Press, 1984.

Hocquenghem, Guy, *Homosexual Desire*, Dangoor Daniella, trans., New York: Schocken, 1980.

Hooker, Evelyn, "The Homosexual Community," in *Sexual Deviance*, J.H. Gagnon and W.S. Simon, eds., New York: Harper & Row, 1967, pp. 176-94.

————, "Male Homosexuals and Their 'Worlds,'" in *Sexual Inversion: The Multiple Roots of Homosexuality*, J. Marmor, ed., pp. 83-107.

Katchadourian, H. A., "The Terminology of Sex and Gender," in *Human Sexuality: A Comparative and Developmental Perspective*, Berkeley: University of California Press, 1979, pp. 8-34.

Katz, Jonathan Ned, *Gay American Almanac*, New York: Harper, 1983.

Kinsey, A.C., W.B. Pomeroy, and C.E. Martin, *Sexual Behavior in the Human Female*, Philadelphia: W.B. Saunders, 1953.

————, *Sexual Behavior in the Human Male*, Philadelphia: W.B. Saunders, 1948.

Kitzinger, Celia, *The Social Construction of Lesbianism*, London: Sage Publications, 1987.

Kinsman, Gary, *The Regulation of Desire: Sexuality in Canada*, New York: Black Rose Books, 1987.

Klein, Fritz, and Timothy Wolf, eds., *Two Lives to Lead: Bisexuality in Men and Women*, New York: Harrington Park Press, 1985.

Krafft-Ebing, Richard von, *Psychopathia Sexualis, with Especial Reference to the Antipathic Sexual Instinct: A Medico-Forensic Study*, Franklin S. Klaf, trans., New York: Stein and Day, 1965.

Lesselier, Claudie, "Social Categorization and Construction of a Lesbian Subject," *Feminist Issues* (Spring 1987), pp. 89-94.

Lewes, Kenneth, *The Psychoanalytic Theory of Homosexuality*, New York: Simon and Schuster, 1988.

Marmor, Judd, ed., *Sexual Inversion: The Multiple Roots of Homosexuality*, New York: Basic Books, 1965.

Masters, W.H. and V.E. Johnson, *Human Sexual Response*, Boston: Little, Brown, 1966.

McGuire, R.J., J.M. Carlisle, and B.G. Young, "Sexual Deviations as Conditioned Behavior: a Hypothesis," *Behavior Research and Therapy* 2 (1965), pp. 185-190.

McIntosh, Mary, "The Homosexual Role," *Social Problems*, 16 (1968), pp. 182-193, reprinted with postscript in *The Making of the Modern Homosexual*, Kenneth Plummer, ed., pp. 30-49, reprinted (without postscript) this volume.

Miller, P.Y. and M.R. Fowlkes, "Social and Behavioral Construction of Female Sexuality," *Signs* 5 (1980), pp. 783-800.

Mohr, Richard, "The Thing of It Is: Some Problems with the Models for the Social Construction of Homosexuality," in *Gay Ideas* (forthcoming).

Money, John, *Gay, Straight and In-Between: The Sexology of Erotic Orientation*, New York: Oxford University Press, 1988.

Murray, Stephen O., *Social Theory, Homosexual Reality*, New York: Gay Academic Union, 1984.

Ortner, S.B. and H. Whitehead, eds., *Sexual Meanings: The Cultural Construction of Gender and Sexuality*, Cambridge: Cambridge University Press, 1981.

Padgug, Robert, "Sexual Matters: On Conceptualizing Sexuality in History," *Radical History Review* 20 (1979), pp. 3-33, reprinted in this volume.

Phelan, Shane, *Identity Politics: Lesbian Feminism and the Limits of Community*, Philadelphia: Temple University Press, 1989.

Plummer, Kenneth, "Going Gay: Identities, Life Cycles and Lifestyles in the Male Gay World," in *The Theory and Practice of Homosexuality*, John Hart and Diane Richardson, eds.

————, *Sexual Stigma*, London: Routledge and Kegan Paul, 1975.

————, "Symbolic Interactionism and Sexual Conduct: An Emergent Perspective," in *Human Sexual Relations: Towards a Redefinition of Sexual Politics*, K. Howells, ed., Oxford: Basil Blackwell, 1982, pp. 223-241.

Plummer, Kenneth, ed., *The Making of the Modern Homosexual*, Totowa, NJ: Barnes and Noble, 1981.

Rich, Adrienne, "Compulsory Heterosexuality and Lesbian Existence," in *Powers of Desire: The Politics of Sexuality*, Ann Snitow, et al., eds., New York: Monthly Review Press, 1983, pp. 177-206.

Richardson, Diane, "The Dilemma of Essentiality in Homosexual Theory," *Journal of Homosexuality* 9 (1983-83), pp. 79-90.

————, "Recent Challenges to Traditional Assumptions about Homosexuality: Some Implications for Practice," *Journal of Homosexuality* 13 (Summer 1987), pp. 1-12.

Roscoe, Will, "Making History: The Challenge of Gay and Lesbian Scholarship," *Journal of Homosexuality* 15 (1988), pp. 1-40.

Rubin, Gayle, "Thinking Sex: Notes for a Radical Theory of the Politics of Sexuality," in *Pleasure and Danger: Exploring Female Sexuality*, Carol Vance, ed., Boston: Routledge and Kegan Paul, pp. 300-309.

————, "The Traffic in Women: Notes on the 'Political Economy' of Sex," in *Towards an Anthropology of Women*, Rayna Reiter, ed., New York: Monthly Review, 1975, pp. 157-210.

Ruse, Michael, *Homosexuality: A Philosophical Inquiry*, New York: Basil Blackwell, 1988.

Schofield, Michael, *Sociological Aspects of Homosexuality*, Boston: Little, Brown, 1965.

Sedgwick, Eve Kosofsky, *Between Men: English Literature and Male Homosocial Desire*, New York: Columbia University Press, 1985.

————, *The Epistemology of the Closet*, Berkeley: University of California Press, 1990.

Simon, William and John Gagnon, "Sexual Scripts," *Society* 22 (November-December 1984), pp. 53-60.

Socarides, C.W., "A Provisional Theory of Aetiology in Male Homosexuality," *International Journal of Psychoanalysis* 49 (1968), pp. 27-37.

Spence, Janet, R.L. Helmreich, and J. Stapp, "The Personal Attributes Questionnaire: A Measure of Sex-role Stereotypes and Masculinity and Femininity," *JSAS Catalog of Selected Documents in Psychology* 4 (1974), p. 43.

————, "Ratings of Self and Peers on Sex Role Stereotypes and Masculinity-Femininity," *Journal of Personality and Social Psychology* 32 (1975), pp. 29-39.

Stern, Simon, "Lesbian and Gay Studies: A Selective Bibliography," *Yale Journal of Criticism* 3 (1989), pp. 253-260.

Storms, Michael, "Sex-Role Identity and Its Relationship to Sex-Role Attributes and Sex-Role Stereotypes," *Journal of Personality and Social Psychology* 37 (1979), pp. 1779-1789.

———, "Theories of Sexual Orientation," *Journal of Personality and Social Psychology* 38 (1980), pp. 783-792.

———, "A Theory of Erotic Orientation Development," *Psychological Review* 88 (1981), pp. 340-353.

Symonds, Donald, *The Evolution of Human Sexuality*, New York: Oxford University Press, 1979.

Taylor, G.R., *Sex in History*, New York: Vanguard, 1954.

Tiefer, Leonore, "A Feminist Perspective on Sexology and Sexuality," in *Feminist Thought and the Structure of Knowledge*, Mary Gergen, ed., New York: New York University Press, 1988, pp. 16-26.

———, "Social Constructionism and the Study of Human Sexuality," in *Review of Personality and Social Psychology*, volume 7, P. Shaver and C. Hendrick, eds., (1987), pp. 70-94, reprinted this volume.

Trumbach, Randolph, "London's Sodomites: Homosexual Behavior in the Eighteenth Century," *Journal of Social History* 11 (1977), pp. 1-33.

Vance, Carol, "Gender Systems, Ideology, and Sex Research," in *Powers of Desire: The Politics of Sexuality*, A. Snitow, C. Stansell and S. Thompson, eds., New York: Monthly Review Press, 1983, pp. 371-384.

Vicinus, Martha, "Sexuality and Power: A Review of Current Work in the History of Sexuality," *Feminist Studies* 8 (1982), pp. 133-156.

Weeks, Jeffrey, *Coming Out: Homosexual Politics in Britain from the Nineteenth Century to the Present*, London: Quartet Books, 1977.

————, *Sex, Politics and Society: The Regulation of Sexuality Since 1800*, London: Longman, 1981.

————, *Sexuality and Its Discontents: Meanings, Myths and Modern Sexuality*, London: Routledge and Kegan Paul, 1985.

Weinrich, James, *Sexual Landscapes*, New York: Charles Scribner's Sons, 1987, chapter 5, reprinted in this volume.

Whitam, Frederick, "The Homosexual Role: A Reconsideration," *Journal of Sex Research* 13 (1977), pp. 1-11.

Whitam, Frederick, and Robin Mathy, *Male Homosexuality in Four Societies: Brazil, Guatemala, the Philippines, and the United States*, New York: Praeger Scientific, 1986.

Williams, Walter, *The Spirit and the Flesh: Sexual Diversity in American Indian Culture*, Boston: Beacon Press, 1986.

Winkler, John, *The Constraints of Desire: The Anthropology of Sex and Gender in Ancient Greece*, New York: Routledge, 1990.